Commodore 64: a visual compendium

Released in January 1982, the Commodore 64 holds a Guinness World Record as the highest-selling home computer of all time, and has sold millions upon millions of units the world over.

Official production ceased in 1992, but its legacy still lives on today. The likelihood is that, as you are reading this, programmers are still making games for it, musicians are still making music for it, and people are still talking about it.

This book has been created to celebrate the visual side of the Commodore 64. It features the stunning pixel art painstakingly created by hand (way before the days of *Photoshop!*), beautiful photography that captures the iconic product design, and a selection of *Zzap!64* cover artworks by artist Oliver Frey. Also included is a series of features, including profiles of key Britsoft developers, interviews with famous C64 artists, a look back at the demo scene, plus a showcase of unreleased titles and the new games being released more than 25 years after the last machine rolled off Commodore's production line.

We hope you enjoy this book as much as we enjoyed putting it together.

Bitmap Books

A huge thanks to all contributors to this book

Graham Axten
Game designer, programmer and graphic artist

Pete Baron
Game designer and programmer

Andrew Braybrook
Game designer and programmer

Steve Brown
Game designer

Stoo Cambridge
Graphic artist

Gary Carr
Graphic artist

David Crane
Game designer, programmer and co-founder of Activision

Stephen Crow
Game designer, programmer and graphic artist

Andrew Davie
Game designer and programmer

Ivan Davies
Graphic artist

Karen Davies
Graphic artist and co-founder of Denton Designs

Steven Day
Graphic artist

Mevlut Dinc
Game designer, programmer and co-founder of Vivid Image

Paul Docherty
Graphic artist

Andy Dyer
Ex-*Commodore Format* reviewer

Andreas Escher
Graphic artist and game designer

Brian Fargo
Game producer and co-founder of Interplay

Simon Forrester
Ex-*Commodore Format* editor

Oliver Frey
Artist and co-founder of Newsfield

Kevin Furry
Game designer and programmer

Martin Galway
Musician

Ron Gilbert
Game designer and programmer

Dave Golder
Ex-*Commodore Format* editor

Matt Gray
Musician

Michael Haire
Graphic artist

Jon Hare
Game designer, graphic artist and co-founder of Sensible Software

Andrew Hewson
Founder of Hewson Consultants

Robin Hogg
Ex-*Zzap!64* reviewer

Paul Hughes
Game designer and programmer

Andy Hutchinson
Ex-*Commodore Format* editor

Robert Jaeger
Game designer and programmer

Steve Jarratt
Ex-*Zzap!64* deputy editor and editor of Commodore Format

Mark Jones
Graphic artist

Roger Kean
Co-founder of Newsfield

Mark W.J. Kelly
Programmer

Kevin Kieller
Game designer and programmer

Phil King
Ex-*Zzap!64* reviewer

Paul Koller
Programmer

Chester Kollschen
Game designer and programmer

John F. Kutcher
Game designer and programmer

Ned Langman
Graphic artist

James Leach
Ex-*Commodore Format* reviewer

Robin Levy
Game designer and graphic artist

David Levine
Game designer

Peter Liepa
Game designer and programmer

Oliver Lindau
Graphic artist

Richard Löwenstein
Game designer, programmer and journalist

Steinar Lund
Illustrator

Archer MacLean
Game designer and programmer

Sean Masterson
Ex-*Zzap!64* and *Commodore Format* reviewer

Jordan Mechner
Game designer and programmer

Alan Miller
Game designer, programmer and co-founder of Accolade

Jeff Minter
Game designer and programmer

Andrew Morris
Graphic artist and game designer

Paul Norman
Game designer and programmer

Michal Okowicki
Programmer

Philip Oliver
Game designer and programmer

Gary Penn
Ex-*Zzap!64* editor and reviewer

Jason Perkins
Game designer, programmer and graphic artist

Simon Phipps
Game designer, programmer and graphic artist

Colin Porch
Programmer

Jacco Van 't Riet
Graphic artist

Julian 'Jaz' Rignall
Ex-*Zzap!64* editor

Hugh Riley
Graphic artist

Andy Roberts
Game designer, programmer and journalist

Stephen Robertson
Graphic artist

John Rowlands
Game designer and programmer

Stephen Ruddy
Game designer and programmer

Antonio Savona
Game designer, programmer and graphic artist

Chris Shrigley
Game designer and programmer

Steve Snake
Game designer and programmer

Mat Sneap
Graphic artist

Chuck Sommerville
Game designer and programmer

Bob Stevenson
Game designer and graphic artist

Trevor Storey
Graphic artist

Jonathan Smyth Temples
Game designer and graphic artist

Stephen Ian Thomson
Graphic artist

Mikael Tillander
Game designer and programmer

Bob Wakelin
Illustrator

Martin Walker
Game designer, musician and programmer

Trenton Webb
Ex-*Commodore Format* editor

Gary Winnick
Graphic artist and game designer

Stuart Wynne
Ex-*Zzap!64* editor and reviewer

Guest reviewers
Mat Allen
Luca Argentiero
Marc Bell
Arnold Blueml
Jerry Bonner
Phil Boyce
Rocco Di Leo
Andrew Fisher
GamesYouLoved
Neil Grayson
Andy Hayes
Tim Nicholls
Dave Perry
Christian A. Schiller
Zack Scott
Audun Sorlie
John Stanley
Kevin Tilley
Andreas Wallström
Andreas Wanda
Matt Wilsher

The demo scene
Pontus Berg
Mike Berry
Antony Crowther
Pete Dabbs
Steven Day
Doug Hare
Daniel Kottmair
David Simmons
Enrico Sturaro

PETSCII gallery
Tero Heikkinen
Tommi Musturi
Martin Völker
Andy Zeidler

Archer MacLean quote courtesy of www.dadgum.com. Alan Miller quote courtesy of www.theguardian.com/uk. Stephen Ruddy *Bubble Bobble* quote courtesy of Frank Gasking and www.C64.com. *Commodore Format* quotes sourced from Commodore Format Archive (commodoreformatarchive.com). Steve Jarratt and Sean Masterson *Zzap!64* quotes sourced from Issue 07 of *RESET* magazine (www.reset.cbm8bit.com). Unreleased Games content by Frank Gasking of www.gamesthatwerent.com. Matt Gray quotes used with permission from www.C64.com. Colin Porch quote used with permission from www.C64.com. David Levine quote courtesy of www.zzap64.co.uk/zzap11/lucas_part2.html

Contents

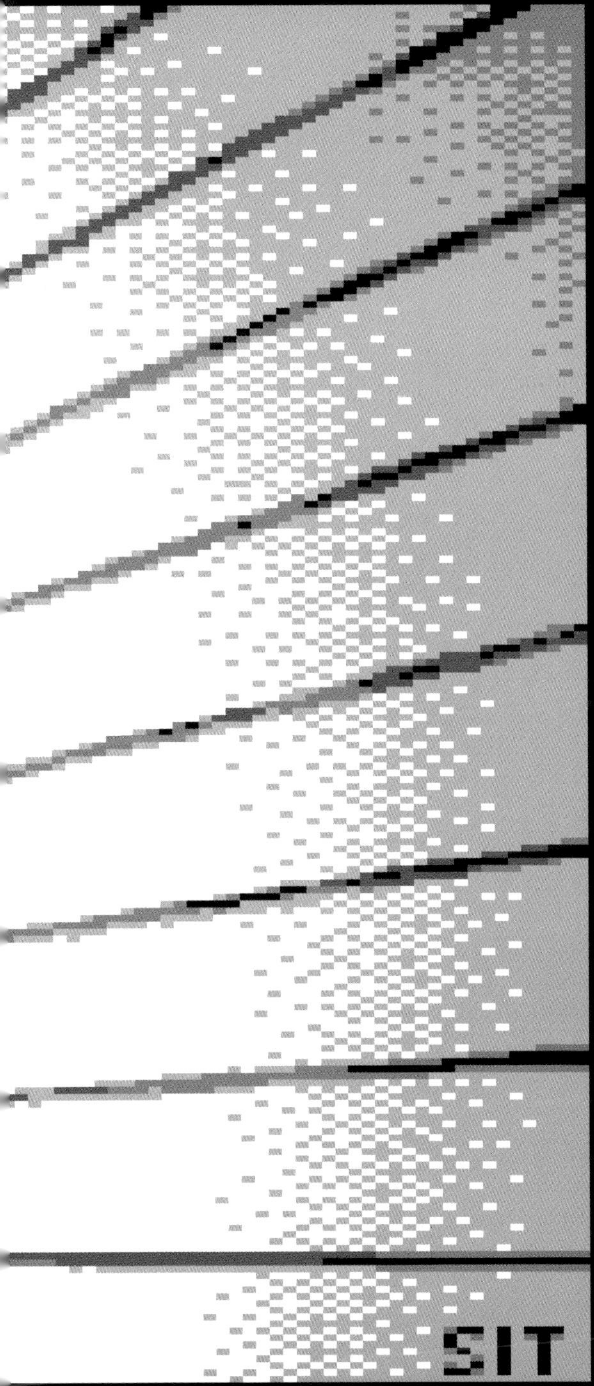

Foreword
by Stoo Cambridge

Here's a question for you: what if the C64 hadn't existed? I know it's a bonkers thought; bear with me. What if ... that whole chapter of computing history we know and love was missing our favourite Commodore box of tricks – no clunky keyboard, no chunky graphics and no sweet-sounding SID chip?

The 64 means so much to so many, the very thought of it not being there – ever – seems absurd. Its very existence has influenced our lives in far-reaching ways, from our friendships and social interactions, the music we enjoy and, for some, even our career choices – all from an interest in this humble 8-bit micro.

Question: what if the C64 had continued to sell through the decades, bringing with it new hardware, peripherals and software titles? Hold on, isn't that what's happened – in a sense? The C64 is amazing in its resilience; Commodore may have bit the dust decades ago, but its famous 8-bit micro still pulls in the crowds. With new machines like the 'C64 DTV', 'The C64 Mini', 'The C64' and the awe-inspiring 'Mega65', I don't think this 8-bit micro is going anywhere soon. Take the retro gaming sites – they're awash with news, previews and reviews of newly developed games waiting to join a library of titles spanning nearly 40 years – wow! I recall that, back in the '80s, home computing was called a fad; thankfully, this fad is showing no signs of being over!

I still get excited listening to classic SID tunes or watching in awe a demo showing visuals even the VIC-II designers would be hard pushed to explain – that's special, that's really special, more so considering that technology today has become so characterless and throwaway.

It's good to see there's life in the old dog yet! Viva C64 forever!

Stoo Cambridge, graphic artist

"It's time to create computers for the masses, not the classes."

Jack Tramiel, founder of Commodore International

Jupiter Lander

Credited as the first game ever released for the Commodore 64, *Jupiter Lander*'s depth of gameplay belies its outwardly simplistic appearance. Indeed, the game is undoubtedly so much more than the sum of its somewhat crude parts. While the objective – landing your intrepid craft on one of the three landing pads – is inherently simple on paper, it's a task made considerably more difficult in practice due to the pixel-perfect collision detection and finely tuned control system. From the demo mode to the innovative zoom-in as your craft nears the landing pads, *Jupiter Lander* is a surprisingly sophisticated game for its time.

Released
1982

Genre
Arcade

Developer
HAL Laboratory

Publisher
Commodore

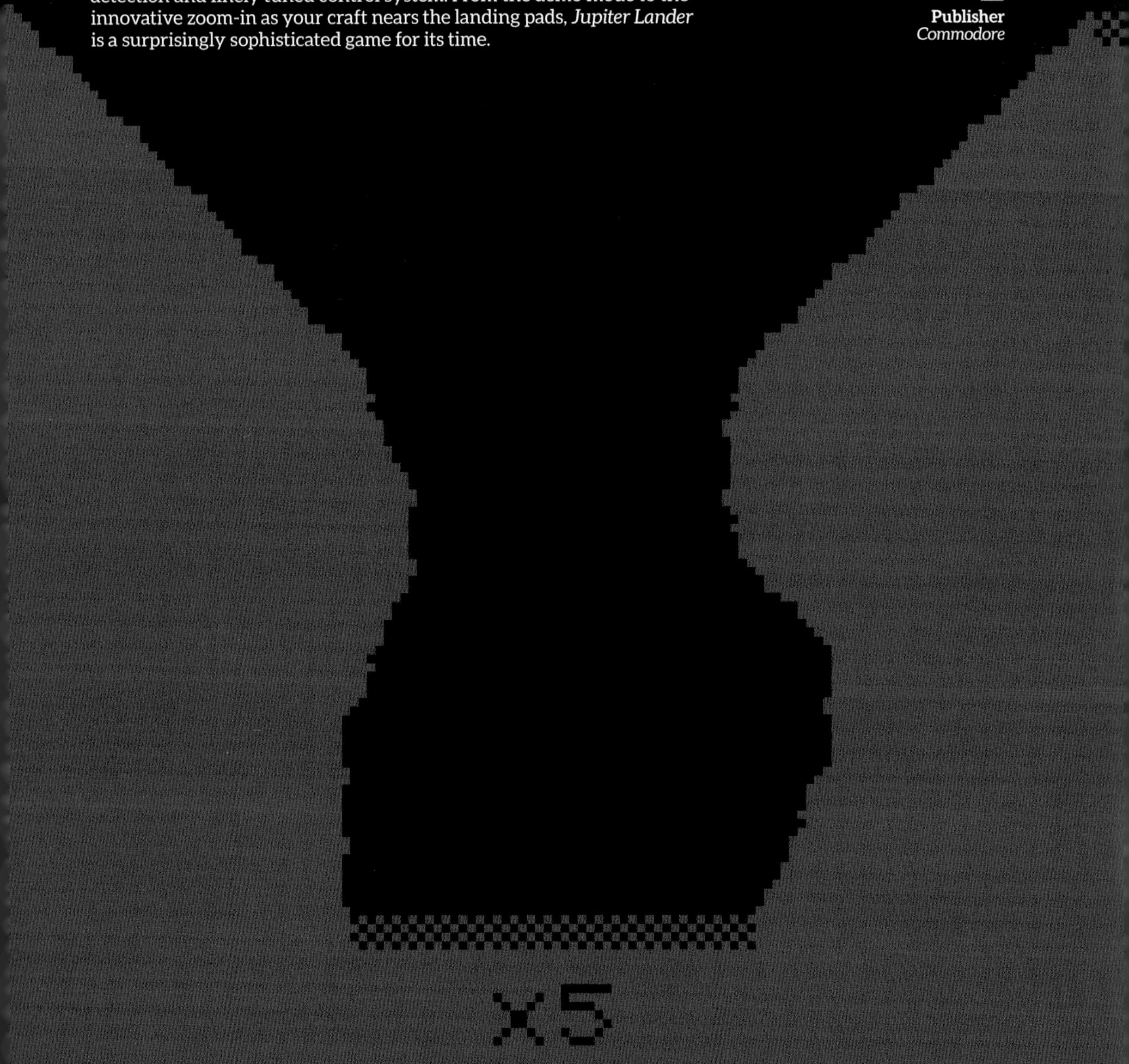

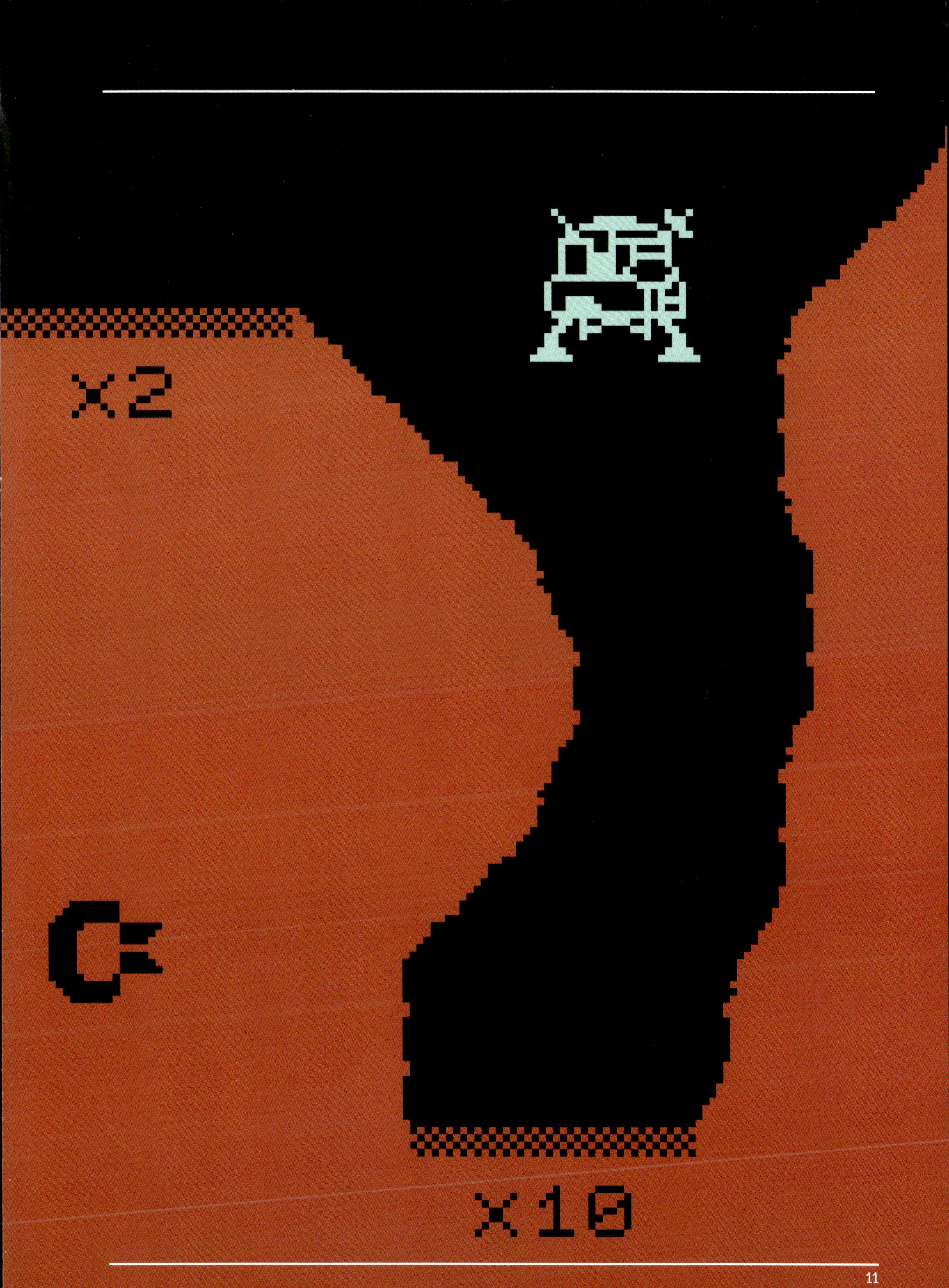
x2
x10

Released
1982

Genre
Shoot 'em up

Developer
Joe Vierra

Publisher
Synapse Software

Fort Apocalypse

"Fly a fully armed helicopter deep into Fort Apocalypse and rescue hostages in this side-on, multi-directionally scrolling cross between an arcade adventure and traditional shoot 'em up. The going is certainly tough as you travel through the four-level fortress – it's packed with hazards, and, if you touch the walls with your helicopter, it explodes. And if that's not enough, there's also the fuel level to worry about too! But while it's not easy, *Fort Apocalypse* is thoroughly enjoyable to play – assuming you're up for its considerable challenge."

Julian Rignall, games journalist

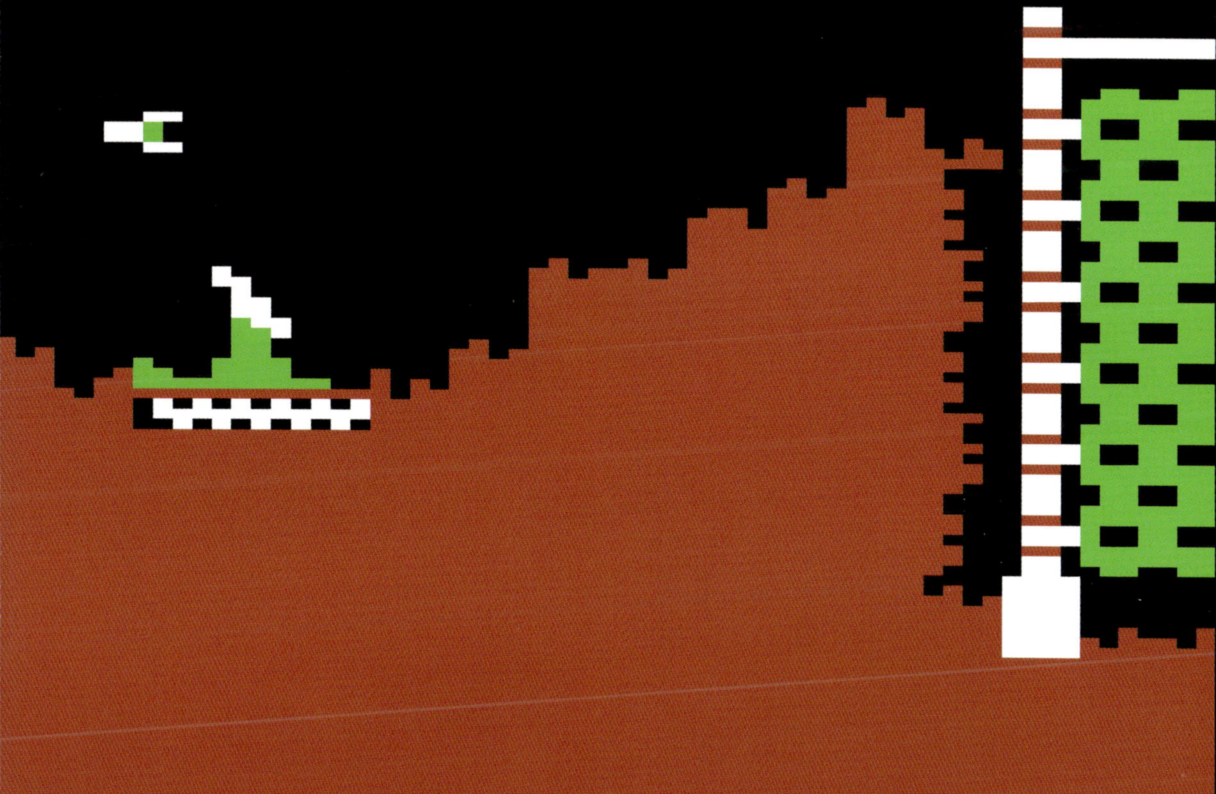

Beach-Head

"When I first saw *Beach-Head* featured on Dutch television back in 1985, it was actually my dad who said 'We need to get this!' We had the greatest time playing it together, especially the artillery shootout where he would call out the distances, and I would do elevation adjustments and fire. The pace of the game and its pressure to take out the enemy quickly were really good, as were the graphics and sound. A true classic."

Martijn Bosschaart, guest reviewer

Released
1983

Genre
Shoot 'em up

Developer
Access Software

Publisher
U.S. Gold

Released
1983

Genre
Scrolling shooter

Developer
Synapse Software

Publisher
U.S. Gold

Blue Max

One of the first waves of games to arrive in the UK courtesy of U.S. Gold, Bob Polin's *Blue Max* places the player in the role of Max Chatsworth, a decorated pilot tasked with bombing three key targets deep inside enemy lines. Naturally, there's all manner of things to obliterate, from buildings and bridges to enemy planes and airfields. There's a multitude of nice touches too, from the anti-aircraft guns spewing flak to the way your plane becomes less responsive as it takes damage (thankfully, you can land at friendly airports for some much-needed repairs). It's relatively short but incredibly tense and rewarding.

"This is one of those games that really takes me back to a great place and time. To this day, whenever I hear *Rule, Britannia!* I still think of *Blue Max*. The game just had so much going on and seemed so wide open for the time. It was akin to *Zaxxon*, but it was deeper. It was one of the few games that were well worth the 15 minutes it took the damn tape to load!"

Jerry Bonner, guest reviewer

Attack of the Mutant Camels

"The idea for *Attack of the Mutant Camels* came from seeing a review of *The Empire Strikes Back* game where the Walkers were described as 'giant mechanical camels'. I thought, 'Why not!?' I was given a US C64, and one of the first things I did with it was write a sprite editor in BASIC and used it to make the giant camel sprites. On a PAL machine, sometimes the camels' bums fall off due to a timing issue. You can tell it's an early game due to the lack of raster scroll."

Jeff Minter, designer and programmer

Released
1983

Genre
Scrolling shooter

Developer
Jeff Minter

Publisher
Llamasoft

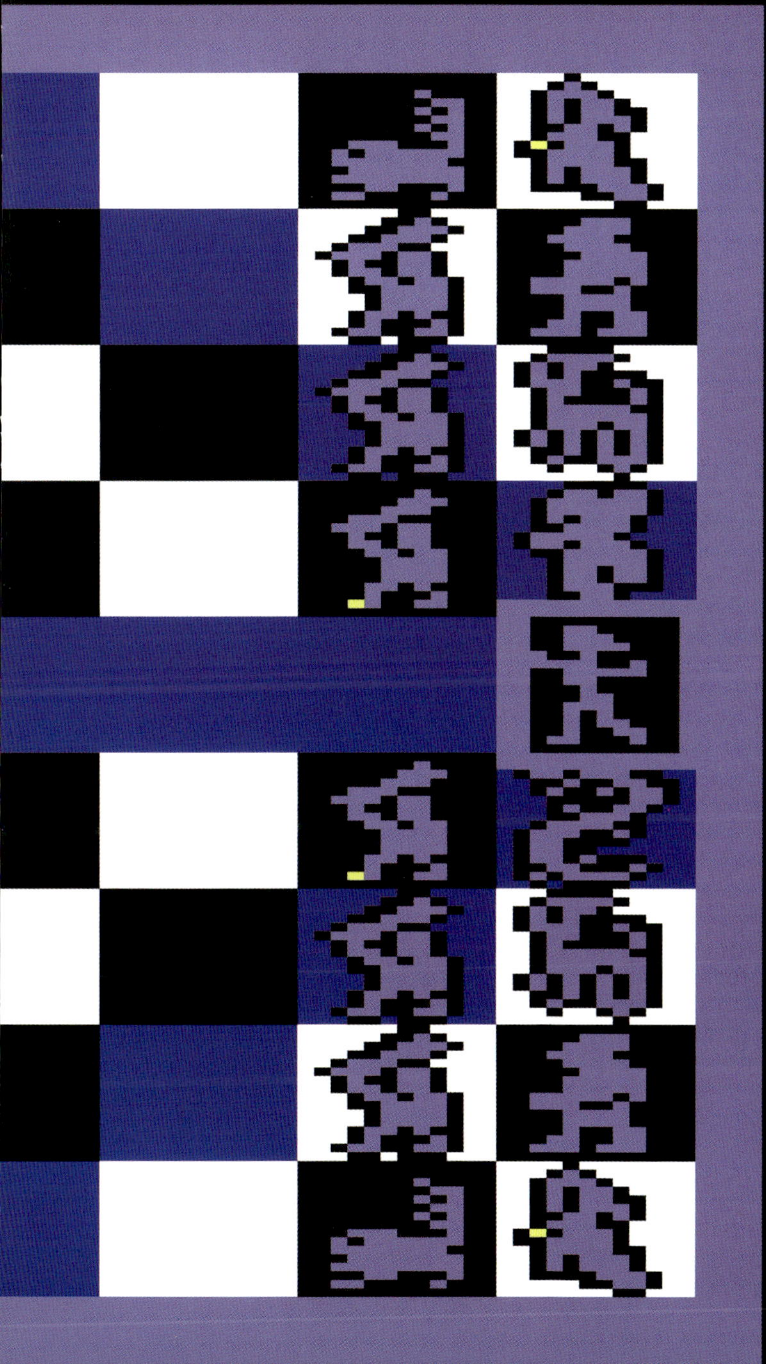

Archon: The Light and the Dark

"*Archon*'s chess-like board hides a more complex game as the Light and Dark sides fight to capture five important 'Power Points' while removing the opposing pieces. But, instead of just taking them, the action switches to a single-screen battlefield where the joystick-controlled creatures fight using their unique abilities. A day-night cycle and magic spells add even more layers to this engrossing strategy game. The sequel – *Archon II: Adept* – added an elemental theme, and the series even gave rise to a UK championship with players attending in costume."

Andrew Fisher, guest reviewer

Released
1983

Genre
Board game

Developer
Free Fall Associates

Publisher
Electronic Arts

Released
1983

Genre
Action

Developer
Paul Norman

Publisher
COSMI

Forbidden Forest

"Because this was my first game and my first programming exercise, I had no rules to follow, and there were no inhibitions. As always, I treated myself as the audience and did whatever I could to excite and surprise myself. One technique was to write complete action sections with lots of random variables without checking each step along the way. I would then run it to experience the whole scene as a viewer instead of a creator. Naturally, things didn't work a lot of the time, but, when they did, that was as close as I could get to an outside perspective."

Paul Norman, designer and programmer

Llamasoft logo by Robin Levy / 2016

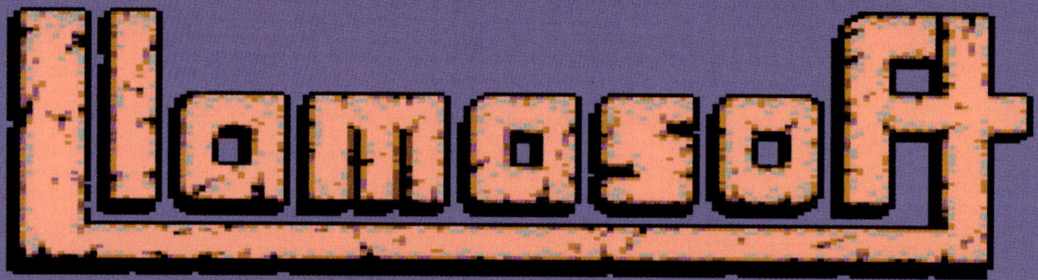

Llamasoft is an independent UK game developer and publisher founded in 1982 by Jeff 'Yak' Minter and has remained proudly autonomous for more than 30 years. Arguably one of the most influential and iconic pioneers of the Britsoft revolution, Minter remained Llamasoft's sole developer for the better part of two decades until Ivan 'Giles' Zorzin officially joined the company in 2004.

A physics major with a passion for arcade games and camelids, Minter began dabbling with programming at college, creating several games for the Commodore PET and a successful version of *Centipede* for the ZX80. When a bout of pericarditis left Minter housebound, he began creating games in earnest for his newly acquired VIC-20. Spotting the potential, a friend offered to handle the business side of selling Minter's various games commercially, and together they formed Llamasoft.

Between 1982 and 1987, Llamasoft developed some of the most original, eccentric and imaginative titles to ever grace a home computer. From simple blasters like *Gridrunner* and *Matrix*, to slick and accomplished shoot 'em ups like *Iridis Alpha*, Minter's desire to create the games he wanted to play resulted in a diverse catalogue of exuberantly eclectic games.

Llamasoft's C64 debut – and one of the first games released for the C64 – was *Rox 64*, a simplistic blend of *Asteroids* and *Lunar Lander* converted from the VIC-20 version in just a single evening. Despite being written in BASIC, *Rox* was both playable and well presented, offering a small glimpse of Minter's future potential. "There is an addictive quality to the game," said *Home Computing Weekly*, awarding *Rox* 3/5. The game would also later appear as a type-in program in *C&VG* magazine.

The company's next title was *Gridrunner*, another VIC-20 conversion programmed in just a matter of days. Eager to produce a *Centipede*-style game but avoid ruffling Atari's legal feathers, Minter gave *Gridrunner* a futuristic angle, adding all manner of enhancements. The result was a frantic, pounding shooter far greater than the sum of its parts. "One of those frenetic shoot 'em ups that keep you coming back for more," said C&VG, while *Home Computing Weekly* dubbed *Gridrunner* "a fast and enjoyable game."

Arriving in early '83, Llamasoft's next outing was *Attack of the Mutant Camels* (*AMC*), a scrolling shoot 'em up inspired by the Atari 2600 game *The Empire Strikes Back*. Tasked with saving Earth from waves of giant, laser-spitting, neutronium-shielded mutant camels, *AMC* aptly demonstrated Minter's coding prowess and abstract imagination. *TV Gamer* magazine called *AMC* "a shoot 'em up with a difference," while *Home Computing Weekly* rated the game at 5/5, adding, "the action is fast and furious. To play it is to appreciate it."

Next out of the Llamasoft stable was *Laser Zone*, another simple yet compelling shoot 'em up converted from the VIC-20 (the company's primary development platform at the time). A twist on the 'bottom shooter' concept featuring an innovative control system – something which would become a Minter hallmark in later years – *Laser Zone* gave the player two ships to manipulate, making the gameplay both challenging and refreshingly different to anything that had come before.

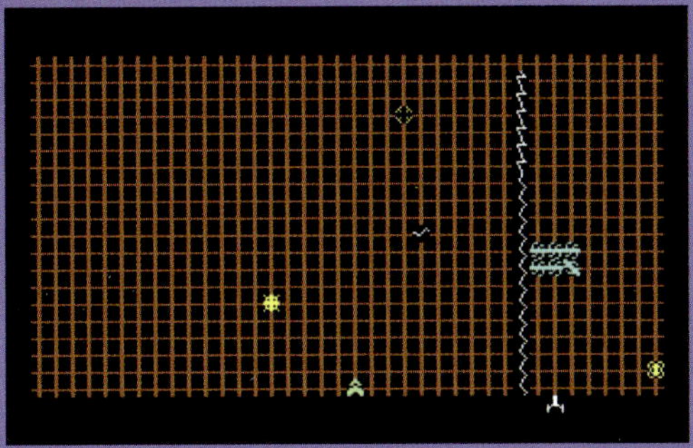

Gridrunner / *1983*

Ancipital / *1984*

Batalyx / *1985*

Iridis Alpha / *1986*

The success of *Gridrunner* in both the UK and USA would lead to the inevitable development of a sequel, *Matrix: Gridrunner II*. While the basic premise remained the same, the gameplay was expanded to encompass new enemies and features in order to reduce repetition; as a result, *Matrix* was even more frantic and chaotic than its predecessor. Noting the game's enhanced sound and visuals, *Home Computing Weekly* gave *Matrix* a commendable 5/5, calling it "an action-packed game."

It was breakfast in a rural farmhouse B&B that would provide the inspiration for Llamasoft's next game *Hover Bovver*, arguably one of Minter's best-loved titles. Set in a typical English country garden, the aim was to simply mow the lawn while avoiding the angry neighbour, a task made a little easier thanks to the player's loyal canine companion. Charming, endearing, packed with humour and extremely polished, *Hover Bovver* scored impressively across the board. "Probably the funniest and most original game in ages," said *Your 64*, awarding the game 90%, while *Commodore User* called it a "masterpiece."

1984 kicked off with *Revenge of the Mutant Camels*, the aptly titled sequel to *Attack of the Mutant Camels*. This time around, players assumed the role of the camels as they fought back against the evil Zzyaxians who had enslaved them in the original game. Much more technically accomplished than its predecessor, *Revenge* was a frantic shoot 'em up loaded with quintessentially English references and irreverent in-jokes. "Commodore ought to give Jeff Minter a medal," said *Personal Computer Games*, while *Your Computer* thought *Revenge* was "a shoot 'em up par excellence."

> *"Arguably one of the most influential and iconic pioneers of the Britsoft revolution."*

Revenge was closely followed by *Hellgate*, the spiritual successor to *Laser Zone*, which would once again pit the player against the invading Zzyaxian forces. Expanding on *Laser Zone*'s innovative dual ship concept, *Hellgate* boasted two pairs of ships, which moved in opposite directions. Initially confusing and more than a little overwhelming, *Hellgate*'s pure and unashamedly chaotic 'shoot-die-repeat' brand of gameplay would ultimately make it one of Minter's most underrated games.

Minter's love of the classic arcade game *Defender* provided the inspiration for Llamasoft's next intergalactic ungulate outing, *Sheep in Space*. A horizontally scrolling shoot 'em up set between two parallel worlds with opposing gravitational fields, *Sheep in Space* was arguably Minter's best blaster to date. "*Sheep in Space* has the usual Llamasoft touches," said *Personal Computer Games*, calling it "a very good mega-zap."

Next came *Metagalactic Llamas Battle at the Edge of Time* (a.k.a. *Meta Llamas*), a deceptively simple shooter that once again pit laser-spitting llamas against evil Zzyaxian hordes in an attempt to defend Earth's outpost on the edge of time. *Meta Llamas* was Llamasoft's only C64 game not programmed by Jeff Minter, coding duties instead falling on the shoulders of Aaron Liddiment. However, having raised the bar considerably with titles such as *Hover Bovver* and *Revenge*, *Meta Llamas* failed to earn the same level of acclaim or notoriety.

Driven by the urge to create a shoot 'em up with more substance, and inspired by arcade adventures like Ultimate's *Atic Atac*, Minter's next game, *Ancipital*, would be his best-received title yet. Featuring Cippy, a character inspired by Brian Aldiss' Helliconia books, and boasting some mind-bending gravity effects, the task was to successfully navigate a 100-screen maze collecting keys and power-ups along the way. *Personal Computer Games* described *Ancipital* as "another classic Minter game," while *Home Computing Weekly* lauded it as "graphically impeccable."

1984 concluded with the release of *Psychedelia*, an innovative 'light synthesiser' that would later play a pivotal role in the direction of future Llamasoft projects. Originally given away for free (and later, as a type-in program in a magazine), Minter was encouraged to develop the concept further and release it as a fully fledged, standalone product. Neither game nor utility, some magazines failed to see the purpose of *Psychedelia*, and as such the reviews were mixed and generally ambivalent.

1985 saw the release of *Mama Llama*, a game which polarised opinion more than any other Llamasoft offering (and subsequently caused a brief rift between Minter and *Zzap!64*). Bold, experimental and thoroughly eccentric, *Mama Lama*'s complexity would far surpass the simplicity and accessibility of Minter's previous games. "It's a very clever and colourful idea," said *Your 64*, calling it "a must for all of his fans." *Zzap!64* rated the game at 59%, suggesting that "even Minter fans may not take to it."

> *"Jeff Minter's C64 output was eclectic, imaginative and unparalleled."*

Llamasoft's return to form would come later that year with the release of *Batalyx*, arguably Minter's most polished and well-rounded game thus far. Comprising six uniquely different sub-games which players could switch between at any time, the slick visuals and unrelenting pace was the culmination of everything Minter had learned to date. "An excellent and incredibly absorbing game," said *Zzap!64*, awarding the game a 'Sizzler' and adding "*Batalyx* is a perfect example of Jeff Minter at his best."

It was almost a year before the arrival of Minter's next game; the blisteringly fast shoot 'em up *Iridis Alpha*. Expanding on ideas from *Sheep in Space*, *Iridis Alpha* featured innovative split-screen gameplay set on opposite sides of a planet, allowing players to switch freely between the two to accomplish their goal. Deep and absorbing, *Iridis* would blow the reviewers' socks off, awarding the game 95% and a 'Sizzler', *Zzap!64* lauded *Iridis Alpha* as "the best shoot 'em up on the 64," while *Your Computer* simply branded it "Jeff Minter at his all-time best."

1987 saw the arrival of Llamasoft's final C64 titles, *Voidrunner* and *Return of the Mutant Camels* (a.k.a. *Revenge II*), both of which were released as budget games via Mastertronic. The third game in the Gridrunner series, *Voidrunner* would elevate the simplistic *Centipede*-style gameplay by adding a squadron of player ships, which would fly in different formations – and fire in different directions – from level to level. Slickly presented and as devilishly addictive as ever, *Voidrunner* was a perfectly formed budget game. *Zzap!64* thought it a "visually stunning shoot 'em up extravaganza" while *Your Commodore* called it "a wild and freaky shoot 'em up."

Revenge II was the third game in Minter's highly successful Mutant Camel series. Once again, players assumed the role of a giant, laser-spitting camel battling to save the Earth from destruction, this time with more than 100 levels and a shop full of useful enhancements and upgrades thrown into the mix. Gorgeous graphics and slick presentation made *Revenge II* the best Mutant Camels game yet – and the perfect C64 swansong. Accordingly, *Zzap!64* awarded the game a 'Silver Medal', simply calling it "superb stuff!"

Llamasoft continued to enjoy a number of successes on platforms such as the Amiga, Atari ST and PocketPC, as well as consoles including the ill-fated Atari Jaguar, Xbox 360 and PlayStation Vita. Llamasoft also released a number of mobile games for iOS devices under the Minotaur Project label.

Inspired by classic arcade games, mentored by a supportive family, and fuelled with tea, Jeff Minter's games were eclectic, imaginative and unparalleled. Indeed, in 2011 *Attack of the Mutant Camels* was one of a handful of games chosen to be featured in 'The Art of Video Games' exhibit at The Smithsonian Institution in Washington D.C. – no small feat for a quiet hippy from Tadley.

Return of the Mutant Camels / *1987*

International Soccer

A regular staple in C64 hardware bundles, Andrew Spencer's seminal seven-a-side soccer sim boasts numerous genre-defining features that were way ahead of their time, from the smooth-scrolling sideline viewpoint to the automatic highlighting of key players. While the chunky expanded sprites seem almost comical, *International Soccer* thankfully has gameplay in spades: the controls are intuitive, the pace fluid, and there are countless hours of fun to be had honing your skills. However, the real joy comes from playing against your friends; indeed, few footy games provide the unparalleled satisfaction of bouncing the ball on your head as you walk it into the net seconds before the full-time whistle.

Released
1983

Genre
Sports

Developer
Andrew Spencer

Publisher
Commodore

Pogo Joe

My connection with computer games started with marketing and package design in the old TRS-80 days. My first game graphics were for *Pogo Joe* circa 1983, a *Q*bert* clone (although I prefer the term 'homage'). Clone or no clone, this was one of the first games built with a 'team' concept: William 'Mike' Denman was the designer/programmer, I did the graphics, and med student Steven Baumrucker created the sound effects and music. I worked on more than three dozen games in my gaming career, and I played *Pogo Joe* more than all the others combined."

Michael Haire, graphic artist

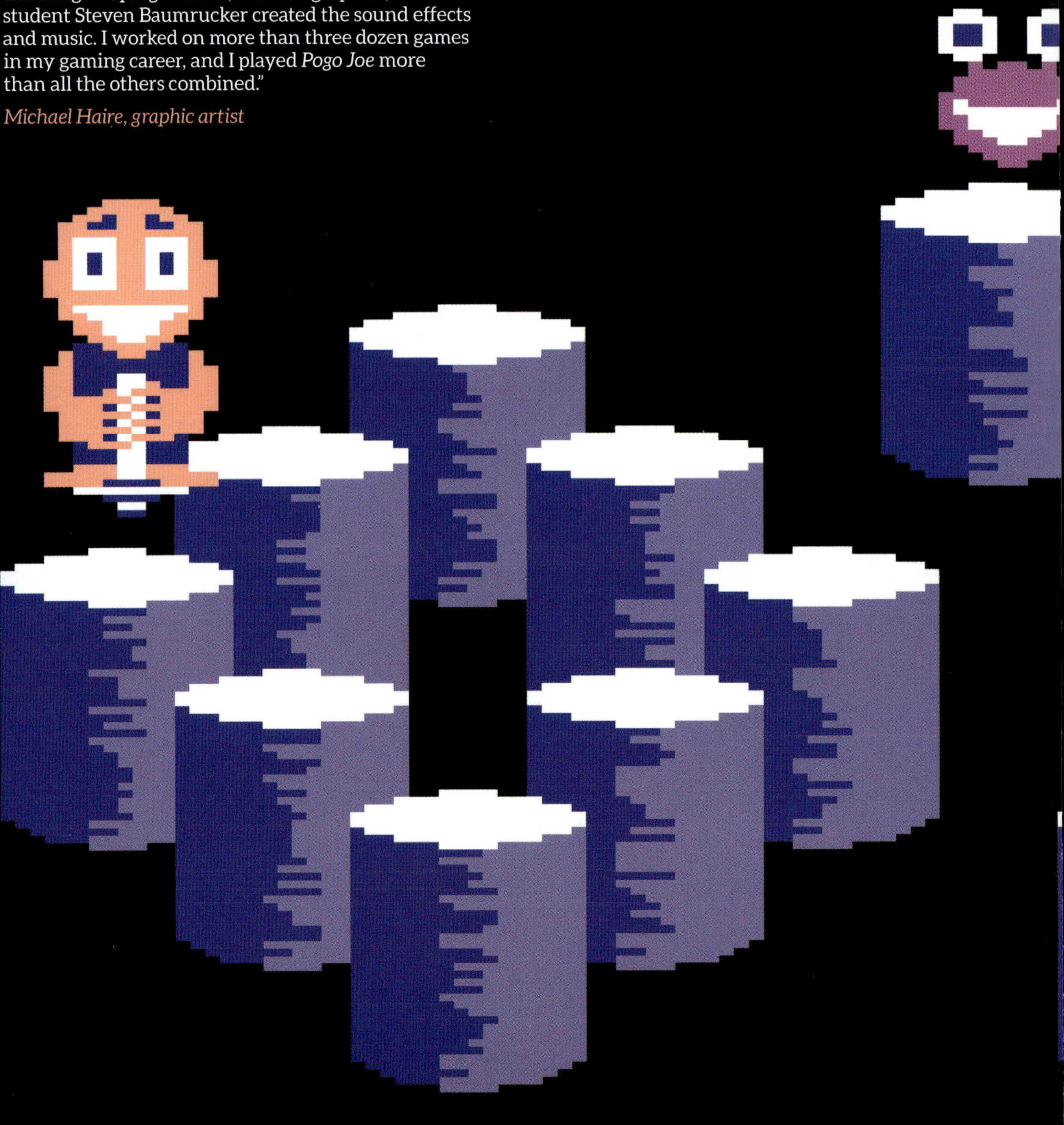

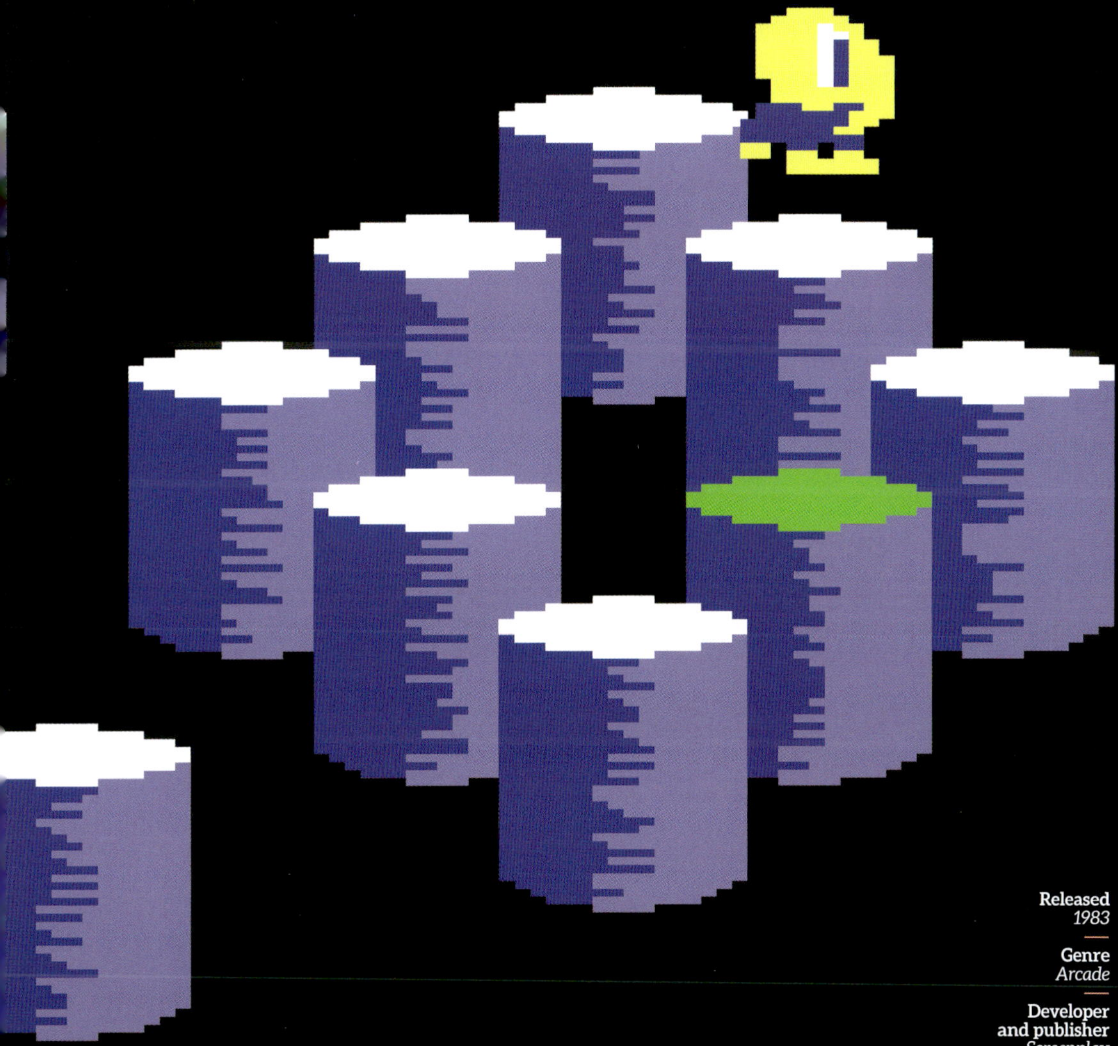

Released
1983

Genre
Arcade

Developer and publisher
Screenplay

Released
1983

Genre
Action

Developer
COSMI

Publisher
U.S. Gold

Aztec Challenge

Developer Paul Norman had a knack for producing brooding and oppressive games with atmospheric soundscapes, and *Aztec Challenge* is certainly no exception. Cast in the role of a hapless citizen of Tenochtitlan, who has been selected as a human sacrifice to appease the gods, your task is to compete in a series of challenges to prove your worth and win your freedom. While the majority of the game's seven levels involve legging it, *Indiana Jones*-style, across multiple trap-laden screens, the opening level, featuring a ziggurat looming large in the distance, remains arguably one of the most iconic moments in C64 gaming history.

"*Aztec Challenge* was originally created by another COSMI programmer in the style of *Mario Bros.* before my arrival. I was asked if I could do a port to the C64, and, for one reason or another, I went off and made a completely new game from scratch that in no way resembled the first, except for the title."

Paul Norman, designer and programmer

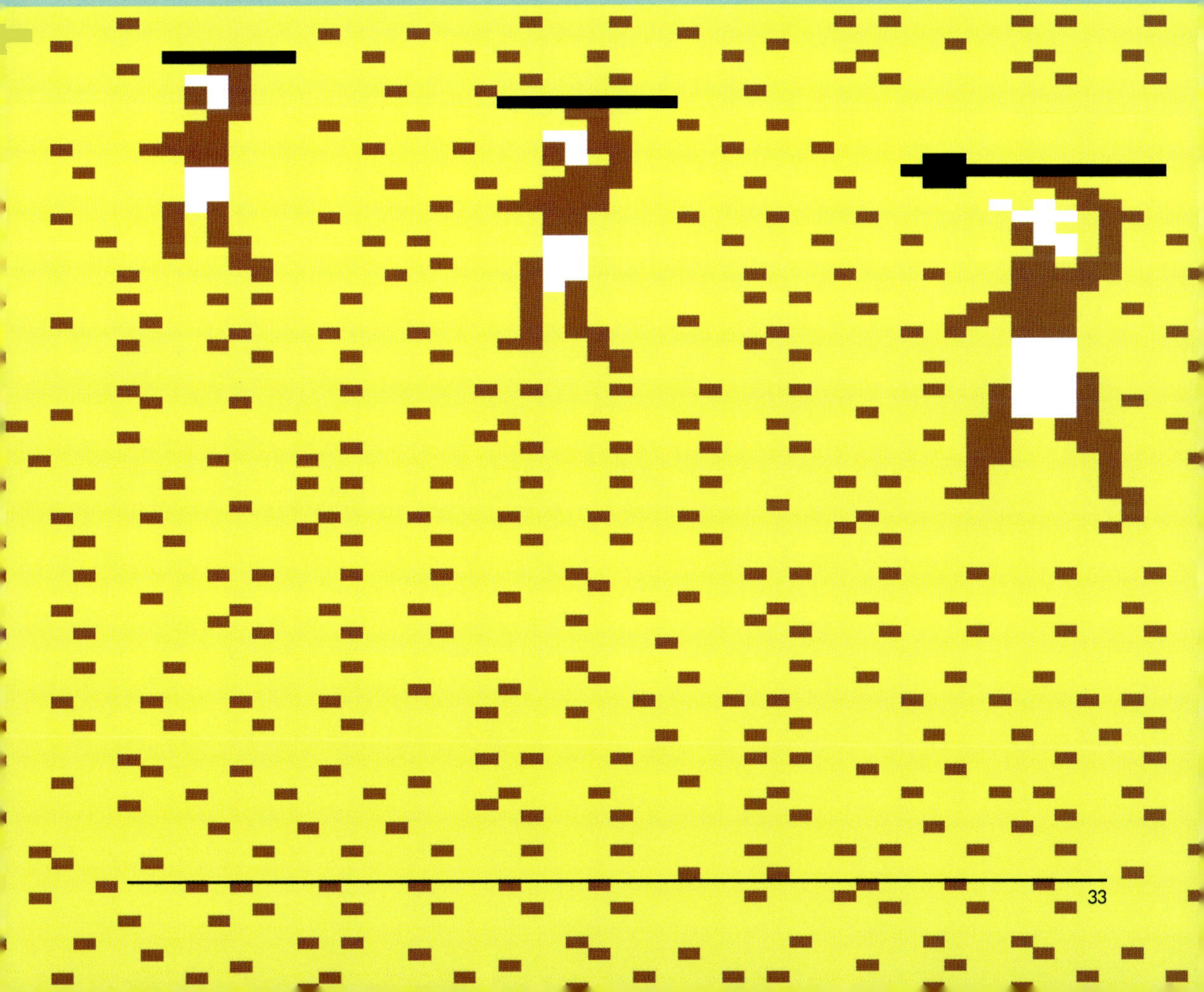

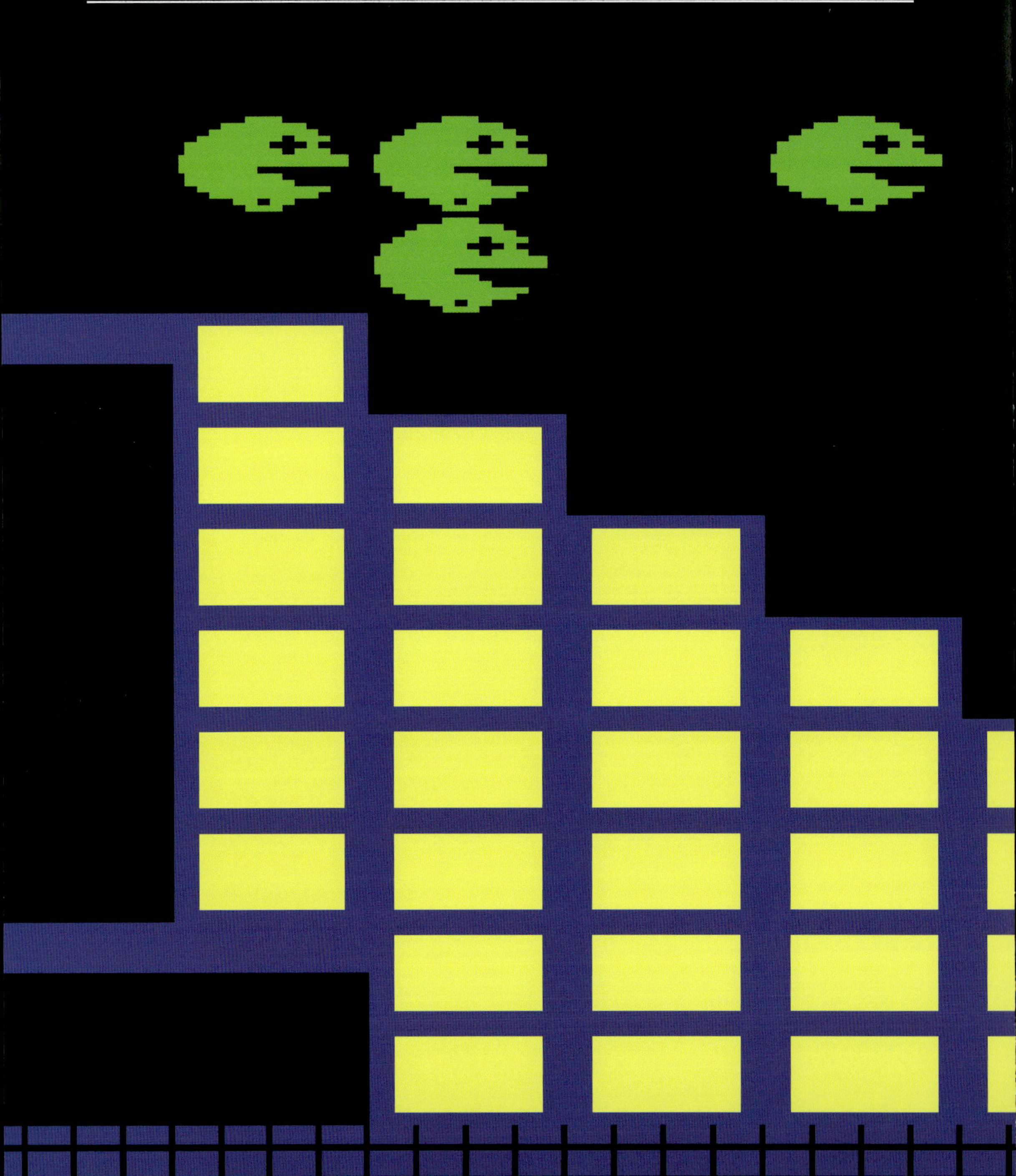

Jack Attack

"In the early summer of 1982, John Traynor and I finalised a 4K VIC-20 cartridge game called *Cubic Critters*. Commodore was interested but wanted to save it as a Gold Medallion game for the soon-to-be-released Commodore 64. Commodore legal felt the *Cubic Critters* name was too close to *Q*bert*, a popular arcade game of the time, so the game was renamed. Commodore insiders felt the red-faced, slightly pudgy character shared some resemblance with Jack Tramiel, president of Commodore, when he was angry. The game was released in 1983 and subsequently nominated for Game of the Year. Only one VIC-20 cartridge still exists."

Kevin Kieller, designer and programmer

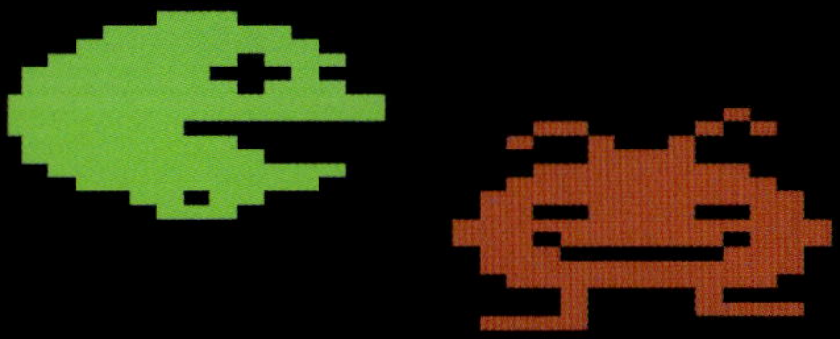

Released
1983

Genre
Arcade

Developers
Kevin Kieller
John Traynor

Publisher
Commodore

Hover Bovver

"Keeping up with the neighbours in the early '80s often involved the purchase of a bright orange Flymo hover mower, but thanks to Jeff Minter's farcical mow 'em up, C64 owners didn't even have to leave the house. Attempting to neatly shear 16 different lawns, players would have to contend with angry neighbours and errant gardeners, with only a demented pooch for protection. Not only was *Hover Bovver* quintessentially English, it was also something of a family affair; Minter conceived the game with his father over breakfast at a country B&B, while the dog was inspired by his mother's dim-witted Afghan hound."

Andy Roberts, games journalist

Released
1983

Genre
Arcade

Developer and Publisher
Llamasoft

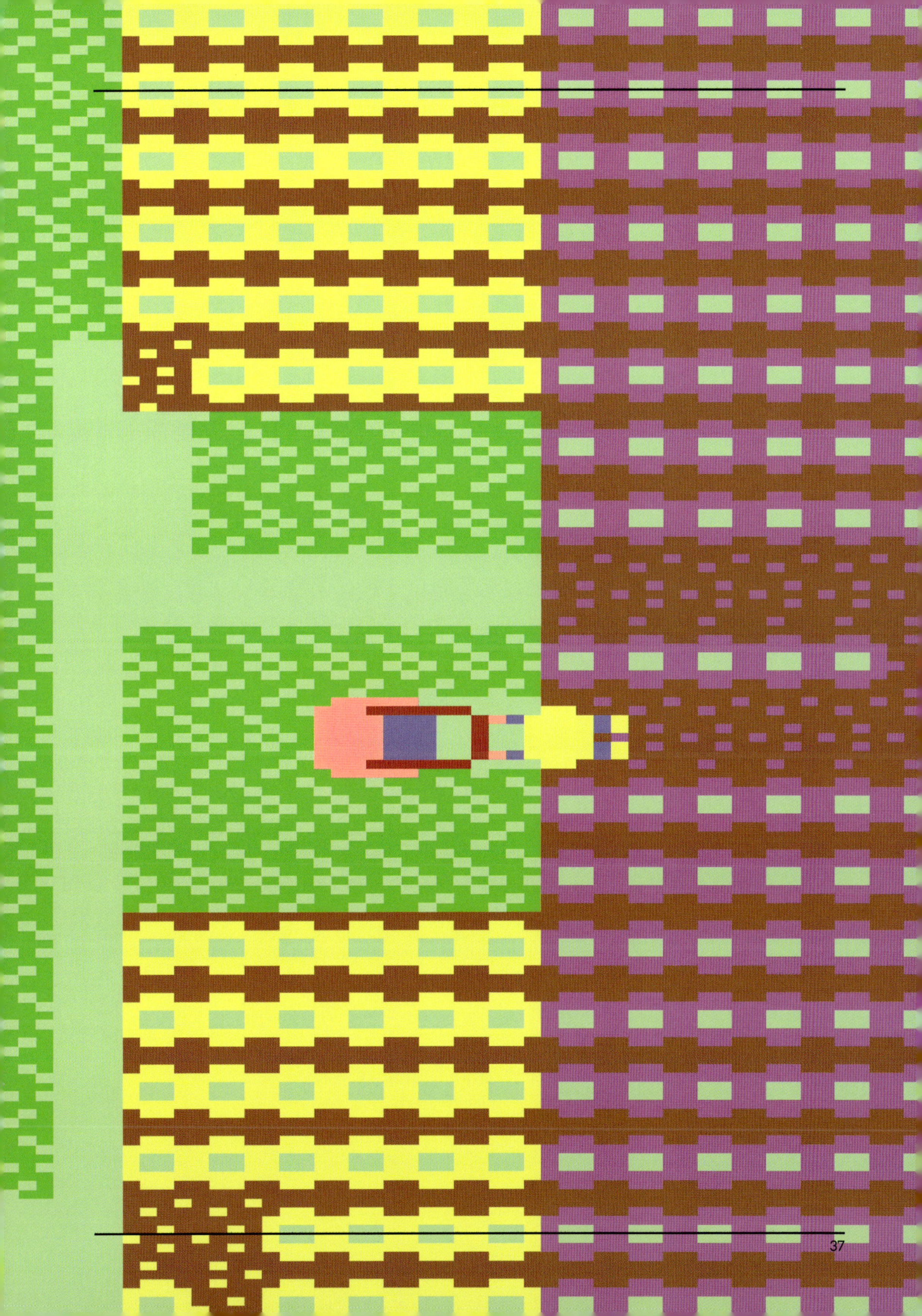

Lode Runner

Originally developed as a monochromatic game with ASCII artwork, programmer Douglas E. Smith took out a loan to buy a colour monitor for a more commercial version that got him signed to Brøderbund. It was comparable with *Boulder Dash* and *Manic Miner* as a subterranean arcade puzzler but distinguished by its sheer speed. Even by the standards of its era, the graphics were minimalistic, but utterly compelling gameplay made it a huge hit."

Stuart Wynne, games journalist

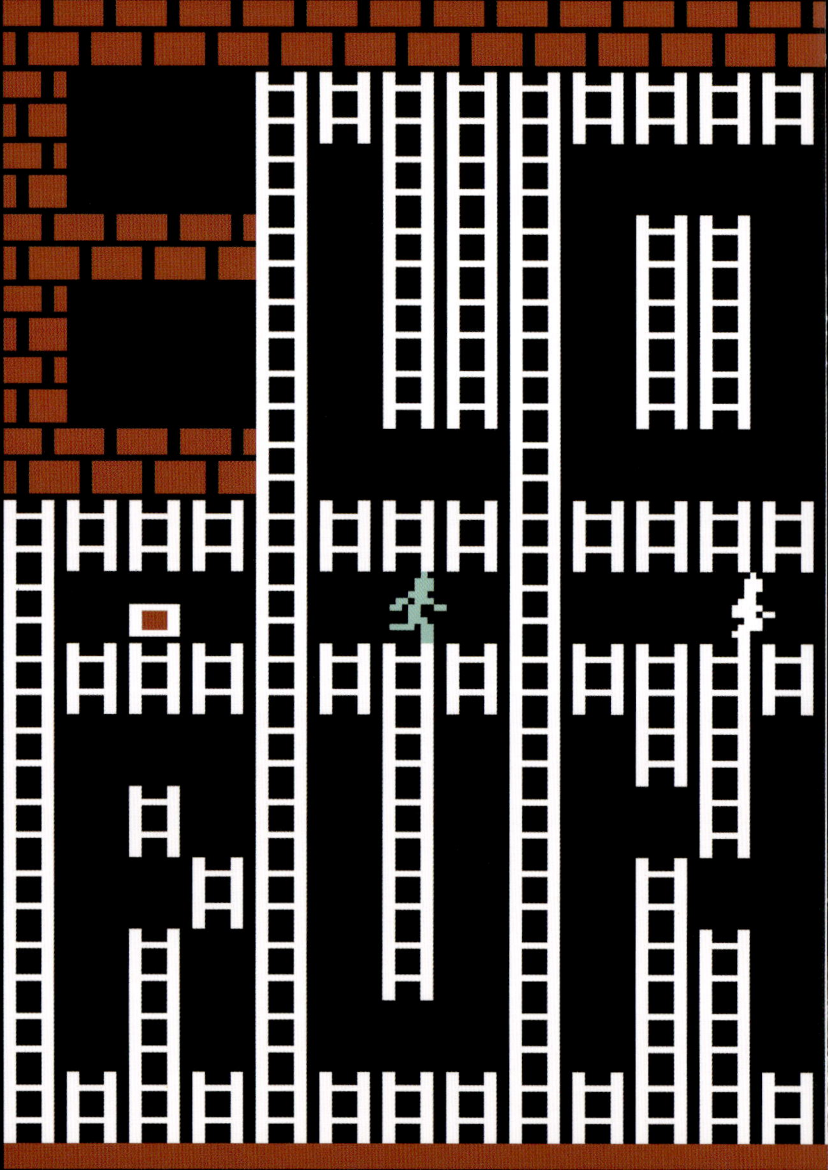

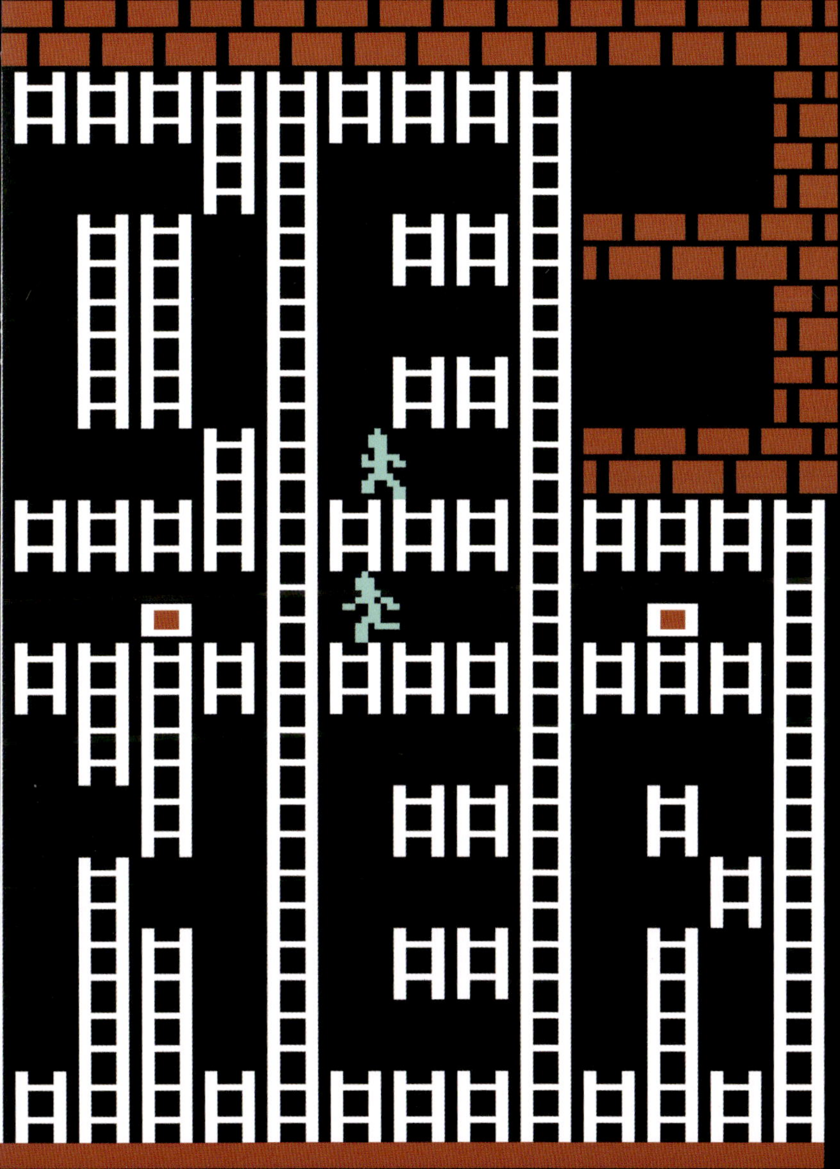

Released
1983

Genre
Platformer

Developer
Douglas E. Smith

Publisher
Brøderbund

M.U.L.E.

"In 1983, game designer Dan Bunten of Ozark Softscape created a game which established computer gaming as a social event way ahead of its time. Turn-based strategy is mixed smartly with action elements, embedded in an intricate economics simulation. Up to four players compete and collude in the colonisation of the distant planet Irata. A plethora of well-balanced random events badger the colonists during their 12-month journey and make each tournament unique. This constitutes the everlasting magic of *M.U.L.E.*"

Christian A. Schiller, guest reviewer

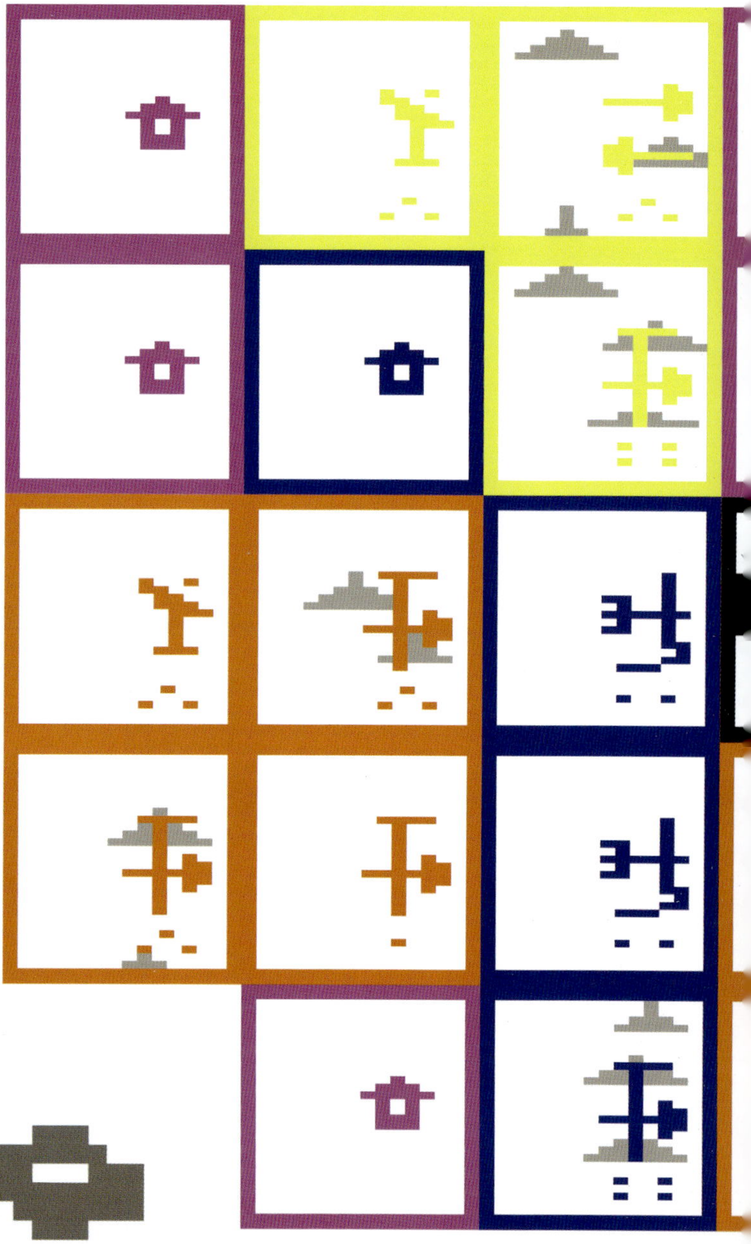

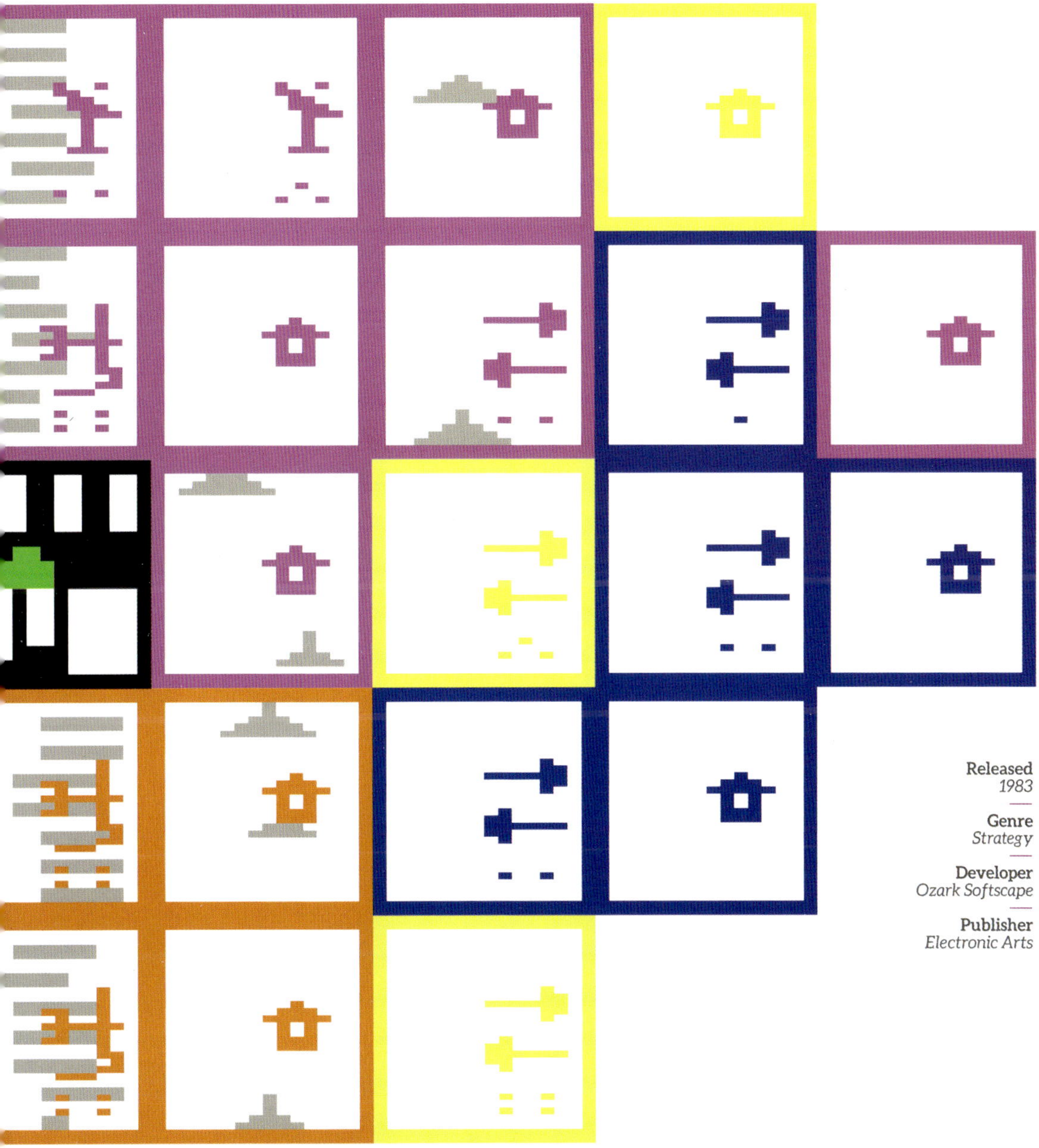

Released
1983

Genre
Strategy

Developer
Ozark Softscape

Publisher
Electronic Arts

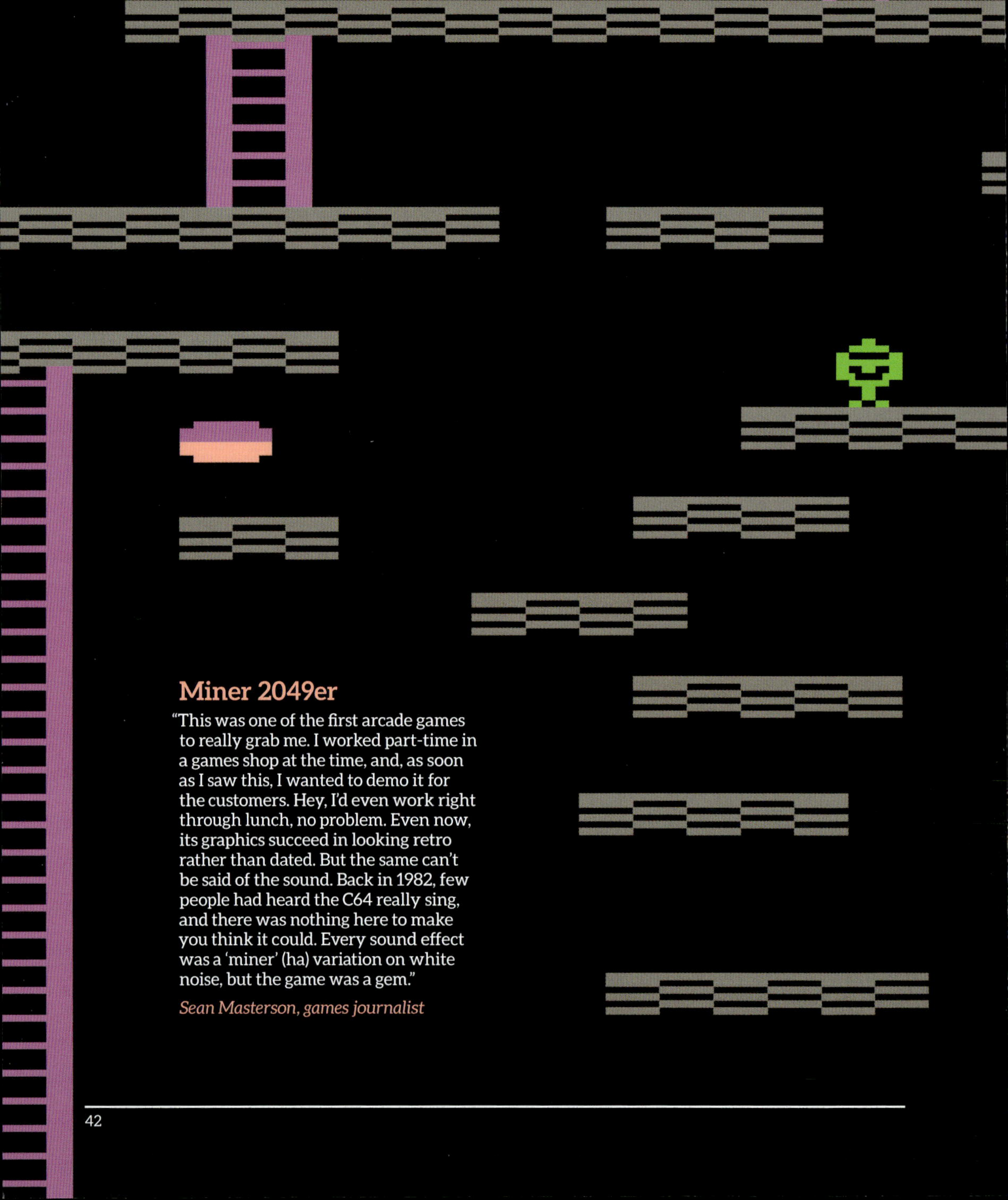

Miner 2049er

"This was one of the first arcade games to really grab me. I worked part-time in a games shop at the time, and, as soon as I saw this, I wanted to demo it for the customers. Hey, I'd even work right through lunch, no problem. Even now, its graphics succeed in looking retro rather than dated. But the same can't be said of the sound. Back in 1982, few people had heard the C64 really sing, and there was nothing here to make you think it could. Every sound effect was a 'miner' (ha) variation on white noise, but the game was a gem."

Sean Masterson, games journalist

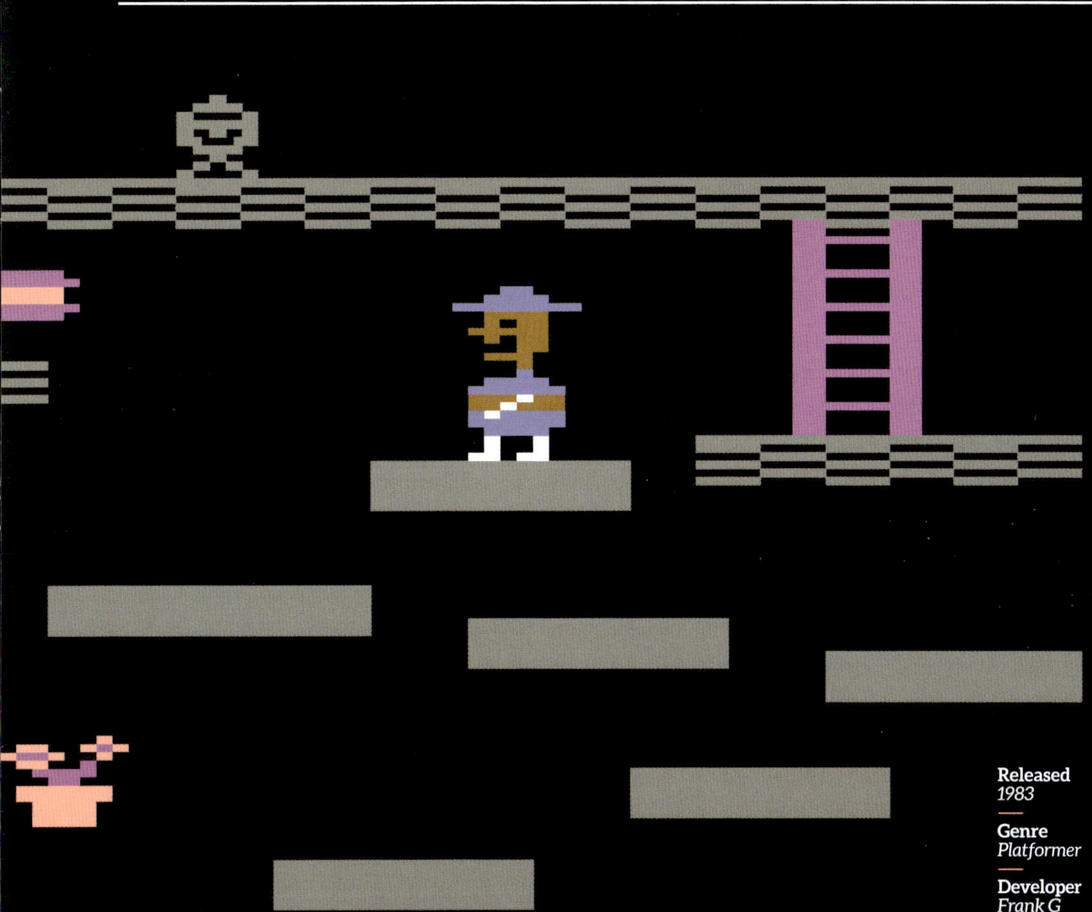

Released
1983

Genre
Platformer

Developer
Frank G

Spy Hunter

"Dun-dun da-dun dada-dun dah-dun. Don't deny humming that immediately when seeing the screenshot, you liar. Bally Midway's vertical scrolling car-based shooter may not have set the world on fire graphically, but every vehicle has a personality and vibe surrounding it, especially the poor cyclists when you nudge them! With smooth scrolling and hard but balanced gameplay, the C64 conversion was arguably more playable than its arcade parent."

Mat Allen, guest reviewer

Released
1983

Genre
Racing

Developer
SEGA

Publisher
U.S. Gold

PORT 1

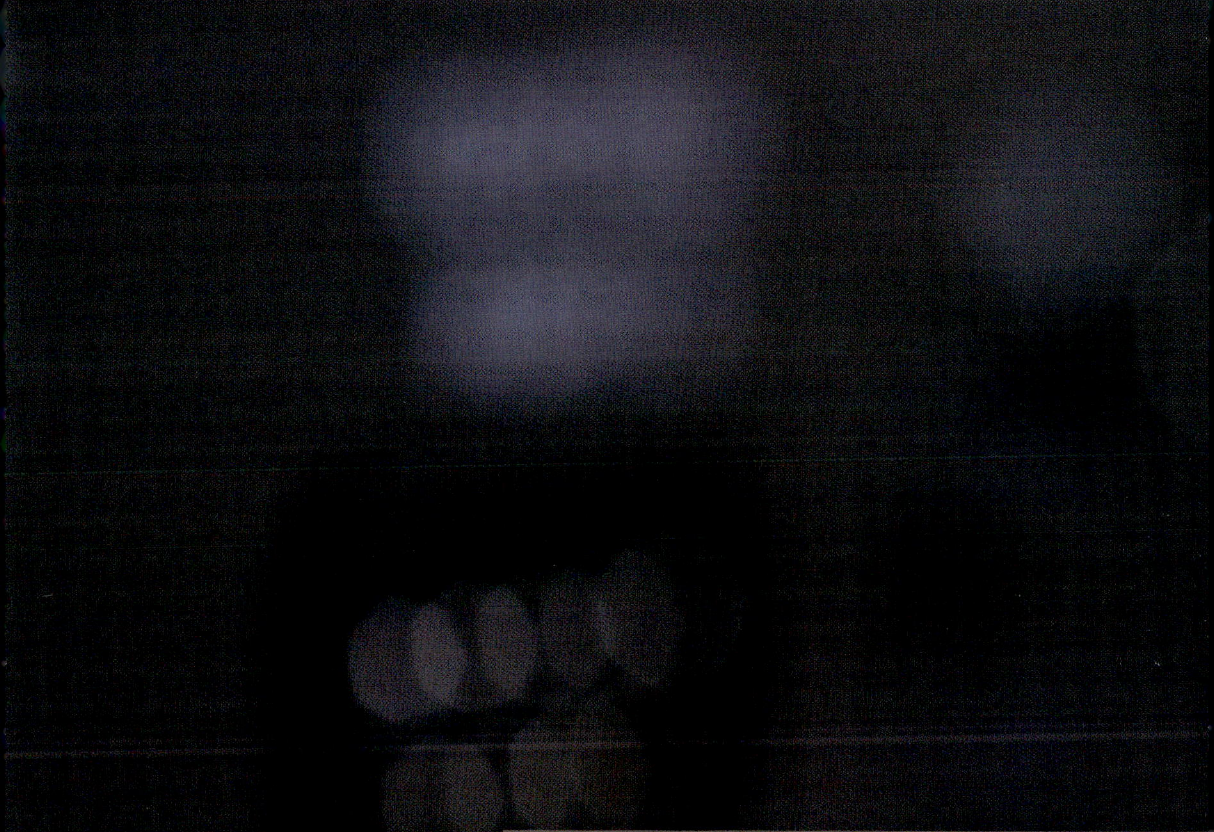

"Everything was a trade-off with C64 art and design; the unholy trinity of memory, speed and quality had to be constantly balanced."

Robin Levy, graphic artist

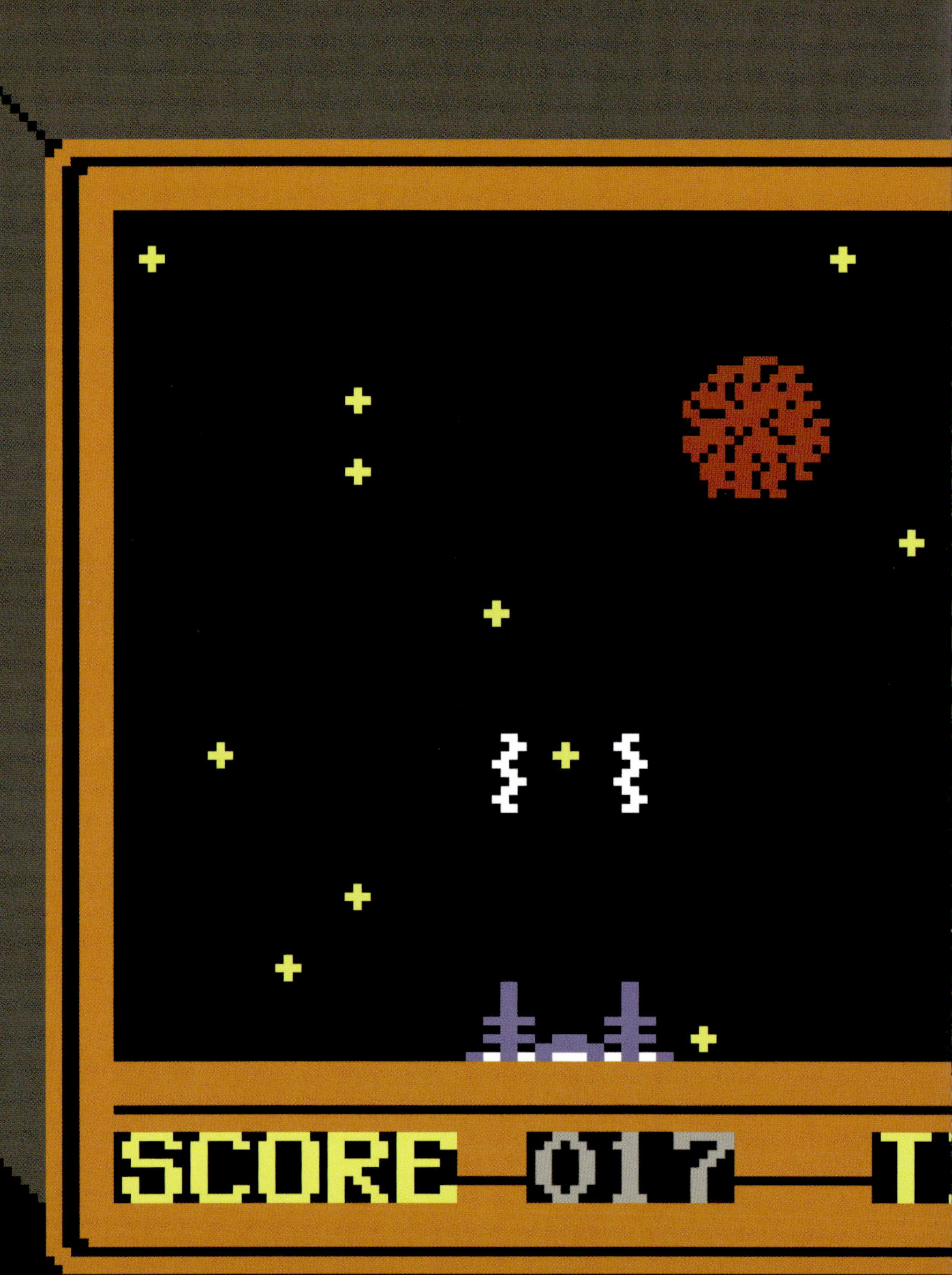
SCORE 017

Lazy Jones

"The clever thing about *Lazy Jones*, in which a bored hotel janitor sticks his nose inside every door he comes across, is that it's actually a collection of familiar arcade games wrapped up in a preposterous portmanteau scenario. Had it been a film, Amicus would have made it. Every time you went through a door, you began playing something closely resembling *Frogger*, *Space Invaders*, *Snake* or whatever. Nevertheless, they mostly succeeded at being moreish. I remember recommending *Lazy Jones* to people on a budget, simply because you got so much for your money. And the music was marvellous: a true testimony to David Whittaker's kung fu."

Sean Masterson, games journalist

Released
1984

Genre
Arcade

Developer
David Whittaker

Publisher
Terminal Software

Released
1984

Genre
Shoot 'em up

Developer
Will Wright

Publisher
Brøderbund

Raid on Bungeling Bay

"The straightforward objective (have helicopter, bomb bad guys) belied its sophistication, which, in hindsight, shouldn't have been the surprise that it was because its developer was Will Wright (who would later go on to create *Sim City*). So I dismissed it the first time I played – but something made me go back to it. Then I saw what the tenacious Bungeling Empire was up to, and I became happily hooked. I remember being intrigued, wondering what the factories might come up with next. What if they could be contained? Nah. Blasting them into their constituent molecules was the only way to go. Nevertheless, there was more to this game than met the eye."

Sean Masterson, games journalist

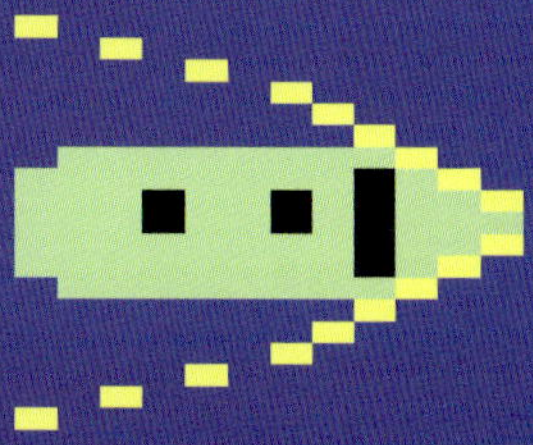

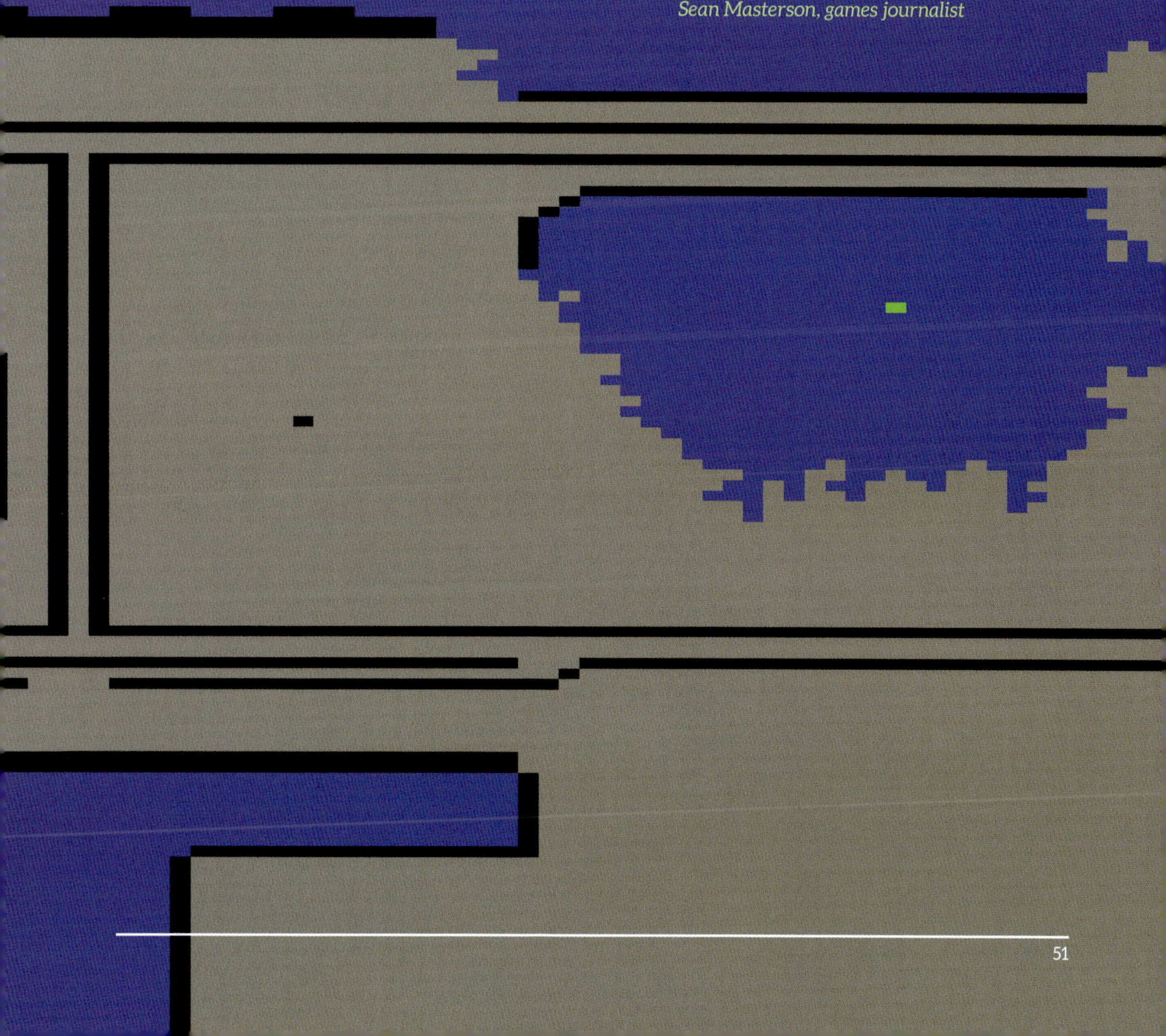

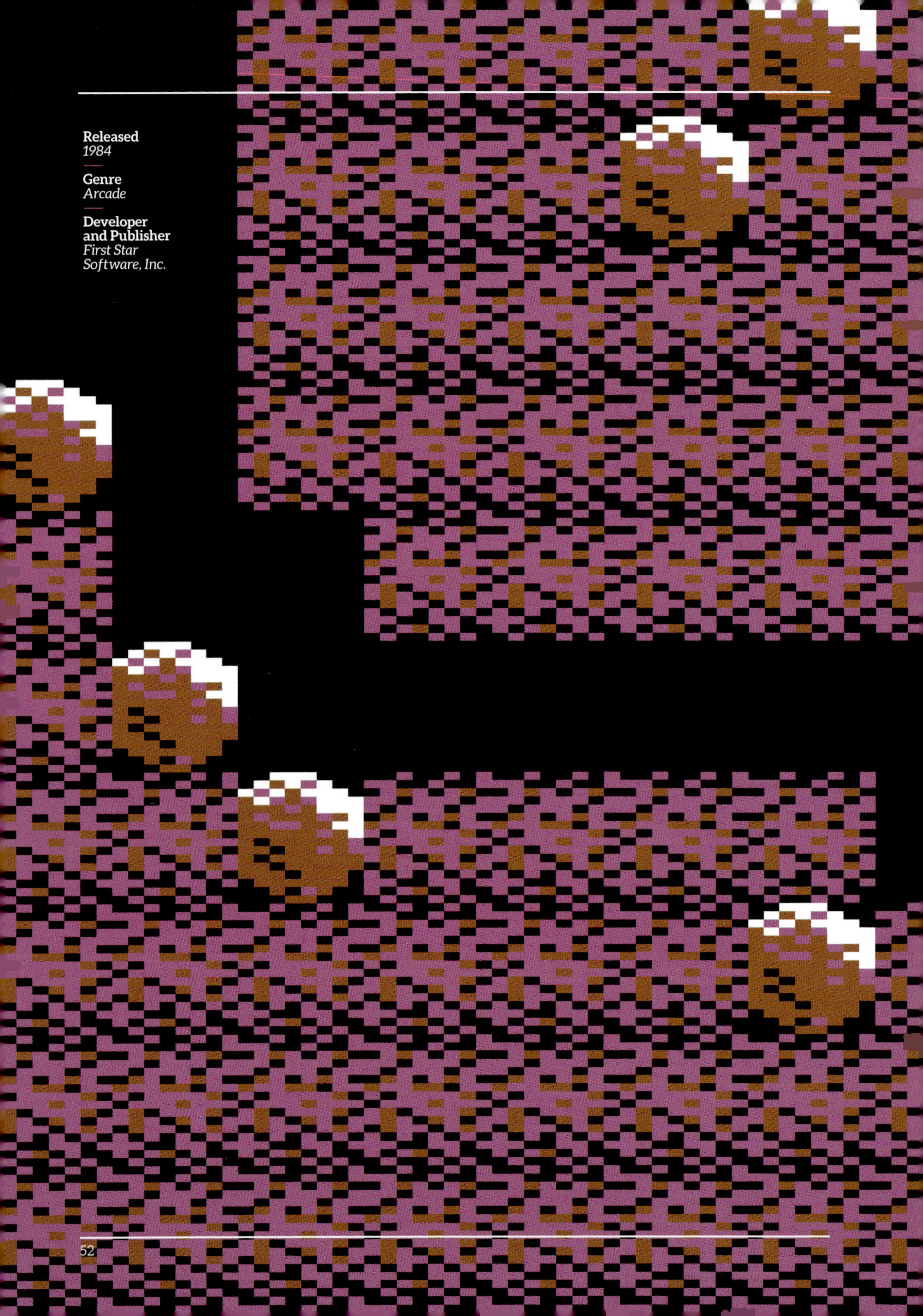

Released
1984

Genre
Arcade

Developer and Publisher
First Star Software, Inc.

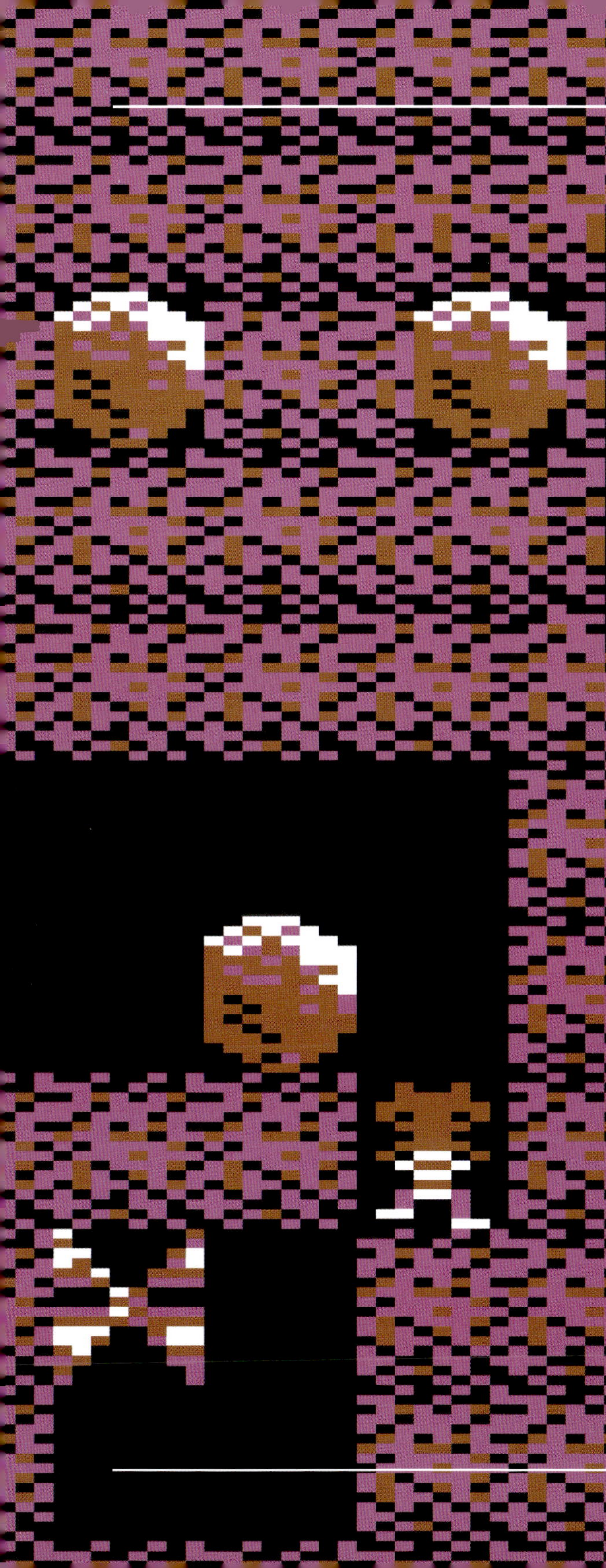

Boulder Dash

"These days, 'creative technology' is almost commonplace, but, back in the day, it seemed relatively rare. *Boulder Dash* was one of the first times in my life when I was able to draw on both my artistic-creative and technical-mathematical sides. It was as if separate poles had merged into a single whole. I wrote the original version for the Atari 400/800, and it was then ported to other platforms by various developers. The C64 conversion was by far the most faithful to the original."

Peter Liepa, original designer

Zaxxon

"My main memory of *Zaxxon* is it being the first game I ever bought for the C64 – and not realising it only worked with a joystick. So, Christmas morning was spent watching the Zaxxon ship repeatedly smack into the first wall while I forlornly bashed the keyboard. Only once the shops reopened and I'd bought one of Kempston's finest was I finally introduced to the horror of this tricky and endlessly repeating isometric shoot 'em up!"

Steve Jarratt, games journalist

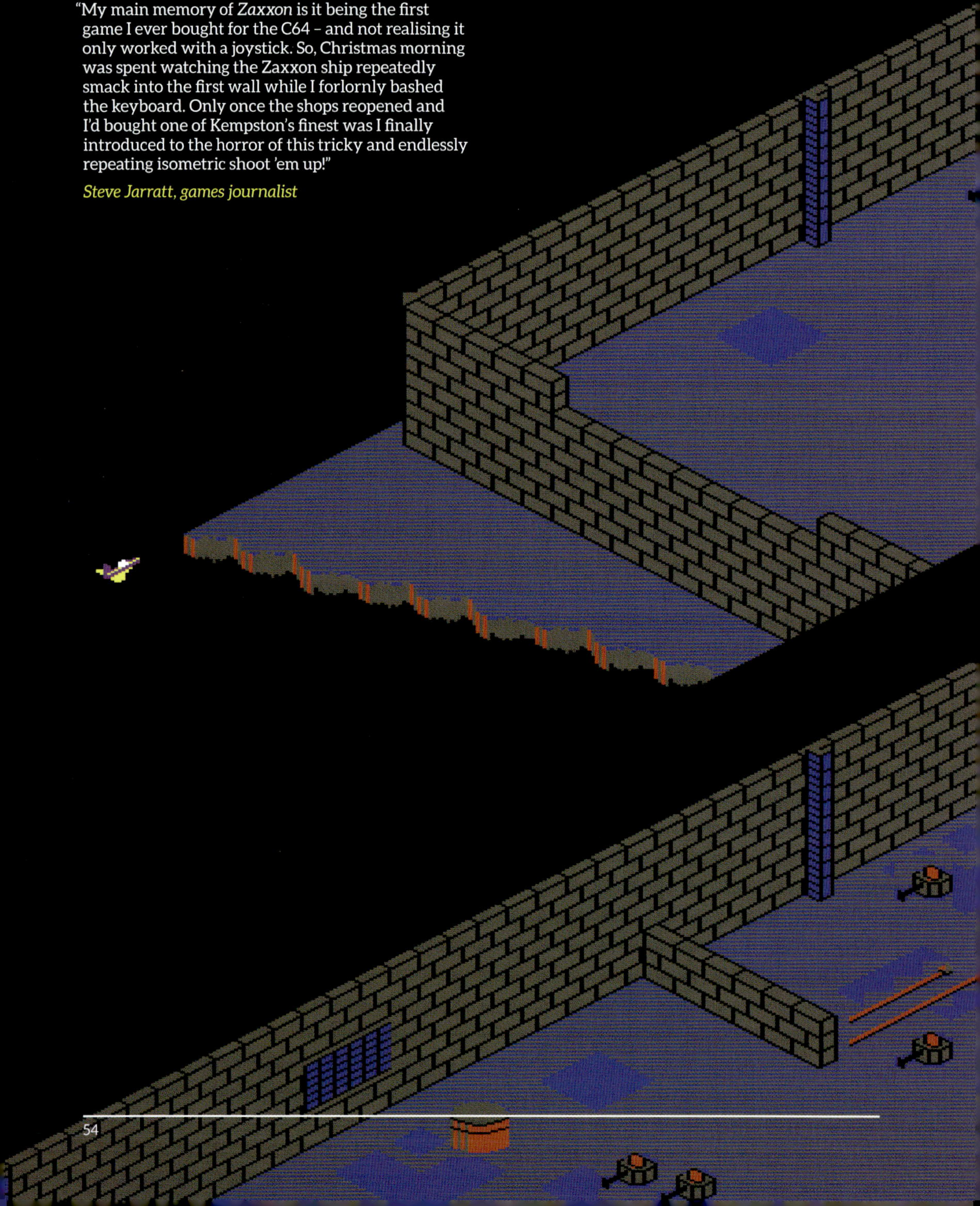

Released
1984

Genre
Scrolling shooter

Developer
Peter Adams

Publisher
Synapse Software

Originally by
SEGA

Released
1984

Genre
Arcade

Developer
SEGA

Publisher
U.S. Gold

Up 'n Down

This faithful conversion of the 1983 SEGA arcade game puts the player behind the wheel of a bouncy red Beetle as it traverses a scrolling isometric landscape collecting coloured flags. Naturally, there are other vehicles on the road to avoid, many of which can be jumped over or landed on. Indeed, those jumping skills will be tested to the max on later levels when gaping chasms appear in the road ahead. Although the C64 version is markedly slower-paced than its arcade counterpart, it's every bit as compelling, aptly demonstrating why SEGA was such an unstoppable arcade powerhouse back in the day.

An interview with **Karen Davies**

Karen Davies began her career working as an artist for Imagine Software on the ill-fated 'Mega Game'* Bandersnatch*. A founding member of Denton Designs, she gained a reputation for her work on seminal titles like* Shadowfire*,* Enigma Force *and* Frankie Goes to Hollywood*, and would later work for Special FX on titles including* Hysteria*,* Firefly *and* Batman: The Caped Crusader*.

Do you remember how you first got interested in art and design?
I always loved art. My earliest memory is from about five when I won an art competition at school. I know I painted a picture although I can't remember what it was, but I did win a set of paints, which I loved. I studied art all the way through school and I knew that was what I wanted to do for a living from an early age. After sitting my A-levels, I attended Liverpool Polytechnic and did a degree in fashion and textiles.

How did your career in the games industry get started?
I was introduced to the games business through my college friend Paula Cain who happened to be married to Steve Cain. After college, I worked in Lyon for a year before moving to London, and that's when I heard from Paula about a company in Liverpool that was hiring graphic artists to work in the games industry. I always fancied trying my hand at some graphic work, so I returned to Liverpool and was lucky enough to be offered a job at Imagine.

You worked at Imagine during its infamous demise; what was that experience like?
Imagine was such a fun and exciting place to work; it felt like it was the beginning of something special. People worked for the love of what they were doing and not just for the money (although some people did get paid very well and there were some lovely company cars). It sounds corny, but your team was like a family; people helped each other, played tricks on each other and, yes, it was really crazy at the end!

What was your first C64 game?
My first game was the ill-fated *Bandersnatch* from Imagine, but the first game I worked on that was actually released was *Shadowfire* from Denton Designs.

You were one of the founding members of Denton Designs; what was that experience like?
Denton Designs was great fun, albeit a bit scary as it was the first time any of us had ever owned a company, and some big commitments were made both personally and professionally. It was sad when Ian Wetherburn left the group, but overall I remember the experience as great fun, especially at the beginning when we would have business meetings with chaps in suits, and all five of us would turn up dressed, let's say, quite casual!

What did a typical day in front of the computer look like for you?
At Imagine, I kept regular hours, working from nine to five and occasionally working late or weekends. Some people, especially the programmers, would work for days without going home, sleeping under their desks and living on junk food (although this was common at Denton Designs and Special FX when a game had to be finished).

At Special FX we would have a time-out around three o'clock in the afternoon to take a break, play a game, or throw paper balls at each other. I was never any good at this game as I throw like a girl and obviously I don't like being hit by paper balls, but it would release a bit of tension and was a welcome distraction from staring at a monitor for eight to ten hours a day.

Which programs did you use to create your C64 art?
The only commercial program I can remember using was the KoalaPad and *KoalaPainter*, which I used to draw loading screens and the icons for *Shadowfire* and *Frankie Goes to Hollywood*.

Did you use any tools that weren't available commercially?
On every game, I typically used an in-house utility that had been written for me. This allowed the graphics to be slotted into the game engine as quickly and easily as possible, so both the programmer and I could see if they worked or not. There may have been a utility that incorporated the KoalaPad, but this may be a wishful thought from back then!

Firefly / *1988*

Looking back, what were the best and worst aspects of creating art for the C64?
The best aspect was, of course, the colours, and the worst aspect the chunky pixels which gave you a big stepped edge to the images. The best way to get around this was to overlay multi-colour sprites with hi-res sprites so that the bottom sprite had colour and the top sprite had definition. I think the first time I used this method was on *Hysteria*, which I worked on with Tony Pomfret.

What was your process? Did you plan on paper, or jump straight in onto the computer?
When I first started, I always used paper. At Imagine Software, I didn't actually have a machine; we worked on paper, and the programmer typed the data in. At Denton Designs, I used paper and computer (paper was good because you could work at home without dragging a computer with you), but before long I was using just a computer. I would sketch and design straight onto the machine because you didn't really know if something was going to work until you saw it on the screen.

"I remember this period with great affection – there was lots of hard work but also lots of laughter."

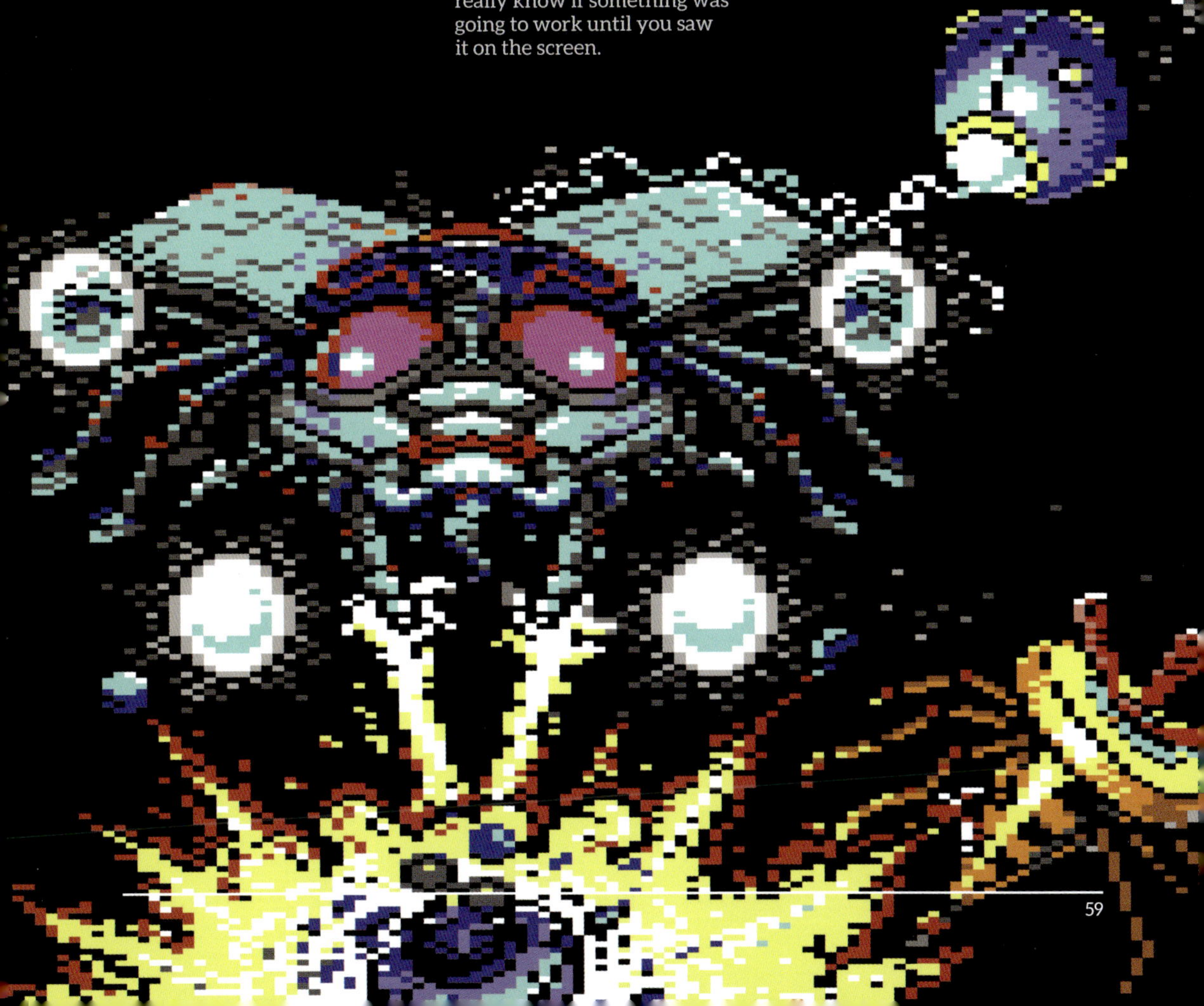

How did your process change throughout your career?
Apart from moving from paper to machine, I would say the main change was research, using more reference for animations and imagery. I resorted back to my art training, where you always start with research and experimentation, time permitting.

What was the development time for a typical game?
The development time would vary, but, typically, I would say two to six months, depending on the game. We always had time constraints, and publishers were usually quite strict as they would have a set release date. Additionally, handing over the game usually meant a final payment, so those deadlines were usually met!

Did you receive much artistic direction, or would you say you had complete freedom?
We would usually have a design, which gave us a general idea as to what was needed, and, if we were developing two versions of the game at the same time, we worked on the imagery together. For example, when we did *Frankie Goes to Hollywood*, I worked very closely with Ally Noble, who did the graphics for the Spectrum version. It's fair to say that anyone in the office could throw in ideas, and, if I thought they worked, I would try them.

When creating C64 art, which aspect did you most enjoy?
My favourite thing to draw was usually the loading screen. I wouldn't have to worry about size, flow or memory, I could just draw. Also, if you were drawing the loading screen, it meant you were at the end of the game, and it was all coming together.

Did you have much input in terms of game design?
I had some input, but it would typically be from an artistic point of view. As I'm not a gamer, I had no place telling people like Joffa Smith, Tony Pomfret, Steve Cain or John Gibson how to design a game! However, I knew I could always put ideas forward.

Did you pay much attention to the various magazine reviews?
I did pay attention to magazine reviews as we always had a good relationship with the press. Whether at Denton Designs or Special FX, it was always good to get a positive review. Of course, I also got mediocre reviews, but I often knew if the review was not going to be good (I just try not to remember those ones!).

If you had the chance to revisit any of your games, what would you change?
If I could go back and make changes, I would probably take a pass on some games, or maybe redo them with hindsight. Sometimes, the weakness was the time frame or design, but, sometimes, I didn't push to get the most out of the programmer or the machine.

Was there anyone working in the industry whose work was inspirational to you?
There are lots of people in the industry I found inspirational, most of them people I worked with including Joffa Smith (a wonderful artist, designer, programmer and a lovely bloke), Steve Cain (an exceptional artist and a good friend), John Gibson (need I say more?), Ian Moran... the list goes on and on.

What C64 games at the time impressed you, or had an influence on your work?
I didn't really follow the C64 scene. I saw games around the office and was occasionally shown the odd game by various people (especially if they thought I should see the graphics). If I had to name specific people, it would probably be most of the artists I worked with; everyone brought something new to the table, and you were always learning.

Outside of games, what were your biggest artistic influences?
I loved movies from an early age, including sci-fi, drama, thrillers, action and adventure. I also became a comic fan when I started working in the game industry, and that was when I became aware of the likes of Frank Miller and Stan Lee. At Denton Designs and Special FX, we also used the photographic books of Muybridge, along with books by illustrators like H. R. Giger, Boris Vallejo and Syd Mead.

Of all the games you've worked on, which are you most proud of and why?
I am particularly fond of *Shadowfire*; not only do I like the graphics, but it also holds good memories as we were just starting Denton Designs,

> *"At Imagine Software, I didn't actually have a machine; we worked on paper, and the data was typed in by the programmer."*

Shadowfire / *1985*

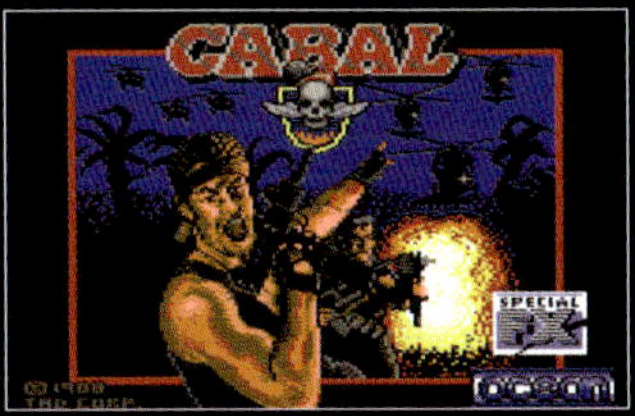

Cabal / *1989*

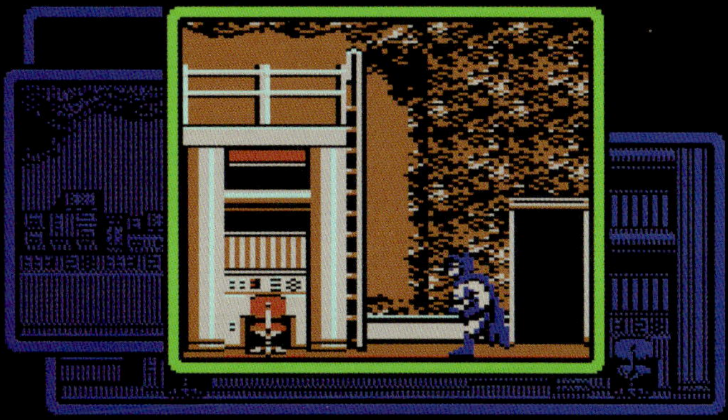

Batman: The Caped Crusader / *1988*

and it was the first game I ever had published. If I could only pick one, it would be *Batman: The Caped Crusader*. I like the animation of the main character and the different windows that opened to mimic comic book panels (that was Joffa's idea).

Were there any C64 games you worked on which sadly never saw the light of day?
Oh yes – *Bandersnatch*! They called it a 'Mega Game' because it was going to be bigger than anything that had been written before. Alas, Imagine went into receivership, and it never saw the light of day.

What was your final C64 game? What made you decide to leave the machine behind?
My last game on the C64 was *Cabal*, released in 1989. Then I moved on to the Amiga. It was bigger and shinier, with more colours and more memory – what was a girl to do?

Was there a C64 game you would have loved to have created the graphics for?
I can't think of any C64 games I wish I could have drawn the graphics for, but there are games that would have been really cool to have been involved in, like *Pokémon* or *Mario* – games that took the world by storm.

What are your favourite games?
I'm ashamed to say I never played computer games. I may have played *Tetris* on the Game Boy while waiting for the kids to come out of school, but that's it really.

What are your standout memories from the C64 era?
I have one or two stories from that period in my life, but whether they should be shared or not is a different matter! I remember this period with great affection – there was lots of hard work but also lots of laughter. I was also lucky to work with some brilliant and funny people, including Robbie Tinman, Ivan Davies and Andy Rixon, to name but a few.

Why do you think the C64 is remembered so fondly?
I really do not know; up until the last few years, I had no idea that people were still interested in these games or this period in gaming. To me, the C64 will always have a special place because it was the beginning of a new chapter and a taste of the possibility of what was to come.

Do you still own a C64?
I don't own a C64, and I don't think I have copies of any of the games I worked on, which is sad, but I know the games are out there, and it makes me smile that people are still interested in them.

What are you up to these days?
These days, I am working as a supply teacher in a local school. I haven't been doing it long, so it's new and exciting, and I am enjoying it. I am hoping it will eventually give me a chance to use my art training.

Released
1984

Genre
Scrolling shooter

Developer
Archer MacLean

Publisher
U.S. Gold

Dropzone

"After getting my degree with the minimum amount of work, I decided to try and produce a game which at least equalled the quality, speed and gameplay of the arcade games of the time. So I took inspiration from *Scramble*, *Defender*, *Stargate*, *Galaxian* and many others and went for it. It took me about six months to come up with something looking so good it could be an arcade cabinet."

Archer MacLean, designer and programmer

Montezuma's Revenge

"I created the original on the Atari when I was 15 years old, which took six to seven months. Shortly after, I was approached by Parker Brothers, who wanted to port it to all of the 8-bit systems. The C64 version was easily the most faithful as they did a great job working with my original source code. I've always had a soft spot for the C64, and, as a developer, I remember being very excited to work on it; 64K RAM was awesome, and the full-colour hardware sprites and audio were a big innovation."

Robert Jaeger, original designer

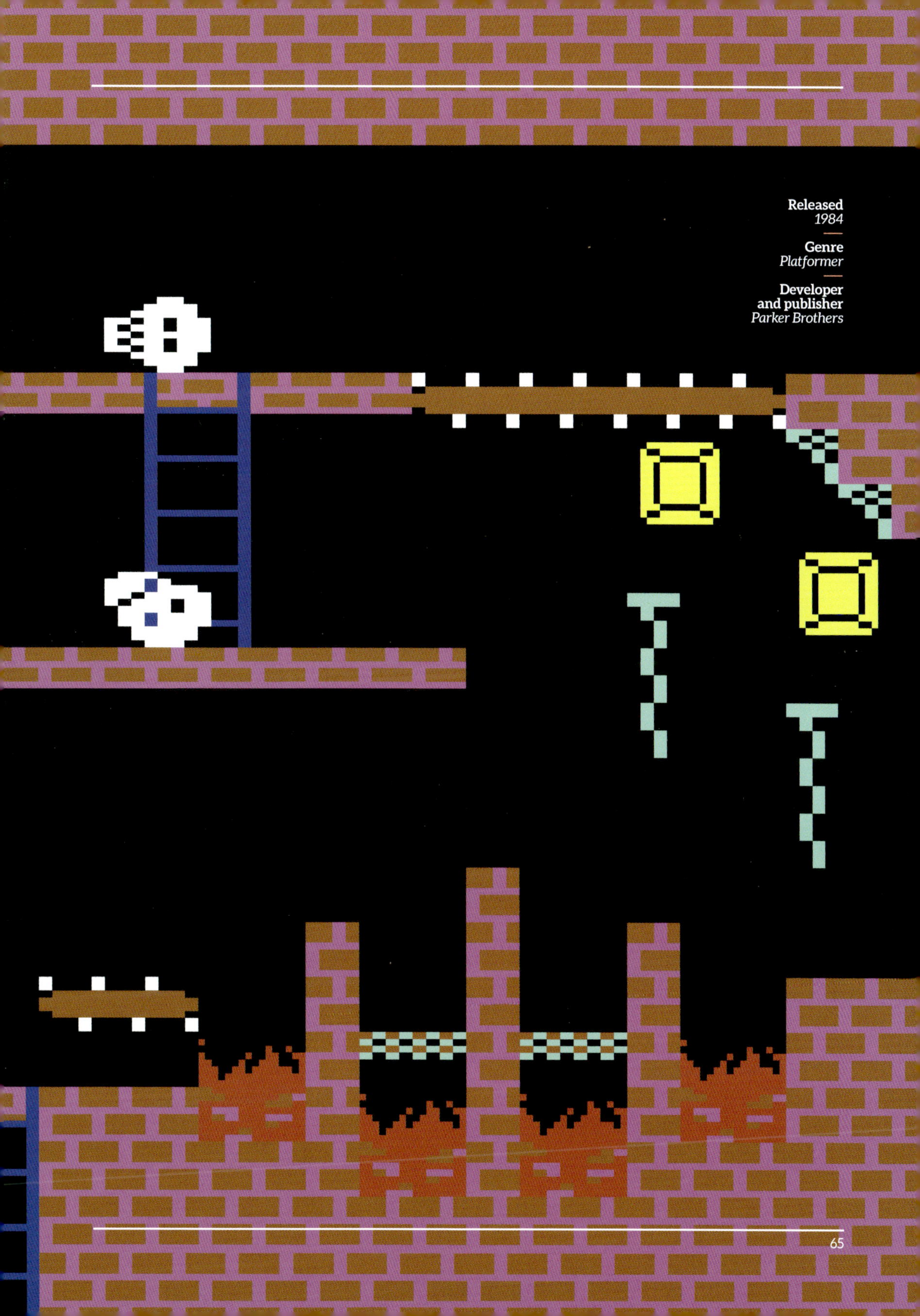

Released
1984

Genre
Platformer

Developer and publisher
Parker Brothers

Bruce Lee

"*Bruce Lee* remains a firm favourite with C64 enthusiasts 30 years after its original release. A unique blend of beat 'em up and platform game, it took players on an epic flick-screen adventure into the heart of a mysterious wizard's fortress to find the secret of immortality. In a novel twist, the game allowed a second player to assume the role of the bad guys and attempt to thwart Bruce's progress; the result was fiendishly fun and extremely addictive."

Andy Roberts, games journalist

Released
1984

Genre
Action

Developer
Datasoft Inc.

Publisher
U.S. Gold

Gyruss

"*Gyruss* was one of the first games I played on the C64. It was a lot of fun and remains so to this day. It was also one of the first copied games I got on disk from a friend at summer camp (I was 12 – gimme a break!) The game is a great arcade conversion, and its difficulty was tweaked to just the right level. *Gyruss* is a true classic and a game I'm looking forward to showing my son when he's old enough to play."

Andreas Wallström, guest reviewer

Released
1984

Genre
Shoot 'em up

Developer
Joe Helleson

Publisher
Parker Brothers

Originally by
Konami

Released
1984

Genre
Racing

Developer
Epyx

Publisher
U.S. Gold

Pitstop II

"*Pitstop II* was something of a technical tour de force back in 1984, with its fast, pseudo-3D courses, convincing car movement and head-to-head split-screen play (although this was offset slightly by the slowest, fiddliest pit stops of all time). The strobing courses and drone of the cars made for a real zen-like racing experience, and I remember having some tense races against the computer opponent. With a Grand Prix mode and multiple tracks, *Pitstop II* really set the mould for modern racing games."

Steve Jarratt, games journalist

Ghostbusters

"Many people remember the title screen of *Ghostbusters* more than the game itself. Artist Hilary Mills drew a perfect *Ghostbusters* logo, and the late Russell Lieblich made an instrumental arrangement of the *Ghostbusters* theme song. Unable to leave it at that, I engineered speech for the C64 in order to enable the game to yell 'Ghostbusters!' Add the song lyrics and a follow-the-bouncing-ball animation, and the title screen became one of the most memorable parts of the game."

David Crane, designer and programmer

Released
1984

Genre
Strategy

Developer
David Crane

Publisher
Activision

Impossible Mission

"Another classic from Epyx, which intoned the gamer to 'Stay a while… Stay forever!' with its amazing digitised speech. *Impossible Mission* was a beautiful exercise in platform gaming, requiring dexterity and timing to guide your somersaulting agent past Elvin Atombender's guardian robots. The level of precision required to complete the game plus the pressure of a countdown timer made it a tense affair – and I still recall the sheer relief as I finally managed to complete the password puzzle and confront the evil genius with just seconds to spare."

Steve Jarratt, games journalist

Released
1984

Genre
Action

Developer
Epyx

Publisher
U.S. Gold

Raid Over Moscow

"*Raid Over Moscow* immersed the player in the 1980s' Cold War conflict between the USA and Russia. As a nuclear missile hurtled toward US soil, the player was tasked with destroying multiple Russian missile silos, infiltrating the Kremlin, and neutralising the nuclear threat. From the *Zaxxon*-inspired attack run to the 3D bazooka section, the game was years ahead of its time, boasting incredible animation and stunning attention to detail that would become classic hallmarks of the Carver Brothers' later games."

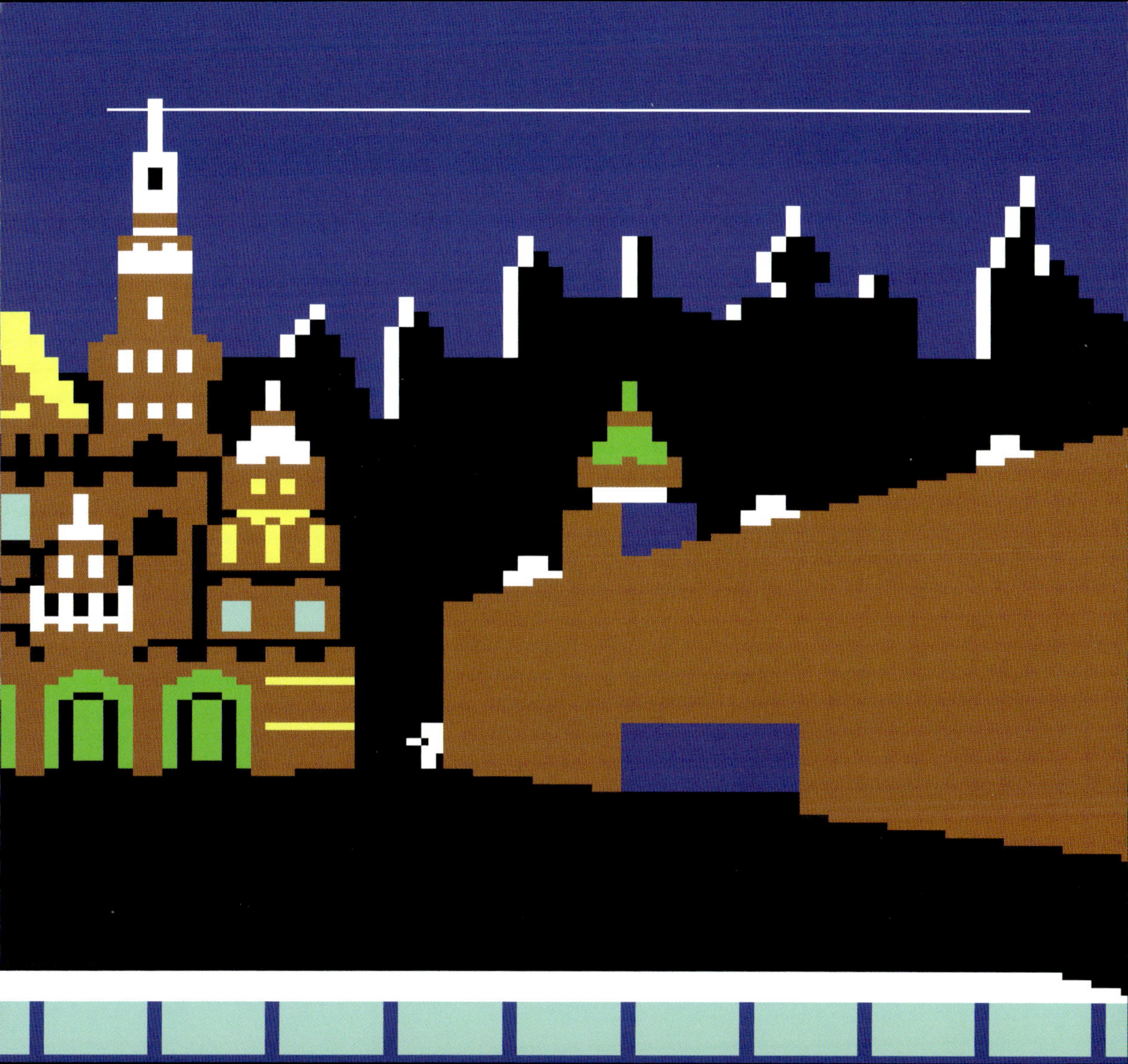

Released
1984

Genre
Shoot 'em up

Developer
Access Software

Park Patrol

"Activision released a solid body of slick, original and playable work in the '80s, including this gem by Tony Ngo, featuring jolly tunes from Russell Lieblich. Your duty as a ranger (a choice of boy or girl) is to patrol the park and pick up litter, avoiding turtles, logs and snakes, and saving drowning swimmers. It's a cute, frenetic, fun medley of running and jumping on land and zipping around the river in a rubber dinghy (which is, curiously, reminiscent of *Defender*)."

Gary Penn, games journalist

Released
1984

Genre
Action

Developer
Tony Ngo

Publisher
Activision

PATROL

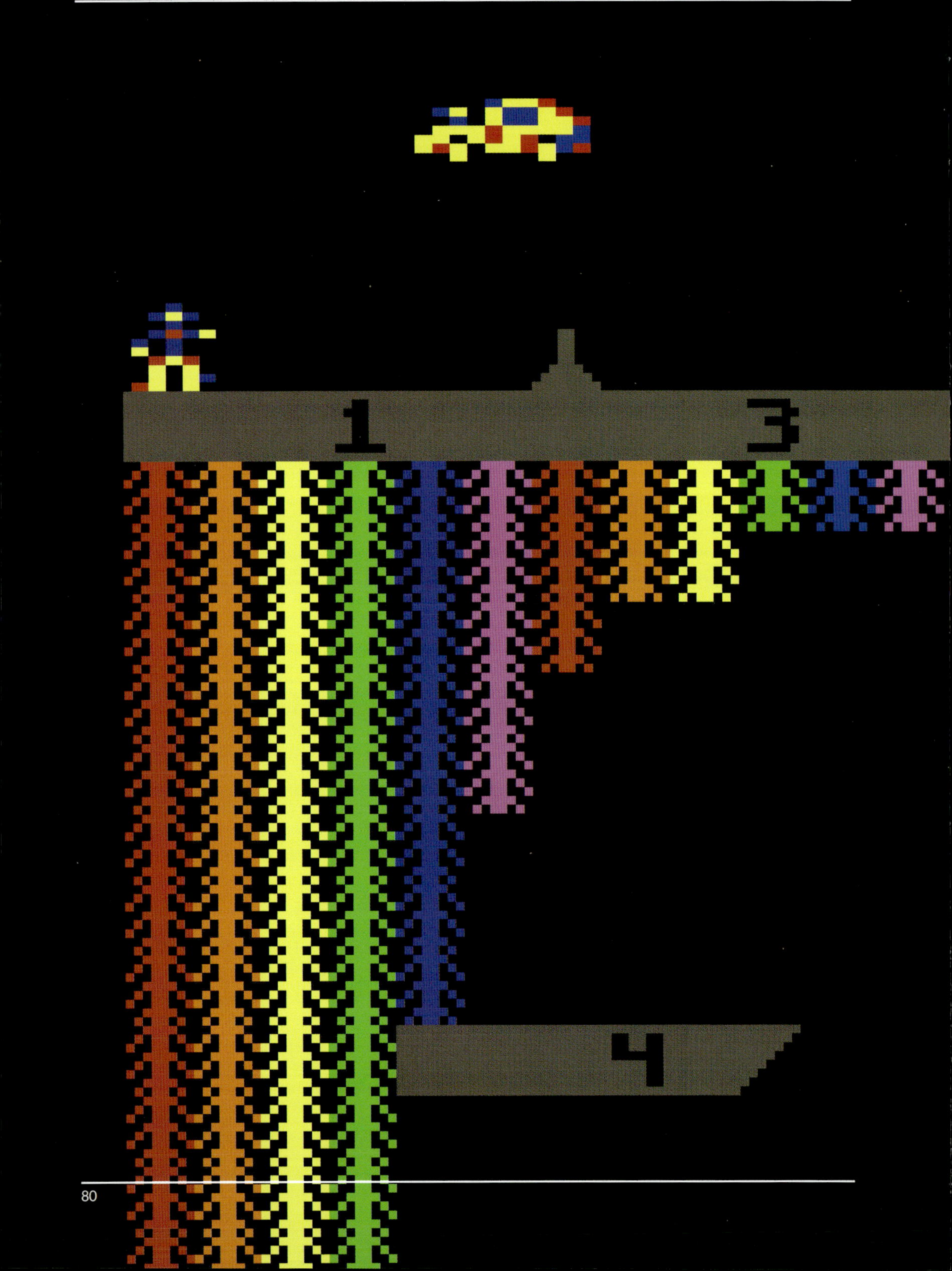
1
3
4

Space Taxi

"I wrote *Space Taxi* in my freshman year at Hopkins. Once I had the initial framework I was building one to two levels per day. When released, it received several awards, industry recognitions and was particularly praised for its digitised speech. The speech saying 'Hey Taxi!' and all the other phrases are actually my own voice captured on homemade electronics and played back at different speeds to create higher and lower pitch voices."

John F. Kutcher, designer and programmer

Released
1984

Genre
Arcade

Developer
John F. Kutcher

Publisher
Muse Software

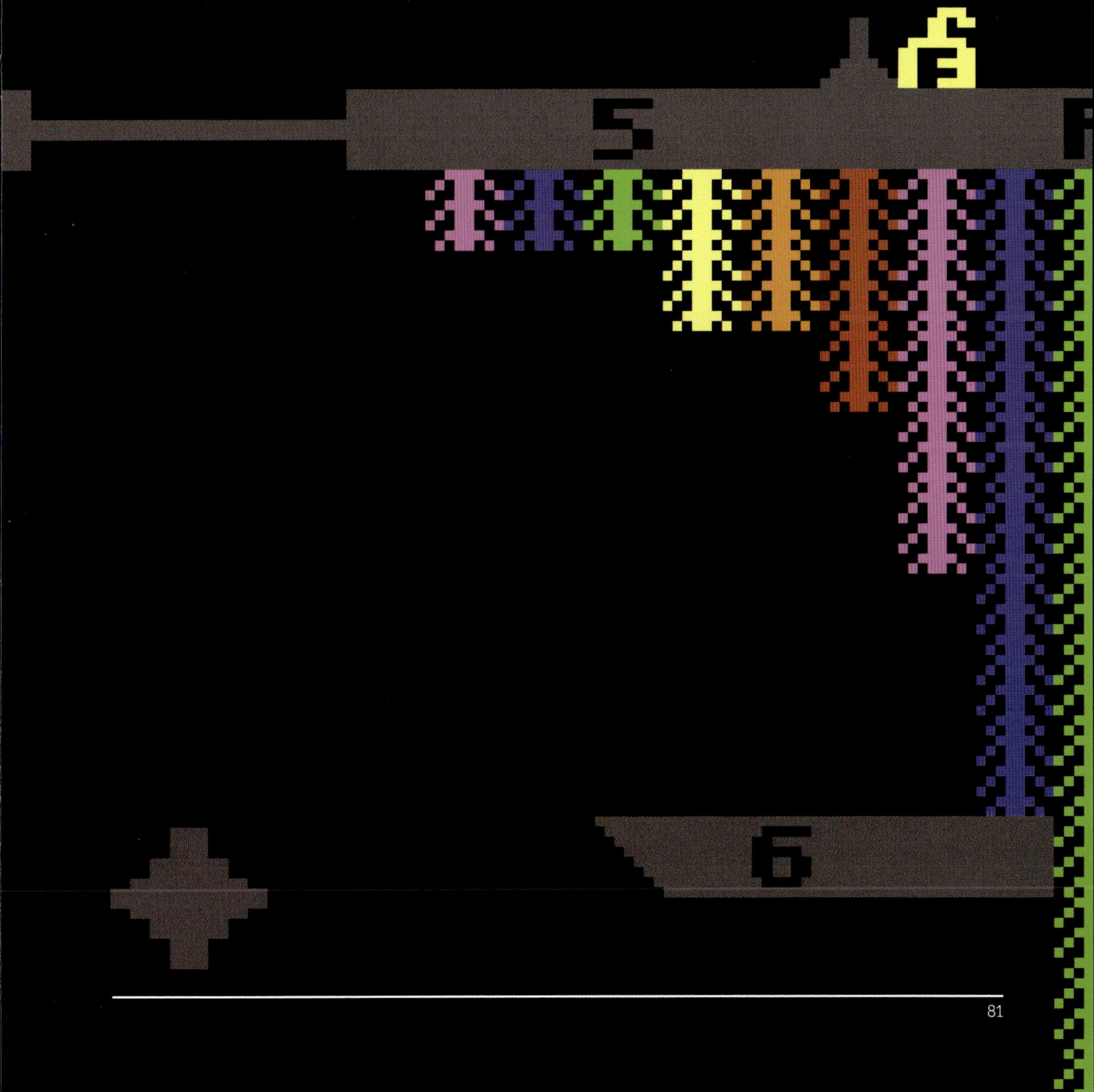

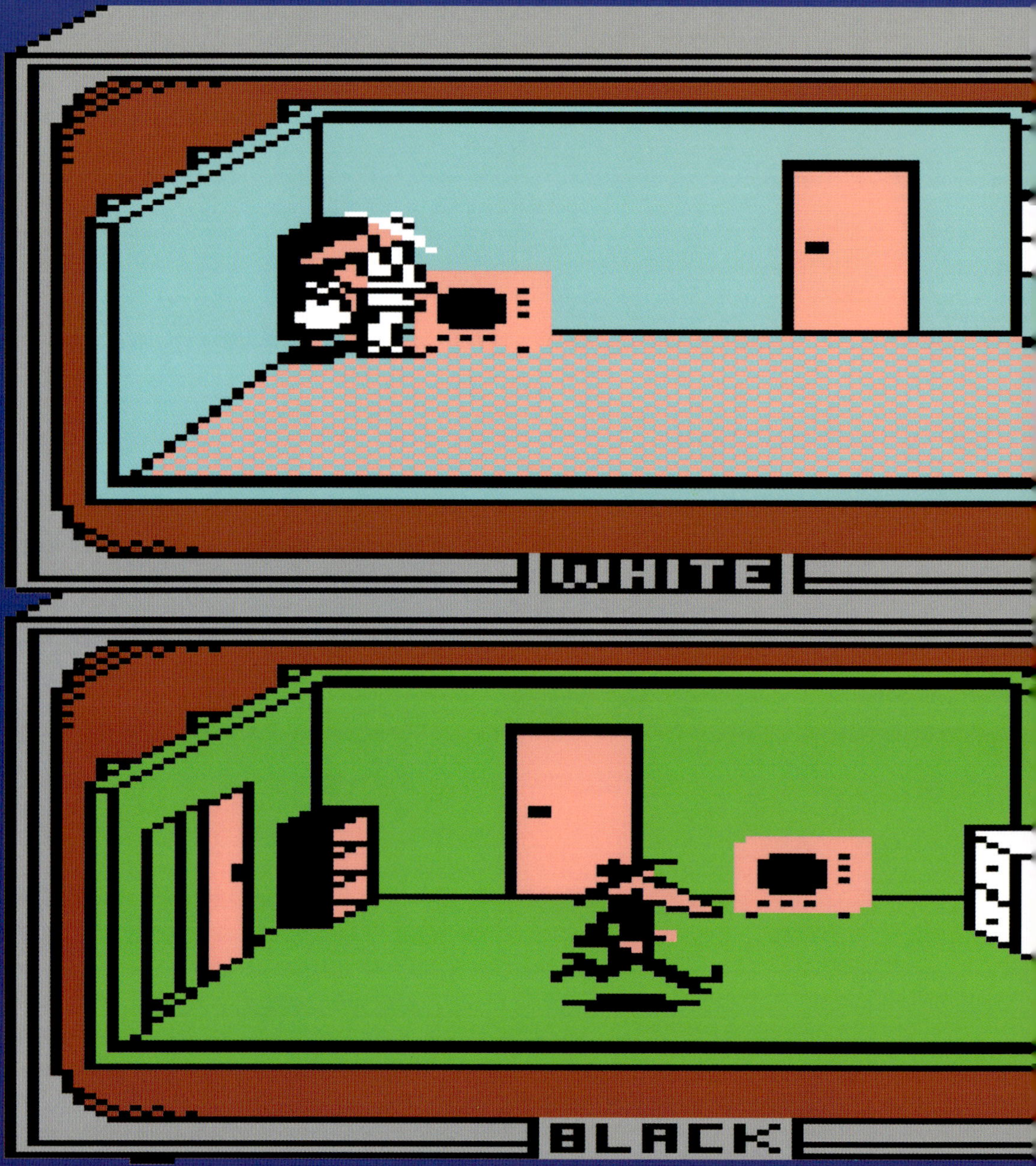
WHITE
BLACK

Spy vs Spy

"Simple, yet characterful line drawings and a text-free, kill-or-be-killed high concept made Mad Magazine's 1961 *Spy vs Spy* strip perfect for 8-bit gaming. First Star Software's split-screen, two-player design and a host of suitably lethal, comedic traps enjoyed smash-hit success and two sequels. 29 years later it was revived on iOS with lavishly updated, full colour graphics that somehow didn't quite match the charm of the 1984 original."

Stuart Wynne, games journalist

Released
1984

Genre
Strategy

Developer
Michael Riedel

Publisher
First Star Software

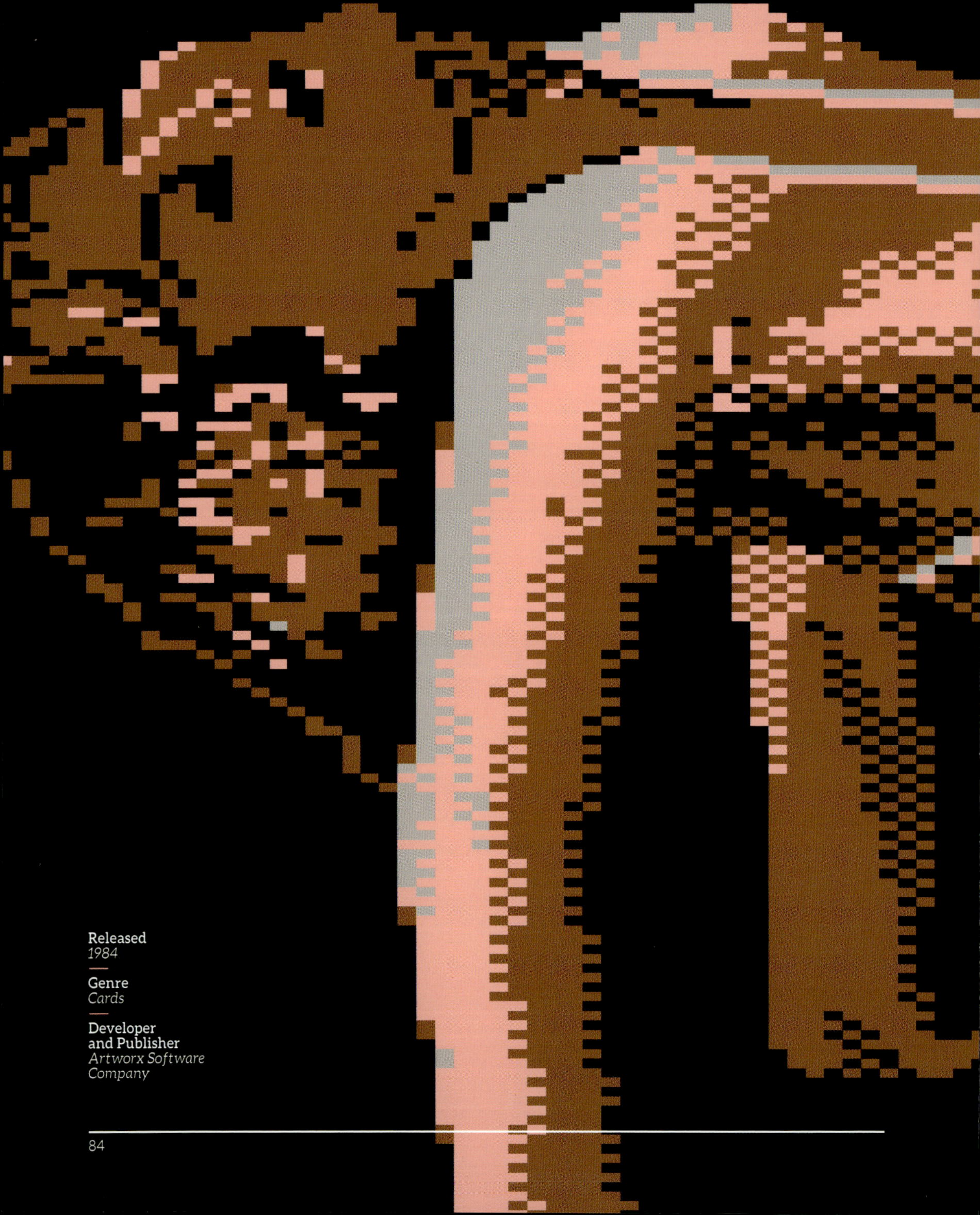

Released
1984

Genre
Cards

Developer and Publisher
Artworx Software Company

game for the C64, and in doing so won the appreciation of many a frustrated teenager. Based around the game of five-card draw poker, the aim is to simply win more hands than your sultry opponent, and in doing so rid them of their clothing. Cheap thrills aside, the game is a fairly decent poker simulation, if a little easy once you've mastered the rules. Thankfully, once you've tired of glaring at Suzi's and Melissa's pixels, additional data disks allow you to take on new opponents like Marlena and Candi (and the slightly less exotic David and Tony).

"I have such fond memories of this game for more than obvious reasons. I remember my friends and me sneaking into the basement to play after *Transformers* refused to load for the 300th time. As a teenager, it was one of the first games I purchased; the nostalgia was worth every penny!"

John Stanley, guest reviewer

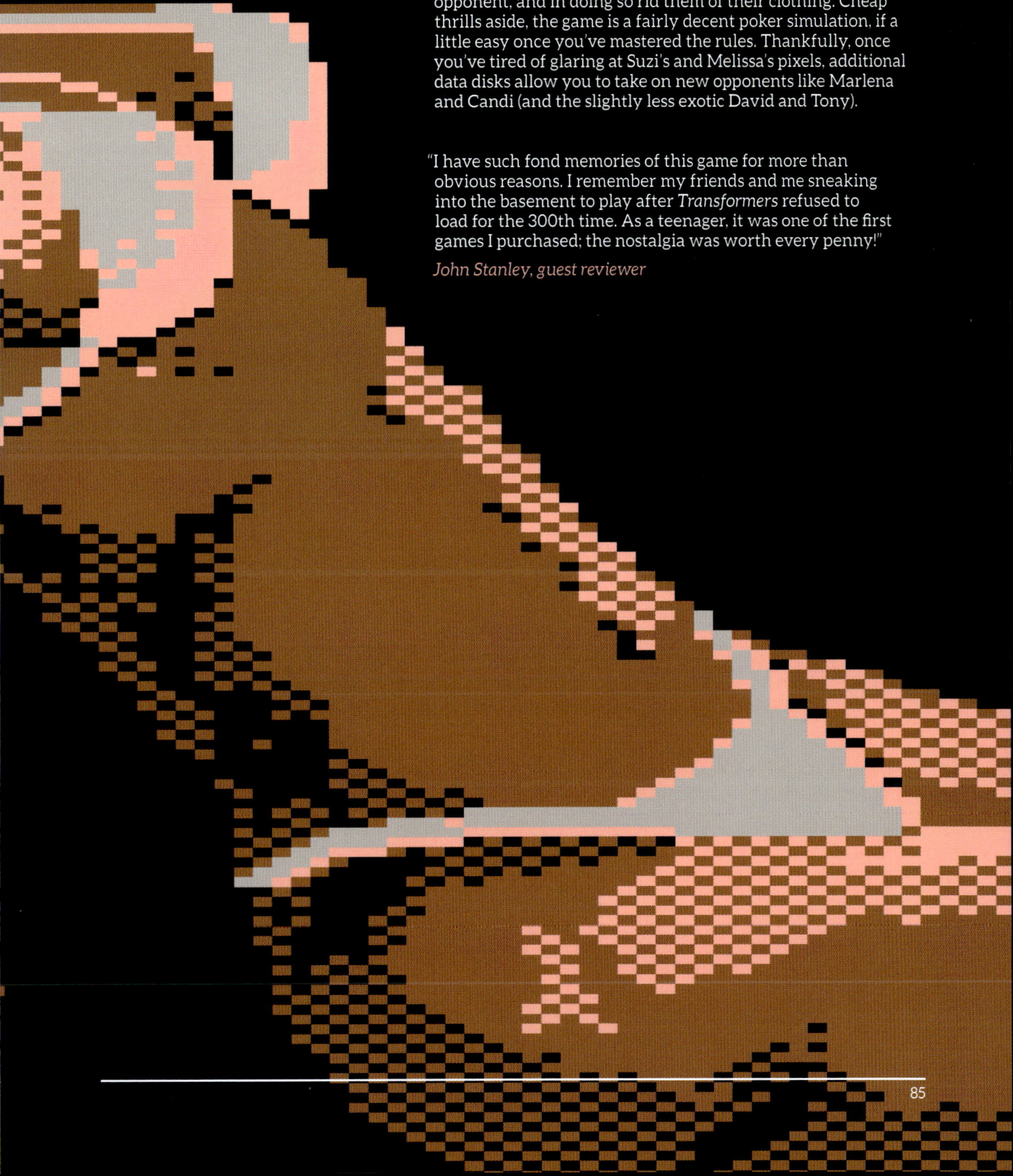

Summer Games

"Whereas the likes of Activision's *Decathlon* focused on the use of blistering brute force to achieve virtual athletic glory, Epyx's approach to a sports simulation was a more sophisticated affair. The detail, fluidity and realism were instantly remarkable, but it was the novel use of more involved control systems that made *Summer Games* so special. Best of all, up to eight people could compete around the same TV."

Gary Penn, games journalist

Released
1984

Genre
Sports

Developer
Epyx

Publisher
U.S. Gold

6581
2183

> "I was able to walk around shows without being mobbed, unlike Rob Hubbard, because I had strived to keep my photo out of the mags, but Rob's was all over the place!"

Martin Galway, musician

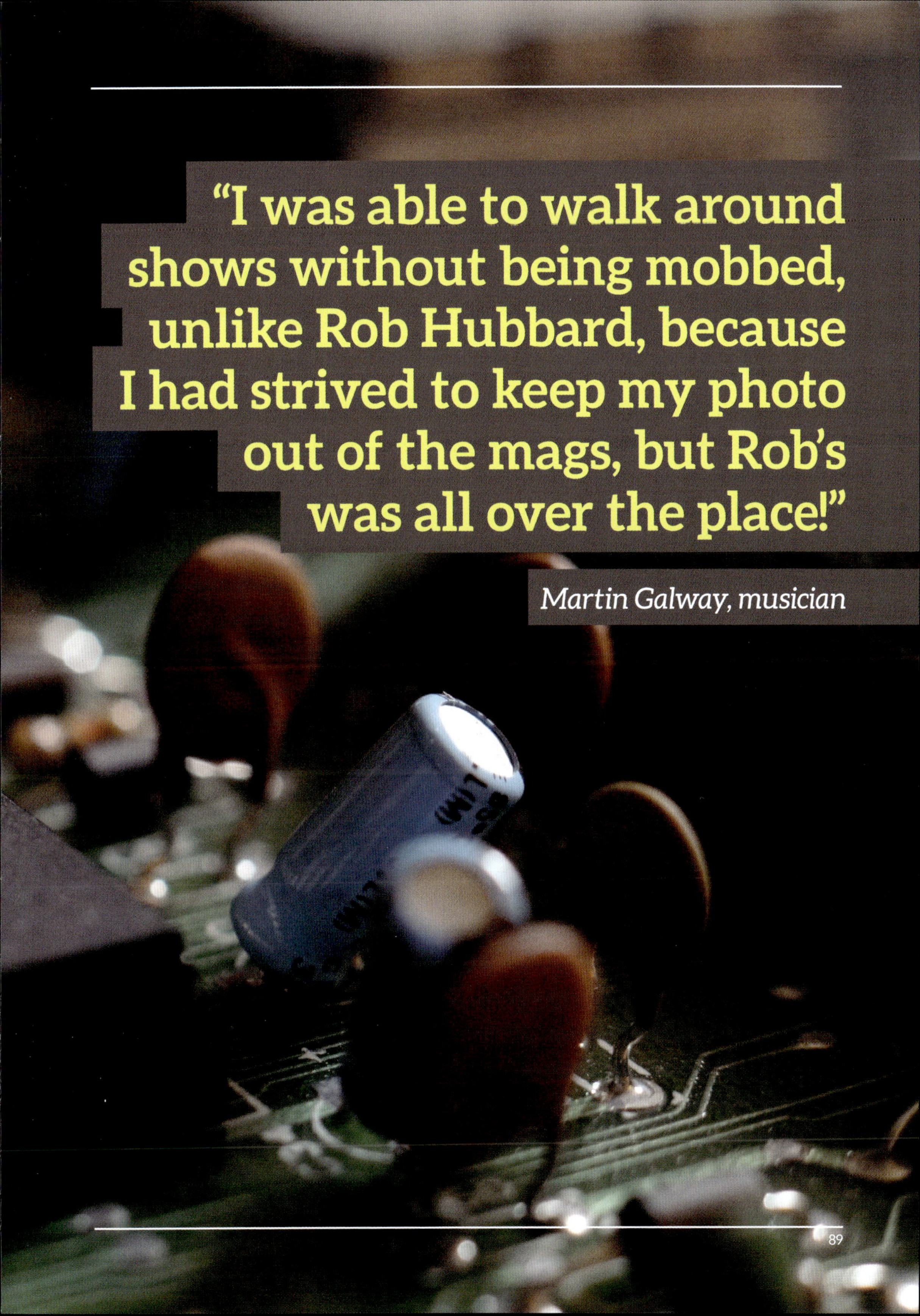

The Last V8

The impending threat of nuclear war in the mid-1980s made for some pretty bleak game scenarios, and *The Last V8* is certainly no exception. Set in 2008, seven years after a global nuclear war, the player's task is to guide a souped-up V8 to safety across the radioactive wastelands. Created by David Darling, this first release on Mastertronic's 'M.A.D.' label is perhaps best remembered for its fuzzy sampled speech, epic Rob Hubbard soundtrack, and brutally unforgiving gameplay. However, if you can master the challenging control system, there's a great deal of fun to be had out in the post-apocalyptic wilds.

Released
1985

Genre
Racing

Developer and Publisher
M.A.D.

400
KPH
x100
RPM

CREATED BY DAVID
DARLING
V8

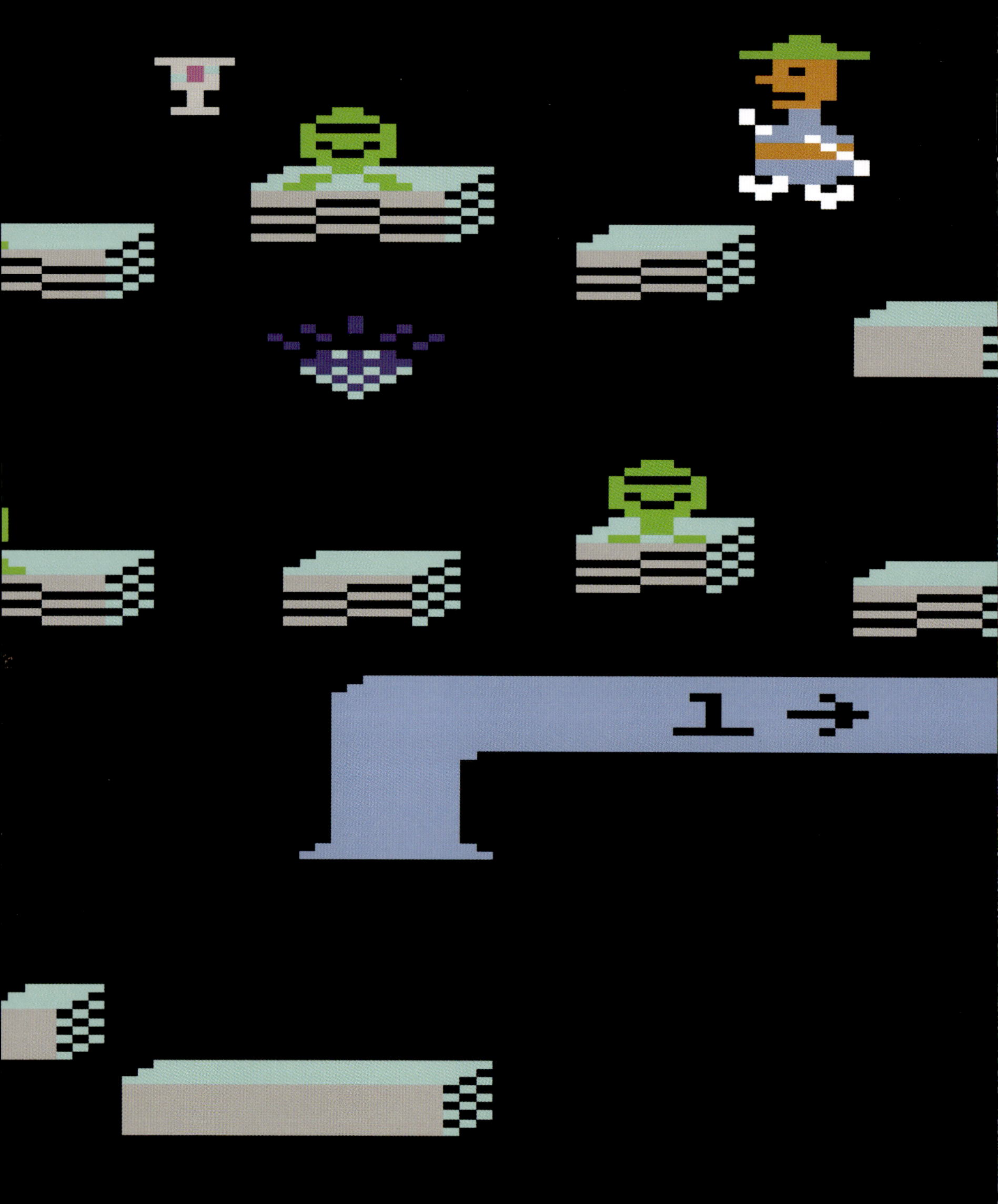
1

Bounty Bob Strikes Back!

"Both Bill Hogue's *Miner 2049er* and this sequel are coarse to the eyes, ears and fingers (and nails-hard to boot). And yet ... there's something about these games that just doesn't let go. The 25 stages see you painting platforms in your wake to win, punctuated by jumping, teleporting, sliding down slopes, climbing ladders and collecting objects to make roaming 'monsters' temporarily killable. The high-score table assembled by little birds is a delight to behold."

Gary Penn, games journalist

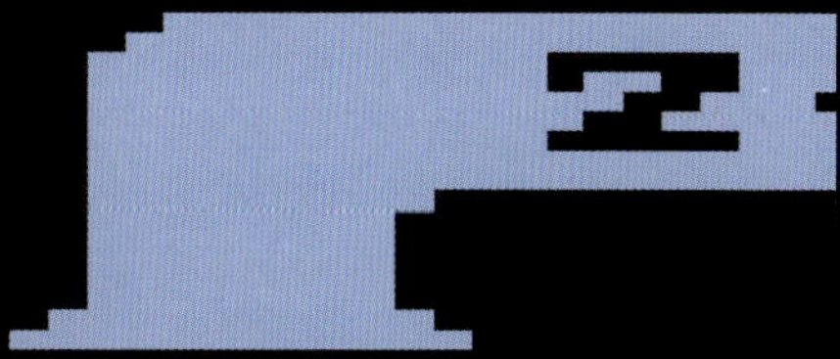

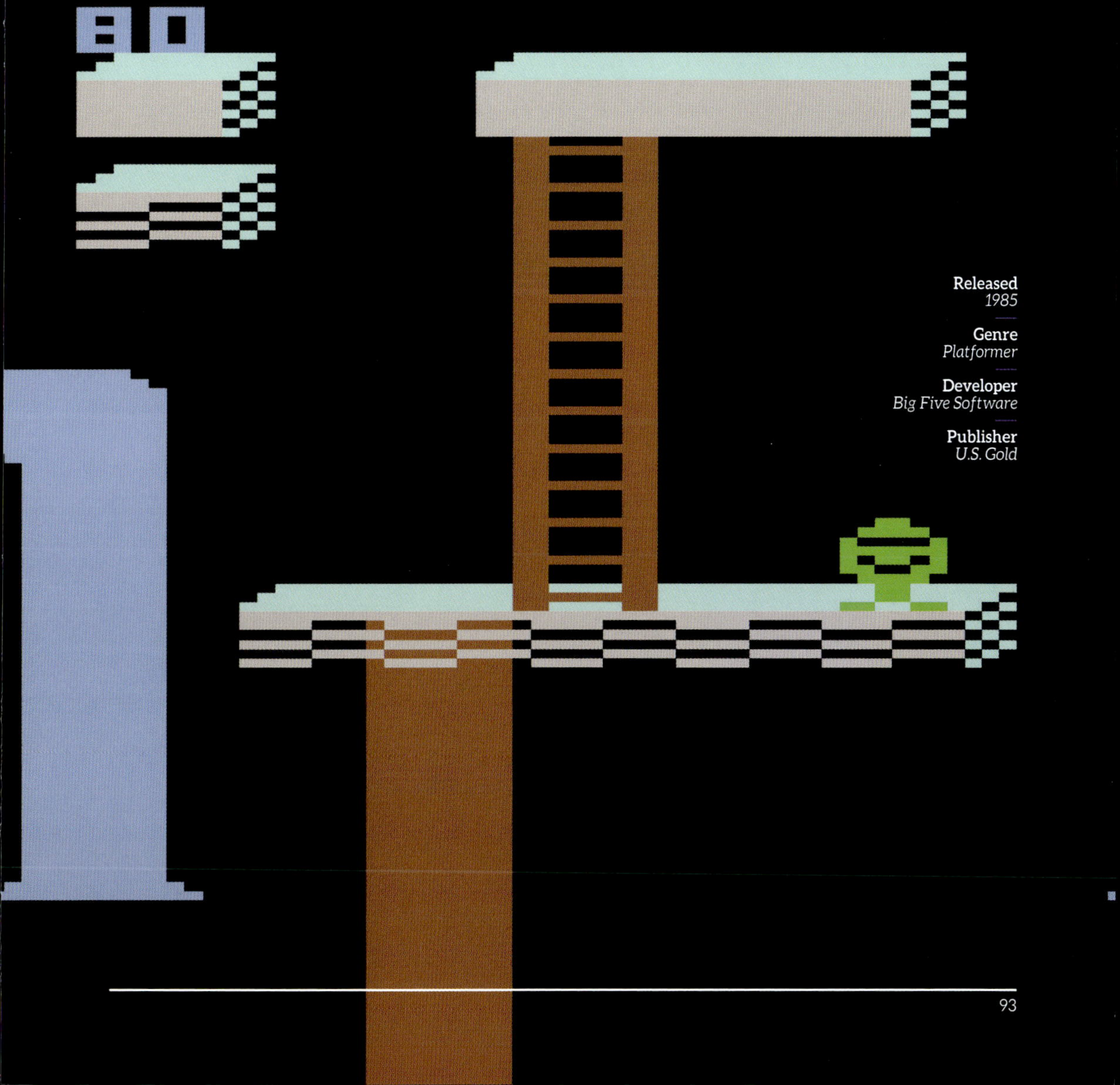

Released
1985

Genre
Platformer

Developer
Big Five Software

Publisher
U.S. Gold

Theatre Europe

Released
1985

Genre
Strategy

Developer
Alan Steel

Publisher
Personal Software Services

Artwork
Oliver Frey

Wizardry

Released
1985

Genre
Adventure

Developer
Steven Chapman

Publisher
The Edge

Artwork
Oliver Frey

THALAMUS

Thalamus was an independent UK computer game publisher originally established in 1986 by Newsfield, the publishing company responsible for the classic games magazines* Crash, Zzap!64, Amtix! *and* The Games Machine. *After Newsfield went into receivership in 1991, Thalamus was subsequently reborn as Thalamus Europe and continued to operate until 1993.

Based out of Newsfield's editorial offices in North London, Thalamus's core team comprised ex-Activision PR manager Andrew Wright and erstwhile Newsfield staff writer Gary Liddon. Their energy, passion, and fresh perspective – coupled with Oli Frey's iconic logo – helped define the company's quintessentially unique and contemporary branding, far removed from the often twee and teen-focused image of the computer games industry at that time.

Between 1986 and 1993, Thalamus released some of the most critically acclaimed games ever to grace the humble C64. Indeed, the company's policy of releasing games only when they were ready resulted in a steady stream of technically advanced and highly polished software. Created by some of the most talented programmers, artists and musicians in the business, many of Thalamus's titles were regarded as gaming landmarks.

Thalamus's debut title was *Sanxion*, a horizontally scrolling shoot 'em up released at the tail end of 1986 and created by the hitherto unknown Finnish programmer Stavros Fasoulas. An unabashedly unforgiving adrenaline-pumping blast through ten alien-infested levels, *Sanxion*'s faultless presentation, innovative split-screen viewpoint and legendary Rob Hubbard soundtrack helped ensure its success. *C&VG* magazine declared the game a 'C+VG Hit', calling *Sanxion* "No-nonsense blasting with some excellent frills", while *Zzap!64* dubbed it "one of this year's better blasts" and awarded the game a coveted 'Sizzler'.

Thalamus's difficult second album proved to be anything but. *Delta*, another horizontally scrolling shooter from Fasoulas, was an epic romp through 32 levels of uncharted space. From the innovative Mix-E-Load, to the lavish graphics, the game oozed polish from every pore. Indeed, *Delta*'s hypnotic soundtrack (inspired by the likes of Philip Glass and Pink Floyd) turned the game into an almost transcendental experience. As well as a *Commodore User* 'Screen Star' award, *C&VG* also branded the game a 'C+VG Hit', adding "With *Delta* you get action with a capital A", while *Zzap!64* declared, "The graphics are superlative, the effects are stunning, and the music is nothing short of amazing."

Not one to rest on his laurels, Fasoulas's third game for Thalamus hit the streets in late '87. *Quedex* (a.k.a. the *Quest for Ultimate Dexterity*), a slick, minimalist arcade puzzle game set across ten increasingly challenging planes, was quite unlike any game that had come before. Boasting the typical

> *"Many of Thalamus's titles were regarded as gaming landmarks."*

Thalamus polish and a thumping soundtrack courtesy of Matt Gray, *Quedex* was Thalamus's best-received title to date. "An original, beautifully designed and superbly implemented puzzle package," said *Zzap!64* as it slapped a 'Sizzler' on the game. Similarly enthused, *Commodore User* gave *Quedex* a 'Screen Star', calling it "the most original game of the year".

During the development of *Quedex*, Messrs Liddon and Wright left the company, to be replaced by ex-Electric Dreams producer Paul Cooper. *Quedex* also marked Fasoulas's final game for Thalamus as he took a hiatus from games development to fulfil his mandatory National Service in Finland. The not inconsiderable task of filling Fasoulas's shoes fell to veteran coder Martin Walker, who had previously programmed a string of C64 games for Quicksilva and Electric Dreams.

Arriving in early 1988, *Hunter's Moon* was a psychedelic, thinking man's shoot 'em up set in deep space. Surrounded by a myriad of mysterious alien structures, players had to use their brains as well as their trigger finger to survive. Beautifully presented and thoughtfully designed, *Hunter's Moon* became an instant classic. "Good-looking, innovative, and challenging", said *Zzap!64*, earning Thalamus another 'Sizzler' in the process, while *The Games Machine* gave *Hunter's Moon* 90%, calling it "a very decent, interesting, addictive game with immense appeal".

The summer of 1988 saw the arrival of *Hawkeye*, a side-scrolling run and gun created by Dutch demo group Boys Without Brains. Despite the game's gorgeous graphics and jaw-dropping parallax scrolling, *Hawkeye*'s simplistic gameplay polarised opinions in the gaming press. "In the playability stakes, it leaves me completely cold", said *C&VG*, giving *Hawkeye* a mere 3/10. Conversely, *Zzap!64* branded the game "an addictive and beautifully presented shoot 'em up of the highest calibre", earning Thalamus the first of many 'Gold Medal' awards.

Delta / *1987*

Hunter's Moon / *1987*

Hawkeye / *1988*

Creatures / *1991*

Armalyte, a horizontally scrolling shoot 'em up created by fledgling developer Cyberdyne Systems. Although touted as the sequel to *Delta* to generate more sales, *Armalyte*'s stunning visuals and refined gameplay ultimately thrust it head and shoulders above every other shooter on the C64. "It's simply the pinnacle of Commodore gaming at present," said *C&VG*, awarding the game 9/10, while *Zzap!64* gave it a 'Gold Medal' award, adding, "If you miss *Armalyte* you're missing one of the best 64 shoot 'em ups of all time."

It was almost a year before Thalamus's next C64 release, *Snare*, a devilishly cunning arcade puzzle game released at the tail end of 1989. A daring quest to retrieve a dead billionaire's prized possession from the heart of a deadly 20-level maze, players needed to master the game's disorientating 90-degree turns in order to navigate the levels safely. *ACE* magazine praised *Snare* highly, calling it "an enjoyable and very addictive game", while *The Games Machine* went as far as branding the game's programmer Rob Stevens as "a cruel, devious son-of-a-bitmapper!".

Thalamus wrapped up the year with *Retrograde*, an absorbing shoot 'em up developed by newcomers Apex Computer Productions and Transmission Software. *Retrograde*'s diverse mix of gameplay styles, coupled with a highly advanced weapons system, was a breath of fresh air in a market starved of decent blasters and saturated with sub-standard arcade conversions and movie licences. "*Retrograde* is a masterpiece of programming," said *Your Commodore*, awarding the game 95%, while *Zzap!64* gave the game a 'Sizzler' and dubbed it "an utterly awesome shoot 'em up".

Originally developed under the name '*Globe Trotter*', *Heatseeker* arrived in 1990 to a somewhat lukewarm reception. Created by Paul O'Malley, who had scored a *Zzap!64* 'Sizzler' with his previous game *Arac*, *Heatseeker* was a unique experience with an environmentally conscious subtext. While *Zzap!64* praised the game's originality and presentation, *Heatseeker* sadly never matched the critical acclaim thrust upon Thalamus's other titles. Disappointing sales led to *Dominion*, the follow-up to *Heatseeker*, being given away free on a *Zzap!64* cover tape.

Thalamus's next release was *Summer Camp*, a game that heralded the company's shift towards the cuter end of the gaming spectrum. Created by the late John Ferrari, who had previously programmed a string of budget games for Mastertronic and Codemasters, *Summer Camp* was a cute 'n' cuddly flick-screen platformer boasting a plethora of neat touches and slapstick cartoon humour. *Your Commodore* gave *Summer Camp* 95%, praising its graphics and playability, while *Zzap!64* called it "a fun-packed challenge with plenty to write home about".

In 1991, Thalamus continued to go from strength to strength with the release of *Creatures*, a hilariously cute and twisted platform game from Apex Computer Productions. Chronicled as a developer diary in *Zzap!64*, *Creatures*' slick implementation and now infamous 'torture screens' ensured the game a much-deserved place in the C64 Hall of Fame. "Overwhelmingly addictive gameplay and amazing attention to detail," said *Zzap!64*, pinning a 'Gold Medal' award on the game, while *Commodore Format* gave *Creatures* 91%, adding, "You'd be daft to miss it."

Swift to capitalise on *Creatures*' immense success, the company (now operating as Thalamus Europe following Newsfield's demise) released *Creatures 2: Torture Trouble* in 1992 to considerable critical acclaim. Now with even more torture screens and a smorgasbord of amazing bonus stages and interludes, the game was a masterclass in C64 game development. *Commodore Format* described *Creatures 2* as "an indispensable feast of frantic fun", while *Zzap!64* gave it a 'Gold Medal' award, saying "colourful, fast and gruesome. But what a laugh!"

Sanxion / *1986*

1992 also saw the release of *Winter Camp*, the sequel to *Summer Camp*, featuring the star of the original, Maximus Mouse. Tasked with saving Camp Nice 'n' Icy from an impending avalanche, players were treated to a delightfully endearing arcade adventure set across eight stages, in what was undoubtedly John Ferrari's finest hour. "*Winter Camp* really outclasses its predecessor," said *Zzap!64*, awarding the game a well-deserved 'Sizzler', while *Commodore Format* thought the game "immensely stylish".

Thalamus's C64 swansong was the wacky cartoon adventure *Nobby the Aardvark*, which hit the streets in late 1992. Created by Genesis Software, Nobby's quest to find the legendary land of Antopia took him through seven diverse levels using all manner of vehicles and weapons. Bursting with detail and humour, *Nobby* was a sure-fire hit with reviewers. "One of the best games of the year," enthused *Zzap!64*, awarding *Nobby* another 'Gold Medal' for Thalamus's trophy cabinet. *Commodore Format* simply stated that "without doubt, *Nobby* is excellent".

But, by the time *Nobby* hit the streets, the sun was already beginning to set on the C64, and a lack of retail interest coupled with rising development costs forced many smaller publishers like Thalamus to focus on the more lucrative 16-bit market.

After releasing a disappointing conversion of *Creatures* for the Amiga and Atari ST, Thalamus Europe finally closed its doors for good in 1993.

In a market dominated by numerous heavyweight contenders, the small but mighty Thalamus managed to assuage the naysayers and forge a reputation as a force to be reckoned with. A perfect marriage of style, substance and technical prowess, Thalamus's back catalogue was home to some of the most unique, innovative, and technically adept games ever to grace the humble Commodore 64.

Thalamus may have gone, but it was certainly not forgotten. As the crowdfunding era began to gain momentum in the early 2010s, industry veteran Andy Roberts saw an opportunity to resurrect the company as Thalamus Digital and bring many of Thalamus's classic C64 games back to life as a set of 'remastered' titles.

Thalamus's return was officially heralded on 29th August 2017, when a teaser trailer for the *Hunter's Moon Remastered* Kickstarter campaign was released via social media. The ambitious project would ultimately reunite many of the original game's core team, including creator and programmer Martin Walker, musician Matt Gray, and graphic artist Robin Levy.

> *"A perfect marriage of style, substance and technical prowess."*

Following a successful crowd funding campaign – and a mere three decades after its original release – *Hunter's Moon Remastered* hit the streets in August 2018, boasting a wealth of updates including new levels, trainer mode, a level editor, and some truly jaw-dropping cinematic sequences that set new standards for C64 animation. "*Hunter's Moon Remastered* is a stunning update," said *Zzap!64*, describing the new additions as "the most incredible array of options and features you'll find in any C64 game". Fittingly, like its predecessor, *Hunter's Moon Remastered* scooped a 'Sizzler' award, scoring a formidable 93% in the process.

Since its inception in 1986, the Thalamus brand has been synonymous with graphical polish, technical excellence, and high production values, with a mere glimpse of the iconic logo sending C64 fans into a frenzy of nostalgia. Judging by the critical response to the first remastered title, Thalamus Digital seems intent on continuing the outstanding legacy of its forebears.

Scarabaeus

"With a *Zzap!64* 'Sizzler' and 96% score, I duly went out and bought this puzzle maze game by European outfit Andromeda Software. Graphically, the 3D mazes were incredibly effective, and the spooky atmosphere was enhanced by some great music, which could be toggled to the sound of your own breathing and heartbeat. Turning a corner directly into the path of poisonous spider was genuinely unnerving. However, the lack of decent instructions meant I never really got anywhere with it; even watching YouTube videos 30 years later, I'm still pretty much stumped!"

Steve Jarratt, games journalist

Released
1985

Genre
Adventure

Developer
Andromeda Software

Publisher
Ariolasoft

Rally Speedway

"Years before seminal racers like *Supercars* and *Slicks* threw their hats into the ring to battle it out for the auspicious title of best top-down racer on the C64, John Anderson's *Rally Speedway* had already beaten most other contenders to the punch. Though not the prettiest in the pageant, what the game lacked in aesthetics, it more than made up for in the playability stakes. With variable weather conditions, a built-in track editor, and scrumptious two-player mode that Saturday afternoons were made for, *Rally Speedway* remains one of the most playable – and horribly underrated – racing experiences on the C64."

Andy Roberts, games journalist

Released
1985

Genre
Racing

Developer
John Anderson

Publisher
Commodore

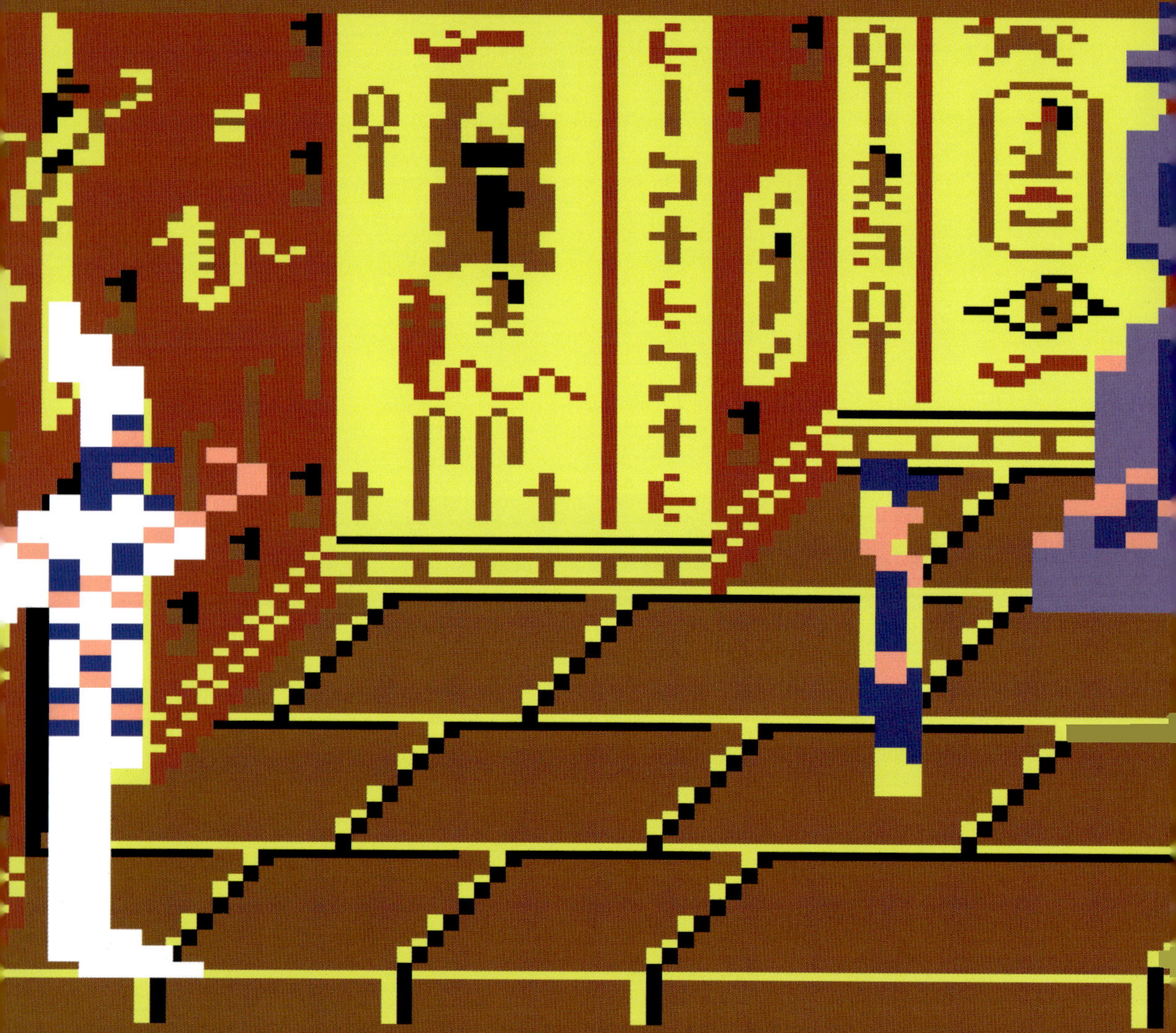

Entombed

"All the Ultimate C64 games were contracted out to third parties; none were written in-house. In fact, it wasn't known until a few years ago who even created the Arthur Pendragon titles. Of the four in question, this is arguably the best, as Arthur finds himself trapped within an Egyptian tomb, looking for an exit without getting squished along the way. Cunning traps, head-scratching puzzles and mummies hunting you down in the corridors await. The graphics are blocky and gaudy, but the torchlight effect was terrific. If only the other games could have been this good."

Mat Allen, guest reviewer

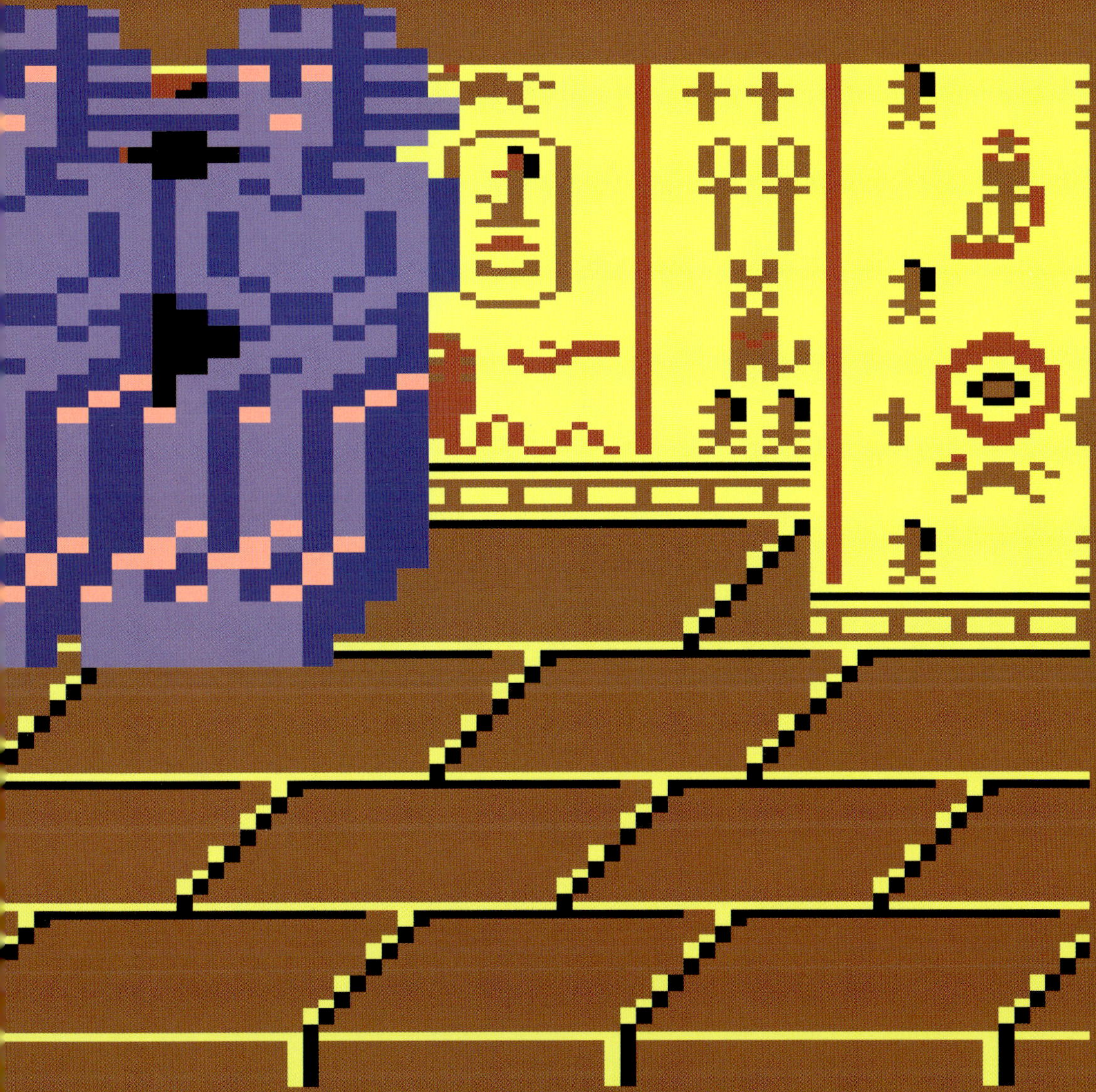

Released
1985

Genre
Adventure

Developers
Dave and Bob Thomas

Publisher
Ultimate Play The Game

"The song I s
Will tell th
Of a cold o

The Bard's Tale: Tales of the Unknown

"The first in a long-running RPG series, *The Bard's Tale* used its small 3D view to portray the action in the city of Skara Brae and its hidden dungeons. Enemy encounters were displayed as a close-up animated portrait as the fight took place. A party could include several character types, notably the Bard, whose magical songs provided important effects (such as light in the darkness). The grind to gain experience unlocked better spells and stronger characters by reporting to the Adventurer's Guild, ready to fight the ultimate villain Mangar in his tower."

Andrew Fisher, guest reviewer

"*The Bard's Tale* came out of my friendship with Michael Cranford as high school *Dungeons & Dragons* players, and it was originally pitched as *Shadow Snare*. Then, later on, EA decided to name it *Tales of the Unknown Vol 1: The Bard's Tale*. After it became a big hit, EA decided it didn't want to lose the value of referencing the Bard, so it dropped the whole '*Tales of the Unknown*' bit altogether."

Brian Fargo, original co-designer

Released
1985

Genre
RPG

Developer
Interplay Productions

Publisher
Electronic Arts

Commodore User masthead by Robin Levy / 2016

First published in October 1983, Emap's Commodore User was one of the earliest C64 magazines to hit British news stands. Originally geared towards the more serious Commodore owner, the magazine would later expand its games coverage in parallel with the burgeoning C64 games market. In 1990, Commodore User was rebranded as CU Amiga, and it eventually closed in 1998.

MARCH 1988
COMMODORE
USER
PHOTON DEATH!
CINERATED!
TRAIN-DERAILED!
ZOR-GUTTED!
REFLY-FRAZZLED!
March 1987 · £1
COMMODORE
USER
310 pta · HFL 5.75
NEMESIS
REVIEWED
WIN A NIGHT OUT WITH THE C.U. TEAM
ARCADES
LE MANS · ROAD TEST
EXPRESS RAIDER
REVIEW AND COMPO
MMODORE
USER
MOLINOS
OLÉ!
£1.10
Nº1 For AMIGA GAMES
JUNE 1988
COMMODORE
USER
HFL 5.90 · DM 5.50
CYBERNOID MAPPED
GREAT GIANA SISTERS
LOVE AT FIRST SIGHT

***Zzap!64* masthead by Robin Levy** / 2016

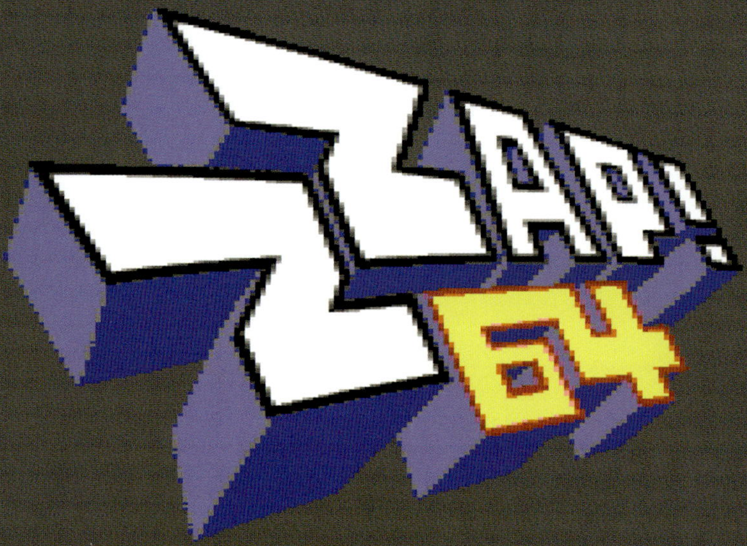

The sister publication to Newsfield's Crash *magazine,* Zzap!64 *made its debut in the spring of 1985. Boasting a strong editorial team, striking design and legendary Oli Frey cover art,* Zzap!64 *went on to become arguably the most influential and iconic C64 magazine of all time. In 1992, the magazine was rebranded as* Commodore Force, *and it eventually closed its doors in early '94.*

"The *Zzap!64* crew were experts at persuading game designers to Ludlow to take part in interviews, forums and game challenges – Crowther, Braybrook, Minter, and the Sensibles come instantly to mind among many other luminaries. I recall Jeff Minter on one occasion holding court cross-legged on the floor in front of the Unicorn Inn's blazing log fire one evening, with half of the customers crowded round like they were attending to some guru from outer space."

Roger Kean

"I think it's fair to say that getting a job on *Zzap!64* completely changed my life. I was probably destined for an anonymous life in the industrial West Midlands, eking out a moribund existence in some menial job (assuming I'd even have one). That all changed when I landed the role of staff writer – my best mate, Ian, genuinely wouldn't believe me when I told him."

Steve Jarratt

"It was my job to review everything that came into the office, and that meant I got to play every game of the period – which helped blur the lines between working and simply having a great time. Indeed, it was so much fun that I'd spend in excess of 16 hours a day at 'Zzap! Towers', writing during the day and then playing games long into the night. It was like having a dream collection of all-time classic video games at my fingertips. No wonder I only left the office to sleep!"

Julian Rignall

"Having multiple reviewers sharing often differing opinions on each title was just one masterstroke that set *Zzap!64* apart. It had a better tips section than any of the competition. It had Oli's brilliant covers. It was just a unique combination of brilliant ingredients, and it was fun. Although I didn't appreciate it properly then, it really was a privilege to have been a small – in more ways than one – part of it!"

Sean Masterson

"One of my most enduring memories of working on *Zzap!64* magazine is sitting at the office playing games morning, noon and night. I'd pretty much run to work every day so that I could pick up the post and see what new releases had come into the office that morning. It was early 1985, and the software industry was going through one of the most exciting times in its history. Innovative new games were being released at an unprecedented rate, making some days feel almost like Christmas. We just didn't know what was going to arrive next, and that made for an incredibly exciting time."

Julian Rignall

"*Zzap!64* was similar to *Crash* in the commitment to the Commodore 64 and the serious scrutiny of new releases, but, in other ways, the magazine was a different beast. We still had the three-reviewers-to-a-game format, but *Zzap!64*'s editorial team comprised fully salaried, full-time employees, unlike the peer-reviewing, part-time schoolboys who wrote up Spectrum games. Over the years, the editorial teams changed, but each brought something new to *Zzap!64*'s unique brand, and each editor took up the cudgels of producing Lloyd Mangram to perfection. Can't say fairer than that!"

Roger Kean

"The office was a total mess: walls were lined with C64 cassettes, boxes of 5.25-inch floppies, broken C64s, joypads, disk drives, power supplies, cables, old TVs and magazines. Likewise, desks were covered in food wrappers, cans of drink, games and ashtrays, and the room was usually filled with cigarette smoke, which just added to the unearthliness of the place. It was like Santa's grotto through the eyes of Tim Burton."

Steve Jarratt

"I never got to the bottom (or they'd have had it soundly tanned) of who actually suspended my desk phone out the window during a lunch break. It was one of those old nine-station, two-tonne affairs, and there it was, hanging by its cord, suspended two floors above Victoria Wine's doorway. Thankfully, you could have held up an elephant with the phone cords of those days, so no hopeful boozer was slaughtered!"

Roger Kean

"Jeff Minter was in the office once for a programmer challenge. While everyone else was watching whoever was playing at the time, Jeff helped himself to a couple of workstations and edited several articles with the aid of find/replace. I can't remember what word he chose – probably something frequently appearing like 'C64' or 'ZZAP!' – and replaced every instance with 'sheep'. Surprisingly, not 'llama', if I remember correctly."

Sean Masterson

"I loved my time at *Zzap!64*, during which I went on some cool press trips (drove a Formula Ford racing car, flew in a light plane, went to a private showing of *RoboCop* before it was out in the cinemas). I also got to play *Tetris* before anyone else in the UK, met some really great developers, and even shagged one of the PR girls. Ah, those were the days ..."

Steve Jarratt

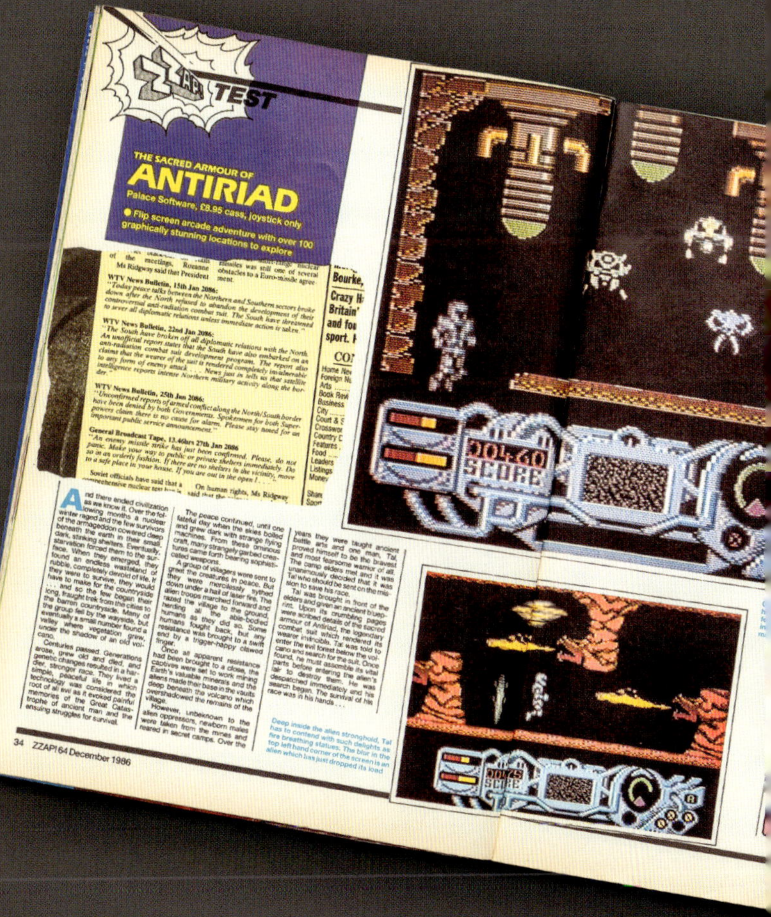

Commodore Format masthead by Robin Levy / 2016

Future Publishing's Commodore Format *hit the streets in September 1990. Despite going toe-to-toe with established heavyweights like* Zzap!64, *within a year,* Commodore Format *had become the leading C64 magazine in Britain, selling in excess of 60,000 copies each month. The last surviving commercial C64 magazine in the UK,* Commodore Format's *final issue was published in 1995.*

"The publishers at the time saw that the Commodore 64 was still a viable machine that was selling plenty of software and had a wealth of potential advertisers. Now I think about it, I do wonder if Chris Anderson, Future's owner, also fancied taking on *Zzap!64*, the mag he helped to launch at Newsfield. Personally, I relished the idea as I was still a huge C64 fan. I think we wrote some good copy and funny lines. Andy Dyer is a remarkably humorous writer and really forced me to raise my game."

Steve Jarratt

"It was all fun, to be honest. The thrill of getting a really good game in and having that as a shared experience was always exciting, but, if anything, it was the less accomplished games that provided the most entertainment. I remember the time we had to review the game of the movie *Dick Tracy*. It was a dreadful game and unfinished. To be fair, I could have written a better game in BBC BASIC. So awful, it was funny."

Andy Dyer

"Every issue would go right to the wire. Bear in mind that, if you wanted to hold the presses, even back in 1990, you were talking a five-figure sum per hour. When you were leaving the office at three in the morning, having made the deadline by minutes, after creating a page from nothing because an advertiser had dropped out at the last second, and you'd written some of the best copy you'd ever produced in the process, you just wanted to punch the air. And, in my case, find somewhere you could still get a drink. God, it was good."

Sean Masterson

“*I do wonder if Chris Anderson, Future's owner, also fancied taking on Zzap!64.*”

SEPTEMBER 1991
£2.20
12
ANIMATORS START HERE — SPRITES ALIGHT ON P44
No.1! BIGGEST AND BEST!
GOT A 64? ★ THEN GET THIS!
Commodore
FORMAT
POWERTESTED
MORE C64 REVIEWS THAN ANY OTHER MAG!
Speedball 2
Escape From Colditz
P.P. Hammer
3D Const'n Kit
Man United
The Ball Game
Over The Net
LOADS MORE...
INJURY TIME!
Future PUBLISHING
Your guarantee of value
INDIANA JONES IV
NEW!
WIN! A FLIGHT IN A PIPER WARRIOR!
GOT A 64? ★ THEN GET THIS!
Commodore
FORMAT
2
NOVEMBER 1990
£1.95
POWERTESTED
Rick Dangerous 2
Midnight Resistance
Ultimate Golf
Wings Of Fury
Snowstrike
Tie Break
Iron man
TWICE THE ACTION!
TWICE THE DANGER!
TWICE THE GAME!

"It wasn't the platform we loved; it was the people who loved it. The C64 was better than anything, but *Commodore Format* and the followers were what made us. Opening reader letters was fun because they got the vibe, and, frankly, we were people talking about a cool thing to people who knew it was cool. Fans of anything are always nice, and to do mags for them was a joy. That they still exist and still remember us as well as the C64 is delightful. And I say this as a jaded old cynic who hates everything."

James Leach

"Preparing the cover tapes was horrible. The stuff would always arrive late and have to be compiled at the last minute. They'd be late back from the duplicators and go out with less testing than we'd have liked… We were magazine folk and never really had the technical skill to make them, and so they still give me the fear to this day. I'm glad everyone liked them, but I still get shivers whenever I see a C15 cassette."

Trenton Webb

"We had a mantra and a truth. The mantra was that the magazine was supposed to be the equivalent of your friend who drops round once a month to play on your computer with you. The truth was that most readers got two games per year: one for birthdays, one for Christmas. It was certainly that way for me growing up – £1.99 games you'd buy with pocket money, but some of these things ran to £20. If I'd have gotten a game for Christmas that turned out to be a pile of pap, I'd have been utterly disappointed. If that'd happened to someone else based on our recommendation, we'd have been mortified!"

Simon Forrester

"I clearly remember the week I took over the tips section, and they decided to send me all of the mail from the *CF* office. Two days later, two enormous padded envelopes arrived at my house; they were the size of pillows and stuffed with hundreds of letters from kids needing help with games. Pretty much every month after that, I would receive a 'pillow' in the mail, and it usually took a day just to open them all. I was 17, living at home, and I got to spend my days playing games and doing what I loved for a national magazine, and I got paid for it. It was tremendous fun."

Andy Roberts

"I remember us talking about giving *Mayhem in Monsterland* 100%. I don't think the team agreed with me, and I don't blame them because it's bat's-arse, isn't it? Nothing is ever completely perfect, is it? But the more I thought about it, the more I became convinced that the score was right. I gave it 100% not because it was perfect but because it was the last great game on the last great 8-bit home computer. It was like its swan-song. I wanted it to go out on a high. What better end can there be for an awesome computer than a last amazing game?"

Andy Hutchinson

"We weren't globetrotting heroes, but we were heroically receptive to good ideas, and, as the C64 waned commercially, the chaps doing homebrews approached us. We did it because we cared. In those days, at Future – unlike now – if your mag went under, you were pretty much assured they would find you another job, so we weren't doing it just to make sure we were employed. We cared."

Dave Golder

Ballblazer

"You have to keep in mind it [*Ballblazer*] preceded all of the other Lucasfilm titles, except *Rescue on Fractalus!*, which was at the same time. I've always wanted to build a device which allowed people to play with invisible forces, such as magnetic fields, and to have these things manifest in such a way that you can actually manipulate forms from action into distance, like you have some kind of mechanism to play with. The original conception of the game was to provide as realistic an environment as possible and to keep people as an important part, it is necessary to involve more than one person in it.

"Then it becomes a social interaction – the computer becomes a, or is in the case of *Ballblazer*, a neutral concurrent medium of interaction between two people. You do not play against the computer or you're not testing your skills or abilities against someone's program but instead you're given an equal opportunity to play against another person."

David Levine, project leader

"From a technical point, I am hugely proud of this conversion from the Atari 800. Working with Kevin Furry (who is still my business partner to this day), we took the custom-built Atari code and ported it to the C64 – something we were told was impossible after another development house had already tried and failed to create the 3D effect. We made a $1 bet with Lucasfilm that we could do it, and, a month later, it was finished. This amazing technical achievement not only wowed the other programmers in the office but also won my boss back his $1!"

Chuck Sommerville, programmer

Released
1985

Genre
Action

Developer
Lucasfilm Games

Publisher
Activision

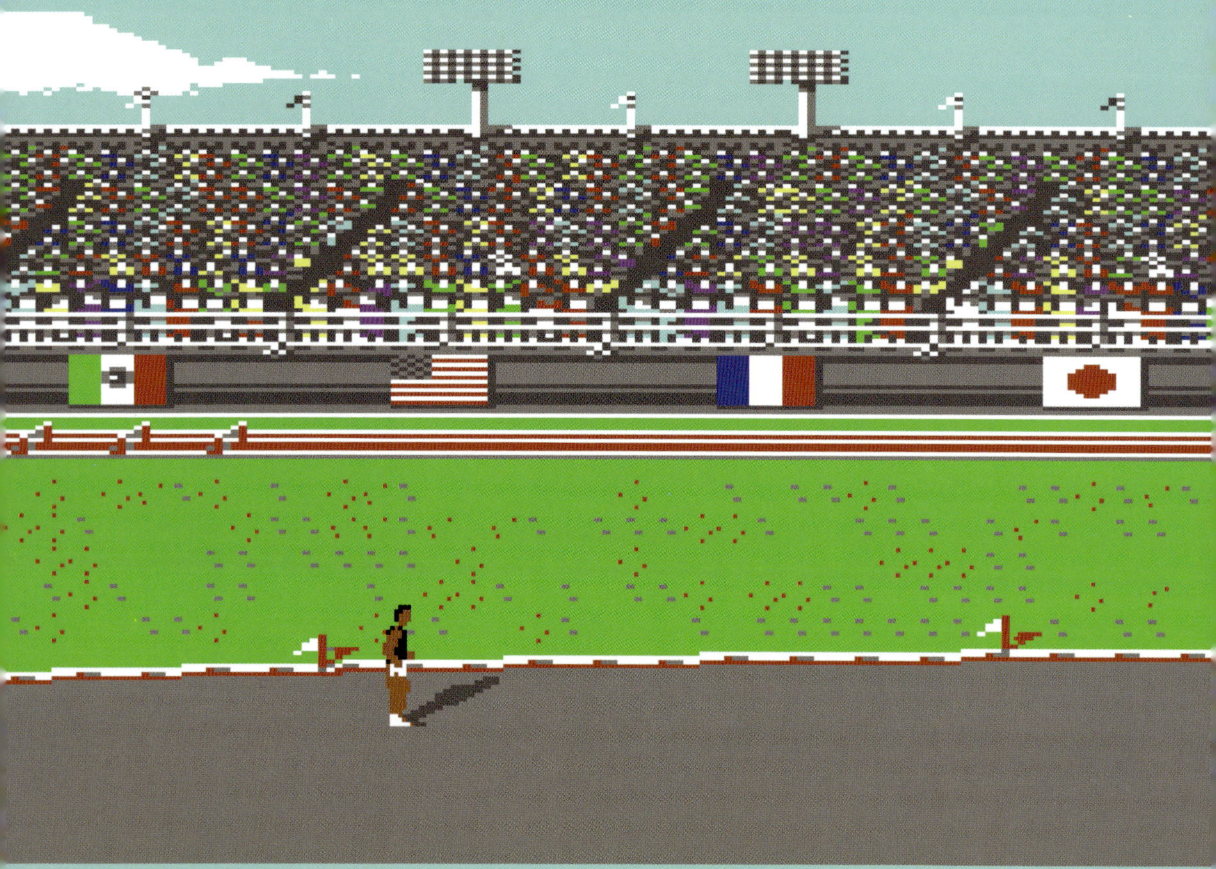

Summer Games 2

"The original *Summer Games* was really popular, and the Epyx marketing department was keen for 'more of the same' with a sequel. As with all games at that time, we started with a brainstorm to choose the events. I got cycling and rowing, and I remember getting loads of grief about the way the wheels looked in the cycling event. The marketing guys kept saying to me, 'The wheels look way too pixellated; they don't look round – can you fix that?' I had the hardest time explaining to them why they were like that."

Chuck Sommerville, designer and programmer

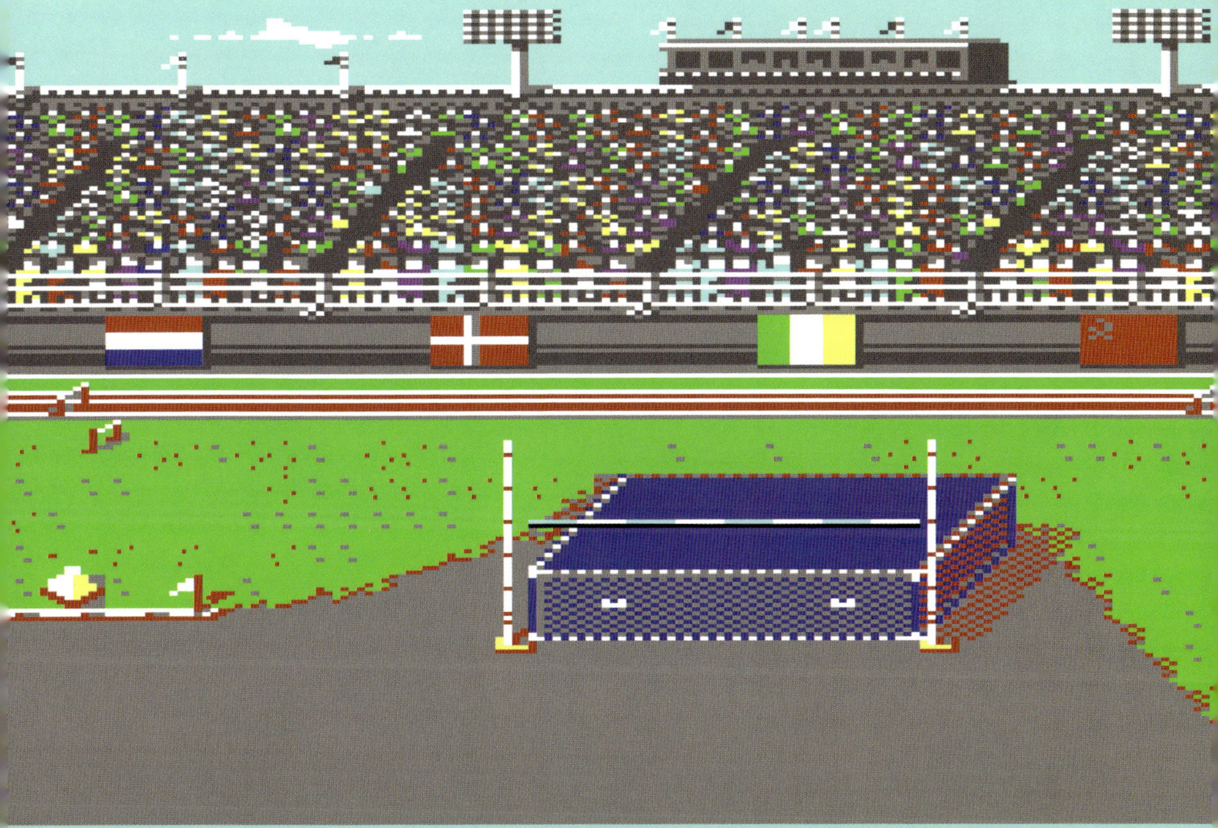

"The sequel to *Summer Games* brought eight new events to the 'Epyx Games' series: cycling, kayaking, triple jump, high jump, javelin, rowing, fencing and equestrian. Like the first game, production values are very high, and Epyx's classic sports title has an excellent visual presentation that's even better than the original *Summer Games*. Each event's mini-game is also very well designed and enjoyable to play, making this collection of sports games an instant classic."

Julian Rignall, games journalist

Released
1985

Genre
Sports

Developer and publisher
Epyx

Gribbly's Day Out

"This was my first original title. Everything was new for me, so I had a lot of ideas but no library of code yet. I wanted to use every trick in the book to make a C64 game that couldn't be implemented on any other machine. I wanted to create a cute character and a game of skill and control. Each level is an eco-system that is being invaded by transforming meanies, with an added twist of the baddest of them all, Seon, lurking somewhere on the level. He gets released when the level's nearly finished to spice things up."

Andrew Braybrook, designer and programmer

"*Gribbly's Day Out* was a simple yet perfectly formed arcade adventure that offered a tantalising taste of things to come from Graftgold. Assuming the role of Gribbly, a cute, one-footed alien from the planet Blabgor, the aim of each level was to rescue a quota of baby Gribblets and return them to the safety of their cave. Boasting incredible attention to detail, from the evolving enemies to Gribbly's dynamic facial expressions, the game was challenging and charming in equal measure, giving way to sheer panic when Seon the mutant Blabgorian was in hot pursuit!"

Andy Roberts, games journalist

Released
1985

Genre
Arcade

Developer
Graftgold

Publisher
Hewson Consultants

Koronis Rift

"Some might say the early C64 releases from Lucasfilm were not so much games but rather showcases for the Californian gamemaker's technical expertise. At its core, *Koronis Rift* is a rather simple sci-fi exploration game with some shoot 'em up elements thrown in for good measure. Travelling a fractally generated planetary surface, you just couldn't believe a C64 would be capable of drawing such convincing, full-screen, multicoloured 3D-landscapes. Understanding the atmosphere and game mechanics presupposed the player had read the printed encyclopedia enclosed in the box though – which explains why *Koronis Rift* hardly got the attention it deserved from game pirates."

Richard Löwenstein, games journalist

"*Koronis Rift* premiered fully bitmapped first-person exploration in real time. As a devil-may-care scavenger, players commanded a modular rover in search of alien technology on an abandoned planet ravaged by weapons tests. Mysterious scraps of equipment the 'Ancients' left behind provided nearly infinite upgrade options that were key to survival in the titular rifts. An otherworldly freedom of choice and movement plus presentational brilliance made *Koronis Rift* a timelessly immersive experience."

Andreas Wanda, guest reviewer

Released
1985

Genre
Shoot 'em up

Developer
Lucasfilm Games

Publisher
Activision

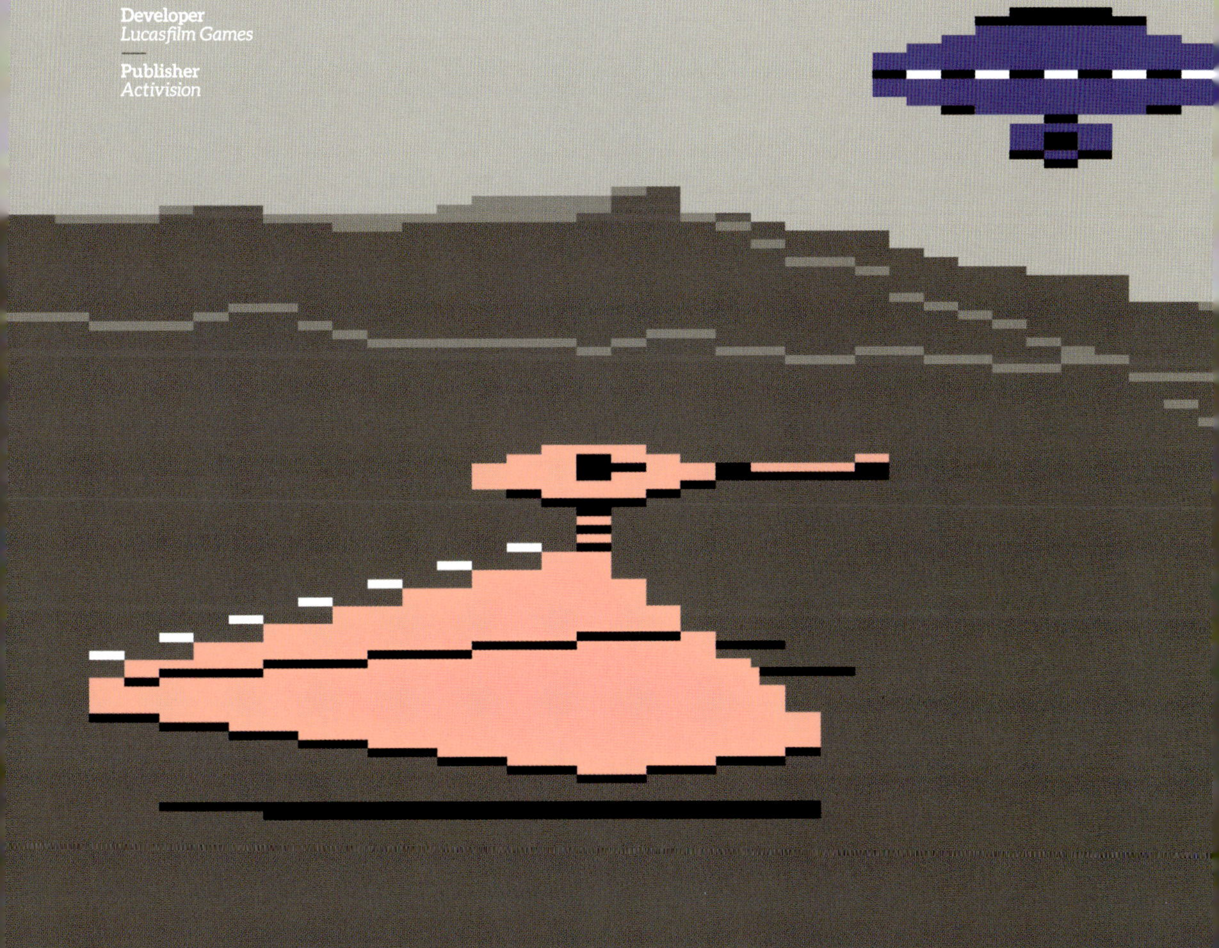

Action Biker

"At first glance, it would be easy to dismiss this as a flimsy budget title hiding behind a snack food licence. Conversely, Mastertronic managed to deliver possibly the first open-world sandbox game, allowing the player an unprecedented amount of freedom to explore the world, collecting various objects to aid them on their quest to win the drag race at the end of the game. Often lambasted for its difficulty level, *Action Biker* was significantly more forgiving than its spiritual successors, *The Last V8* and *Red Max*."

Andy Roberts, games journalist

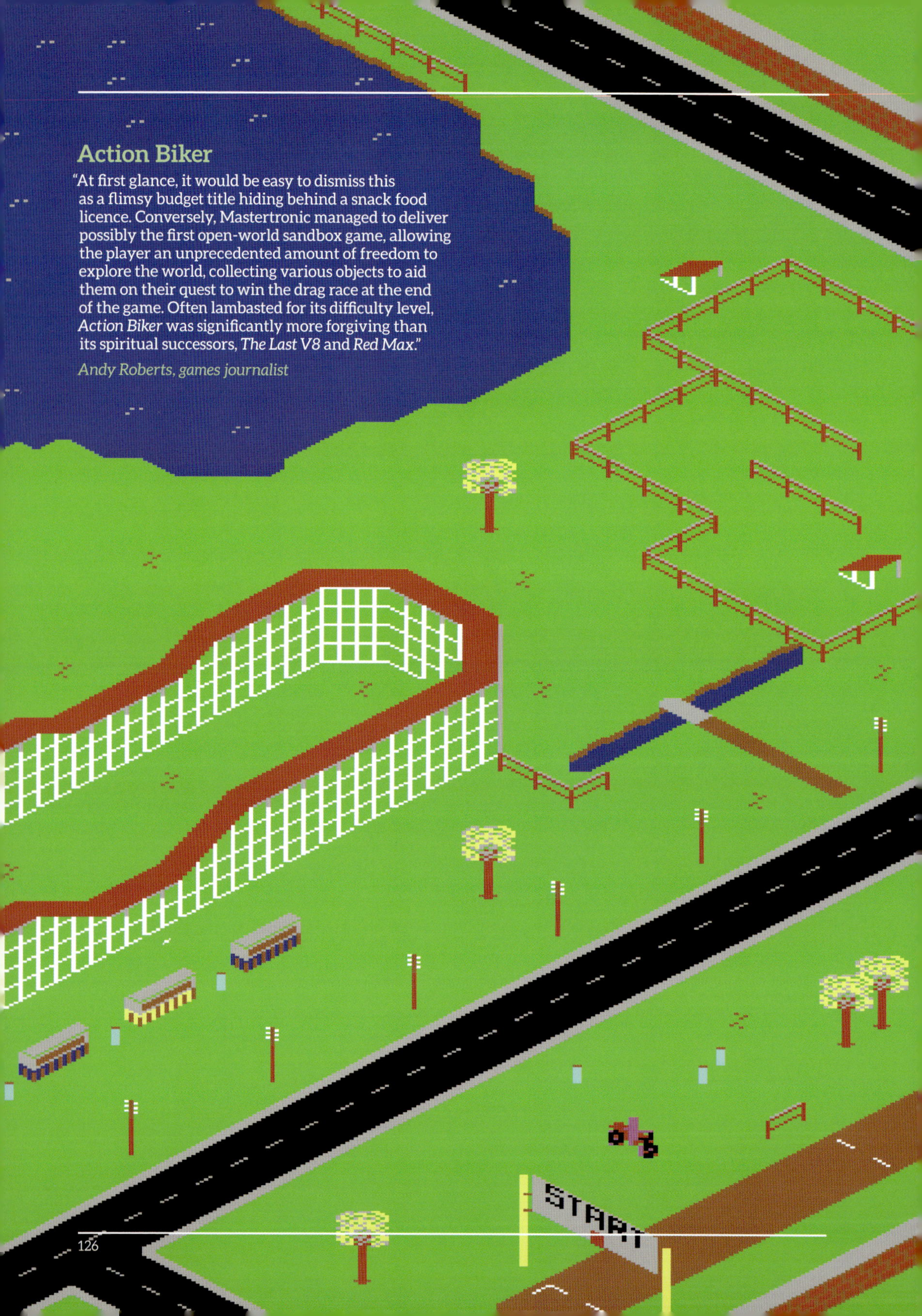

Released
1985

Genre
Action

Developer and Publisher
Mastertronic

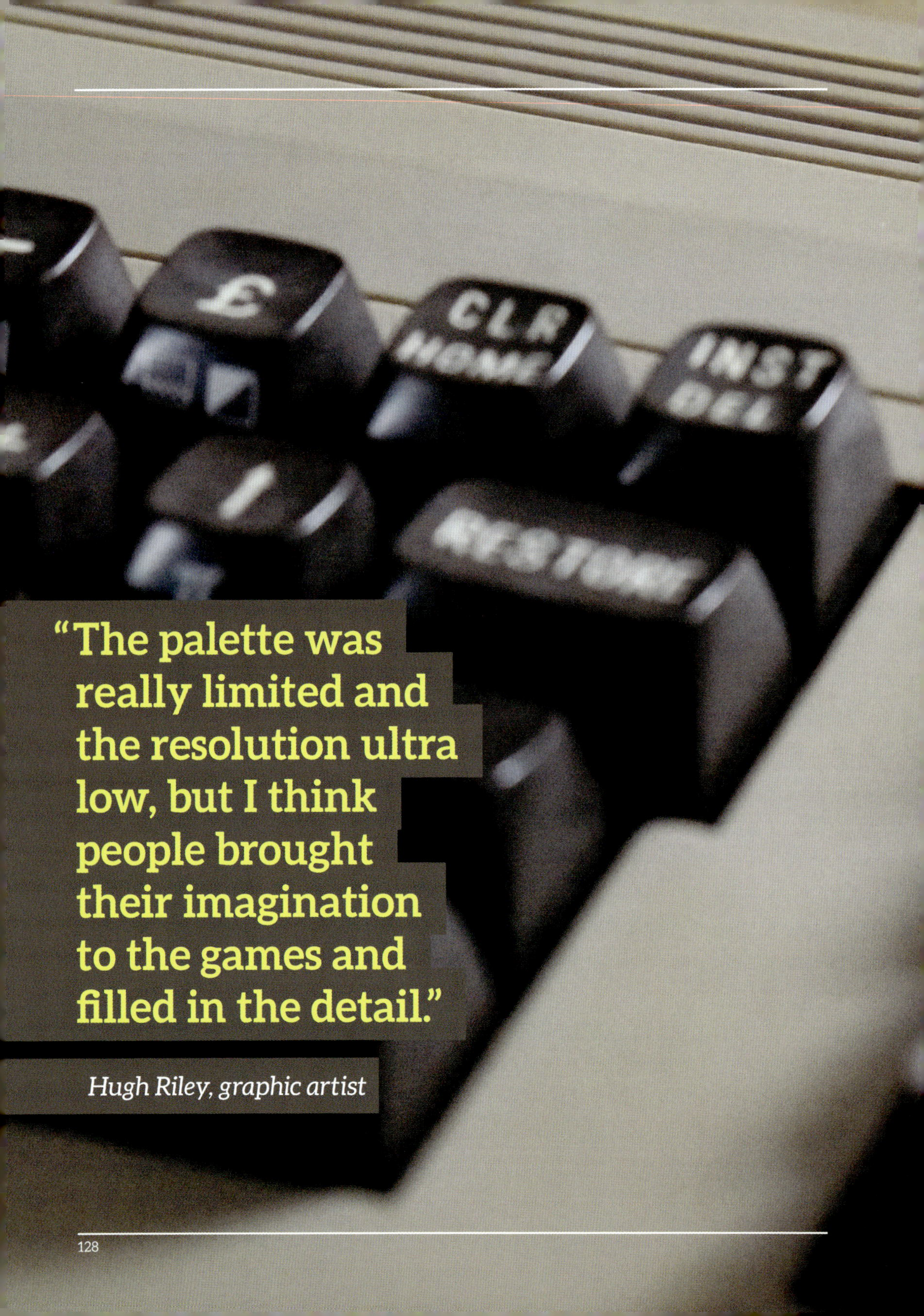

"The palette was really limited and the resolution ultra low, but I think people brought their imagination to the games and filled in the detail."

Hugh Riley, graphic artist

POWER

Released
1985

Genre
Racing

Developer
Rick Koenig

Publisher
Electronic Arts

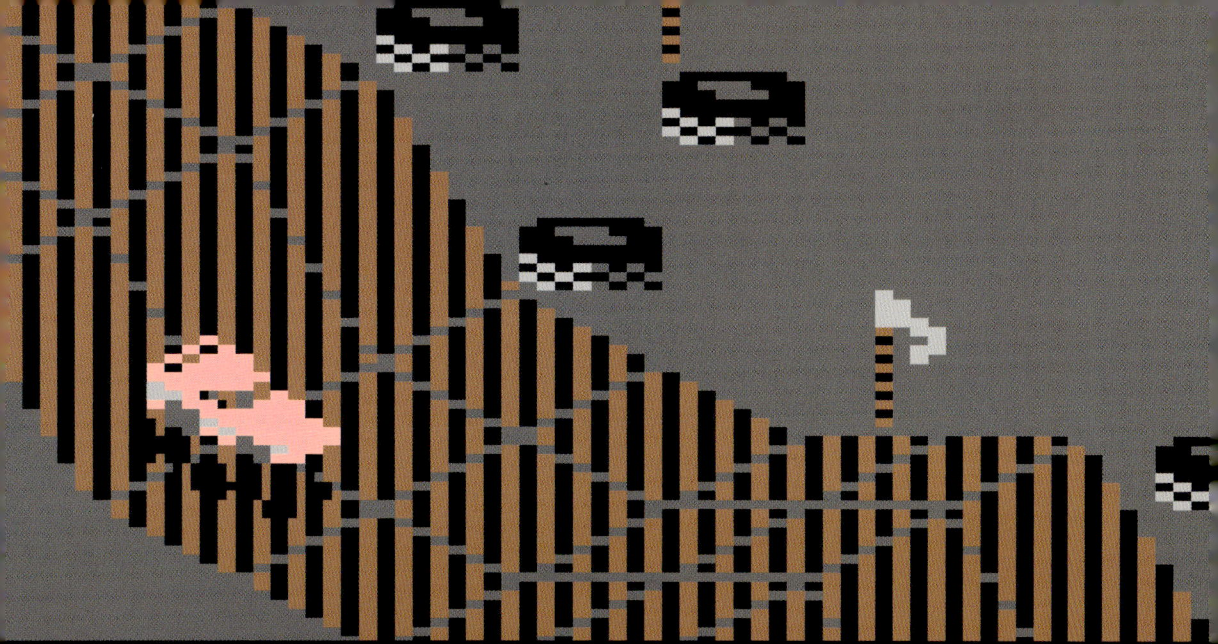

Racing Destruction Set

"As well as being a thoroughly enjoyable one- or two-player isometric racing game, this early Electronic Arts release also enables players to design and create their own race tracks, complete with elevation changes, unique gravity settings and different road conditions. Making new tracks is a breeze with the intelligently presented course editor, and you're able to race a variety of different vehicles, ranging from a lunar rover and racing cars to a motocross bike. Brilliant fun!"

Julian Rignall, games journalist

Beyond the Forbidden Forest

Released
1985

Genre
Action

Developer
COSMI

Publisher
U.S. Gold

Artwork
Oliver Frey

Beach-Head II: The Dictator Strikes Back

Released
1985

Genre
Shoot 'em up

Developer
Access Software

Publisher
U.S. Gold

Artwork
Oliver Frey

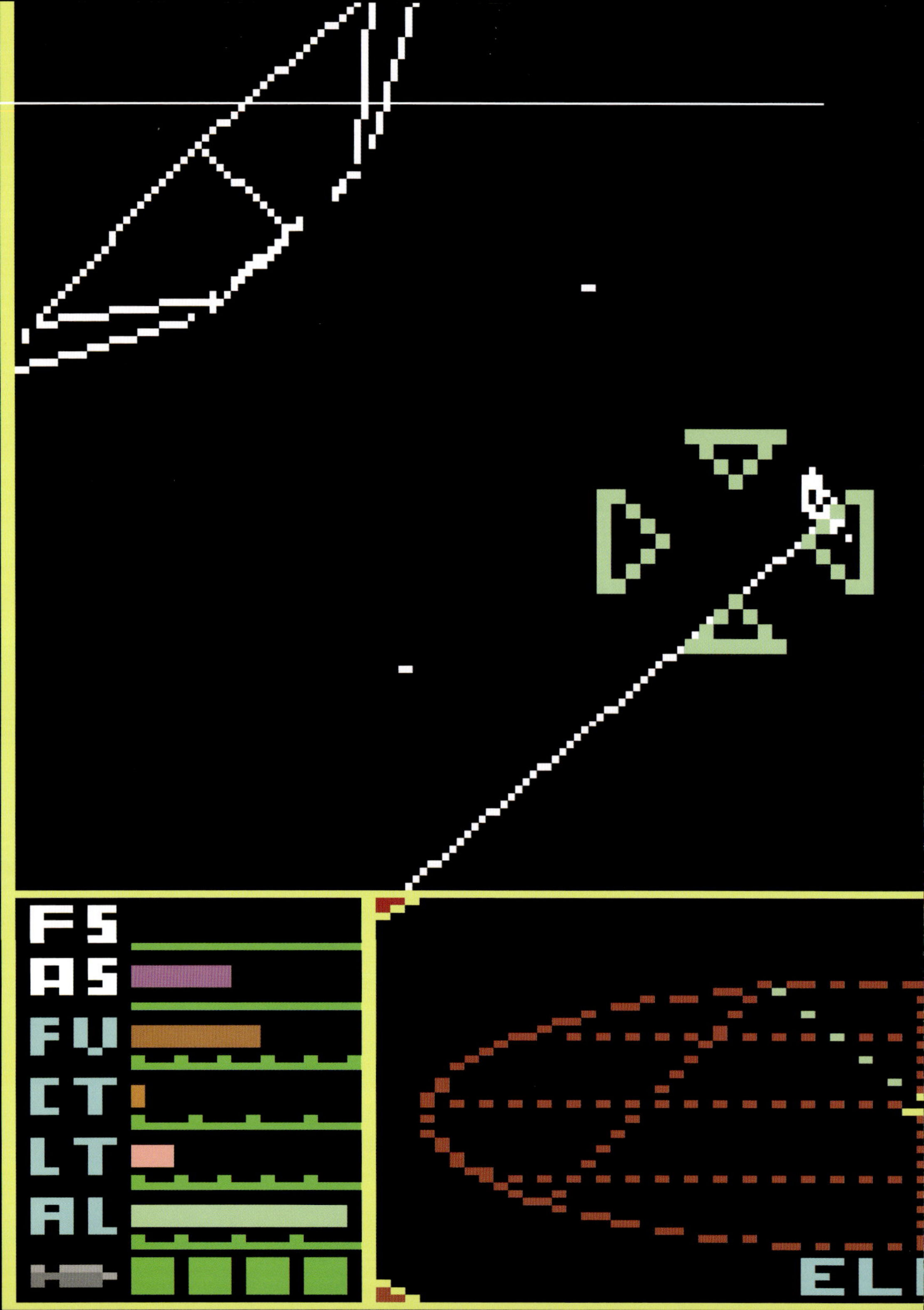
FS
AS
FU
CT
LT
AL

Elite

"Though *Zzap!64* hadn't even launched, Firebird took the magazine's imminent arrival seriously enough to send Colin Fuidge all the way to our offices in Yeovil. There was never any doubt from the first moments of playing the game – Bob Wade was only dragged away after six hours of non-stop gaming – that *Elite* would be *Zzap!64*'s first cover, now an iconic image, painted by Oliver Frey. Looking back, the reactions to *Elite* were spot on, and it has continued to be a game which fascinates generations."

Roger Kean, co-founder of Newsfield

Released
1985

Genre
Simulation

Developers
David Braben
Ian Bell

Publisher
Firebird

"Let that word sink in for a moment ... *Elite*. Cover game of Issue 1 of *Zzap!64* Gold Medal material right from the off, 30 years ago – 30! The nostalgia and allure of *Elite* is still immense, as is seen with anticipation for *Elite: Dangerous*. *Elite* promised infinite space to explore, combat and a sense of wonder, and it delivered in style. 3D was never the forte of the C64, and it's awfully lonely out there with minimal sound too, but, hey, it's space after all. We were, however, enthralled. *Elite* paved the way for space games like no other. Awesome."

Robin Hogg, games journalist

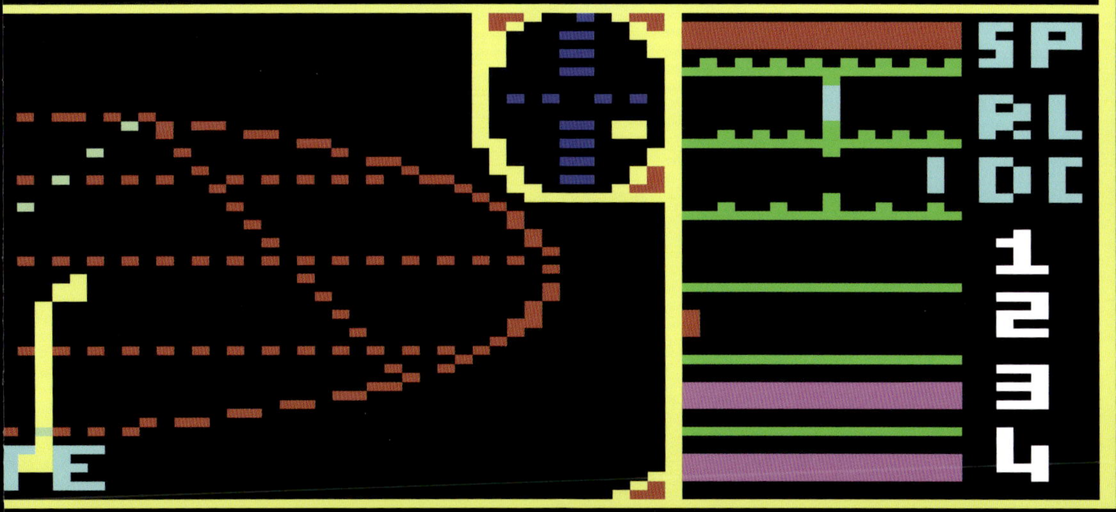

The Eidolon

After discovering the Eidolon in the abandoned laboratory of missing scientist Dr. Joseph Agon, you are transported into a mysterious metaphysical world populated by all manner of strange and ethereal creatures. The aim of each level is to find three jewels which unlock the barrier between you and the gigantic dragon guarding the exit, but, to earn those jewels, you'll need to dispatch the caves' other inhabitants through the strategic use of coloured fireballs, each with a unique purpose. By literally turning the fractal technology from *Rescue on Fractalus!* on its head, the Lucasfilm team managed to create arguably one of the most immersive first-person experiences on the C64.

Released
1985

Genre
First-person shooter

Developer
Lucasfilm Games

Publisher
Activision

"The team – Gary Winnick, Charlie Kelner and myself – played ideas off of each other to create *The Eidolon*. Gary's characters were the key elements of the game, and the remainder were mazes, fractals and effects. Ron Gilbert and I joined the games group to provide C64 expertise, and we created some impossible effects. *Eidolon* used full-screen sprites and particle models which were revolutionary at the time."

Kevin Furry, programmer

Hyper Sports

After Konami's relentless button-basher *Track & Field* took the arcades by storm in 1983, it was quickly followed by *Hyper Sports*, which offered armchair athletes the chance to participate in several new events, such as swimming, skeet shooting, long horse, archery, triple jump, and weightlifting. While there's some frenzied joystick waggling involved, some events thankfully rely more on reflexes and timing, allowing players a momentary respite for their aching wrists. Though it lacks the nuance and sophistication of other sports franchises of the time, it's an amazingly authentic arcade conversion and a fine example of what a talented team of developers could cram into just 64k.

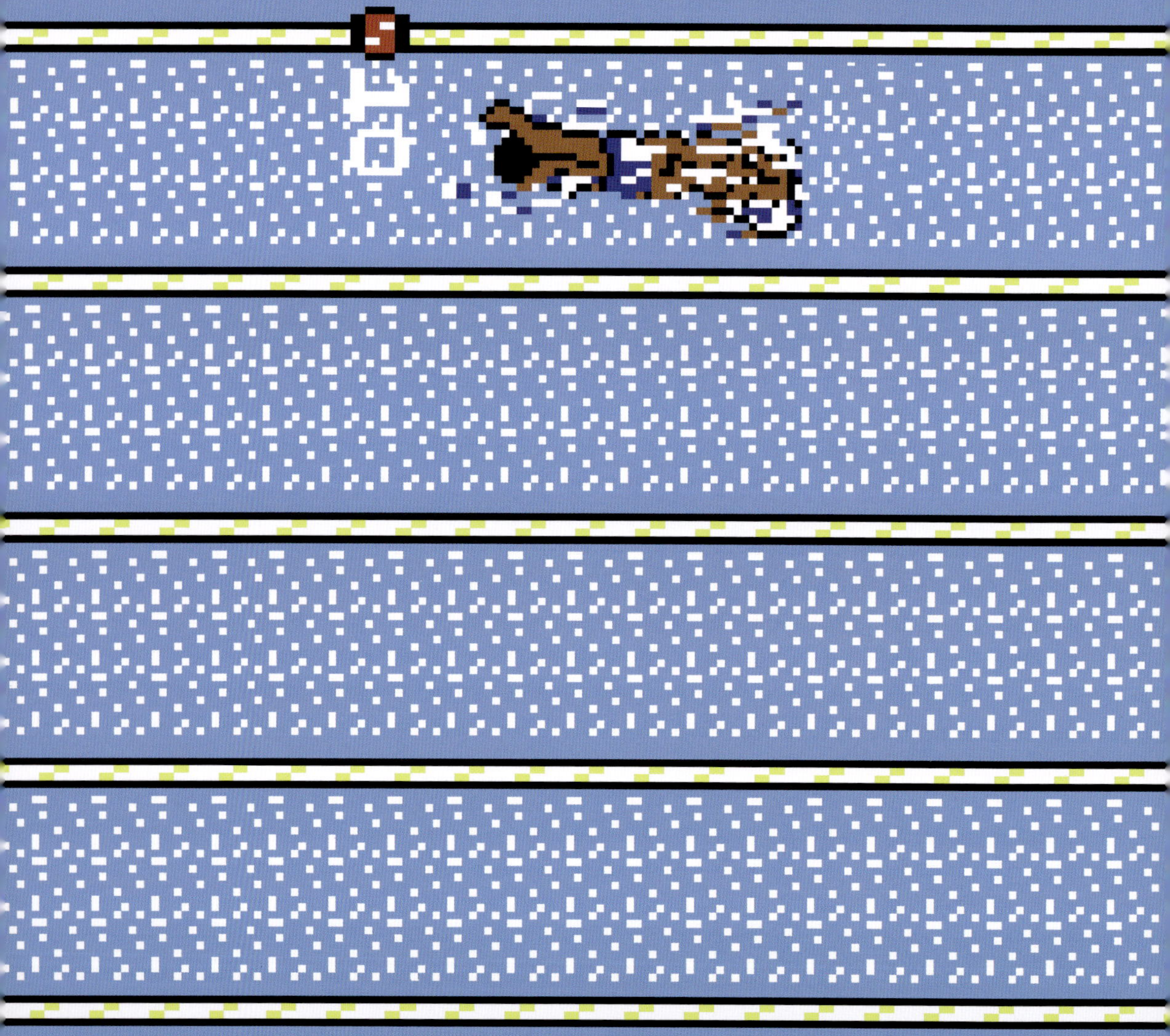

"I decided to adapt Vangelis's main score from *Chariots of Fire* for the game, but I didn't tell anyone I was doing it. I did it completely from memory as I'd never seen the movie or bought the score. So this was 'unlicensed' per se, and, when I was about halfway through it, David Collier decided it was a good idea to bring David Wood in for a listen. He didn't even wait for the playback to finish and walked off … to go get on the phone and get the licence! For the loading music, I composed what I thought was an anthemic celebration. It was 1985, and disco was still in my mind, so I took the opportunity to make it a high-energy danceable piece – the first part of the tune is kinda mysterious, and the second section is the soaring danceable anthem."

Martin Galway, musician

Released
1985

Genre
Sports

Developer and Publisher
Imagine

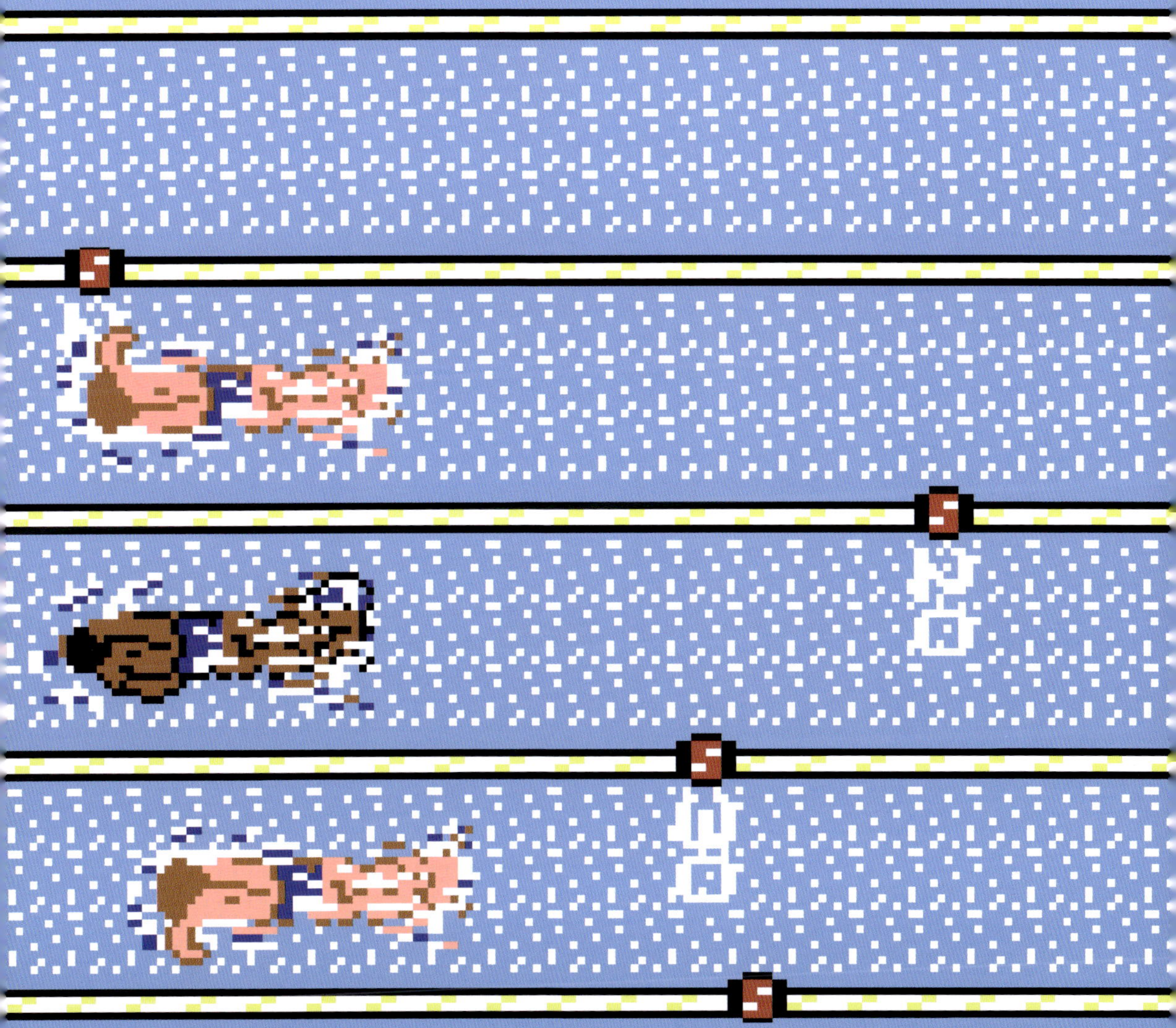

Cauldron

"It would be amusing to think that Palace Software looked at arcade shooter *Defender* and thought 'Yeah, it's good, but it's not quite 'witchy' enough', and came up with *Cauldron*. The truth, though, is that this was instead a clever attempt to fuse two gaming genres – in this case, shooting and platforming – and the results were… interesting. All of this was tempered by the pain of the excruciatingly high-difficulty level, which was harsh even by old-school standards. More trick than treat."

Andy Dyer, games journalist

Released
1985

Genre
Action

Developer and Publisher
Palace Software

Kikstart

Long before console games like *Trials HD* had us screaming at the TV in frustration, Mastertronic's humble motorcycle trials simulator had already earned a place in the C64 hall of fame. Despite its budget heritage, *Kikstart*'s gameplay is extremely nuanced: learning the correct speeds for each obstacle – not to mention the angle of the bike – is critical to your success, and, though the penalties are steep, the thrill of making it through a course with zero faults is nothing short of exhilarating. Throw in a simultaneous two-player mode and *Kikstart* quickly becomes one of the best two-player experiences on the C64.

"Shaun Southern's affectionate, unofficial tribute to the BBC television show *Kick Start* (the original Mr. Chip release even featured a take on the programme's theme tune) is the spiritual forerunner to the contemporary Trials series. A motorbike is used to negotiate eight different courses, including the likes of rough terrain, tyres, cars and buses. Striving for the smoothest possible ride to shave off valuable split seconds from records became an obsession."

Gary Penn, games journalist

Released
1985

Genre
Racing

Developer
Mr. Chip Software

Publisher
Mastertronic

START
HIC-

Released
1985

Genre
Action

Developer and Publisher
Taskset

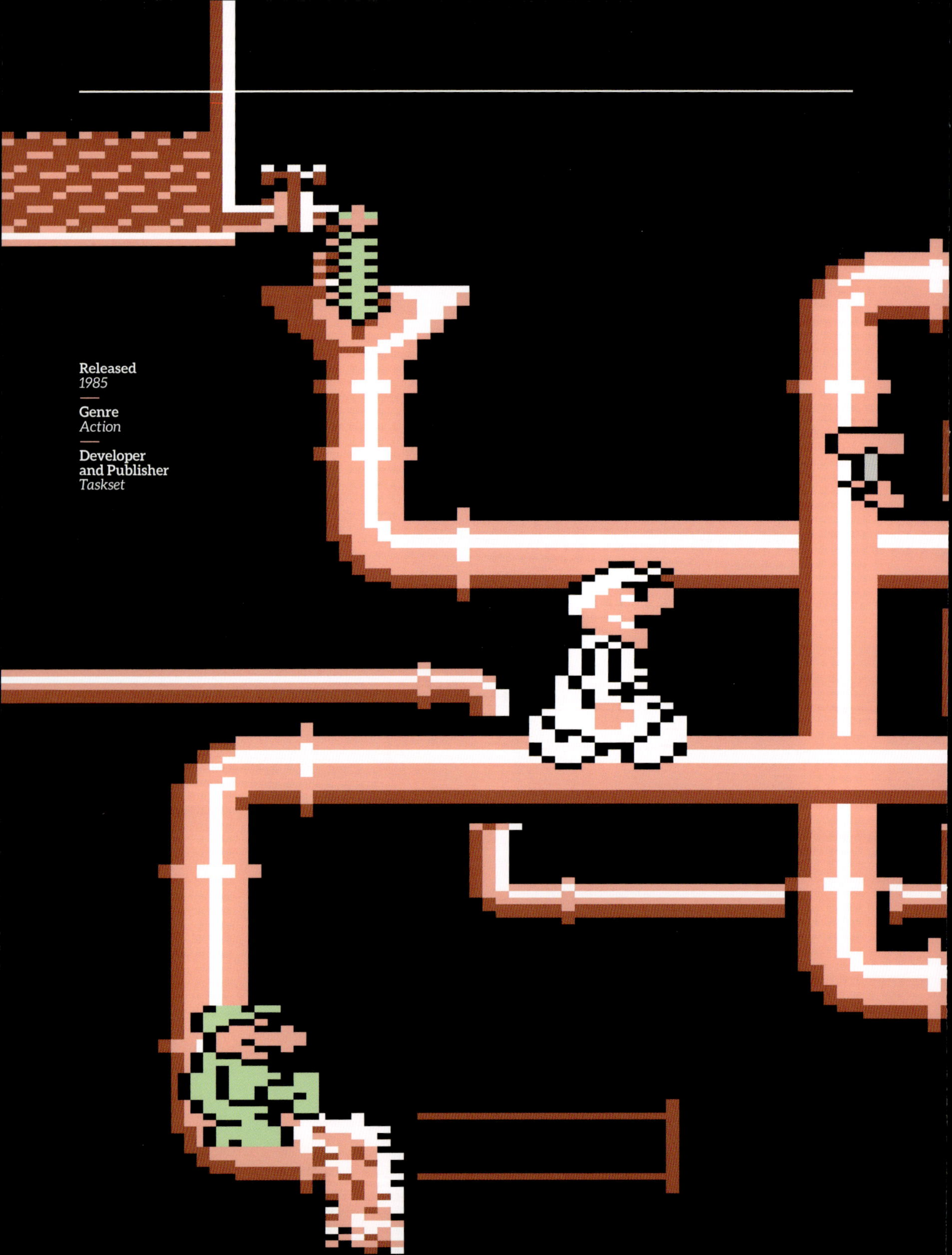

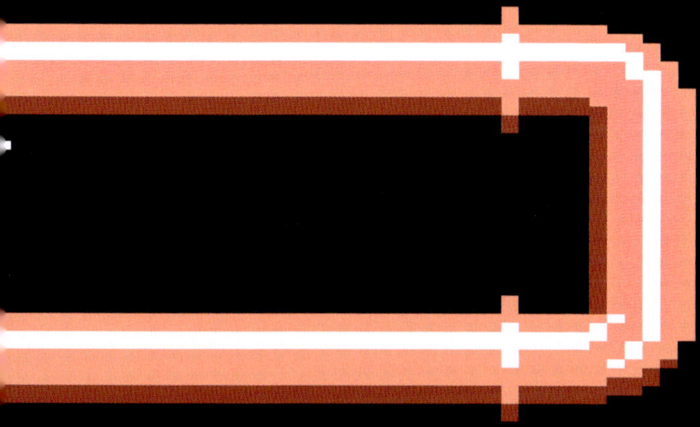

Super Pipeline II

Your role as Foreman Fred is to ensure the smooth running of the pipeline and fill a designated number of barrels on each of the game's 16 increasingly hectic levels. Naturally, there's all manner of adversaries throwing a spanner in the works, from drills and hammers that make holes in the pipes to lobsters and caterpillars which merely serve as an annoyance. Thankfully, there's an unlimited supply of expendable workmen who can be guided around the pipeline to fix leaks or even used strategically as a human shield. The end result is a perfect storm of chaos, with every aspect of the game finely tuned to produce the maximum amount of panic.

"Sheikh Aleg has a problem, and thus so do you, in keeping his pipelines free from sabotage and interference. The various tools and fauna may look cute, but they'd soon as rip a hole in the pipes and yourself, given a second chance. Nothing that your unlimited supply of Freds can't fix, however, with their trusty Irish screwdrivers. I swear though that lobster ended up moonlighting in *Great Giana Sisters* later…"

Mat Allen, games journalist

Mercenary

"Before *GTA*, before *Oblivion* and *Skyrim*, there was Paul Woakes's *Mercenary*. A true open-world, sandbox action-adventure game crammed into the C64. The wireframe vector graphics were visually minimalist, but the gameworld was incredibly rich and engaging, with side-quests and a variety of vehicles to pilot and mysteries to solve as you sought to escape from planet Targ. Few C64 games grabbed me like *Mercenary* did, with its slick 3D graphics, clever twists and wry wit. It gave me a rare glimpse of the future of gaming that wouldn't be fully realised for well over a decade."

Steve Jarratt, games journalist

Released
1985

Genre
Adventure

Developer and Publisher
Novagen Software

Monty on the Run

The third in the Monty Mole series, this is probably one of the best-loved C64 titles, helped in no small part by an epic Rob Hubbard soundtrack. In his quest to outrun the authorities, Monty's adventure would take him through a maze of intricately crafted screens, collecting essential items and somersaulting from platform to platform. Like many British games from the 1980s, *Monty* gave subtle nods of respect to the Zeitgeist – and the occasional 'up yours' to the establishment."

Andy Roberts, games journalist

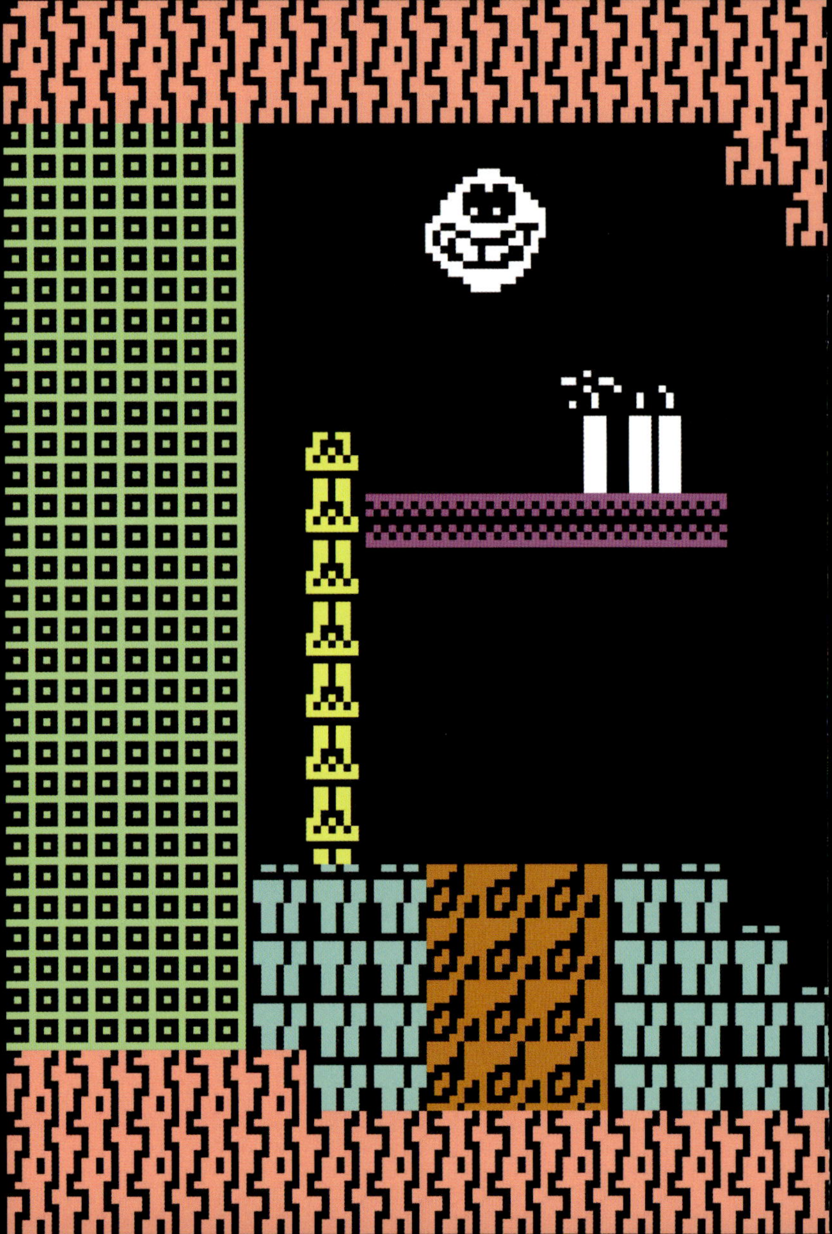

Released
1985

Genre
Platformer

Developer
Micro Projects

Publisher
Gremlin Graphics

The Way of the Exploding Fist

"*Fist*'s graphics were as realistic as they were elegant, and the digitised sound effects made every round powerfully physical. Its intuitive controls allowed for a natural flow of moves and blocks, so that the computer game karatekas' actions alone determined a fight's outcome: the grin over the first successful roundabout kick is still etched on players' faces. A historic, seismic release in 1985, the depth of gameplay and immersion became the yardstick by which the evolving beat 'em up genre would be judged."

Andreas Wanda, guest reviewer

Released
1985

Genre
Fighting

Developer
Beam Software

Publisher
Melbourne House

Released
1985

Genre
Sports

Developer
Epyx

Publisher
U.S. Gold

Winter Games

"After the sublime and sweaty pleasures of *Summer Games* and its sequel, the third in the series sees a cool change of venue and climate to host seven new events. Once again, Epyx excels with a visually lush virtual sports convention that's just as slick, tight and compelling an experience as its precursors."

Gary Penn, games journalist

Frankie Goes to Hollywood

"*Frankie* was a game that felt very different for the time. It was very visual and music-based, taking a lot of references from the pop group. I think we were all very happy with the way the game and the graphics turned out. My only regret is the lack of a talking moose in the murder mystery game, something Paul Morley (representative of the band) said no to! Who doesn't want a talking moose head in a game, giving out clues!?"

Karen Davies, graphic artist

Released
1985

Genre
Adventure

Developer
Denton Designs

Publisher
Ocean

Released
1985

Genre
Simulation

Developer
David Crane

Publisher
Activision

Little Computer People

"Few people realise that the *Little Computer People* disk already had a custom person on it. This was done by imprinting a unique serial number on each disk to seed their personality. In order for the personality to persist from session to session, a sector of 'brain' data was written to the disk during the game. Beginning in December, if the person played a record, there was a chance that he would play Christmas music. The likelihood increased every day until Christmas Day. Since many kids got their copy of *Little Computer People* as a Christmas gift, many owners never discovered this fact!"

David Crane, designer and programmer

Karateka

"I created *Karateka* while attending Yale in the early 1980s. My goal was to create a game that was visually sophisticated yet so easy to play that even a non-gamer could immediately pick up the joystick and become addicted. *Karateka*'s success proved to me (and to my parents) that this could be a legitimate career. It helped me decide, right after college, to go on and make *Prince of Persia*. I was lucky to have Robert Cook to do the Commodore 64 port; he had a great eye for detail in graphics and sound."

Jordan Mechner, original designer

Released
1985

Genre
Scrolling beat 'em up

Developer
Jordan Mechner

Publisher
Brøderbund

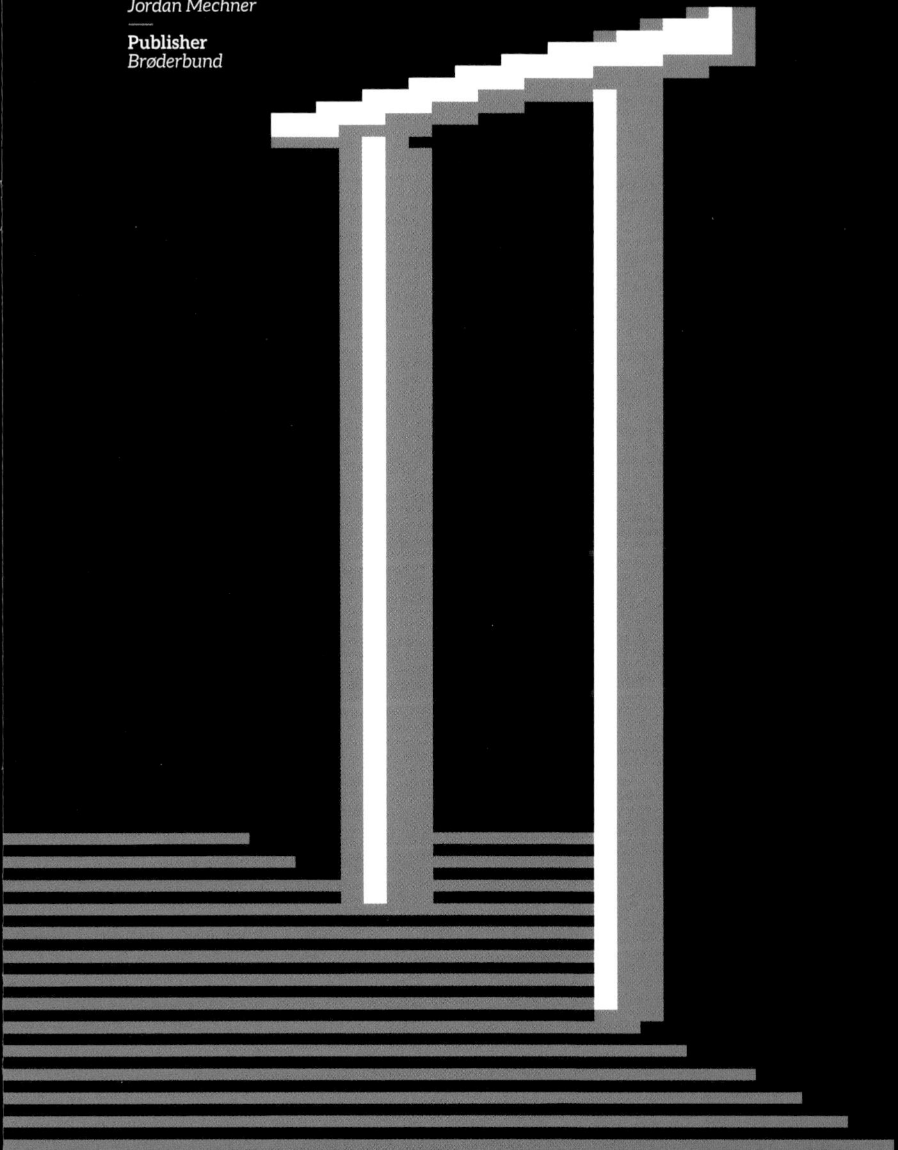

Law of the West

"The most interesting game I designed was *Law of the West*. I incorporated a system in which the player could do bad things – could shoot lots of people – but it had consequences. And I think that was interesting – to develop a darker story. I also tried to have all the characters react differently to you, depending on what you had done previously."

Alan Miller, designer and programmer

Released
1985

Genre
Adventure

Developer and Publisher
Accolade

ALERT.
001

Paradroid

"This was our second title for the C64 after *Gribbly's Day Out*, so it was important for us to deliver a great product. The Paradroid diaries in *Zzap!64* had created some good publicity ahead of launch, and, fortunately, Andrew Braybrook delivered a phenomenal game. *Paradroid* has a beautifully elegant design and is wonderfully balanced. It wasn't actually our biggest ever hit but has certainly become something of a cult classic."

Andrew Hewson, founder of Hewson Consultants

"Using some of the code systems that I had for *Gribbly's Day Out*, this time, I wanted an atmospheric battle aboard a space ship. The game design was written on a small piece of blue notepaper, which Steve (Turner) found recently but was sadly water-damaged. Remarkably, most of the design just worked first time, so the game turned out as originally imagined. The firing mode I wanted didn't work, though, so it was changed, twice, at the eleventh hour to a more traditional system. Also, the blueprint look that I originally envisaged was changed to a bas-relief look, without using multi-colour mode."

Andrew Braybrook, designer and programmer

Released
1985

Genre
Shoot 'em up

Developer
Graftgold

Publisher
Hewson Consultants

"Loading games on the tape drive took ages back then, so I thought it would be quite unsettling and dramatic to have a large bold eye staring at you as the game loaded."

Bob Stevenson, graphic artist

Thing on a Spring

One of the games responsible for Gremlin Graphics' meteoric rise to fame, *Thing on a Spring* became a cult classic thanks in part to its eponymous mascot and groundbreaking Rob Hubbard soundtrack. Your job is to collect pieces of a magical jigsaw scattered around the evil goblin's factory while avoiding the denizens that will sap your precious oil supply. Along the way, you'll also have to locate five switches to activate various gadgets like lifts and escalators, which allow you to reach previously inaccessible areas. Despite its simplistic appearance, *Thing on a Spring* is one tough cookie, and you'll need ninja-like skills (and zen-like patience) to master the controls and ultimately reach the final confrontation.

"Development wasn't going so well on a new C64 game Gremlin was trying to make. We agreed to take on the development and were told we had six weeks to finish it! Around the same time, Rob Hubbard had sent us a flyer asking, 'Want great music in your games?'. Yes, we did! As Rob was unemployed at the time, we had to pay for his train travel to meet with us, but he soon delivered on his promise and sent the first draft of the now famous *Thing on a Spring* title track."

Jason Perkins, designer and programmer

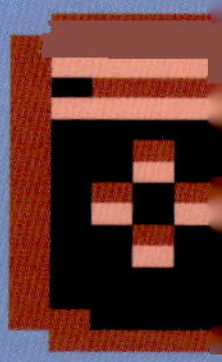

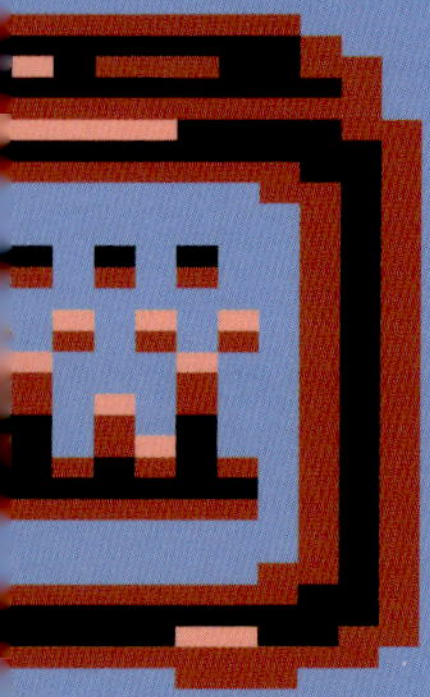

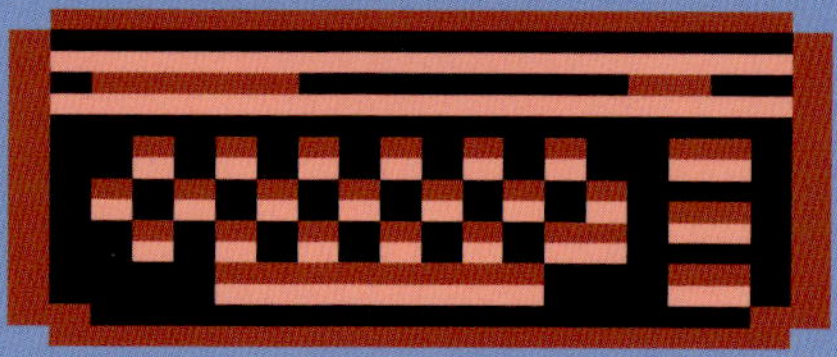

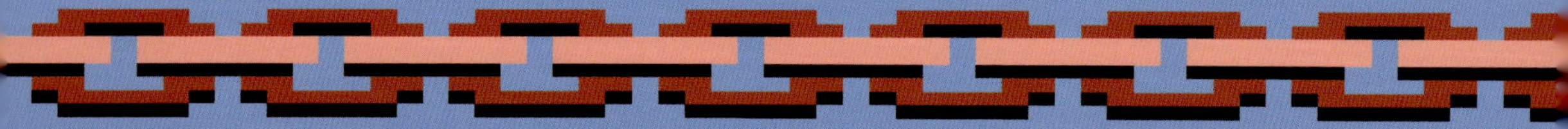

Released
1985

Genre
Platformer

Developer
Micro Projects

Publisher
Gremlin Graphics

Released
1985

Genre
Adventure

Developer
Applied Systems Engineering Inc.

Publisher
U.S. Gold

Time Tunnel

"I look back fondly on the times that I, a gnome, explored eras such as the Stone Age, Colonial Salem, and an Intergalactic Spaceship. The experience of finding scriptures scattered across time was mesmerising. Maybe it was because *Time Tunnel* was my first adventure game. Maybe it was because the puzzle-solving was shrouded by mystery and accompanied by infectious melodies. Regardless, during my quest to become King of the Gnomes, I was truly lost in time."

Zack Scott, guest reviewer

Ghosts 'n Goblins

"Capcom's 1985 arcade smash-hit featured exactly the sort of lavish, richly detailed sprites to push the C64 to its limits. In truth, it would take four years and an upgraded (1MB) 16-bit Amiga to fully capture the coin-op, but it was the C64 game with its cut-down levels and ferocious difficulty that was a titan of its era and the perfect game for bragging rights over the rival Sinclair Spectrum."

Stuart Wynne, games journalist

Released
1986

Genre
Action

Developer
Chris Butler

Publisher
Elite Systems

Originally by
Capcom

Green Beret

"The arcade game had next to no music at all – just a few jingles between levels and such. I started with the loading music and imagined the desolation of a place torn apart by war, where plants and flowers started to regrow, and beauty has returned. For the high-score tune, I implemented an unlicensed version of Jerry Goldsmith's tune from *The Great Escape* - this appears to be unused if you actually play the game … not sure what happened there (apart from the obvious, it was a bad idea!) Finally, I had left the title screen to last and really had no idea what to do. I started with a big intro and went into a pretty terrible dance track that I wasn't happy with at the time – and have only grown to like less as the years have gone by! It's pretty hard to listen to it, and any time anyone has spent effort doing a remix or arrangement of it, I feel sorry!"

Martin Galway, musician

Released
1986

Genre
Run and gun

Developer and Publisher
Imagine

Originally by
Konami

Green Beret

Released
1986

Genre
Run and gun

Developer and Publisher
Imagine

Artwork
Oliver Frey

Leaderboard

Released
1986

Genre
Sports

Developer
Access Software

Publisher
U.S. Gold

Artwork
Oliver Frey

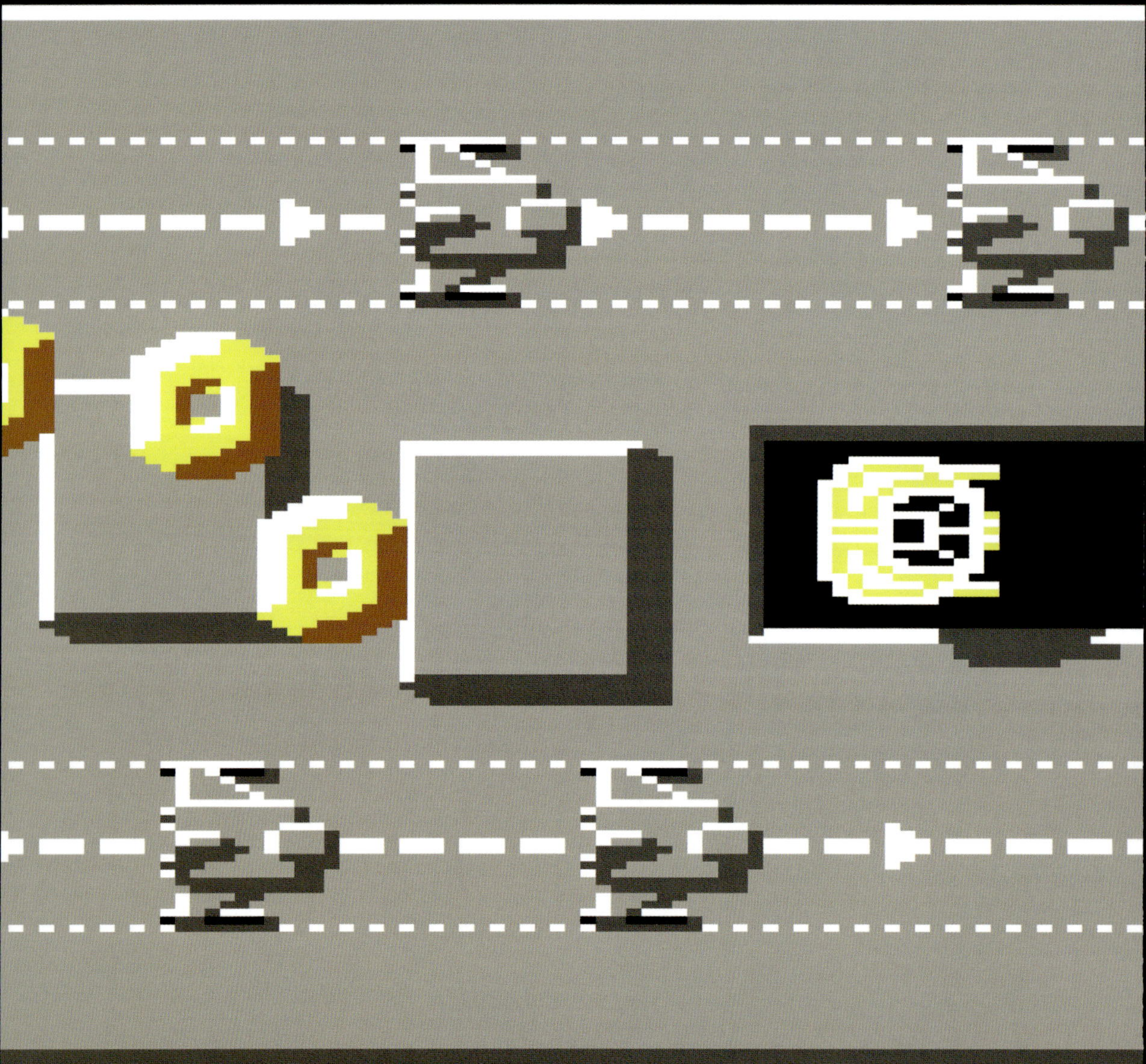

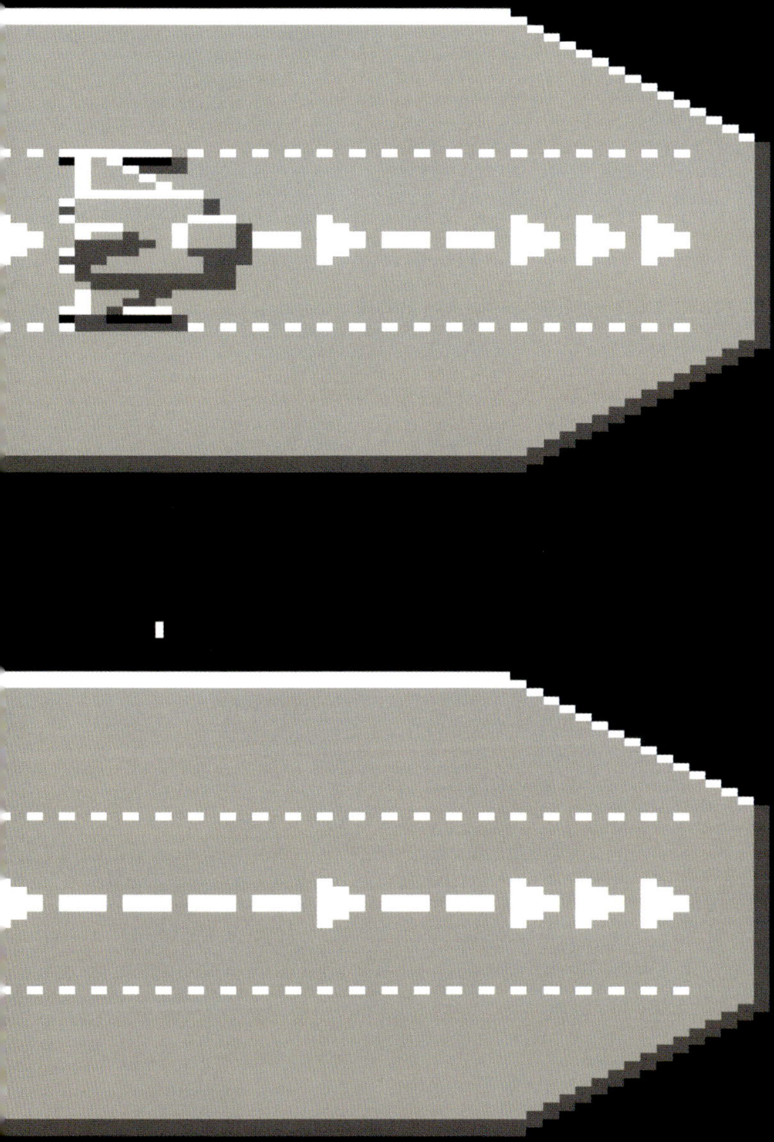

Uridium

"I knew *Uridium* was going to be UK number one before we even shipped it; such was the reception in the press. I'd stayed up all night helping to pack cassettes, but, the next evening, I sank into the darkest feeling of despair. It had been a colossal effort, and I just couldn't imagine how we could ever repeat it. The game was a total smash – probably Hewson's biggest ever hit – and had a big influence on our thinking for subsequent titles."

Andrew Hewson, founder of Hewson Consultants

"I was keen to get the arcade speed and look, which required a bit of simplification of the scrolling routine, and a new way of getting lots of movement on the screen by using the background characters for bullets. I also wanted an agile spaceship that could loop and roll. We had bought a sprite and character set editor by this time, so I spent a long time animating the Manta spaceship. I used to design graphics while waiting for the code to compile, about 30 minutes a pop: I was using two C64s at a time!"

Andrew Braybrook, designer and programmer

Released
1986

Genre
Scrolling shooter

Developer
Graftgold

Publisher
Hewson Consultants

Revs

Arriving at a time when most racing games on the C64 were fairly primitive *Pole Position* variants, Geoff Crammond's peerless Formula 3 racing sim was laps ahead of the competition. With its intricately modelled 3D tracks and unconventional analogue controls, *Revs* is a true simulation in every sense of the word, and you'll need to pick through the incredibly detailed manual before you're even remotely ready to tackle your first lap of Silverstone or Brands Hatch. However, it's all about the engine's revs, not the vehicle's overall speed, and, once you've mastered steering and changing gears, *Revs* truly comes into its own as a quintessential racing simulation.

Released
1986

Genre
Racing

Developer
Geoff Crammond

Publisher
Firebird

77
FIREBIRD

The Pawn

"At the 1986 Novotel trade show in London when I was 18, I boldly proclaimed to the boss of Magnetic Scrolls that I could make *The Pawn* look just as good on C64 as it did on the ST and Amiga! She surprisingly said, 'Prove it!', and we struck a deal a few days later. It required me to hand-pixel each of the 30 images from scratch as that was the only way to get close to the quality required. I was humbled and learnt a huge amount from that project."

Bob Stevenson, graphic artist

Released
1986

Genre
Text adventure

Developer
Magnetic Scrolls

Publisher
Rainbird

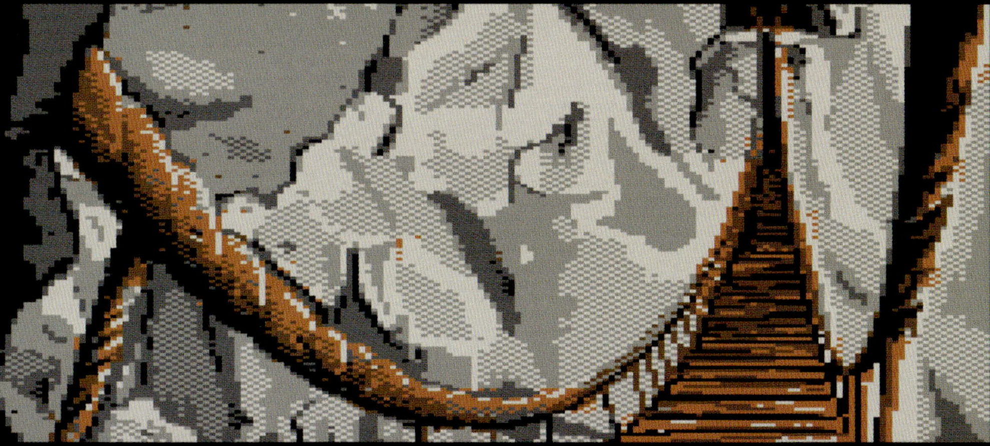

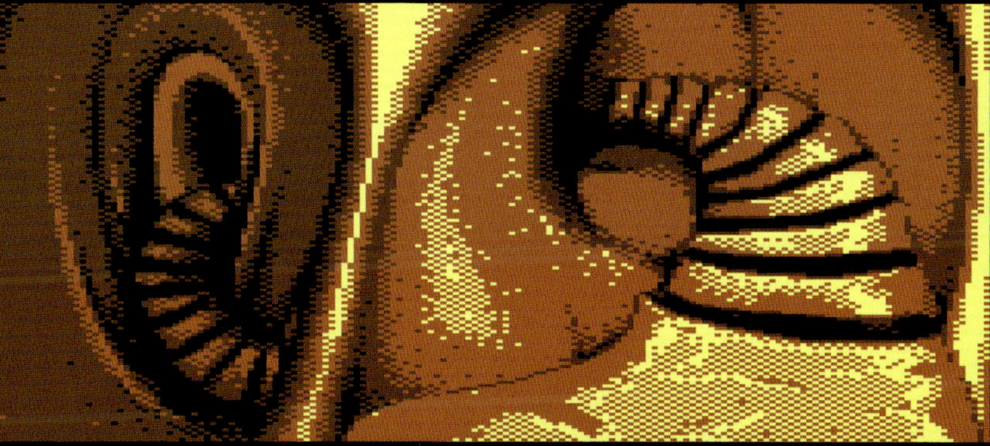

Rambo: First Blood Part II

"The size of the freely accessible play area is impressive. It's even possible to destroy houses and trees, and, due to the opponent's superiority, a downright survival feeling sets in. Anyhow, *Rambo* always remained in the shadow of the similar shooter, *Commando* since the gameplay was rather plain and frustrating at times, ending after ten minutes at the latest. Nevertheless, the atmosphere of the movie was skilfully captured, especially through the adaptation of the original soundtrack."

Oliver Lindau, guest reviewer

"I went and bought a pre-recorded cassette of the official score by Jerry Goldsmith and listened to it over and over. The game's title tune was an arrangement of the main *Rambo* theme, but I was actually influenced by the night-time stalking-around scenes in the movie, and made it spooky and dark. For the loading music, however, it never occurred to me to use more music from the movie! I came up with an original piece and programmed a morse code routine with a pitch that was musical notes in a tune, quickly launched into an anthemic prog-rock style, and continued in a military direction, so it kind of spells out an infantryman's experience, being excited about going to war, seeing it and living through it, and realising it's a lot grimmer coming out at the other end as a survivor."

Martin Galway, musician

Released *1986* / **Genre** *Run and gun* / **Developer and Publisher** *Ocean*

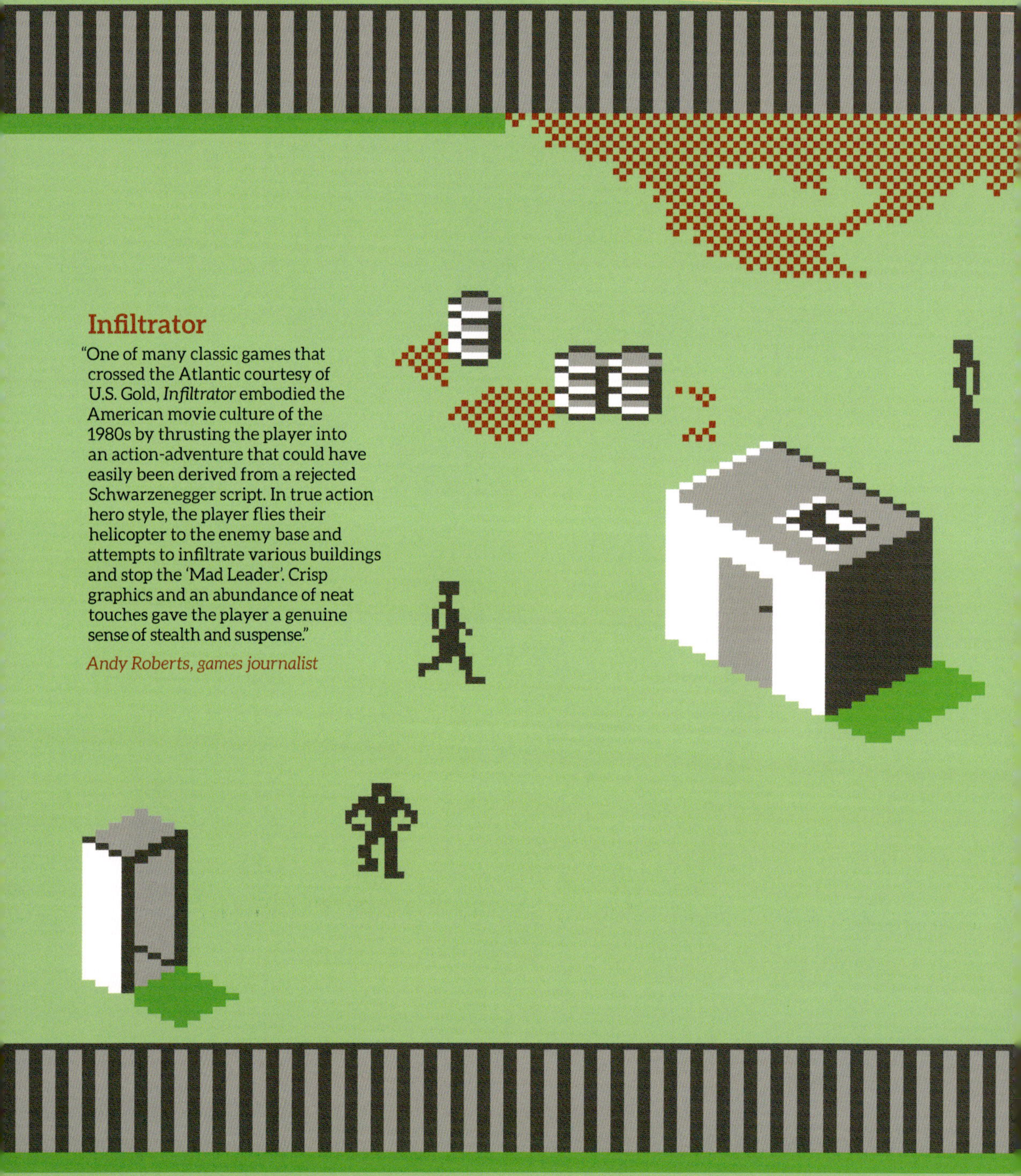

Infiltrator

"One of many classic games that crossed the Atlantic courtesy of U.S. Gold, *Infiltrator* embodied the American movie culture of the 1980s by thrusting the player into an action-adventure that could have easily been derived from a rejected Schwarzenegger script. In true action hero style, the player flies their helicopter to the enemy base and attempts to infiltrate various buildings and stop the 'Mad Leader'. Crisp graphics and an abundance of neat touches gave the player a genuine sense of stealth and suspense."

Andy Roberts, games journalist

Released
1986

Genre
Simulation

Developer
Chris Gray Enterprises

Publisher
U.S. Gold

Released *1986* / **Genre** *Scrolling shooter* / **Developer** *Sensible Software* / **Publisher** *Ocean*

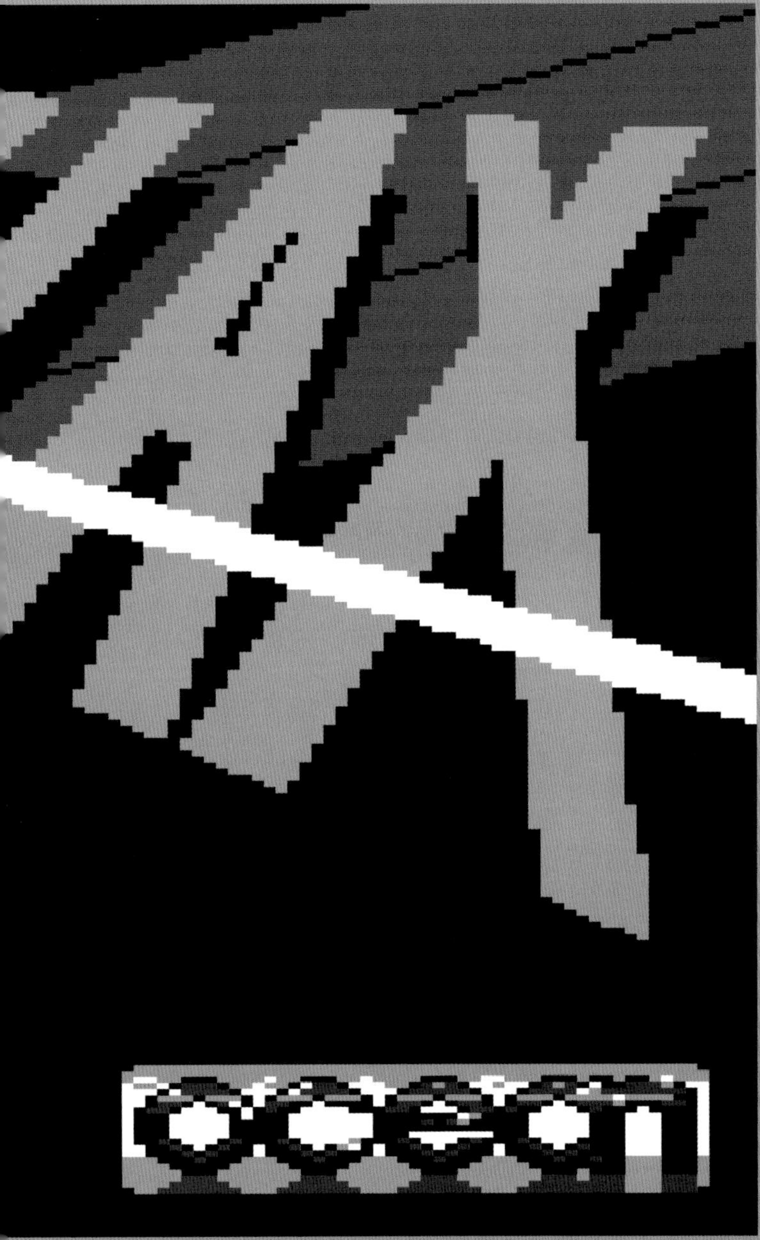

Parallax

"*Parallax* was our first game as Sensible Software. Signed up by Ocean in our first-ever business meeting, we went home with a cheque for £1,000 and smoked cigars in the dinner carriage of the train on the way home to Essex ... pity the royalty cheques never followed. The first time I heard Martin's music for this game, the hairs stood up on the back of my neck – it was incredible. This was our lucky break."

Jon Hare, designer and graphic artist

"Gary Bracey popped his head around the door and said, 'Mart, could you see what this game is? Some developer sent it in, and we're a bit busy.' It was *Parallax*. So I was the first person to see it outside of Sensible Software. I obviously thought it was worth publishing, showed it to Gary, and the rest is history. I took my C128D home on the bus and worked on it for two weeks. I definitely wanted it to be a big tune, so I started off with a deceptively simple intro motif and built it up. Little did I know, it would be like 8 minutes long – it certainly was a long ramp into the melody! The crazy ending of the title tune was the result of some SID experiments I had been doing. Ocean's graphics programmers had long been sending illegal commands to the VIC-II to see what it could do, and I started trying out undocumented SID waveforms, basically issuing commands that weren't in the manual to see what kind of sound came out. To me, it was like pulling the curtain away and revealing a big machine that had been playing the music."

Martin Galway, musician

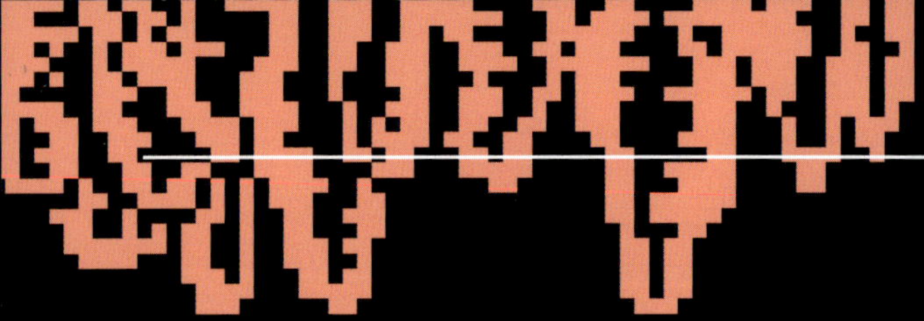

Starquake

"I created *Starquake* initially on the Speccy, and then it was converted over to the C64. I worked closely with the programmer at Bubble Bus Software on the conversion to ensure it played as closely as possible to the original. I also programmed the sound engine and probably created most of the sound effects and the music for the C64 version. It was also fun to put more colour into the graphics than the limited Spectrum palette allowed."

Stephen Crow, original designer

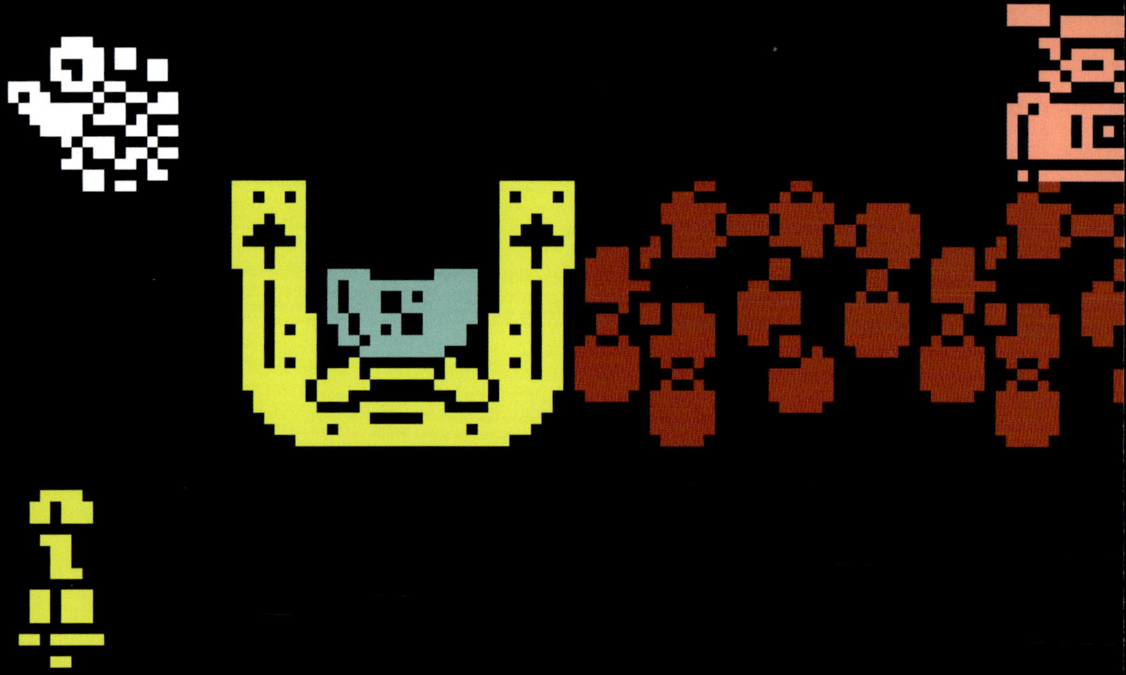

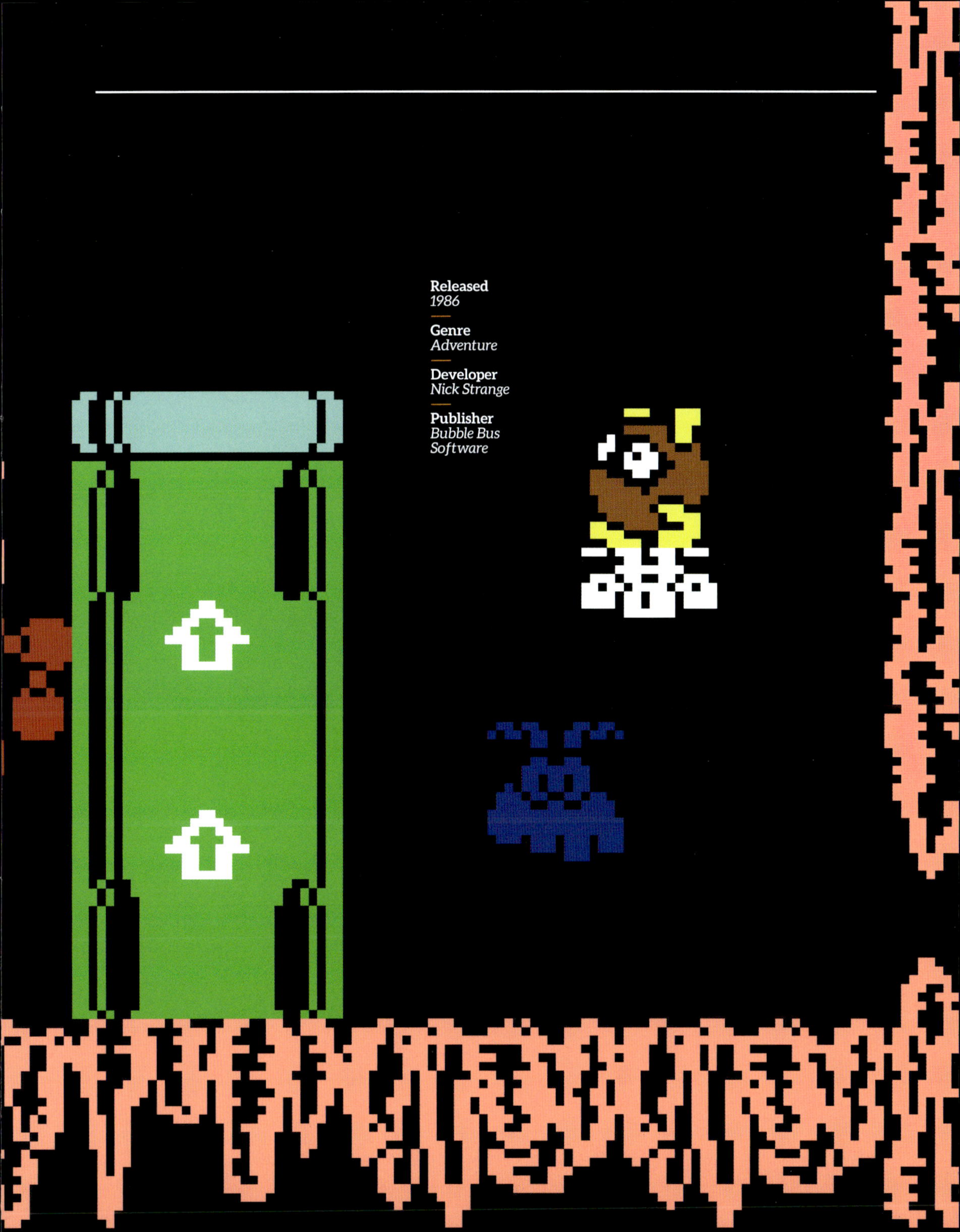

Released
1986

Genre
Adventure

Developer
Nick Strange

Publisher
Bubble Bus Software

Thrust

"I'd been seduced by vector graphics coin-ops like *Asteroids* and *Battlezone*, and I loved the way they emulated real-world physics. So, when *Thrust* appeared on the C64, I was totally blown away (not to mention, it cost a measly two quid at the time). Rather than being restricted by the resolution of sprites or a game's clunky collision detection, *Thrust*'s fluid control system allowed you to play with a remarkable level of freedom and precision. The levels may have been fiendishly designed, but your biggest enemies were momentum, inertia and sheer blind panic."

Steve Jarratt, games journalist

"Few games on the 64 made use of Newtonian mechanics – and even fewer as impressively as *Thrust*, which makes the fact that this physics-fuelled fun was a budget release all the more 'WTF'. Yes, *Thrust* smells like Atari's *Gravitar*, but it's so much richer in flavour thanks to the inventive addition of spice: an orb to extract from each planet; a weighty orb attached by a rigid cable to your ship to radically affect its handling and make for some remarkable sphincter-clenching moments as you navigate the increasingly tight, twisty and deadly caverns."

Gary Penn, games journalist

Genre
Arcade

Developer
Jeremy Smith

Publisher
Firebird

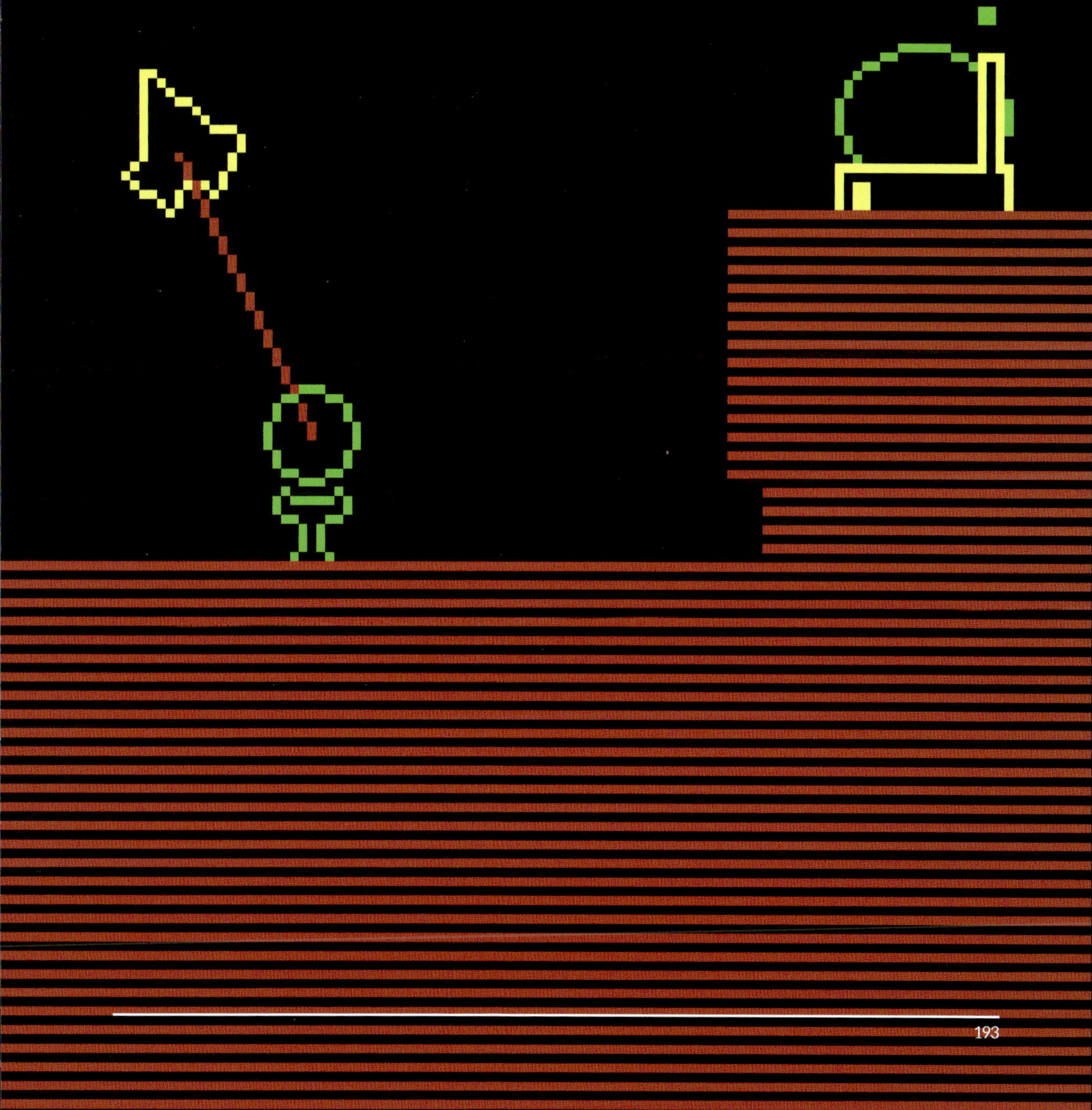

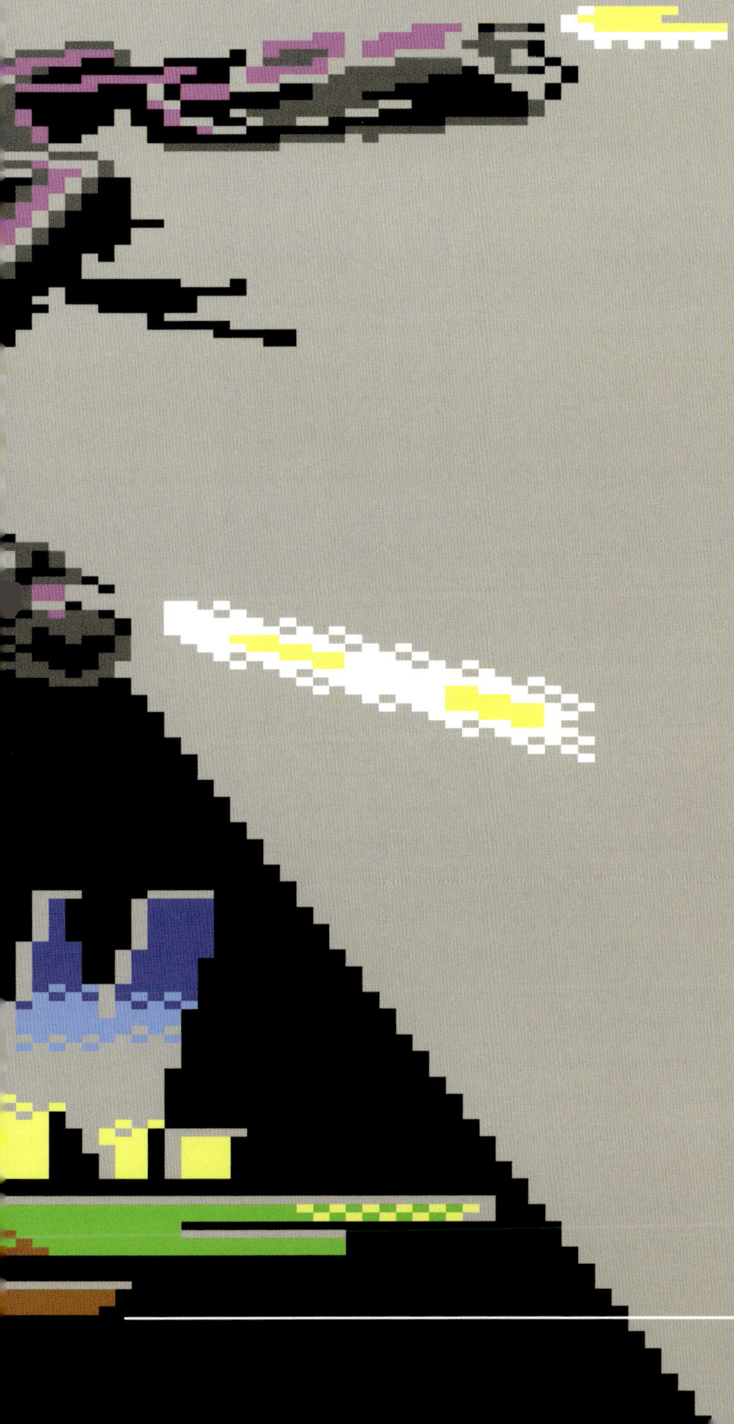

Sanxion

As a pilot for the Sanxion Corps, it's your sworn duty to defend Earth from an imminent alien invasion which, as you might expect, involves flying through multiple levels annihilating everything in your path. There's no upgrades or power-ups to speak of, but, thankfully, your ship is equipped with a radar which alerts you to incoming attack waves. There's also an innovative training session after each level which allows you to rack up valuable bonus points. Despite being hard as nails, *Sanxion* is a pounding shoot 'em up that oozes polish, from the silky-smooth parallax scrolling, slick graphics, and atmospheric sound design, to the legendary Rob Hubbard loading music.

"Thalamus had Bob Stevenson lined up to do the *Sanxion* loading screen, but he couldn't commit to it as he was too busy doing other work. I knew Bob pretty well, and, on a few occasions, he was kind enough to recommend me for work. The actual loading screen was an overnight job; I just copied the Oliver Frey artwork as best I could! Looking back on it now, it's pretty crude as I was still learning about pixelling at the time, but it's nice that it's remembered fondly."

Mat Sneap, graphic artist

Released
1986

Genre
Scrolling shooter

Developer
Stavros Fasoulas

Publisher
Thalamus

WARH
SIR'86

Warhawk

"When Firebird entered the budget market with their £1.99 Silver range, they really upped the quality, releasing some highly playable games that offered great value for money. One of the best releases was Proteus Development's *Warhawk*, a vertically scrolling sci-fi shooter with an amazing Rob Hubbard soundtrack. As I loved drawing spaceships, the game really played to my artistic strengths, so inspiration for the loading screen was easy to find, and it became one of my most famous pieces. I remember this took about 14 hours to draw, compared with six to eight hours for my previous screens."

Stephen Robertson, graphic artist

Released
1986

Genre
Scrolling shooter

Developer
Proteus Developments

Publisher
Firebird

Palace Software logo by Robin Levy / 2016

London-based Palace Software was an independent developer and publisher founded in 1983 by Peter Stone and Richard Leinfellner. Its core team was comprised of programmers Stan Schembri and Rob Stevens, artists Steve Brown, Dan Malone and Jo Walker, plus musician Richard Joseph. Palace Software was eventually sold by parent company Palace Group to the French-owned Titus in 1991.

In 1983, Peter Stone and Richard Leinfellner worked at The Video Palace, a video shop based in central London. The shop began selling computer games at the cusp of the Britsoft revolution, and, when game sales began to increase exponentially, the duo saw the lucrative potential of developing games themselves. Stone approached Palace Group's head honcho Nik Powell, the project was greenlit, and Palace Software was born.

Between 84 and 91, Palace's core team of talented developers produced some of the C64's most memorable games, including *Cauldron*, *Barbarian* and *The Sacred Armour of Antiriad*. The company also published several games and utilities from other talented developers – including Sensible Software and Denton Designs – on its Outlaw label.

Palace's C64 debut title was *The Evil Dead*, a spooky arcade adventure based on the 1981 Sam Raimi movie to which Palace owned the home video rights. Narrowly skirting the controversy that surrounded the movie's ban in the UK, the C64 version was closer in spirit to *Atic Atac* than a gory horror fest, and the reviews were generally favourable. "*The Evil Dead* isn't nearly as evil as it sounds," said *Personal Computer Games*, while *Commodore Horizons* thought the game was "an excellent debut from Palace Software."

Keen to replicate *The Evil Dead*'s success, Palace's next title was intended as a movie tie-in based on John Carpenter's *Halloween*, a plan that fell by the wayside when the limitations of the subject matter became all too apparent. However, suitably inspired by witches and pumpkins, artist Steve Brown decided to take the game in a new direction and by assimilating Brown's love of platformers with Leinfellner's affection for shoot 'em ups like *Defender*, the concept for *Cauldron* was born.

> “ Antiriad's *post-apocalyptic theme and stunning presentation resulted in one of the best flick-screen platformers on the C64.* ”

Cauldron subsequently hit the streets in the spring of 1985 to considerable acclaim. A sprawling arcade adventure which seamlessly blended two different styles of play, the game was an epic witch hunt to track down the elusive ingredients required to rid the world of the evil 'Pumpking'. *Cauldron* scored impressively across the board: "The graphics are bewitching," said *Your 64*, while *Zzap!64* called it "an excellent combo of zapping, leaping and exploring", earning Palace its first 'Sizzler' in the process.

Cauldron's success led to the inevitable 1986 sequel *Cauldron II: The Pumpkin Strikes Back*. Keen to give the fans something new but retain a sense of continuity, *Cauldron II* flipped the concept, this time casting players in the role of a pumpkin on a quest into the heart of the evil Witch Queen's castle. Coded by the late Stan Schembri, the game was crammed with neat touches and, like its predecessor, hard as nails. "*Cauldron II* looks good, sounds good, and plays even better," said *Zzap!64*, earning Palace another 'Sizzler', while *Your Commodore* said, "It has all the hallmarks of a classic."

Palace's next game was *The Sacred Armour of Antiriad*, which arrived just in time for Christmas '86. Derived from artist Dan Malone's love of comic books and his desire to mesh the ancient with the futuristic, *Antiriad*'s post-apocalyptic theme and stunning presentation resulted in one of the best flick-screen platformers on the C64. "Rather like Christmas, games from Palace arrive once a year," said *Your Computer*, awarding the game 5/5. *Zzap!64* was similarly impressed, slapping a 'Sizzler' on *Antiriad* and calling it "a really slick and polished arcade adventure."

Barbarian II: The Dungeon of Drax / *1988*

Cauldron / *1985*

The Sacred Armour of Antiriad / *1986*

1987 saw the release of the bloody hack 'em up *Barbarian*, inspired by artist Steve Brown's love of the *Conan the Barbarian* books, comics and movies. Always keen to try something new, the result was a visceral and brutal sword-fighting game with authentic fantasy overtones. Ironically, it would be the game's packaging featuring a scantily clad Maria Whittaker – rather than the game's decapitation move – which would ultimately generate the most controversy. *Zzap!64* called it "the definitive man-to-man combat game," while *C&VG* declared *Barbarian* "an unashamedly bloodthirsty hack 'n' slash combat game".

Barbarian was closely followed by the quintessentially British *Stifflip & Co.*, an innovative icon-driven graphic adventure created by Binary Vision, the team behind such groundbreaking C64 games such as *Zoids* and *The Fourth Protocol*. Years ahead of its time and packed with bally splendid humour, *Stifflip & Co.* was unanimously well-received. "If you're a games player desperate for something different then take a look at *Stifflip*," said *C&VG*, while *Your Commodore* called it "the very best of British ingenuity and programming".

Palace wrapped up the year with the release of Sensible Software's *Shoot 'em up Construction Kit* (*SEUCK*), arguably one of the most innovative programs ever produced for the C64. The debut title on Palace's newly formed Outlaw label, which had been established specifically to publish titles from other developers, *SEUCK* was not only a slickly programmed game creation tool; it was also a masterclass in user-friendly product design. "There's no doubt that *SEUCK* is an exceptional piece of software," said *Zzap!64*, awarding *SEUCK* a much-deserved 'Gold Medal'.

1988 would herald the release of *Troll*, the second title on Palace's Outlaw label. Created by Denton Designs, the company previously responsible for classics such as *Shadowfire* and *Enigma Force*, *Troll* was a quirky action puzzle game featuring an endearing troll called Humgruffin. Despite the game's fantastic presentation, *Troll*'s unorthodox 3D landscape and gameplay quirks would ultimately leave a bad aftertaste. "*Troll* is certainly a brave try at a different sort of game," said *C&VG*, whereas *Zzap!64* called it "an unusual and moderately appealing game marred by excessive emphasis on luck".

Palace's next release was *Rimrunner*, a futuristic shoot 'em up featuring a race of elite insectoid warriors tasked with patrolling the surface of various planets astride impressively animated reptilian 'Runners'. Despite its striking visuals and impeccable presentation, *Rimrunner*'s relatively simplistic gameplay gleaned only average review scores. "Style merchants Palace pack another knockout punch with their latest offering," said *C&VG*, awarding *Rimrunner* 8/10 and branding it "a nifty little game."

The sequel to Palace's most commercially successful game to date, *Barbarian II: The Dungeon of Drax* appeared at the tail-end of 1988, developed by newcomers Rob Stevens and Jo Walker. Eager to expand on the original game rather than simply giving players more of the same, Palace propelled the genre to new heights by adding two different player characters, multiple fantasy-inspired foes and a large, explorable world.

Barbarian II would go on to repeat the heady success of its predecessor, earning a string of accolades including a 'C+VG Hit', *Commodore User* 'Screen Star' and a 'Gold Medal' from *Zzap!64*.

Barbarian: The Ultimate Warrior / *1987*

Rimrunner / *1988*

The attention to graphical detail is phenomenal," said *Zzap!64*, while *Commodore User* called it '[a] brilliant hack 'em up, which sets new standards for the genre".

In 1989, Palace's innovative 8-bit output began to take a back seat as the company turned its focus on the booming Amiga and Atari ST markets. Its next C64 title, *Cosmic Pirate*, was a conversion of the highly acclaimed 16-bit game, developed by Zippo Games (a.k.a. The Pickford Brothers) and released as a budget title on the Byte Back label. Aptly described as '*Asteroids* on steroids', *Cosmic Pirate*'s depth and budget price tag proved to be a winning formula. *Zzap!64* said, "Compared to the chronic simplicity of most budget releases, this is a welcome surprise," while *C&VG* thought it "fast, smooth, and pretty good fun".

Despite a noticeable lack of internally developed 8-bit titles, Palace saw a brief return to glory in the summer of 1990 with *International 3D Tennis* (*I3DT*), a unique top-spin on the sporting genre developed by Sensible Software. Boasting incredible 3D vector graphics and an innovative control system that enabled players to focus on their shots rather than struggling to reach the ball, *I3DT* was a welcome shot in the arm for the stagnant sports genre. Scooping multiple awards including a *Zzap!64* 'Sizzler', *C&VG* called *I3DT* "a breakthrough both in tennis simulations and programming," while *The Games Machine* thought it "one of the best computer sports games ever".

Palace's final release came in 1991 in the form of *Swap*, a delightfully uncomplicated puzzle game that would beat similar puzzlers like *Bejeweled* to the punch by a clear decade. Despite the simplistic gameplay, the slick presentation and variety of options enabled *Swap* to hold its own amongst other puzzlers of the time. "It's pretty, slick, and undoubtedly very clever," said *Commodore Format*, while *Zzap!64* called it "compulsive stuff for puzzle fans".

Despite an impressive portfolio of successes on various formats, Palace was sold to the French publisher Titus in 1991 as The Palace Group shed its various subsidiaries to focus on movie production. Palace effectively became Titus's UK office, and several projects that were in production – including the highly ambitious *Barbarian III* – would ultimately never see the light of day.

One of the great British success stories of the Britsoft era, Palace's relatively diminutive size was far outweighed by its ability to consistently churn out quality software. Driven by the urge to create games that were original, innovative and unique, Palace's impressive back catalogue is home to some of the most iconic and accomplished games of all time.

> "Barbarian II *would go on to repeat the heady success of its predecessor.*"

10th Frame

"Developed by Access Software, this follow-up to *Leaderboard* swaps golf greens for the wooden lanes of ten-pin bowling and does it brilliantly. I'd been bowling in a league for a while, and so this was right up my alley. Using a similar control system to *Leaderboard*, you positioned your bowler and then set the speed and 'hook' or spin of the ball. Animation of the character and the pin-fall was great, and obtaining a strike was just as satisfying as the real thing. *10th Frame* is a cracking little simulation."

Steve Jarratt, games journalist

Released
1986

Genre
Sports

Developers
Roger and Bruce Carver

Publisher
Access Software

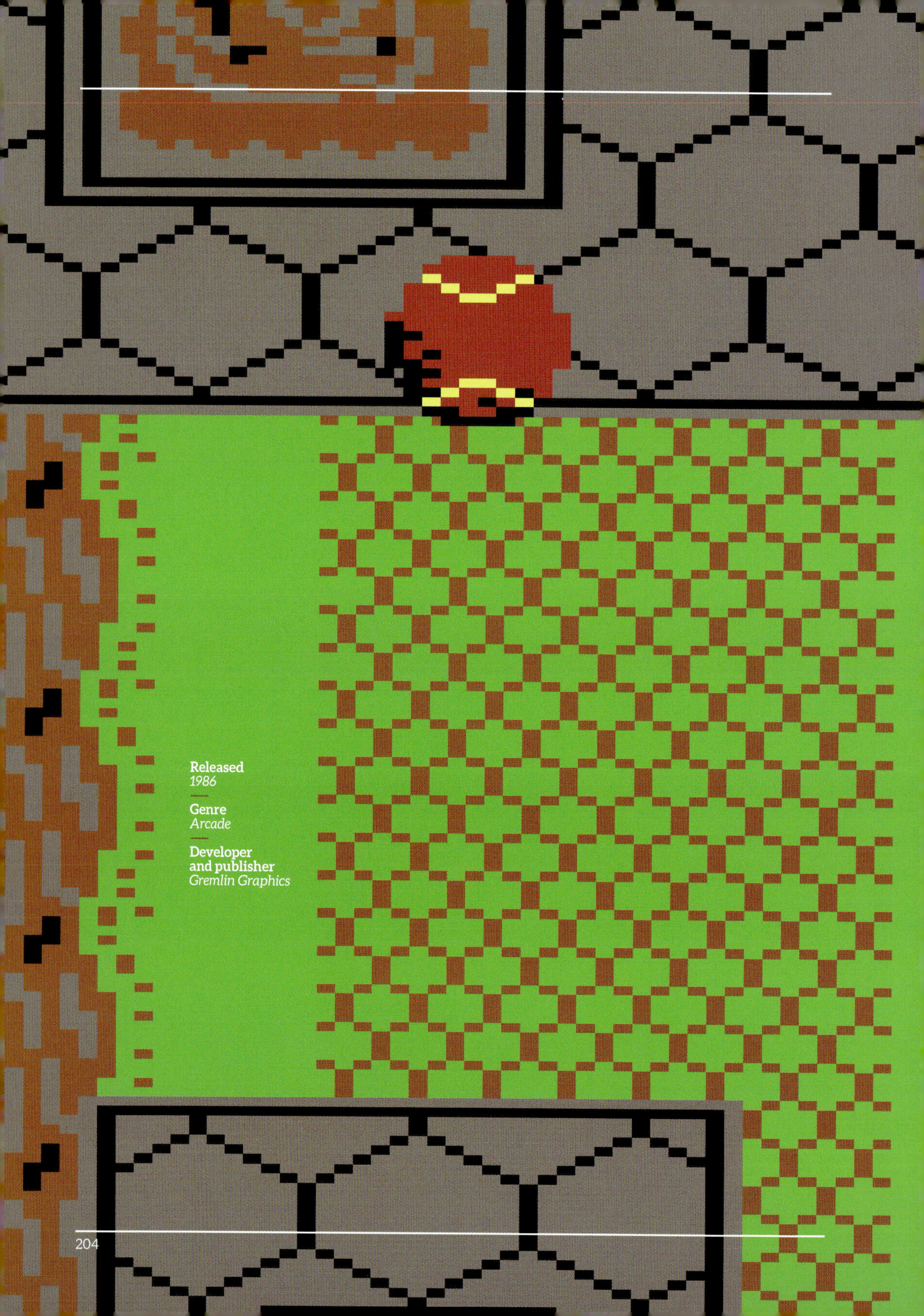

Released
1986

Genre
Arcade

Developer and publisher
Gremlin Graphics

Bounder

"*Bounder* was created one sunny English summer's day when Rob Toone, Andy Green and myself were hanging out at a local park, playing some tennis and doing what teenagers do. We'd all been making little games by ourselves and felt it was time to collaborate. We knocked some ideas around for a while and decided a *Marble Madness*-type game with a rolling tennis ball would be cool. The idea slowly changed, and we ended up with a pretty solid idea for a game, starring a bouncing tennis ball having to navigate a scrolling puzzle level where any misplaced bounce would mean a swift and novel death."

Chris Shrigley, designer and programmer

PETSCII gallery

An intrinsic part of Commodore's DNA, the PET Standard Code of Information Interchange – affectionately known as 'PETSCII' – is the eclectic series of shapes and lines branded onto the C64's keys. In the right hands, however, these crude symbols can be crafted into stunningly beautiful imagery that almost defies belief. Undoubtedly, it is C64 art in its purest form.

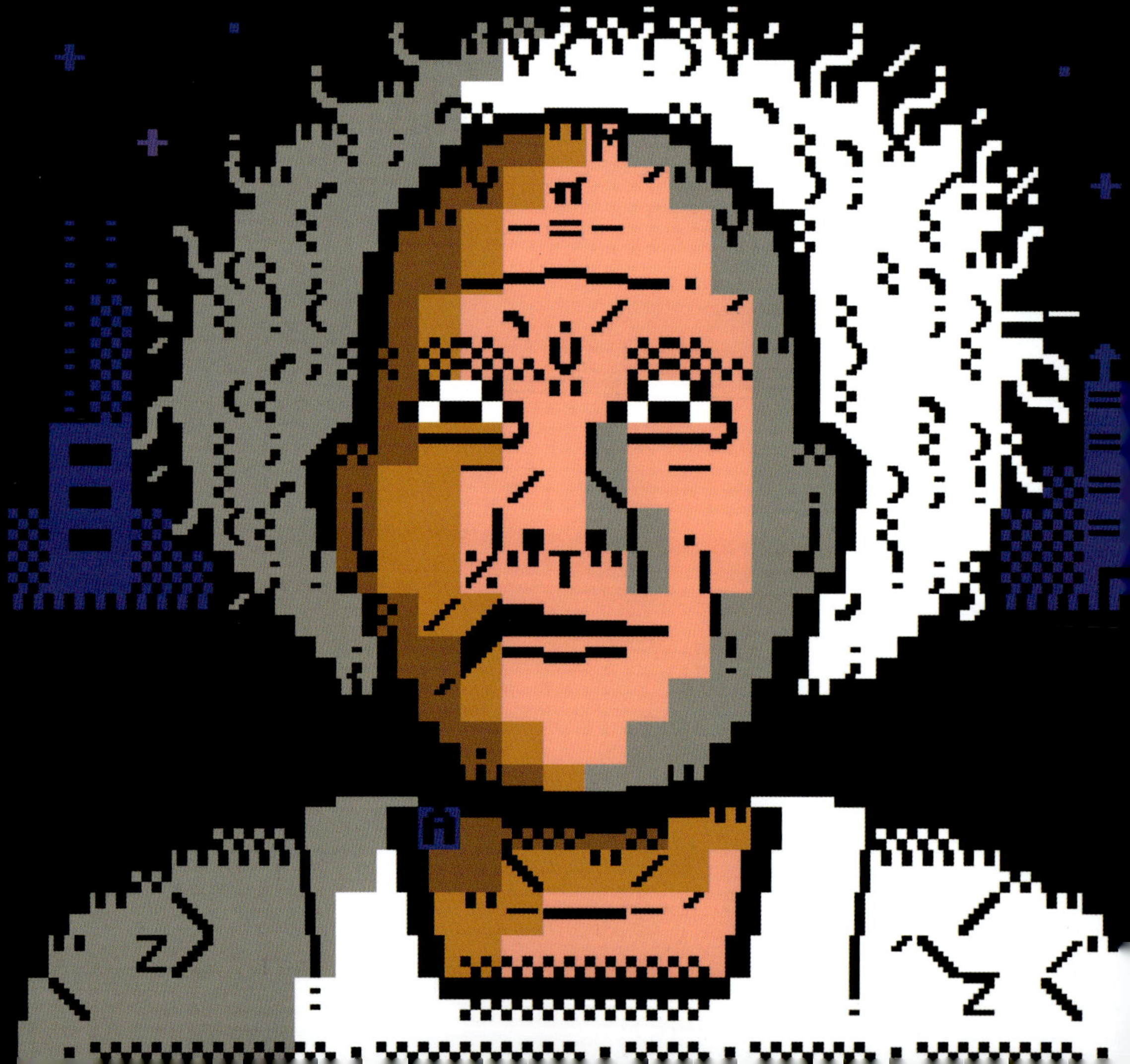

Great Scott / *Shine* / *2018*

Rekall Inc. / *Shine* / *2017*

SixShots / *Electric* / *2016*

Alice in PETSCIIland / *Dr. TerrorZ* / *2019*

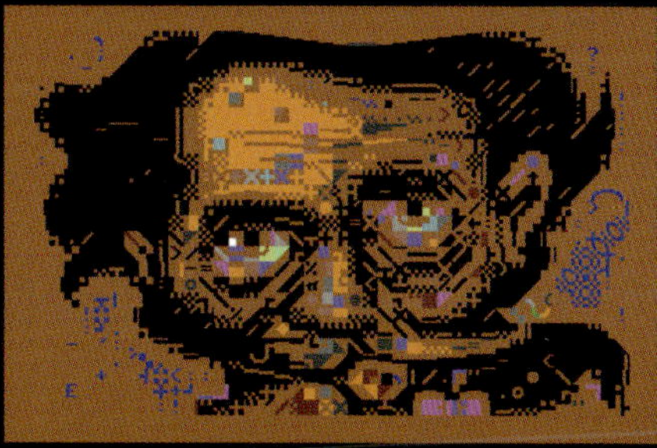

Strindberg / *Electric* / *2017*

Planet of Zoo / *Electric* / *2017*

Armakuni Returns / *Shine* / *2020*

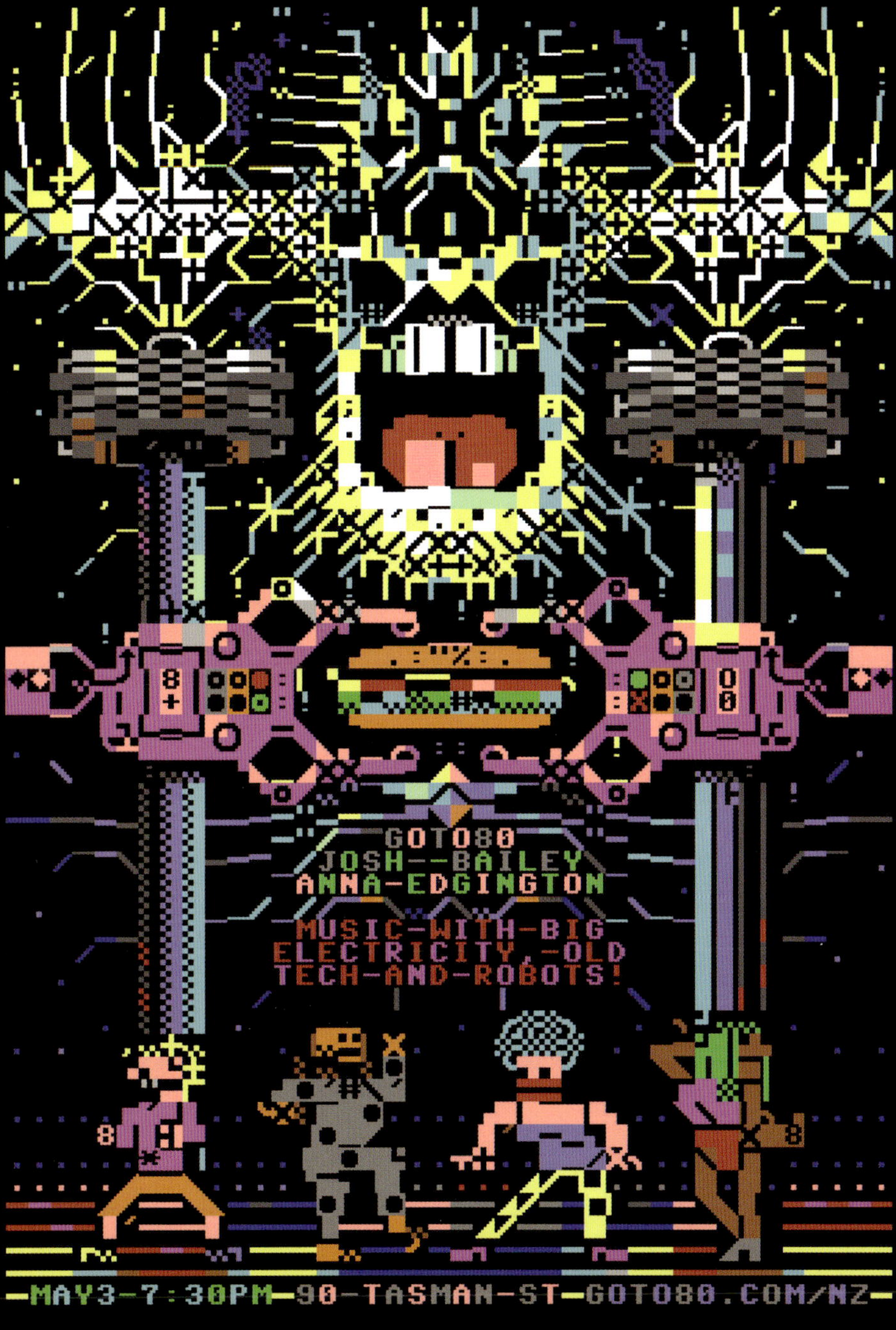
GOTO80
JOSH--BAILEY
ANNA-EDGINGTON
MUSIC-WITH-BIG
ELECTRICITY,-OLD
TECH-AND-ROBOTS!
-MAY3-7:30PM-90-TASMAN-ST-GOTO80.COM/NZ-

Hairy / *Electric / 2017*

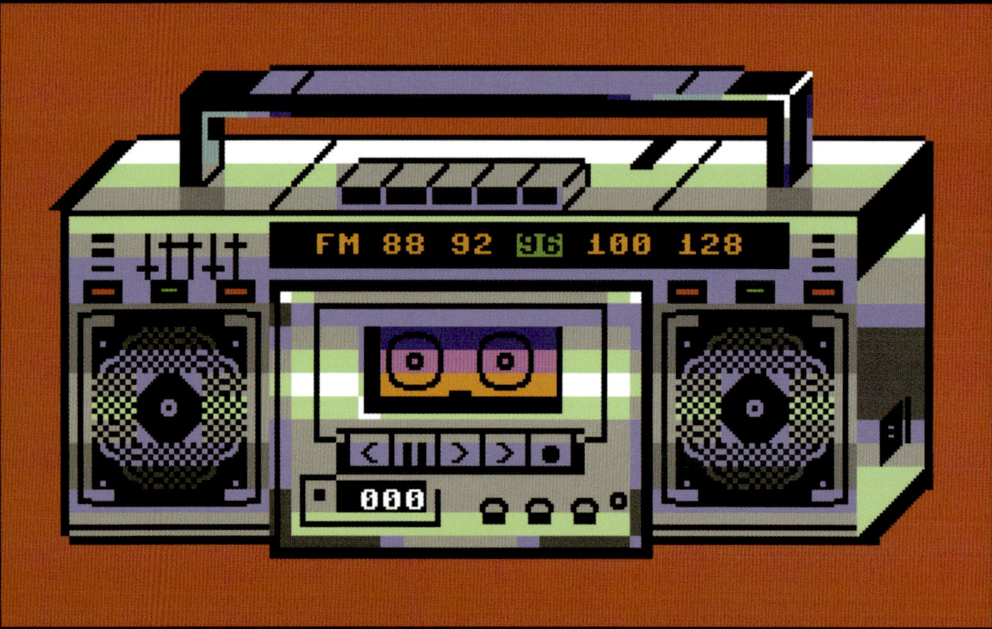

SIDBlaster / *Dr. TerrorZ / 2019*

Clone of Aztec / *Phat-Phu / 2020*

Green Goblin / *Shine / 2018*

Released
1986

Genre
Scrolling shooter

Developer and Publisher
Imagine

Originally by
Nichibutsu

Terra Cresta

"Imagine were responsible for some of the worst arcade conversions on the C64 – and some of the best, with the adaptation of Nichibutsu's vertical shoot 'em up *Terra Cresta* arguably taking the lead. There are three reasons to play it: because it's driven by Martin Galway's atmospheric rhythms; because coder David Collier crammed tons of arcadey objects, colours and smoothness in; and because it's an amazingly playable test of skill. Seldom did you to fight so hard to survive against waves of enemy aggressors; manoeuvring through a rain of enemy projectiles almost feels like a ballet."

Richard Löwenstein, games journalist

The Sacred Armour of Antiriad

Released
1986

Genre
Action adventure

Developer and publisher
Palace Software

Artwork
Oliver Frey

Gauntlet

Released
1986

Genre
Action

Developer
Gremlin Graphics

Publisher
U.S. Gold

Artwork
Oliver Frey

World Games

"The follow-up to the *Winter* and *Summer Games* titles sees the player travelling around the world, participating in a series of more unusual sports events. There's weight lifting (Russia), slalom skiing (France), log rolling (Canada), cliff diving (Mexico), caber toss (Scotland), bull riding (USA), barrel jumping (Germany), and sumo wrestling (Japan). While *World Games* boasts some of the best graphics of any of the 'Games' series, what makes this one really stand out is its superb gameplay: each mini-event is a real joy to play."

Julian Rignall, games journalist

Released
1986

Genre
Sports

Developer and publisher
Epyx

Released
1986

Genre
Racing

Developer and publisher
Epyx

Super Cycle

"There are echoes of *Outrun* and *Pitstop* in *Super Cycle*, and, looking back, it was a really obvious racing game to make. Even so, it was brilliantly put together and deliciously playable. You had to use as much of the width of the road as you could, which was often easier said than done, with racers and other hazards suddenly appearing just a few pixels ahead. Dangling from your bike after a dangerously close overtaking manoeuvre made many races white-knuckle rides. It's a great example of deceptively simple, ridiculously addictive gameplay."

Sean Masterson, games journalist

"I remember seeing *Super Cycle* on the shelves and begging my father to buy it for me. Luckily, he did. The game was horrendous to load from tape, but, in those days, I was too excited about the next track to care – I could always get a cocoa while I waited, couldn't I? Everything about *Super Cycle* was great. The smooth gameplay, the music and the excellent inlay cover had me hooked for a very long time."

Andreas Wallström, guest reviewer

INST DEL
CLR HOME
RESTORE
RETURN

"The C64 punched above its weight on a number of levels, and it's a real icon of '80s culture."

Stephen Ian Thomson, graphic artist

An interview with **Stephen Robertson**

Stephen Robertson was one of the C64's most prolific loading screen artists – famously signing his loading screens with 'SIR' (a nice play on his initials). He established a strong reputation on Compunet with his tribute screens and freelanced for various publishers including Firebird and Rack-It, producing countless classic loading screens for games such as **Warhawk, MicroRhythm, Cybernoid, Eliminator** ***and*** **I, Ball.**

How did you first get interested in computers?
My first computer programs were written in maths lessons at school using optical cards (we had to write the program in binary by filling in the 'holes' with soft pencils). In the sixth form, I did O-level Computer Studies, mainly using BBC computers. I decided I had to get my own computer, and, as I only had a black-and-white TV (and a limited budget), I went for a Sinclair ZX81.

When I left school, I got a training position at a computer shop, spending one day a week at college doing a computer course. I wanted to get a BBC, but a college friend convinced me that a C64 was just as good if you had the *Simon's Basic* cartridge. I saved up for a C64, but there was a shortage of C2N Datasettes, so I was limited to typing in programs and losing them when the machine was turned off! I eventually managed to get a cassette recorder, disk drive and 1702 monitor, so I could finally use the machine to its full potential.

How did your career in the games industry get started?
At the computer shop where I worked, we got a bunch of Touch Tablets for the Atari 8-bit computers. I borrowed a computer and tablet and started doodling some pictures. When I brought the pictures into work, my colleagues were impressed, so I started using them to demo the tablets, and we sold loads of them.

When I got a C64, I tried a friend's KoalaPad Touch Tablet and decided I had to have one. A schoolboy who visited the shop wanted to sell his KoalaPad, so I bought it from him for £50 (I eventually made that back twice over from selling my first piece of art). I started doing some pictures, including tributes to movies such as *Star Wars* and *Ghostbusters* and games like *Koronis Rift*, *Thing on a Spring* and *Monty on the Run*.

I sent demo disks to a few companies, including Activision UK, and, shortly afterwards, I received a phone call from Oxford Digital Enterprises which was making a Titanic game. Activision's Rod Cousins had given them my name, and they wanted me to draw a loading screen showing the Titanic crashing into an iceberg.

What was your first C64 project?
The loading screen for *R.M.S. Titanic*. Oxford Digital Enterprises said they could offer me £100 and asked if that was reasonable. As I was earning £50 a week at the time, I said that was "very, very reasonable", which was a massive understatement! Later, I started working for Firebird doing screens for their C64 budget range.

What did a typical day in front of the computer look like for you?
I was mostly freelance in my early career. During the day, I worked in a computer shop, so the C64 art was a nice way to make extra money. Most of my work was done during evenings and weekends; I'd just sit in front of the computer and draw (when I wasn't playing games, and I played games a lot). I'd also visit computer clubs or work on Compunet demos with friends.

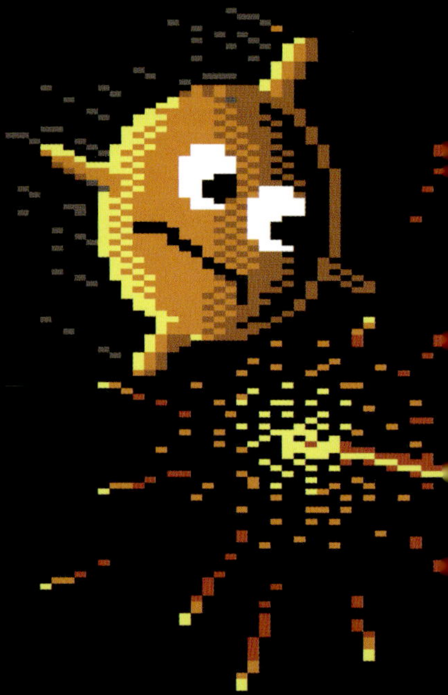

I, Ball / *1987*

You were quite active during the Compunet era; what was that like?
It was an amazing time – nothing like it had been seen before. Compunet really thrived on user content and interactions, so there was this incredible competition to upload better and better content. The demos and pictures were really inspiring. However, most of my skills were honed just doing pictures for pleasure myself, much of which happened before I joined Compunet.

Which programs did you use to create your C64 art?
I used Audiogenic's *KoalaPainter* along with its Touch Tablet. It was a pretty powerful piece of software, although the flood fill was very slow. I also used *Sprite Machine* by Anirog to draw and animate sprites.

Did you use any tools that weren't available commercially?
For displaying my pictures for demo purposes, I wrote a custom machine code loader and used a compression program (or 'cruncher') to reduce the file size. This was important for uploading to Compunet as the upload speeds were very slow. I also soldered an Atari Touch Tablet stylus to my KoalaPad as the stylus was more precise and had a button for drawing (which the KoalaPad stylus lacked). This was a big convenience and made drawing much easier.

Looking back, what were the best and worst aspects of creating art for the C64?
The C64's multicolour bitmap mode (typically used for loading screens) could only handle three foreground colours in each 4x8 pixel square, plus a global background colour. This wasn't as restrictive as the Spectrum, but it was still tricky to get lots of colours in a small area.

For in-game graphics, you had to use the character-based modes, but you only had 256 characters to create your backgrounds, so games would tend to use a lot of repeated graphics, and it was difficult to do anything complex. The Touch Tablet made it easier to draw bitmap art, whereas sprites and character-based graphics had to be created using a joystick or keyboard controls, which was a lot trickier.

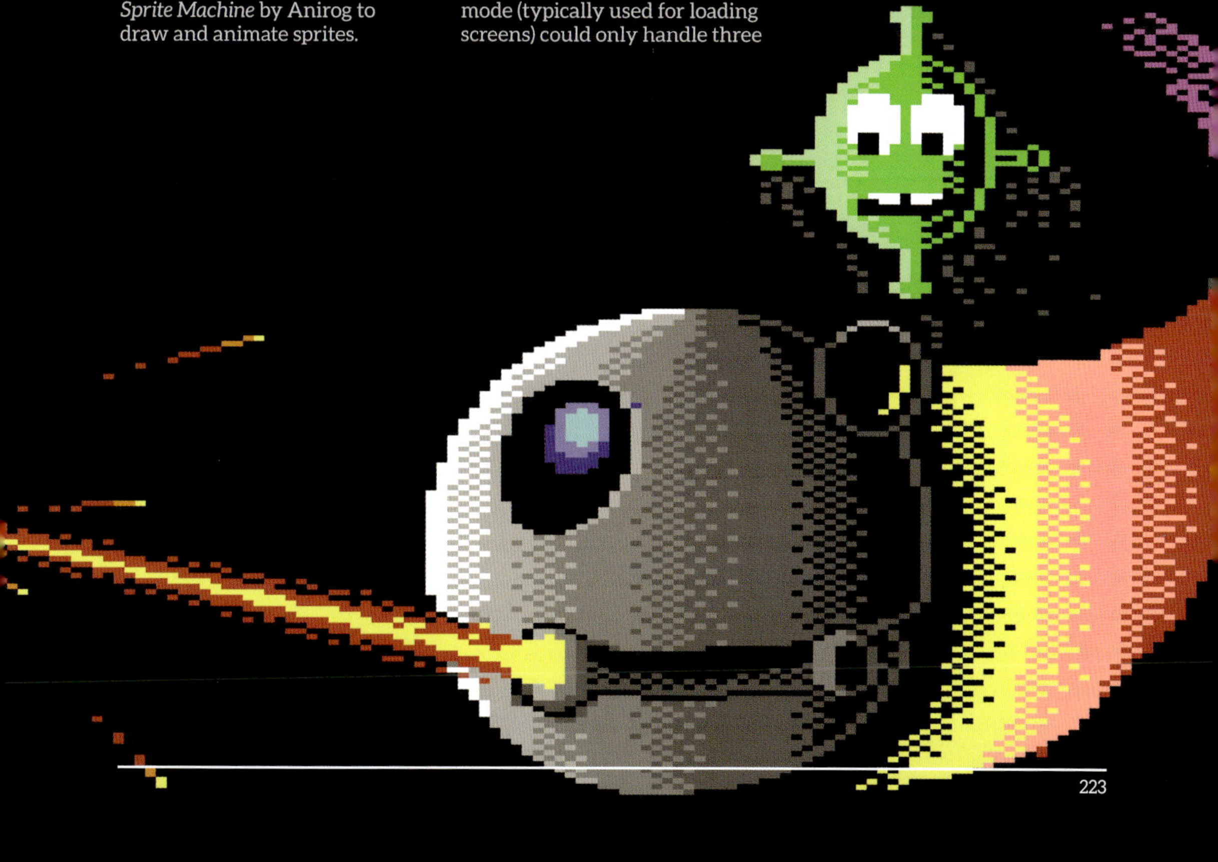

“I remember being ecstatically happy when I got the phone call from Firebird asking me to work for them.”

What was your process? Did you plan on paper, or jump straight in onto the computer?
I just started drawing. I'd use the line drawing function to define the rough outlines, then use the flood fill to fill in areas of colour, and finally, I'd zoom in and refine it. All detailing, shading and stippling was done in zoom mode, pixel by pixel, which was quite time-consuming. Once I'd drawn a picture, I'd look at it from a distance and even upside down: this would show up any errors (such as wonky perspective) that you couldn't see when it was right in front of you.

How did your process change throughout your career?
On the C64, it didn't really change at all. When the Amiga and ST arrived, I had to adjust to using a mouse, but the tools – such as *Deluxe Paint* and *OCP Art Studio* – were much more advanced.

What was the development time for a typical loading screen?
I generally had a deadline to hit. This could be quite tricky when I couldn't get inspiration from the game, or if a picture was especially tricky to draw.

Did you receive much artistic direction, or would you say you had complete freedom?
I occasionally had a bit of art direction. For example, I had to change the *R.M.S. Titanic*'s portholes from white to yellow, and Firebird wanted a really big logo on the first screen I did for them. For projects where I didn't have any box artwork as a guide, I was pretty much free to do whatever I liked, and even when I did have box artwork, I was generally free to do my own interpretation.

When creating C64 art, which aspect did you most enjoy?
As I tended to specialise in bitmap graphics and loading screens, I didn't really enjoy doing sprites or character-based backgrounds as it was very limiting and I couldn't use the Touch Tablet.

Did you have much input in terms of game design?
It depended on the job and the game, really. In the C64 era, I didn't have much influence over the game design itself as my job was simply to draw the graphics; that sometimes involved putting the levels together, although I didn't design the actual level layouts, just the graphic detail.

Did you pay much attention to various magazine reviews?
Loading screens didn't typically factor into magazine reviews, but occasionally one of my screens would be printed alongside a review, which I found very cool.

If you had the chance to revisit any of your games, what would you change?
I'd fix the wonky perspective in my *Uridium* tribute picture and the rear wheel in the *Marauder* loading screen!

Was there anyone working in the industry whose work was inspirational to you?
In the C64 era, I was inspired by artists like Bob Stevenson and programmers like Andrew Braybrook. I was also a massive fan of musicians like Rob Hubbard, Martin Galway, Fred Grey and David Whittaker; their work, in particular, was very inspiring. The magazine *Zzap!64* was also massively influential.

What C64 games at the time impressed you, or had an influence on your work?
Early games like *Forbidden Forest* made a big impression despite the relatively crude graphics (especially as my previous computer was a ZX81). *Impossible Mission* was another with its amazing graphics and incredible synthesised speech, as was *Uridium*, which must have had some influence on me as I eventually drew a tribute picture.

Outside of games, what were your biggest artistic influences?
In the early days, my favourite movies were *Star Wars*, *Alien* and *Aliens*, so they were a huge influence. I'm a big fan of sci-fi movie design in general. In the '70s and '80s, my main sci-fi influences were artists like Chris Foss, Peter Elson and Angus McKie; I loved their craggy, colourful, detailed spaceships and otherworldly vistas.

Were there any C64 games you worked on which sadly never saw the light of day?
I did a bit of work for a *Judge Death* game that was never released and also worked on a prototype for *Nigel Mansell's Grand Prix Challenge* (the only thing that survived was the loading screen).

What was your final C64 game? What made you decide to leave the machine behind?
The last picture I worked on was *Gribbly's Day Out*. After that, the C64 work dried up. By that point, I was already more interested in the Amiga and went on to do graphics for *Cybernoid* on the Atari ST and Amiga.

Was there a C64 game you would have loved to have created the graphics for?
I would have loved to have done more loading screens for full-priced games. The trouble was Firebird had Bob Stevenson do their full-priced screens, and Hewson mainly gave me budget releases. At one point, I was asked to do the graphics for a C64 shoot 'em up for a fellow Compunetter who was a very talented programmer, but he landed a job at Ocean, and the project never happened. It's interesting to think how different my career might have been if that project had gone ahead and been successful.

What are your favourite games?
It has to be *Elite*. I played that game obsessively for weeks to get to Elite status, and I was the sixth person in the UK to do so. I even won a copy of the game in a competition at a computer show; you had to get the highest number of credits in two dockings. I came second, narrowly missing out on winning a disk drive.

What are your standout memories from the C64 era?
I remember being ecstatically happy when I got the phone call from Firebird asking me to work for them. Seeing games with my graphics in them on the store shelves was a massive thrill, too.

Why do you think the C64 is remembered so fondly?
The C64 was a massive step up from earlier micros of that era: better keyboard, more memory, hardware sprites, the amazing SID chip, and it was cheaper than its competitors. Plus it had so many creative games and demos. In the UK, Compunet really helped build a community around the machine, which fostered the exchange of ideas and created an incredible drive to really push the envelope of what the machine could do (including things that Commodore didn't even know it could do!).

Do you still own a C64?
Yes, I still have my original C64 with the disk drive, monitor, tape deck and the Touch Tablet I used to draw all my C64 art. It still works, though it's getting a bit poorly, and the disk drive won't read disks any more.

What are you up to these days?
I now work as a senior designer for a major games studio working on AAA games – a slightly different experience from doing loading screens in the 8-bit era!

> *"Once I'd drawn a picture, I'd look at it from a distance and even upside down."*

Eliminator / *1988*

Marauder / *1988*

Released
1986

Genre
Action puzzle

Developer and Publisher
Electric Dreams Software

Spindizzy

While similarities to *Marble Madness* are inevitable, *Spindizzy* manages to stand apart from other isometric action puzzlers of the time thanks to its incredible scope, depth, and complexity. Your task is to chart a mysterious new dimension using GERALD, a remote-controlled, shape-shifting gyroscope. Time is of the essence, but, thankfully, mapping a new room or collecting one of the many diamonds will reward you with extra time to complete the mission. However, to reach those diamonds, you'll need to use your trusty gyro to flip switches to activate lifts, skim across ice and water, and bounce on trampolines to reach higher areas. Although initially demanding, once you've mastered the controls, *Spindizzy* is an incredibly rewarding experience.

"Continuing my fascination with 3D graphics, *Spindizzy* immediately caught my attention for its angular Escher-like levels, and visual similarity to the *Marble Madness* coin-op. This flick-screen action puzzler tasked you with exploring a vast network of mazes in control of a gyroscopic device called Plexity. Your task is to chart a mysterious new dimension using GERALD. Sadly, the game's sensitive control system and overall difficulty meant I never got more than a few screens into the game's 400-plus areas! But that didn't stop me from returning to it just to experience its unique visual style."

Steve Jarratt, games journalist

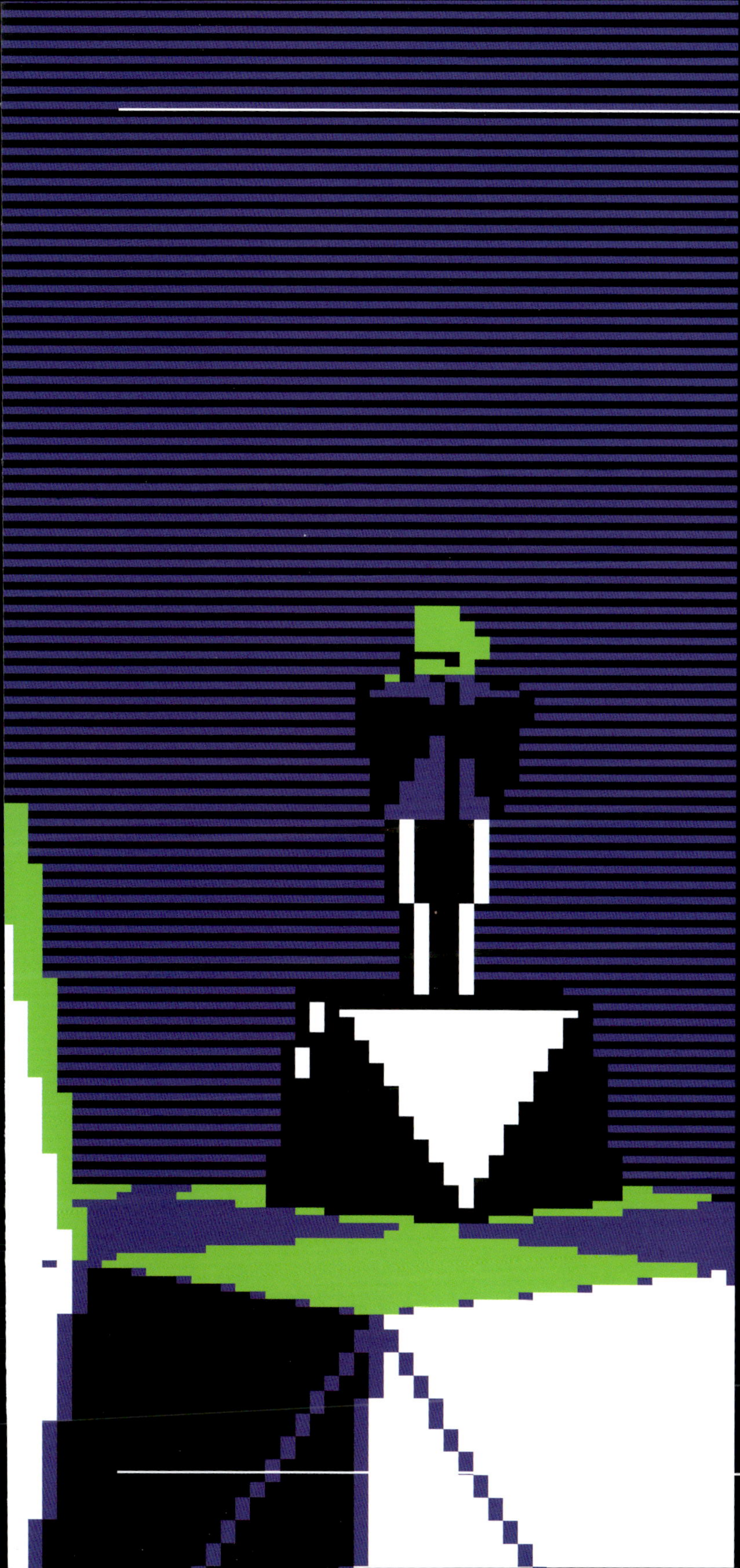

The Sentinel

"The C64 played host to some extraordinary games, but one of the most innovative and atmospheric was *The Sentinel*. It delivered a tense game of cat and mouse, as you transported yourself around each abstract landscape in order to reach higher ground than that on which the Sentinel stood. Absorb the landscape's custodian, and you moved on to the next level. As one of the first fully polygonal 3D games, it was a standout in its day, and the unhurried speed of the camera only served to make the game even more suspenseful. If someone updated this for the iPad, I'd buy a copy tomorrow."

Steve Jarratt, games journalist

Released
1986

Genre
Strategy

Developer
Geoff Crammond

Publisher
Firebird

Slap Fight *Imagine*

Laser Squad *Blade Software*

Time Machine *Vivid Image*

Firefly *Special FX*

Stormlord *Hewson Consultants*

First Samurai *Vivid Image*

Short Circuit *Ocean*

Tetris *Andromeda Software*

Game Over *Dinamic*

Turrican *Rainbow Arts*

Starglider *Rainbird*

Solomon's Key *Probe Software*

Iron Lord *Ubi Soft*

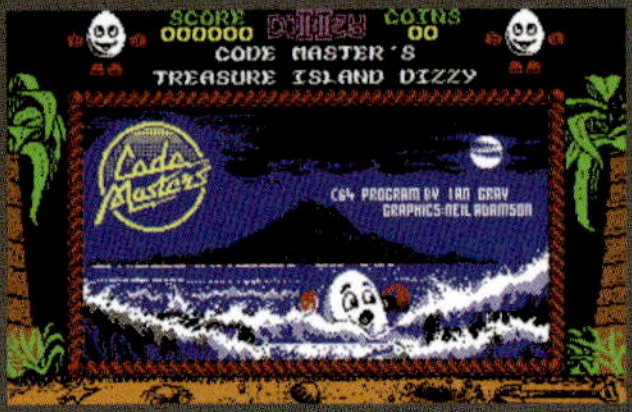

Treasure Island Dizzy *Codemasters*

R-Type *Rainbow Arts*

Brave Starr *Probe Software*

Batman: The Caped Crusader *Special FX*

BMX Kidz *Firebird*

Soul Crystal *Starbyte Software*

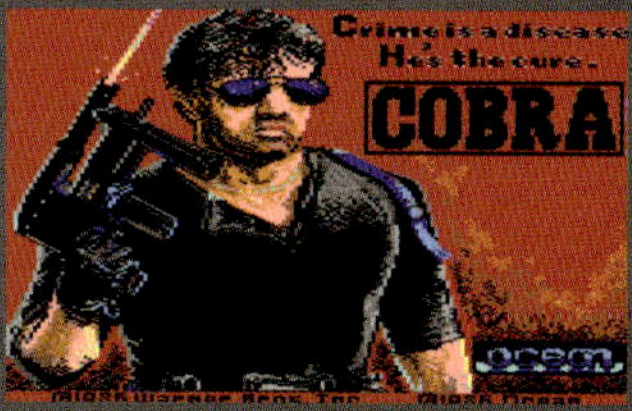

Cobra *Ocean*

Star Wars *Vektor Grafix*

Miami Vice *Ocean*

Space Harrier *Elite Systems*

Head over Heels *Ocean*

Kane *Mastertronic*

Green Beret *Imagine*

Cybernoid II *Hewson Consultants*

Retrograde *Apex Computer Productions*

Rastan *Imagine*

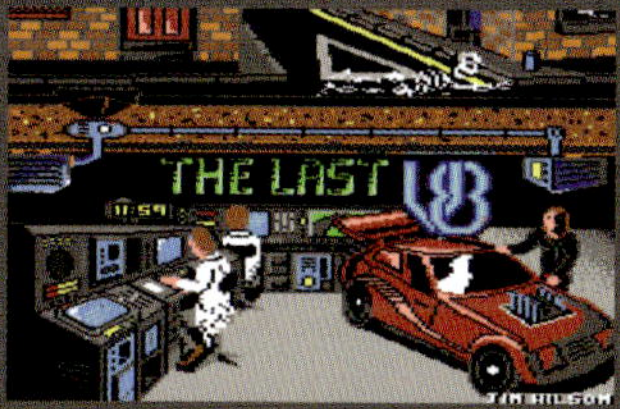

The Last V8 *Mastertronic*

The Staff of Karnath *Ultimate*

Druid II *Electralyte*

Phobia *Image Works*

Platoon *Ocean*

Gremlins 2: The New Batch *Elite*

Robin of the Wood *Odin Computer Graphics*

Gunship

"When MicroProse released *Gunship* in 1986, military airborne warfare was hip. Kids loved action movies, like *Iron Eagle* and *Top Gun*, with iconic pilots and high-tech aircraft. The AH-64 Apache was just introduced by the US Military, and MicroProse made it possible to operate this state-of-the-art combat helicopter at home! As you would expect from MicroProse, the attention to detail was incredible, and the package content very comprehensive. *Gunship* truly set new benchmarks."

Rocco Di Leo, guest reviewer

Released
1986

Genre
Simulation

Developer and Publisher
MicroProse Software

Zoids

Released
1986

Genre
Action

Developer and publisher
Martech

Artwork
Oliver Frey

Apollo 18: Mission to the Moon

Released
1987

Genre
Simulation

Developer and publisher
Accolade

Artwork
Oliver Frey

Pirates!

"My last big C64 game was Sid Meier's *Pirates!* Sid pushed beyond the confines of military sims to pursue a lifelong interest in the so-called Golden Age of Piracy. An action-adventure game, the player could sword fight, sail, attack enemy vessels and interact with the denizens of the Spanish Main. Every screen was restricted to a character set of no more than 127 unique characters using the C64's (less than ideal) palette of 16 colours. The team spent less than nine months on the game from launch to publication."

Michael Haire, graphic artist

"I wanted so badly to be good at this game. On paper, it was the perfect combination of strategy, puzzle and arcade game, woven together into one gloriously original package. However, I never seemed to get the knack of avoiding violence, so it was only ever a matter of time before I was skewered by an arcade action swashbuckling sequence. This game of adventure on the high seas was forever taking the wind out of my sails. I persevered and spent many a long evening in the service of some colonial power, but I was ultimately unable to sate its avaricious appetite."

Sean Masterson, games journalist

Released
1987

Genre
Action adventure

Developer
Sid Meier

Publisher
MicroProse Software

Buggy Boy

"Never judge a book by its cover. At first sight, *Buggy Boy* looks like a simple obstacle racing game with rough, bulky graphics and sound which would rather fit a slot machine. The gameplay, however, is particularly fluent, and the race tracks are built brilliantly. The carefully placed bonus flags, time bonuses and jumps tempt the player to try risky manoeuvres again and again, which means it's the player themselves causing the level of difficulty in this incredibly addictive game."

Oliver Lindau, guest reviewer

Released
1987

Genre
Racing

Developer
Bob and Dave Thomas

Publisher
Elite Systems

Originally by
Tatsumi

Bop'n Rumble

"The brief from Fred (Milgrom) for *Bop'n Rumble* was a scrolling beat 'em up with huge sprites – something not common on the C64 due to memory limitations. He even wanted the whole screen to shake when you threw someone! David Pentecost, Russel Comte and I went away and just made the game up as we went along. In hindsight, the fact you had to beat up blind people and old grannies was pretty politically incorrect! The huge sprites in the game were achieved using some pretty neat tricks that we were doing at the time. I think we pretty much nailed Fred's brief."

Andrew Davie, designer and programmer

Released
1987

Genre
Scrolling beat 'em up

Developer
Beam Software

Publisher
Melbourne House

HEAD
OVER
HEELS

Head over Heels

"I was dragged down to the Ocean dungeon to take a look at *Head over Heels* so I could get a good look at the characters in order to be able to create the cover art. It was a lot of fun to work on, even though I didn't have a clue what the game was about. The sheer weirdness of the characters made the job an absolute pleasure! The squares in the background were removed for the initial release but were left intact for the Hit Squad version. Creator Jon Ritman bought the original art from me a few years later."

Bob Wakelin, artist

"In this exceptionally well-designed isometric arcade adventure, the player takes control of not one but two different heroes. Each has its own distinct abilities: Head can jump higher than Heels and can fire doughnuts to paralyse enemies, while Heels can carry items and climb onto certain obstacles that are inaccessible to his partner. The player must use these complementary skills to solve puzzles across the game's 300 rooms in an attempt to liberate a number of enslaved planets under the rule of an evil emperor."

Julian Rignall, games journalist

Released
1987

Genre
Arcade

Developer and Publisher
Ocean

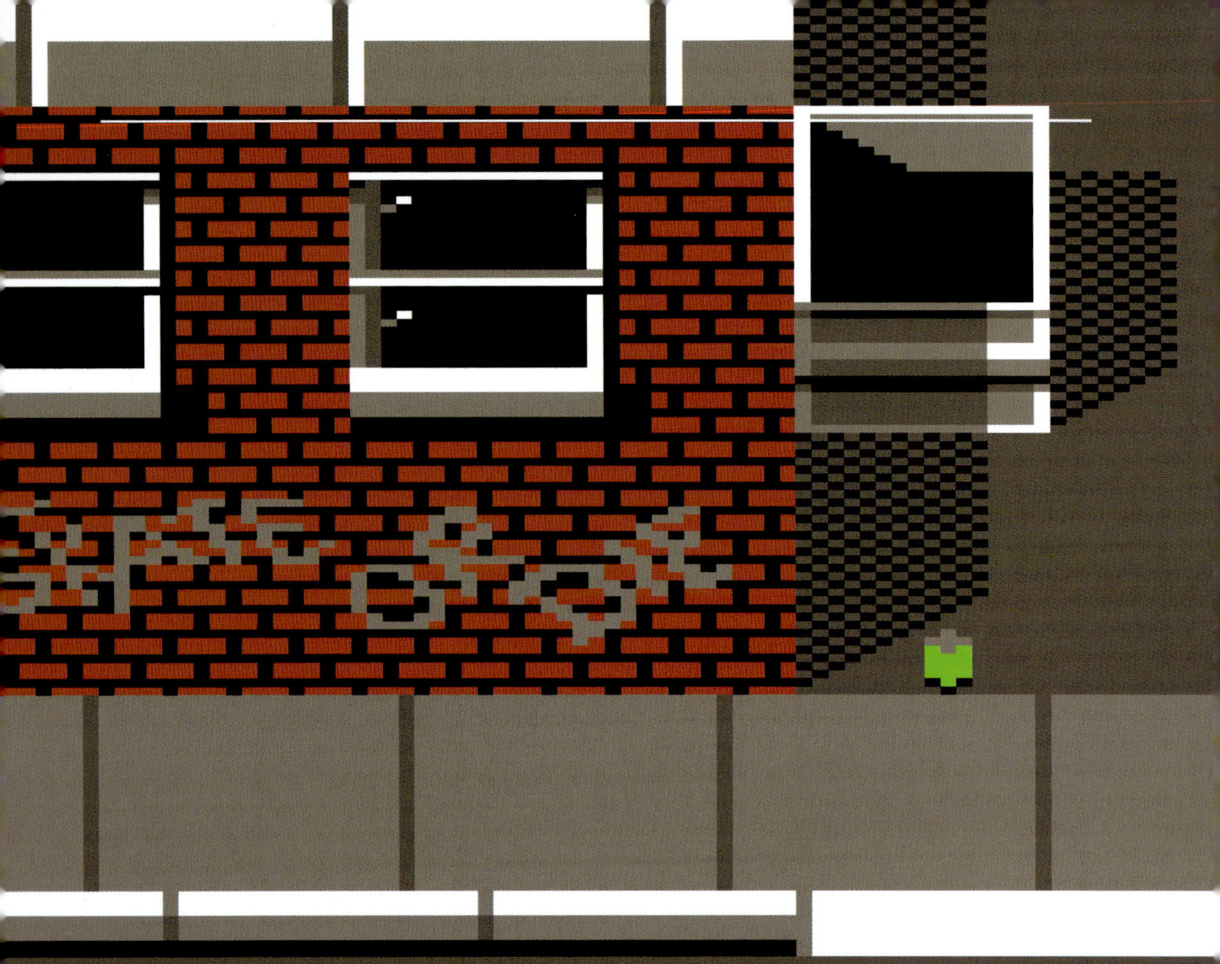

Skate or Die!

"Long before Tony Hawk's series brought extreme skateboarding to a new generation of gamers, we had this. Fairly simple in its execution, you had half-pipe, ramp, racing and street settings, along with something that resembled a giant kitchen sink dropped into someone's back garden. In these, you could wow your opponents or just wipe out, leaving your skateboard to briefly soldier on by itself. To be honest, though, despite its well-deserved success, it never grabbed me. What I remember it most fondly for is Rob Hubbard's masterfully crafted intro music. Even if you're as cack-handed as me, it's worth firing it up just for that."

Sean Masterson, games journalist

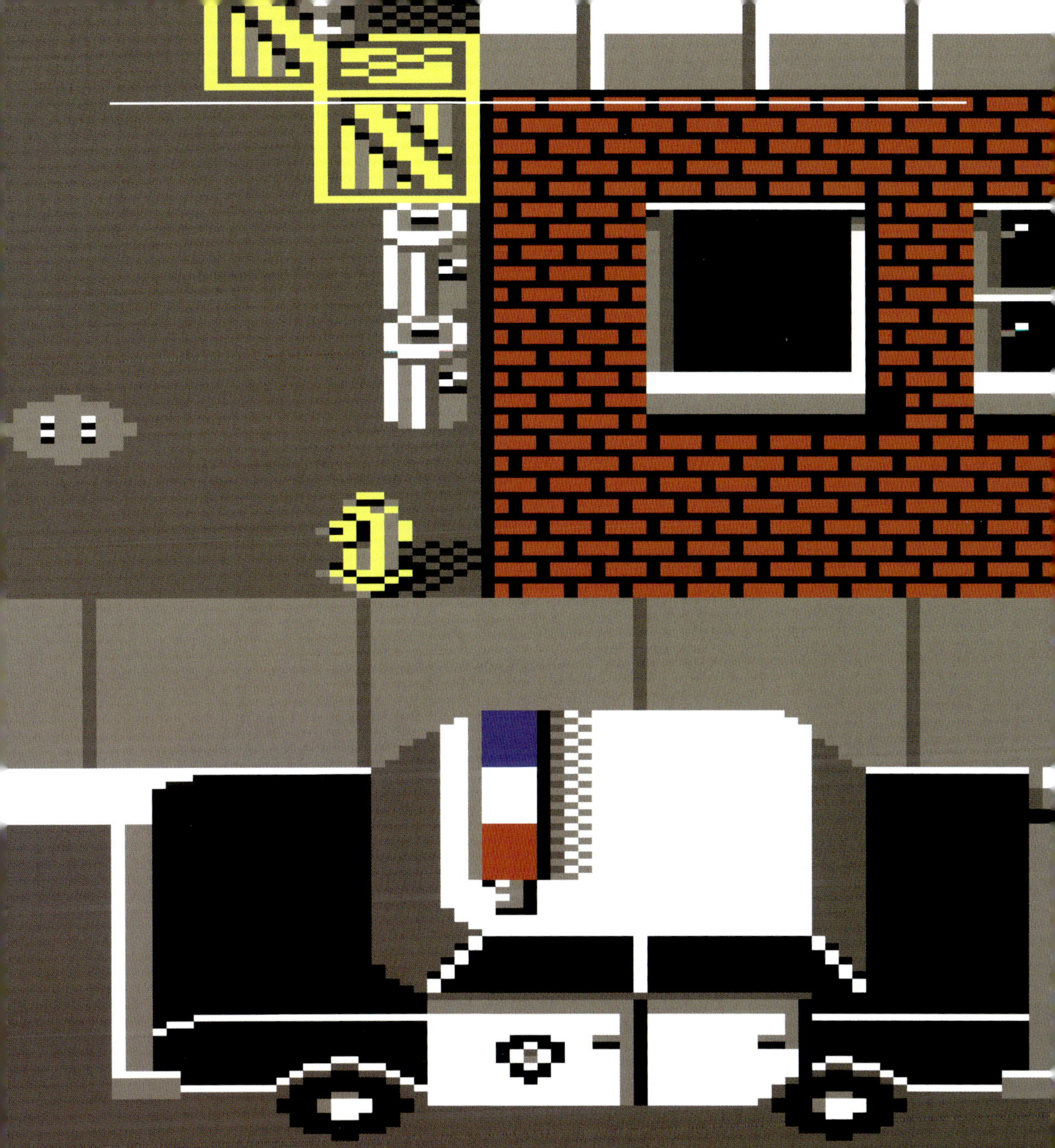

Released
1987

Genre
Sports

Developer and publisher
Electronic Arts

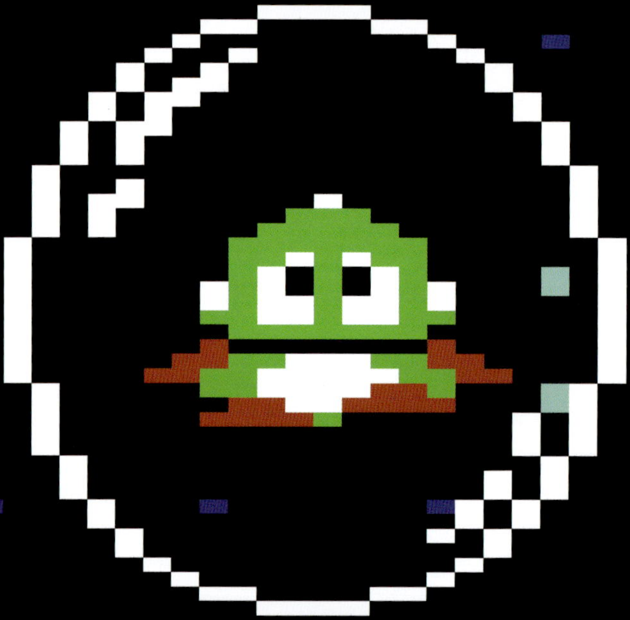

Bubble Bobble

This stunning conversion of Taito's 1986 arcade game sees our intrepid heroes, Bub and Bob, attempting to rescue their girlfriends from the clutches of the evil Baron Von Blubba. Set across 100 increasingly hectic levels, the dragons must use their bubble-blowing ability to trap the various enemies before bursting said bubbles and collecting the myriad of pickups left in their wake. For fans of the arcade original, everything's here, from the two-player mode to the maddeningly twee music to the plethora of pickups and special abilities, all somehow crammed into a single load. As arcade conversions go, *Bubble Bobble* is nothing short of a masterpiece.

"*Bubble Bobble* was just such a fantastic arcade game that to get anywhere near the playability of the original would make a good C64 game. Typical of the time, the conversion took around three months. I was very happy that we managed to get all the levels in, although we did have to lose some presentation content and some sprite images."

Stephen Ruddy, programmer

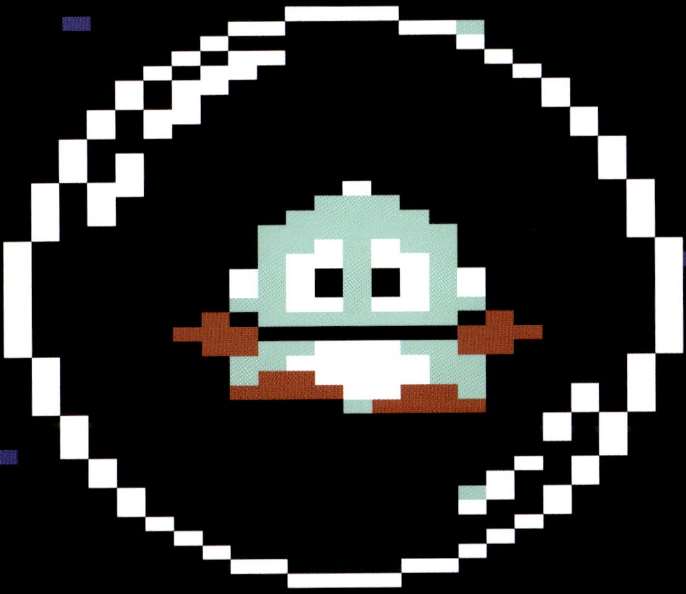

Released
1987

Genre
Arcade

Developers
Software Creations

Publisher
Firebird

Originally by
Taito

Released
1987

Genre
Point-and-click adventure

Developer and Publisher
Lucasfilm Games

Maniac Mansion

The game that single-handedly pioneered the point-and-click adventure genre as we know it, *Maniac Mansion* follows a group of teenagers led by Dave Miller as he attempts to rescue his girlfriend Sandy from Dr. Fred's basement laboratory. While the nuts and bolts of the game is standard adventure fare, everything is underpinned by a genuine sense of tension – not to mention a killer sense of humour – as you try to avoid bumping into the various members of the Edison family. The end result is a beautifully crafted homage to B-movies and horror flicks, and, with multiple ways to complete the game, you'll be itching to return to the mansion time and time again.

"The Commodore 64 is quite possibly the greatest computer ever built, and *Maniac Mansion* would not exist without it. Its combination of simplicity, sophistication and limitations provided the perfect storm of creative and technical innovation that allowed *Maniac Mansion* to go on to define the point-and-click genre. It was a joy and wonder to program and will forever remain my favourite computer."

Ron Gilbert, co-designer and programmer

The Last Ninja

"I saw an image where a ninja fighter blended in with a dark background, and it was then that I recognised that the eyes surrounded by the black of the mask immediately conveys 'ninja' without any more information needed. I used a mirror to study my own eyes as a reference and utilised a small pipette to put water drops on my forehead to get the look of beads of sweat. In those early days of video games, I was using paints, inks and airbrushes to create artwork."

Steinar Lund, artist

Released
1987

Genre
Action adventure

Developer and Publisher
System 3

Defender of the Crown

"Oh, *Defender of the Crown*. How I loved your visual splendour. This was a game that fired my imagination and forced me to believe that games could be epic, cinematic and important. Unfortunately, it was scuppered by cripplingly slow loading tapes. Fancy a 60-second sword fight? Wait a couple of minutes. Invade a neighbouring Kingdom? You might have to wait another ten minutes. How well have you done? No fricking idea, I went and had a cider down the skateboard park half an hour ago. A great idea conceived too early, perhaps."

Andy Dyer, games journalist

Released
1987

Genre
Strategy

Developers
Master Designer Software

Publisher
Cinemaware

Released
1987

Genre
Scrolling shooter

Developer
Stavros Fasoulas

Publisher
Thalamus

Delta

Set in an uncharted backwater of space known as Delta, your mission is to wipe out the Hsiffian Khanate after diplomatic relations break down. And thus begins 32 levels of solid shoot 'em up action set across a variety of beautifully realised levels, from ancient temples and meteor storms to beautifully animated ocean planets and fiery suns. Destroying key attack waves will earn credits which can be used to purchase weapons and upgrades for your ship, although learning precisely which upgrades to collect will take time and patience to figure out. Crammed into a single load, *Delta* is a marvel of minimalistic game design polished to the highest possible standard.

"Packing arcade-quality graphics and boasting a scintillating soundtrack by world-famous SID composer Rob Hubbard, Stavros Fasoulas's *Delta* is a classic side-scrolling shooter that plays as good as it looks. What's really impressive, though, is the huge amount of sprites that you encounter across its 32 levels of action: there are swarms of enemies to battle, making this one of the most hectic and challenging shooters on the Commodore 64."

Julian Rignall, games journalist

IK+

"Sometimes games just come together; they have everything. For a fighting game of the '80s, *IK+* was one of them. It had the awesome soundtrack by the legendary Rob Hubbard and an animation and fighting system that Archer MacLean made worth mastering – and timing was everything. As a young gamer, becoming the very best at this was crucial as the two-player mode was great fun (almost as much as the cheats available). Drop your pants in an instant!"

GamesYouLoved, guest reviewer

Released
1987

Genre
Fighting

Developer
Archer MacLean

Publisher
System 3

Released
1987

Genre
Racing

Developer
Mr. Chip Software

Publisher
Mastertronic

Kikstart II

"Within months of leaving school, I started as a trainee at Mr. Chip Software. I immediately played everything they'd produced and worked out, in my mind, how it could all be better. At first, I made small contributions to various projects, but I wanted to co-author my own game, which I eventually did on the sequel to Shaun Southern's *Kikstart*. I had ideas for new obstacles and features, plus a track designer, but, most importantly, everything would be redrawn. It was my first game, and it reached No.1 in the charts. Start as you mean to go on!"

Andrew Morris, co-designer and graphic artist

Released
1987

Genre
Scrolling shooter

Developer
Martin Walker

Publisher
Thalamus

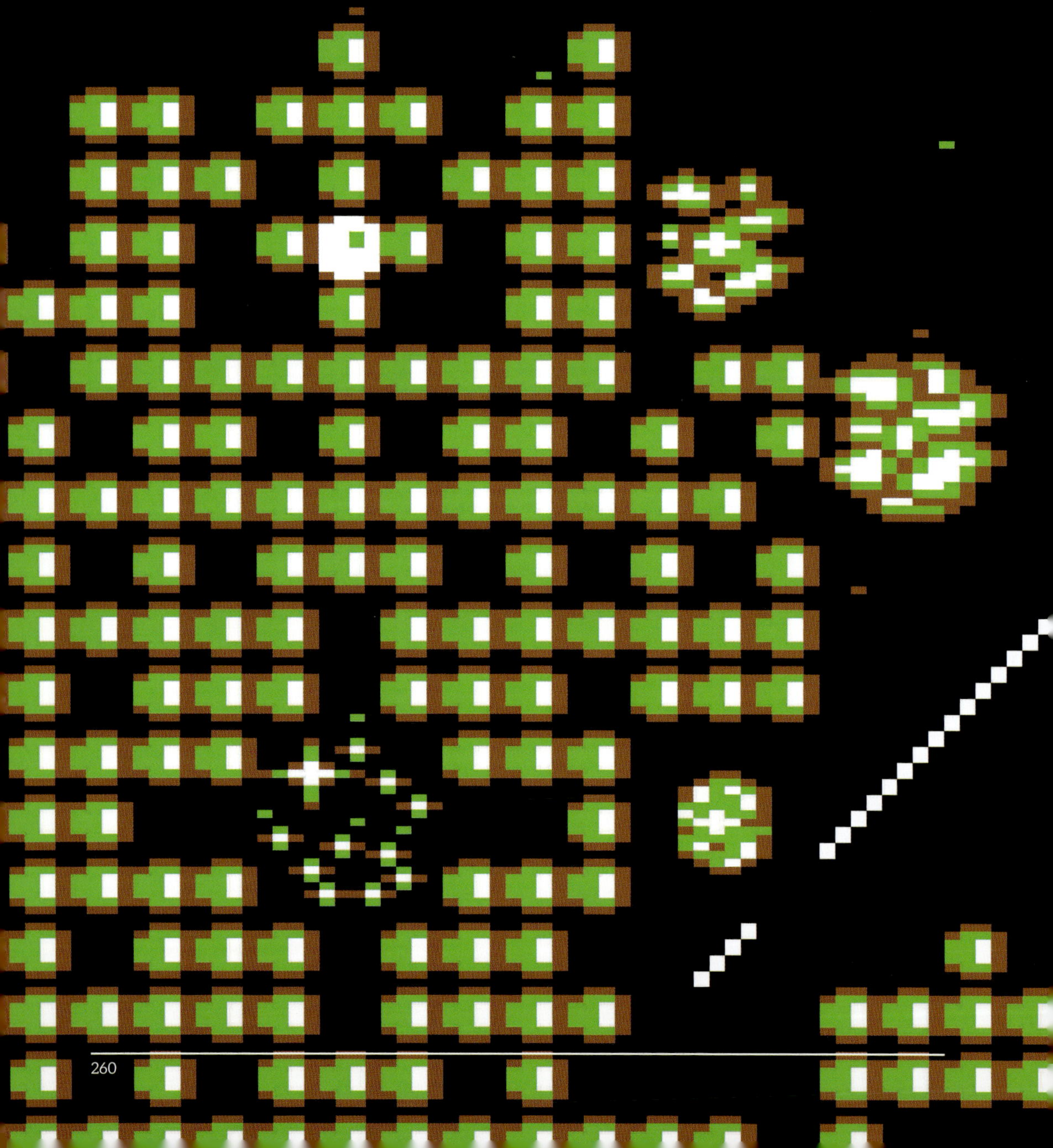

Hunter's Moon

After venturing too close to a black hole, you find yourself lost in deep space surrounded by hive-like alien cities. The only way back home is to blast through the hives and retrieve the starcells, keeping one eye on the workers who quickly repair any damage inflicted by your laser cannons. Thankfully, your Hunter craft is equipped with perma-shields, adjustable engines, and a handy radar to help you locate starcells even when you're flying blind. Technically accomplished and dripping with neat touches, from the wide array of worker types to the incredible sound design, *Hunter's Moon* is a game that demands a measured balance of strategic planning and psychotic blasting.

"*Hunter's Moon* was a joy to create, but I was particularly pleased with my 'computerised Spirograph' approach to level creation, which managed to cram a massive 128 different levels into very limited memory. Each level had eight worker cells in different start positions and pointing in different directions, and then they were given instructions to travel a specific distance, then to turn by a specific angle, and repeat the process indefinitely to create the hive structures. Easy when you know how!"

Martin Walker, designer and programmer

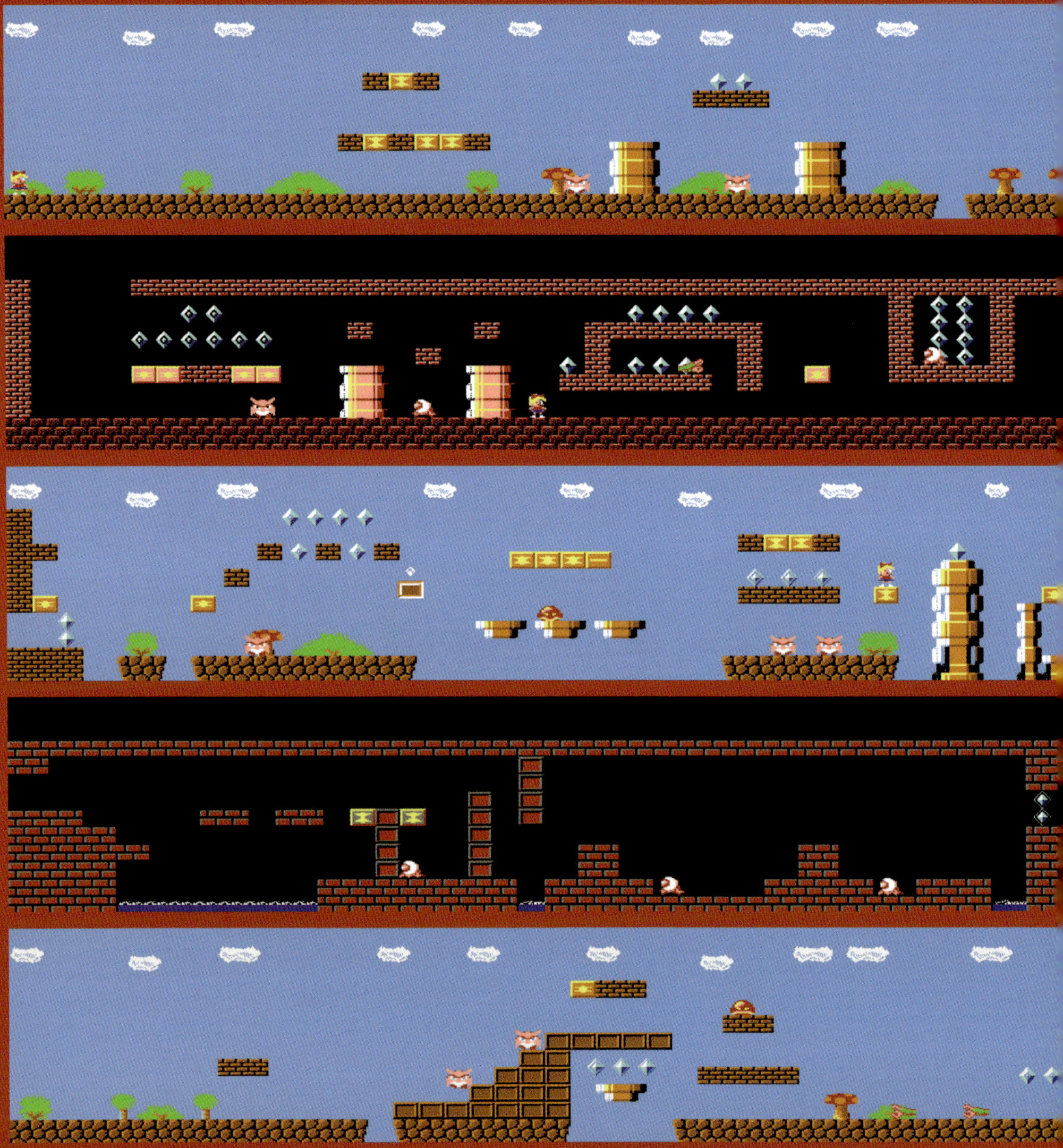

The Great Giana Sisters

"When I first saw *The Great Giana Sisters* running on a Commodore 64, it completely blew my mind, and it was the first game I played from beginning to the end. For me, this was the first platform jump and run game ever! In addition to the more-or-less simple graphics, the sound from audio magician Chris Hülsbeck made the game a great experience. Only later, when I saw *Super Mario* for the first time did I realise that *Giana Sisters* looked somehow similar…"

Luca Argentiero, guest reviewer

Released
1987

Genre
Platformer

Developer
Time Warp Productions

Publisher
Rainbow Arts

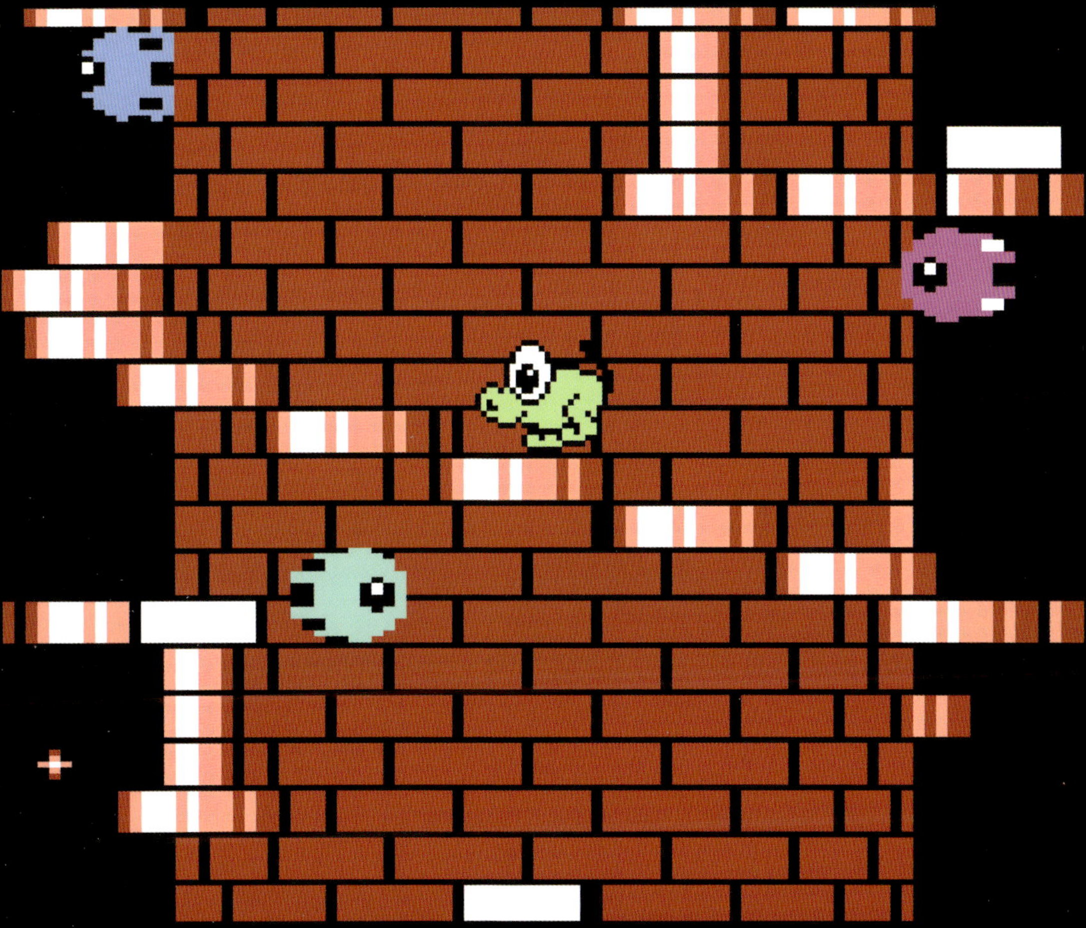

Released
1987

Genre
Action

Developer
John M. Phillips

Publisher
Hewson Consultants

Released
1987

Genre
Sports

Developers
Bruce and Roger Carver

Publisher
Access Software

World Class Leaderboard

After cutting their teeth on classics such as *Beach Head* and *Raid over Moscow*, the Carver brothers set their sights on creating the definitive golfing simulation. *World Class Leaderboard* is undoubtedly the pinnacle of the Leaderboard series, featuring four new courses including Cypress Creek, Doral Country Club, St Andrews, and the fictional Gauntlet Country Club. As a sports simulation, it's impeccable, from the innovative power and snap controls to the wide selection of clubs and irons. However, it's the game's ambience and leisurely sense of pace that makes it such a joy to play. Indeed, tackling 18 holes on the C64 is almost as relaxing and meditative as the real thing.

"*World Class Leaderboard* would have to be not only the best golf sim on our beloved bread bin, but the best sports sim full stop. Bruce and Roger Carver created the most wonderfully playable game, which I still play regularly with my father. It's clearly a massive technical achievement on the C64, with stunning animation and depth of gameplay. The slow screen redraw and slight unpredictability of where the ball will land (even with a perfect shot!) just add to the charm and help make *World Class Leaderboard* a timeless classic, an enormous challenge and great fun to play even today."

Kevin Tilley, guest reviewer

“Getting to work on the C64 felt like a step up from our prior constraints, and certainly, I remember feeling like the scrolling backgrounds were unique and state-of-the-art.”

Gary Winnick, graphic artist and game designer

Released
1987

Genre
Shoot 'em up

Developer
Simon Nicol

Publisher
Martech

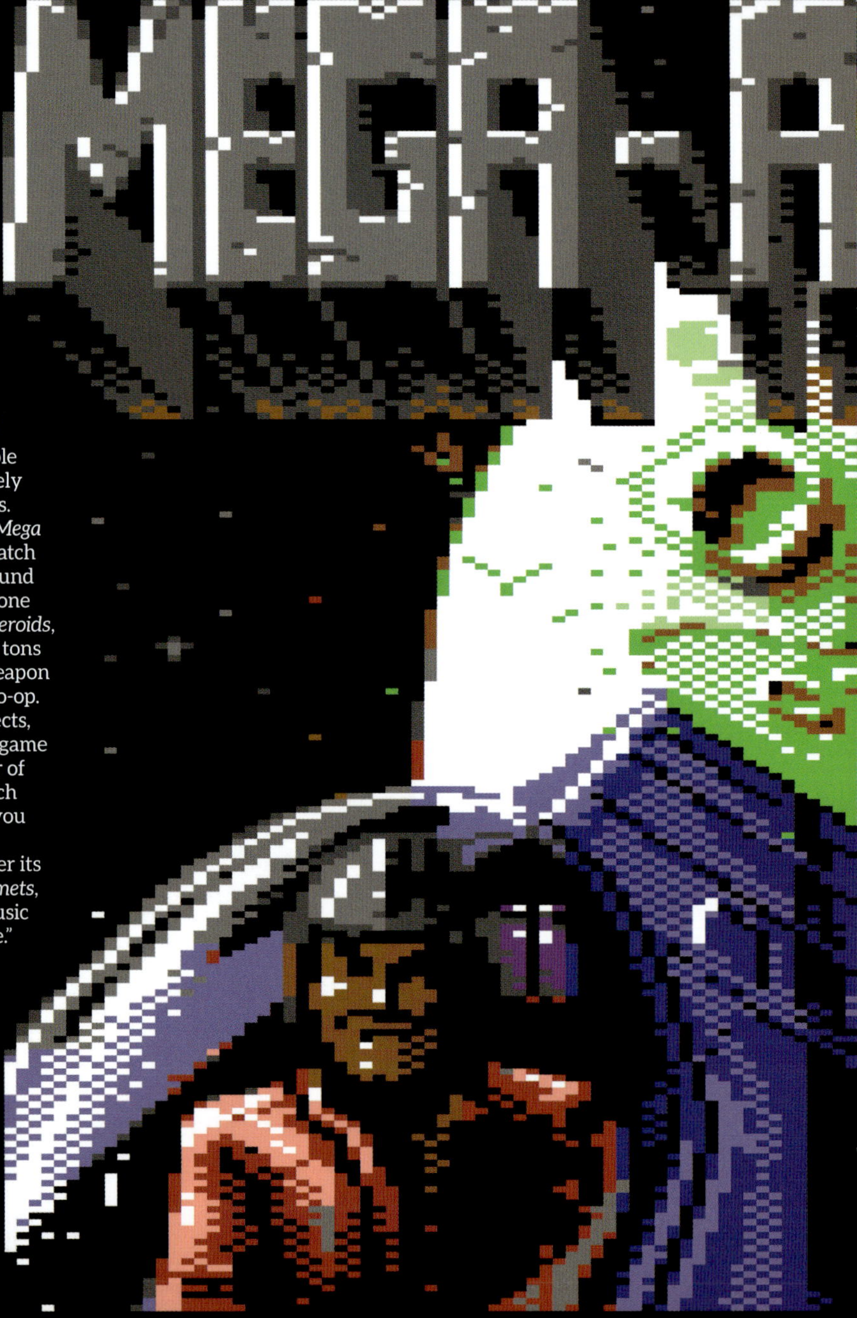

Mega Apocalypse

Now this is a perfect example of a game which almost solely relies on its audible qualities. In doing so, Simon Nicols's *Mega Apocalypse* is the perfect match to the C64's amazing SID sound chip. At its core, it's just a clone of Atari's space shooter, *Asteroids*, but it's put on steroids with tons of aggressors, speed-ups, weapon add-ons and a two-player co-op. The crazy mix of sound effects, Rob Hubbard music and in-game speech samples adds a layer of chaos to the gameplay, which is finely balanced to make you fight for the top slot of the high-score table. Some prefer its 1985 predecessor, *Crazy Comets*, because of its more pure music experience – but you decide."

Richard Löwenstein, games journalist

POCALYPSE
BY
Simon Nicol
BOB

Arkanoid

"*Arkanoid* was my first professional piece of work (I'm still going after almost 30 years!), so I've a big soft spot for it. We had the arcade machine near my dungeon corner (Ocean was below street level; we could just see out and watch people's feet as they passed by), and I got rather good at it. I remember playing the thing all the way through so we could get a videotape of it, then I could use that video and the much-used pause button to try to match the graphics. All hi-tech stuff!"

Mark Jones, graphic artist

Released
1987

Genre
Arcade

Developer and publisher
Imagine

Software Creations

Software Creations was an independent UK developer based in Manchester. Founded in 1987 by ex-Ocean programmer Richard Kay, the company would later expand to include Stephen Ruddy, Mike Ager, Andrew Threlfall and the legendary Follin brothers, Tim, Mike and Geoff. After producing a string of critically acclaimed games for numerous computers and consoles, the company was eventually sold in 1994 to Rage Software.

Richard Kay began his career in Ocean Software's warehouse, where his interest in game development began to grow. After learning to code on the BBC Micro, he landed a job as a programmer with Ocean before the lure of the Air Force pulled him away. Despite the urge to become the next *Top Gun*, Kay's reputation led to a steady stream of offers from publishers that were too good to refuse; Kay advertised for staff in the *Manchester Evening News*, Stephen Ruddy responded, and the rest is history.

During its seven-year reign from 1987 to 1994, Software Creations was responsible for arguably the finest arcade conversions ever to grace a home computer. Authentic, playable, and technically adept, titles such as *Bubble Bobble*, *Ghouls 'n Ghosts*, and *Bionic Commando* were skilfully crafted by some of the C64's finest talent, affirming Software Creation's reputation as the go-to conversion house.

> “Software Creations was responsible for arguably the finest arcade conversions ever to grace a home computer.”

Creations began life as a developer-for-hire, creating low-key titles for publishers such as Tynesoft and Firebird. The company's debut title, *The Big KO*, was a tongue-in-cheek boxing simulator converted from the BBC version (which had successfully landed programmer Stephen Ruddy a job with the company). Despite the game's appealing price tag and endearing charm, *The Big KO* hit the canvas. "This simply isn't a knockout," said *Commodore User*, calling it "a sub-standard boxing sim".

The company's next title was *Kinetik*, an eccentric arcade adventure converted from the ZX Spectrum. While the aim of the game was standard fare for hardened adventurers, the laws of physics – and the taxing control system – would change on every screen, throwing multiple curveballs at the player. "If you like your games to be tough, then you'll enjoy *Kinetik*," said *Your Commodore*, branding it "an extremely difficult game to play", while *Zzap!64* thought it "a nice idea which fails to entertain".

Kinetik was quickly followed by *The Mystery of the Nile*, a charming platformer set in the Arabian desert. Featuring three distinct characters which players could switch between at any point, the game was well-received despite its visual similarities to its Spectrum counterpart. "Neither engrossing or addictive, but there's fun to be gleaned," said *Zzap!64*, while *Commodore User* praised the large, bright graphics, calling it "a lively game that's big enough and challenging enough to provide many hours of play".

Creations continued its bumper first year with *Denarius*, a vertically-scrolling shoot 'em up developed by new recruits Mike Ager and Andrew Threlfall. Set across 16 increasingly challenging levels, the game was a solid budget blaster boasting a neat parallax star effect. Praising the game's high level of polish, *Zzap!64* described it as "a colourful and noisy shoot 'em up". *Commodore User* was equally enthusiastic, calling it "a very impressive piece of programming".

The company's relationship with Firebird ultimately led to Creations landing the contract to convert Taito's *Bubble Bobble* coin-op to the C64. Developed by Stephen Ruddy, *Bubble Bobble* retained all of the arcade machine's key features, including 100 levels and a fabulous two-player mode. The end result was a near-perfect arcade conversion, a tour-de-force in programming, which raised the bar for home computer conversions and established Creations as a force to be reckoned with.

Released in October 1987, *Bubble Bobble* dominated the computer magazines of the time, with the C64 version picking up a string of accolades including a *Commodore User* 'Screen Star' and *Zzap!64* 'Gold Medal'. "Firebird's done an ace job of converting Taito's hit coin-op," said *C&VG*, awarding the game 9/10. Indeed, the game scored an unprecedented 97% in *Zzap!64*, which simply called it "a superlative conversion".

1988 kicked off with the release of *Agent X II*, a Mastertronic budget title set across three different levels (a platformer, a horizontally scrolling shoot 'em up and a *Breakout* clone). Quirky and eclectic, the game's high point was undoubtedly the stunning Tim Follin soundtrack which *ACE* magazine thought "hypnotic and otherworldly".

Hot on the heels of *Agent X II* came *Black Lamp*, a medieval-themed platformer that cast players in the role of Jester Jack on a quest to recover the kingdom's protective Black Lamp from a blaze of evil dragons. Converted from the 16-bit machines, the game sported some fantastic visuals and an incredible progressive-rock soundtrack. *Commodore User* called *Black Lamp* "very professionally produced", while *Zzap!64* thought it "extremely challenging, very addictive and comes thoroughly recommended".

Another Mastertronic title swiftly followed in the form of *Scumball*, a delightful arcade adventure created by newcomer Martin Howarth. Reminiscent of the classic C64 game *Starquake*, *Scumball*'s redeeming features – neat visuals, accessible gameplay, and budget price tag – were a winning combination. *Zzap!64* said it was a pleasant mix of genres, adding, "it may be derivative, but it's neat, attractive and fun to play."

Bubble Bobble / *1987*

Bionic Commando / *1988*

Creations fans eager for another quality coin-op conversion had their prayers answered in the summer of '88 when *Bionic Commando* made its debut on U.S. Gold's Go! label. A staggeringly authentic port of the Capcom arcade game set across five huge levels, *Bionic Commando* would retain all the playability – and the hallmark grappling hook – of the original, not to mention treating C64 owners to some of the best music ever squeezed from the SID chip. As well as a *Commodore User* 'Screen Star', the game picked up a 'Sizzler' from *Zzap!64* which called the game "horrendously good fun". *The Games Machine* was similarly enthusiastic, labelling *Bionic Commando* 'a top-notch conversion".

Overall, 1988 would prove to be a prolific year for Software Creations, with the company producing eight different C64 titles, including conversions of SEGA's *Body Slam* and Taito's *Sky Shark* (the US version of *Flying Shark*), as well as original budget titles for Mastertronic and Firebird including the *Combat School*-inspired *Raw Recruit* and a conversion of Clive Brooker's Spectrum racing game *War Cars Construction Set*.

The year concluded with the release of *Psycho Pigs UXB*, a conversion from the Jaleco coin-op marred by a controversial ad campaign dubbed by one magazine as "puerile and sexist". Promotional gripes aside, however, most reviewers would enjoy the frivolous arcade gameplay. "Not bad for a few chuckles," said *Zzap!64*, while *The Games Machine* thought it a "compelling, playable game".

Released in 1989, *Peter Pack Rat* would be Creations' final budget release for the C64. A simplistic platform collect 'em up, *Peter Pack Rat* was a solid conversion of the Atari arcade game with a bargain price tag. "Solid budget entertainment for old-fashioned gamers," said *Commodore User*, while *Zzap!64* concluded with, "No frills, no fancy bits with knobs on, just good, plain fun."

Creations' relationship with Go! continued with the release of *LED Storm*, an adrenaline-pumping racer in the *Spy Hunter* mould converted from the Capcom coin-op. Another masterwork from Stephen Ruddy, the relentless gameplay, thumping soundtrack and stunning parallax scrolling helped the game scoop numerous awards including a *Games Machine* 'Star Player'.

"Easily one of the most playable racing games ever," said *Zzap!64*, awarding *LED Storm* 94% and a much-deserved 'Sizzler', while *ACE* simply called it a "superb arcade conversion".

The year closed on a high with the arrival of *Ghouls 'n Ghosts*, the second game in Capcom's *Ghosts 'n Goblins* series and, more poignantly, programmer Stephen Ruddy's swansong on the C64. Expertly programmed, the C64 conversion followed Sir Arthur's quest across five stages to rescue his future bride, and boasted an incredibly atmospheric soundtrack courtesy of Tim Follin. *Zzap!64* awarded *Ghouls 'n Ghosts* 96% and a 'Gold Medal', calling it "a masterpiece of a conversion", while *ACE* simply dubbed it "U.S. Gold's shoot 'em up in shining armour".

1990 saw the release of one of Creations' most ambitious projects to date, a conversion of Data East's *Sly Spy: Secret Agent*. Beautifully presented and packed with a multitude of *James Bond* references, the game was both extremely diverse and incredibly faithful to the arcade version. "Fast-paced, exciting, and easy enough to get into," commented *Zzap!64*, while *Commodore Format* said, "None of it is particularly spy-like, but all of it is rather good fun."

Ghouls 'n Ghosts / *1989*

The company wrapped up 1990 with *Puzznic*, a simplistic puzzle game spread across an impressive 144 different levels and converted from the Taito coin-op. Deceptively simple to learn but devilishly tricky to master, *Puzznic* scored highly across the board. *Your Commodore* gave the game a 'YC Fun One' award, calling it "fiendishly difficult". *Zzap!64* was similarly impressed, calling *Puzznic* "a superb puzzle game" and adding another 'Sizzler' award to Creations' mantlepiece.

> *Software Creations steadily gained a reputation as one of the UK's premiere game developers.*

Software Creations' final C64 title was arguably one of its finest: the seminal arcade adventure *Gauntlet III: The Final Quest*, released in 1991. Presented in isometric 3D with stunning visuals, the game expanded on *Gauntlet*'s hack 'n' slash gameplay by adding RPG-like quests for players to tackle. Awarding *Gauntlet III* a 'Sizzler', *Zzap!64* called it "unmissable", while *Commodore Format* said, "If you're mad about monster mashing, you ought to give it a try."

After a multitude of incredibly successful games on various home computer formats, Software Creations made the inevitable transition to consoles with the NES and SNES. However, as the sun began to set on the 16-bit consoles – and with greater challenges ahead for the games industry – the decision was made to sell the company to Rage Software. Following rapid expansion in the late 1990s, Rage began publishing its own titles, but spiralling costs and a run of poor sales saw it close its doors in 2003.

From humble beginnings of creating budget games, Software Creations steadily gained a reputation as one of the UK's premier game developers. Tackling virtually impossible conversions with confidence and aplomb, the company made the arduous process of squeezing mammoth arcade experiences into humble 8-bit computers look like child's play.

64

64

64

POWER

f 1
f 2
f 3

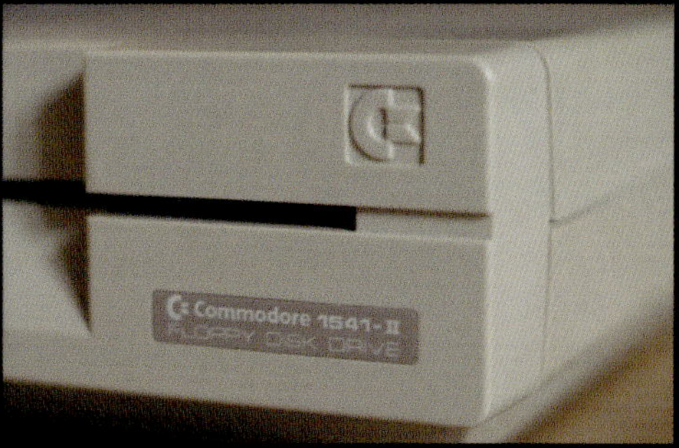
Commodore 1541-II
FLOPPY DISK DRIVE

POWER

C64

POWER
DRIVE

CONTROL

Platoon

Released
1987

Genre
Action

Developer and Publisher
Ocean

Artwork
Oliver Frey

Shoot-'Em-Up Construction Kit

Released
1987

Genre
Utlity

Developer
Sensible Software

Publisher
Outlaw Productions

Artwork
Oliver Frey

SCORE:000600 INVADE

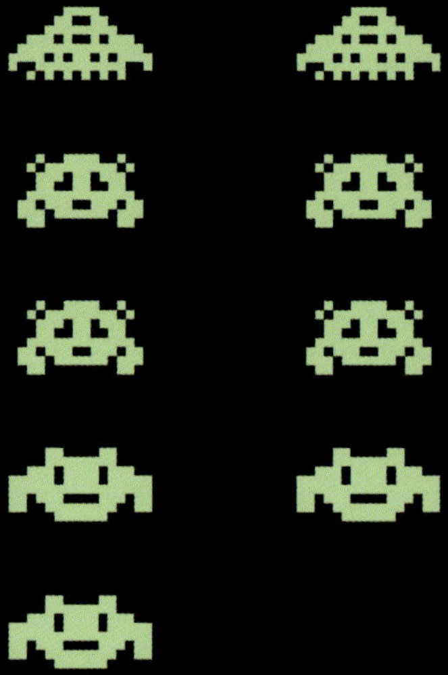

Invade-a-Load

"Two for the price of one, and no more boring load times. Not only a genius idea but a piece of technical mastery, *Invade-a-Load* allowed us to play a game – *Space Invaders* no less – while the main game was loading. Of course, we often stopped the tape to carry on playing as it was sometimes better than the game it was hooked onto. And what a great way to stick two fingers up to your Speccy mates who never had such luxuries. With the mighty Hubbard providing the soundtrack, *Invade-a-Load* deserves to be considered a classic."

Matt Wilsher, guest reviewer

Released
1987

Genre
Shoot 'em up

Developer
Richard Aplin

Publisher
Mastertronic

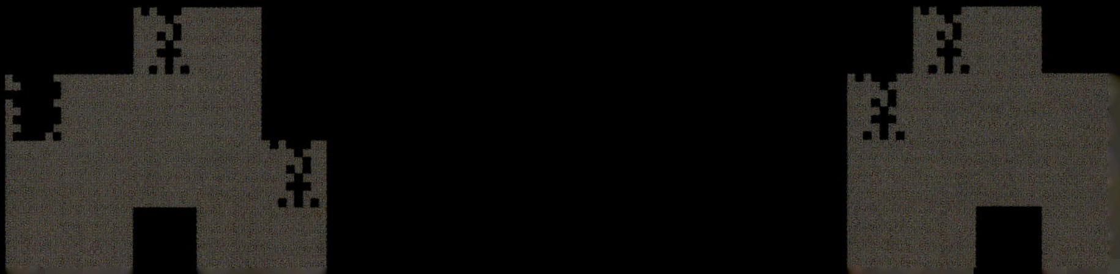

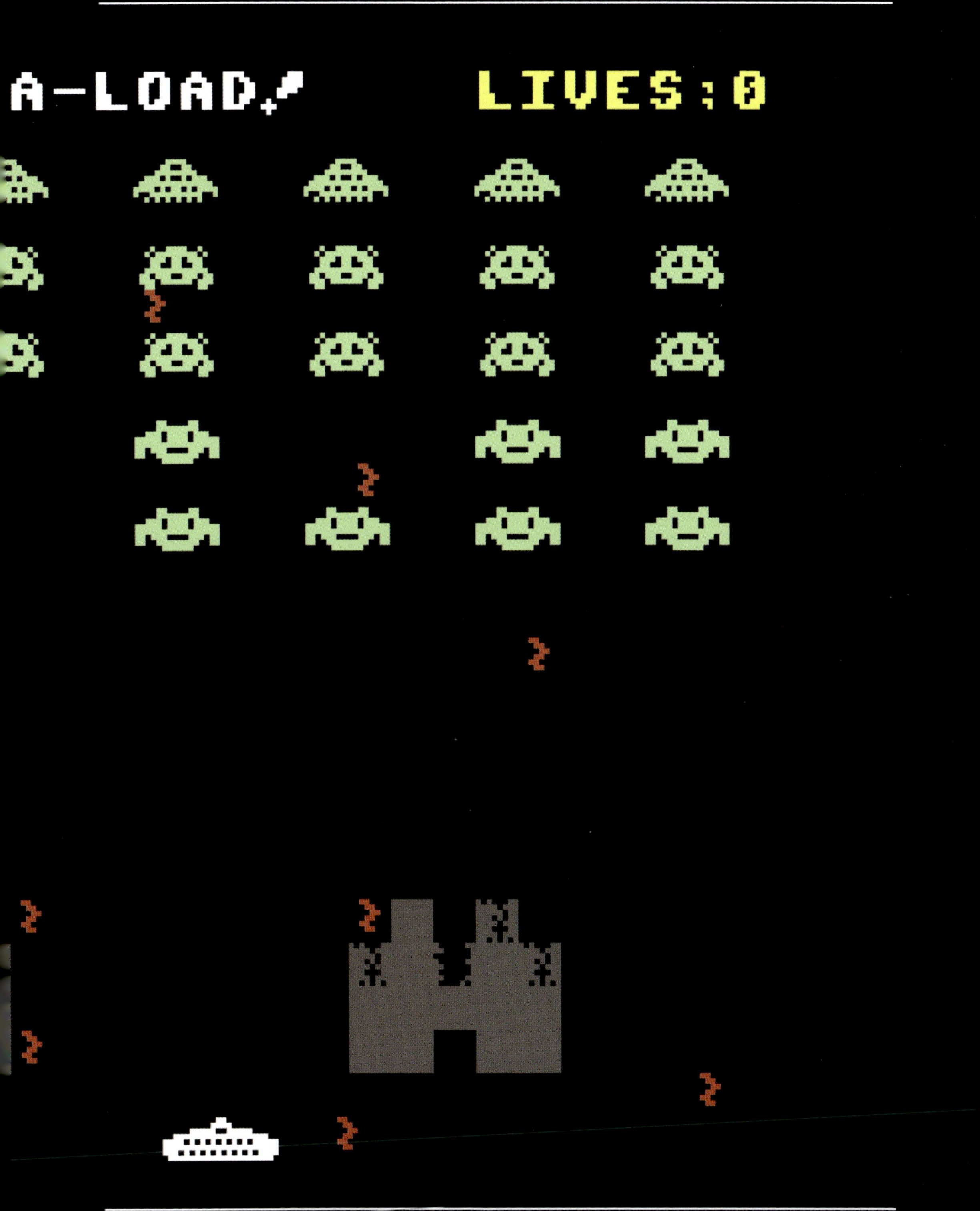
A-LOAD.
LIVES:0

Bangkok Knights

"We decided it would be novel to have huge characters, something that was unheard of at the time. I figured out we could use double-sized multi-colour sprites for the character and colour block-out, and use normal-sized sprites on top to anti-alias. It kind of worked (in a blocky way), but the sprite editor I was using couldn't handle this combination, so animation was tortuously difficult. I was quite pleased with my caricature of Mark Cale as 'Killa Kale', and I enjoyed making the font, but, in hindsight, I'm less pleased with the backgrounds."

Hugh Riley, graphic artist

"Sometime in November 1987, I got a phone call from Mark Cale of System 3 asking if I could provide a loading track for *Bangkok Knights*, but they needed it next week. Rob (Hubbard) had done the in-game, but I think he was departing for the US and didn't have time to do another track. This was a big opportunity – to effectively stand in for my SID hero. There was also the tempting prospect of perhaps working on the sequel to *The Last Ninja* the following year. I went up to their Hampstead offices in London the following week with my loading track for *Bangkok Knights*. Mark listened to it and approved it, and then we went for a drink, where he offered me an exclusive contract to work for System 3. I said yes, and that was that. In mid-January of 1988, I started work on *Last Ninja 2*."

Matt Gray, musician

Released
1987

Genre
Fighting

Developer and Publisher
System 3

An interview with **Paul Docherty**

***A self-taught artist and bastion of the mid-'80s Compunet scene, Paul 'Dokk' Docherty is widely regarded as one of the C64's best-loved pixel artists. Better known for his accomplished loading screens, which graced games such as* IK+, Druid 2, Quedex, Hammerfist *and* Exile, *he also produced graphics for several chart-topping titles including* Vendetta, BMX Kidz *and* Dominator.**

How did you first get interested in computers?
I grew up in a neighbourhood in Edinburgh that was a bit shady at the time, so, when I discovered computers, it was a relief to not have to deal with the world outside. My first computer was the VIC-20, with its massive pixels and weird aspect ratio. It was a couple of years before I upgraded to the Commodore 64, and maybe a year later, I joined Compunet, which was a real revelation – it hadn't occurred to me until that point that computer art was something I could do myself.

I got a copy of *Paint Magic* from Roosta, a friend I met online, and I started creating images using a joystick. I was really into comic book illustration at the time, but art on the computer hooked me very quickly. I really liked working within the limitations of the C64 graphics chip, and I liked the way images looked on a CRT. The glow was seductive. At the time, it felt like the future.

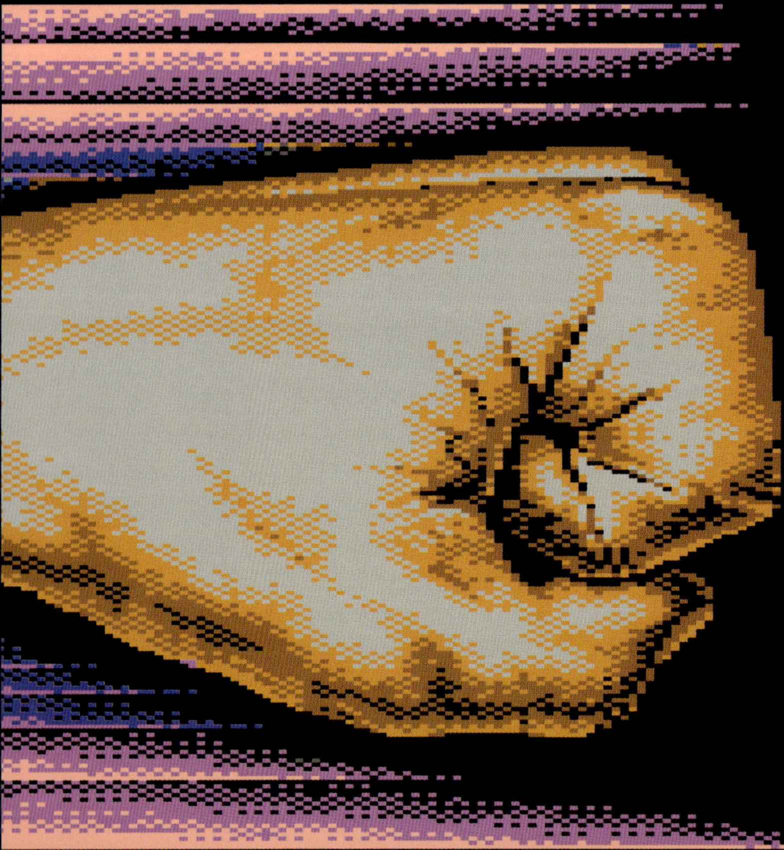

You were quite active during the Compunet era; what was that like?
Through Compunet, I met some local C64 users, and I dabbled in the demo scene, getting involved in an Edinburgh demo crew called Pulse Productions, where I met Graham Hunter. That was when the idea of computers being a career started to percolate. We started developing a side-scrolling shoot 'em up, and someone suggested that I could make money by doing graphics for game companies. There was money in loading screens, apparently.

How did your career in the games industry get started?
I know I sent around a demo disk with my early images, but my first opportunity came through a friend who knew Rich Hare. Rich recommended me to English Software to create

a loading screen for a game he was working on called *Leviathan*. Work was still thin on the ground, though, and it wasn't until *Zzap* published a picture of mine in the Christmas 1986 issue that I started getting real attention.

> "I got a huge kick out of seeing my pictures printed in Zzap!64 *for the first time.*"

What was your first C64 project?
Leviathan was the first loading screen I did. I don't recall how long it took, but my first attempt was not great. That was when Rich [Hare] gave me the best advice anyone could give an artist just starting out: it didn't matter what the artwork looked like, it was my job to deliver an exciting loading screen and to interpret the artwork in whatever manner I saw fit to make that happen. It was a terrific learning experience.

You worked on several demos with Graham Hunter; what was the experience like?
Graham and I called ourselves Radix Developments just to mess about making Compunet demos, really. We did a few scrolling message demos where I would mess about with some graphics ideas. I think it was the demo we did called *Blue Eyes* that got the attention of Paul Cooper who was scouting for new talent for Thalamus. That's how we got to do the loader for *Quedex*.

What did a typical day in front of the computer look like for you?
While I was still working from my parents' house, I would work late into the night because it was quieter and there were fewer distractions, but once I moved to London, I kept more typical office hours.

Which programs did you use to create your C64 art?
The main program I remember using was *Paint Magic*. The sprite editor I used for *BMX Kidz* was pretty primitive, but somebody took pity on me and passed along a much more sophisticated one that allowed for overlaying and mixed resolutions. By the time I did *All Terrain Gardener*, I was doing some incredibly complex 128-frame animations with high-res outlines.

Did you use any tools that weren't available commercially?
I remember using John Twiddy's '*Integrator*' tool to build the maps in *Vendetta*, which would construct screens from basic elements. The problem was, I would get really granular with the elements. For example, I'd build a wall with a single brick element that would repeat over and over, and consequently, the screens would take ages to render.

After a while, someone sat me down to take another look at *The Last Ninja* to see how Hugh Riley had done it. Hugh used bigger elements with the odd detail or two to create variety, and, at that point, I could see where I was going wrong. Once I figured that out, everything moved a lot smoother.

Looking back, what were the best and worst aspects of creating art for the C64?
I liked the C64 for its limitations, such as the tiny, constrained palette and limited resolution. The tools were always crude, but I didn't know what good tools were until much later, so I didn't really know there was another way of doing things.

What was your process? Did you plan on paper, or jump straight in onto the computer?
I would draw straight into the paint program like a sketchbook. I wasn't classically trained, so working in a different medium first seemed superfluous.

How did your process change throughout your career?
I'm still the same way now: I work in the delivery medium so that I always know what the finished product is going to look like. That didn't change the entire time I was working in video game graphics.

What was the development time for a typical game?
It often varied. Working as a freelancer was pretty chaotic, often with project managers mostly leaving me to my own devices until deadlines loomed. Working full-time at System 3 was a bit different in that I was sharing the office with other project teams, so there was a lot of feedback and a lot of support from peers. Deadlines were always a problem, regardless.

Did you receive much artistic direction, or would you say you had complete freedom?
When I did loading screens for Probe and Firebird, typically they'd provide me with the box artwork and let me interpret that for the C64 screen as I saw fit. Usually, the art was designed for a vertical box, but the Commodore screen was horizontal, so it could be tricky getting the elements to fit and still interact in a meaningful way.

When creating C64 art, which aspect did you most enjoy?
I enjoyed working on loading screens as the process was really simple, and the client usually gave me carte blanche, which wasn't really the case for in-game graphics. Loading screens were what I was best at, too, so it was a very relaxing task. But I liked all of it really, all the different disciplines that go into creating an overall look for a game.

Did you have much input in terms of game design?
Working with programmers like Gary Liddon on *Tyger Tyger* and Dave 'Ubik' Korn on *All Terrain Gardener* were extremely collaborative processes, whereas *Dominator* was less so because the level maps had already been built by Jason Perkins and Hugh Riley, and I was just creating the sprites.

Did you pay much attention to the various magazine reviews?
I got a huge kick out of seeing my pictures printed in *Zzap!64* for the first time. That was very cool: Bob Stevenson's *Druid* artwork on one page, my picture of *Judge Dredd* on the facing page. I was a big fan of Bob, so that was a big deal for me. Beyond that, I didn't really pay attention to reviews; if something received a bad review, I probably already had a good idea that what I did was inferior. That said, I can't deny that I loved the acclaim when I got it.

If you had the chance to revisit any of your games, what would you change?
Tyger Tyger had a horrible palette that I would reconsider nowadays, but, on the whole, the work I did back then reflected the kind of decisions I was making at the time.

Was there anyone working in the industry whose work was inspirational to you?
Yes, Bob Stevenson was my benchmark for excellence in C64 graphics, and I think most people felt the same way. He had a keen eye and a crisp style that was elegant and simple. I was also a fan of Hugh Riley, whose style was very much the opposite: loose and organic. Gary Liddon was a big influence, and working with him opened my eyes to what game design could be. I was also a fan of the Cyberdyne Systems guys; I loved *Armalyte*, so it was great when we connected at System 3. Working with people who genuinely loved gaming was always a pleasure.

What C64 games at the time impressed you, or had an influence on your work?
I was a big fan of side-scrolling shoot 'em ups like *Armalyte*, *Delta*, *IO* by Doug Hare and Bob Stevenson, and that crazy C64 version of *Salamander* that Bob worked on.

Of all the games you've worked on, which are you most proud of and why?
Doug Hare and I did the C64 version of *Exterminator* for Audiogenic, a bizarre arcade game that involved disembodied hands shooting down bugs and such as they flew towards you. The reviews I read assumed the graphics were digitised from the original, but I hand-rendered everything to make the best use of the C64's graphical peculiarities. I was especially proud of how those graphics turned out.

Trantor: The Last Storm Trooper / *1987*

Leviathan / *1987*

> **“Bob Stevenson was my benchmark for excellence in C64 graphics. He had a keen eye and a crisp style that was elegant and simple.”**

Were there any C64 games you worked on which sadly never saw the light of day?
I worked on a couple of games for Firebird – *All Terrain Gardener* and *Tyger Tyger* – neither of which got published. *Tyger Tyger* was never actually completed, as far as I know. [NOTE: a 50% complete version was tidied up by Jani Tahvanainen and Henrik Jansson, and released as a playable demo in 2014.]

What was your final C64 game? What made you decide to leave the machine behind?
The final C64 graphics I did were for *Exile* in 1991. I was a huge fan of Jeremy Smith's game *Thrust*, so I was very happy to work on *Exile*. At that time, I was already working on 16-bit platforms – the demand for C64 graphics was in steep decline, so there were fewer opportunities to work on that format.

Was there a C64 game you would have loved to have created the graphics for?
At the time, I was jealous that Bob Stevenson got to create the screens for *The Pawn*, but, on the whole, I didn't think about what other people were doing. I would have liked to have worked on games like those that Sensible Software was doing – *Wizball* and the like – but there was only one SensiSoft. Doing the graphics for a Jeff Minter game would have been cool, too.

What are your favourite games?
Hunter's Moon by Martin Walker, which I found incredibly relaxing for some reason. It had a lovely atmosphere to it. Occasionally, I'll fire up the emulator every now and again to play it.

What are your standout memories from the C64 era?
I remember the business being a bit chaotic and exploitative, and being a freelancer that young was pretty wretched for me because I didn't have any business sense. But I also met some great people along the way, some of whom I still keep in touch with to this day, so, in the end, I just chalk it all up to experience.

Why do you think the C64 is remembered so fondly?
I think the resurgence of interest in 8-bit graphics and chip-tunes brings a lot of people back to the C64. There was some great stuff being done back then that feels crude and raw in the age of Ultra HD and FLAC audio. It feels so limited now – quaint and antique – but, at the time, we felt like pioneers.

Do you still own a C64?
When I was at System 3, the artist Tony Hagar needed to borrow my C64 and colour monitor for a project he was working on. I left System 3 and basically lost touch with him, so I never got it back. If you're reading this, Tony…

What are you up to these days?
I worked in video games until 1999, graduating from the Amiga and Atari ST to ultimately work on 3D PC gaming. The business had really changed by then, and, in the end, I felt I needed to move on. I'm now a film editor working in New York City, and I was an editor on the 2014 documentary *Jodorowsky's Dune*.

Black Lamp / *1988*

Savage / *1988*

Combat School

"Failing to get a decent time in the Iron Man race level resulted in a punishment of push-ups, where you had to waggle your joystick as fast as you could. My friend Marcus and I were on the floor laughing because the push-up sound effect sounded like a cow mooing! Because we were on the floor and unable to play, the game ended, and we had to start all over. And we did – again and again. We waggled our joysticks so much, sweat was running down our backs; it was as close to real combat school as we got back in those days!"

Andreas Wallström, guest reviewer

Released
1987

Genre
Sports

Developer and publisher
Ocean

Originally by
Konami

Released
1987

Genre
Action

Developer and publisher
Gremlin Graphics

Deathwish 3

"This is seriously violent, and the fact that my parents had no idea I was playing such a gruesome game was all the more exciting. Mowing down enemies with guns and rocket launchers wasn't just the aim of the game, but it's all I cared about. What about the old grannies wandering about? They were fair game too, but leave them alone, and they got their handbags in on the action! Luckily, there was someone on hand to clear up the mess, dragging dead folk off the screen as efficiently as a fast food restaurant cleaner. Utter mayhem that served little point, but, my word, it was fun."

Matt Wilsher, guest reviewer

Released
1987

Genre
Action puzzle

Developer
Stavros Fasoulas

Publisher
Thalamus

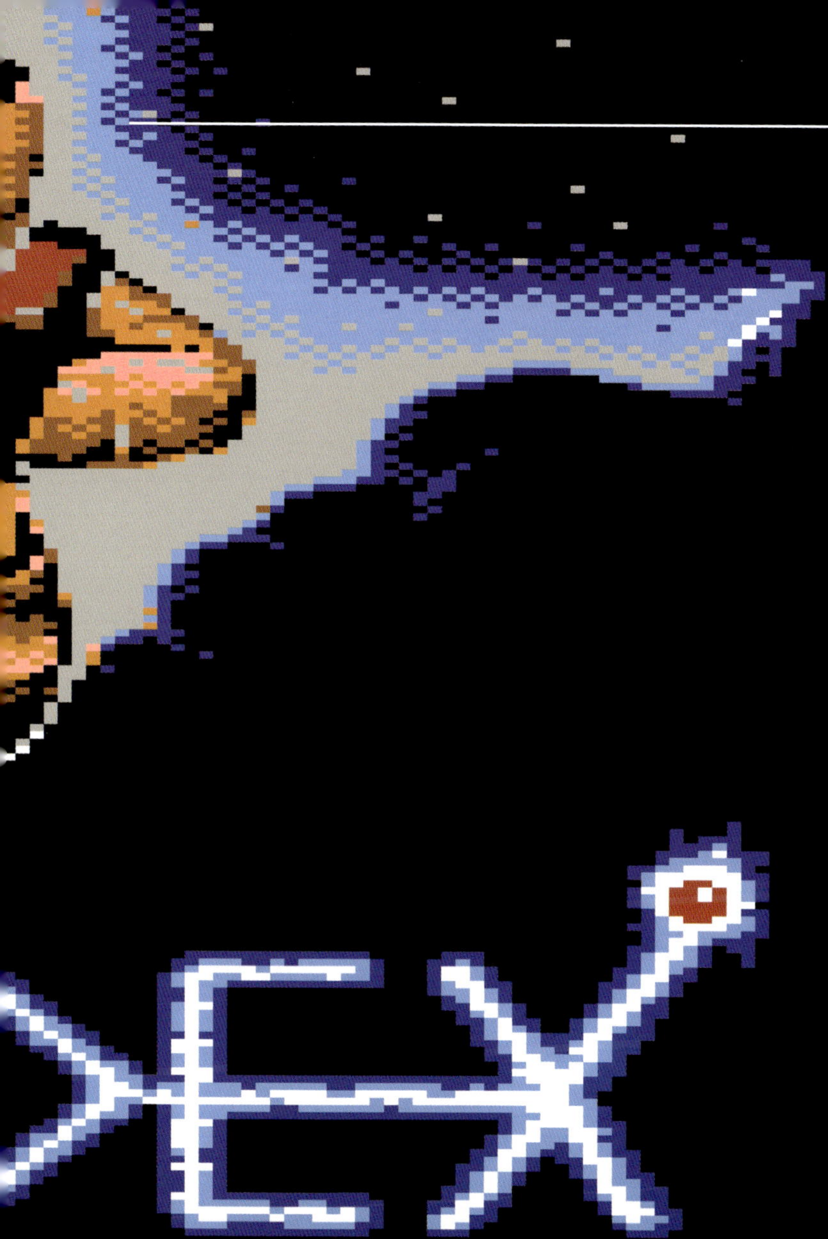

Quedex

"Flesh tones were always tricky on the C64, but that never stopped me from trying. The irony that I was drawing a hand holding a joystick by hand using a joystick was not lost on me! Almost all the graphics I created on the C64 were with *Paint Magic* and a Kempston Competition Pro joystick. It was the daftest and most laborious technique for creating graphics, but, on the C64, I never did it any other way."

Paul Docherty, graphic artist

"*Quedex* came about because Paul Docherty and/or Graham Hunter passed one of my Compunet demos on to Paul Cooper at Thalamus. They wanted to use it for the loading sequence, but it had been written on *Soundmonitor*. Somehow, they managed to get it to play while the game loaded. The in-game tunes needed to be written in such a way that, if a sound effect played, it didn't destroy the music too much. Stavros Fasoulas and Paul Cooper drove up to my parents' house where I basically had the top floor of a bungalow to myself. Stavros loaded up his game demos and went through what was needed. I think it took me about two weeks to do all the tunes and FX. Working for such a big name in the industry definitely opened up more doors."

Matt Gray, musician

"Painting in pixels was never more magical for me than when I was sitting in a darkened room with just a joystick hooked up to the C64 and the cathode ray tube glowing in front of me."

Paul Docherty, graphic artist

Krakout

Gremlin's take on *Breakout* turns the block-breaking genre on its side and throws in a variety of enemies (including floating heads and swarms of killer bees), psychedelic scrolling backdrops and funky Ben Daglish tunes. When we reviewed it in *Zzap!64*, it had the unfortunate drawback of turning up just after *Arkanoid*, which we all loved; although quite pretty, Gremlin's effort just seemed clumsy and derivative by comparison."

Steve Jarratt, games journalist

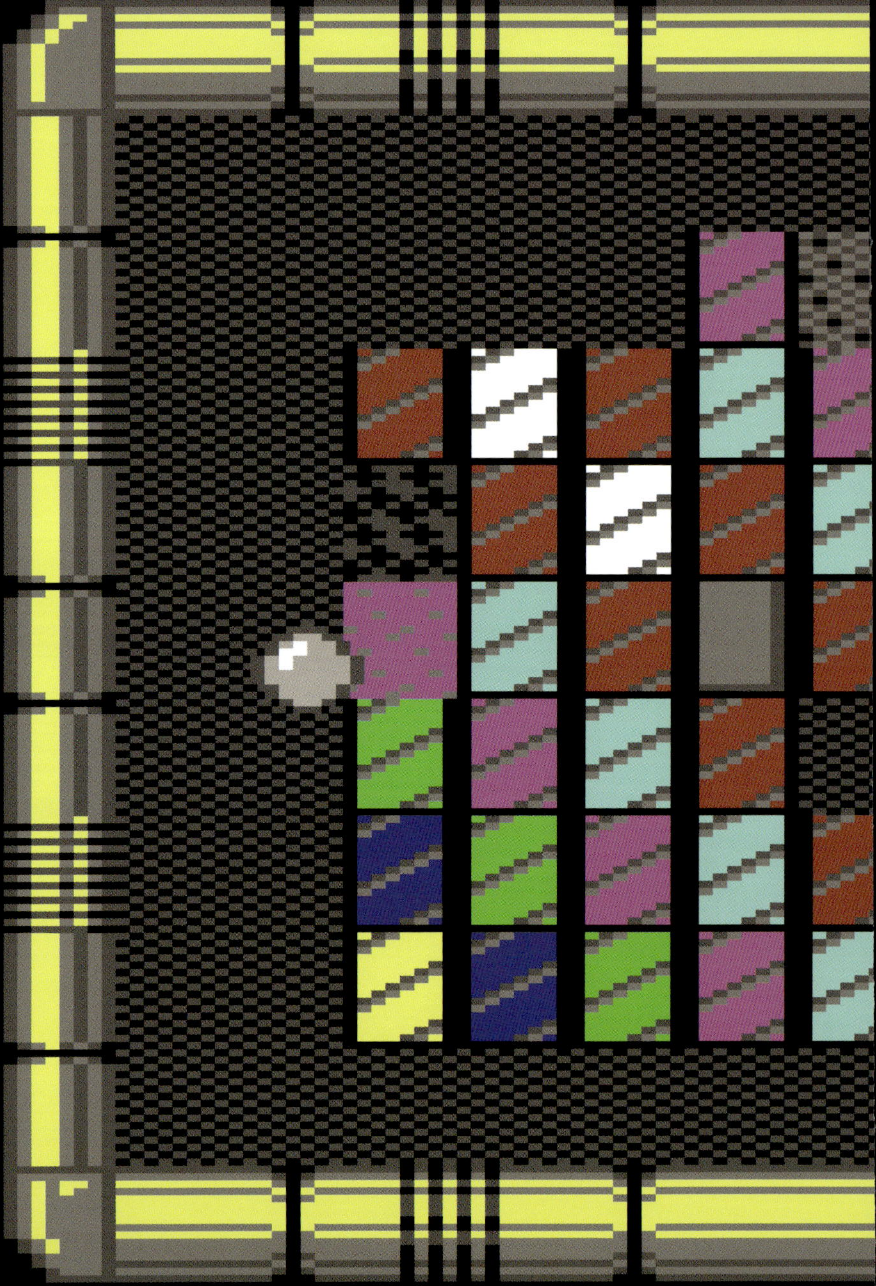

Released
1987

Genre
Arcade

Developer
Andy Green

Publisher
Gremlin Graphics

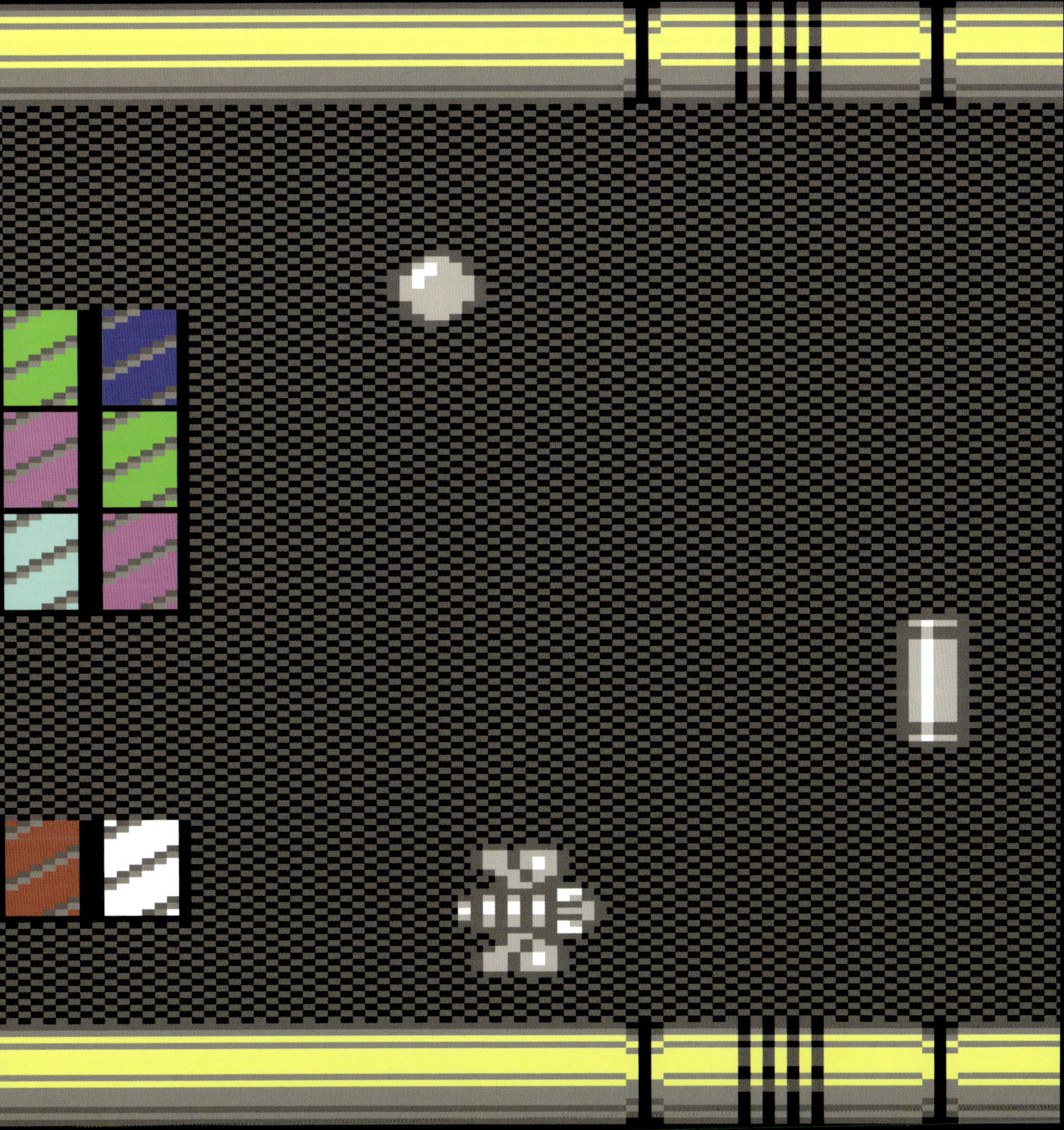

Released
1987

Genre
Sports

Developer and publisher
Epyx

California Games

"When designing *California Games*, I remember we had a big brainstorm with the team and were all putting event ideas onto a big whiteboard. Skateboarding was hot at the time, so we decided we had to do something with it. I was also a keen skater and decided that a side-view half-pipe event would work really well from a technical aspect. To create the skater animation frames, we used Epyx's innovative animation tool called *'Wilbur'*, which was created especially for the equestrian event in *Summer Games*. It got its name from a TV show in the '50s that featured a talking horse whose owner was called – you guessed it – Wilbur".

Chuck Sommerville, co-designer and programmer

Released
1987

Genre
Scrolling shooter

Developer
Sensible Software

Publisher
Ocean

Wizball

"This 'Game of the Decade' was Inspired by *Dropzone* and *Nemesis*. One day, I got to Chris's house, and he showed me this weird bouncing ball control he'd invented. I drew a stupid grinning green head, and *Wizball* was born. Chris added loads of weapons, and I came up with the landscape colouring idea, so we added paint bubbles to catch. The paint-collecting orbiting satellite SFX sounded like 'meows', so we called it 'Catellite'."

Jon Hare, co-designer and graphic artist

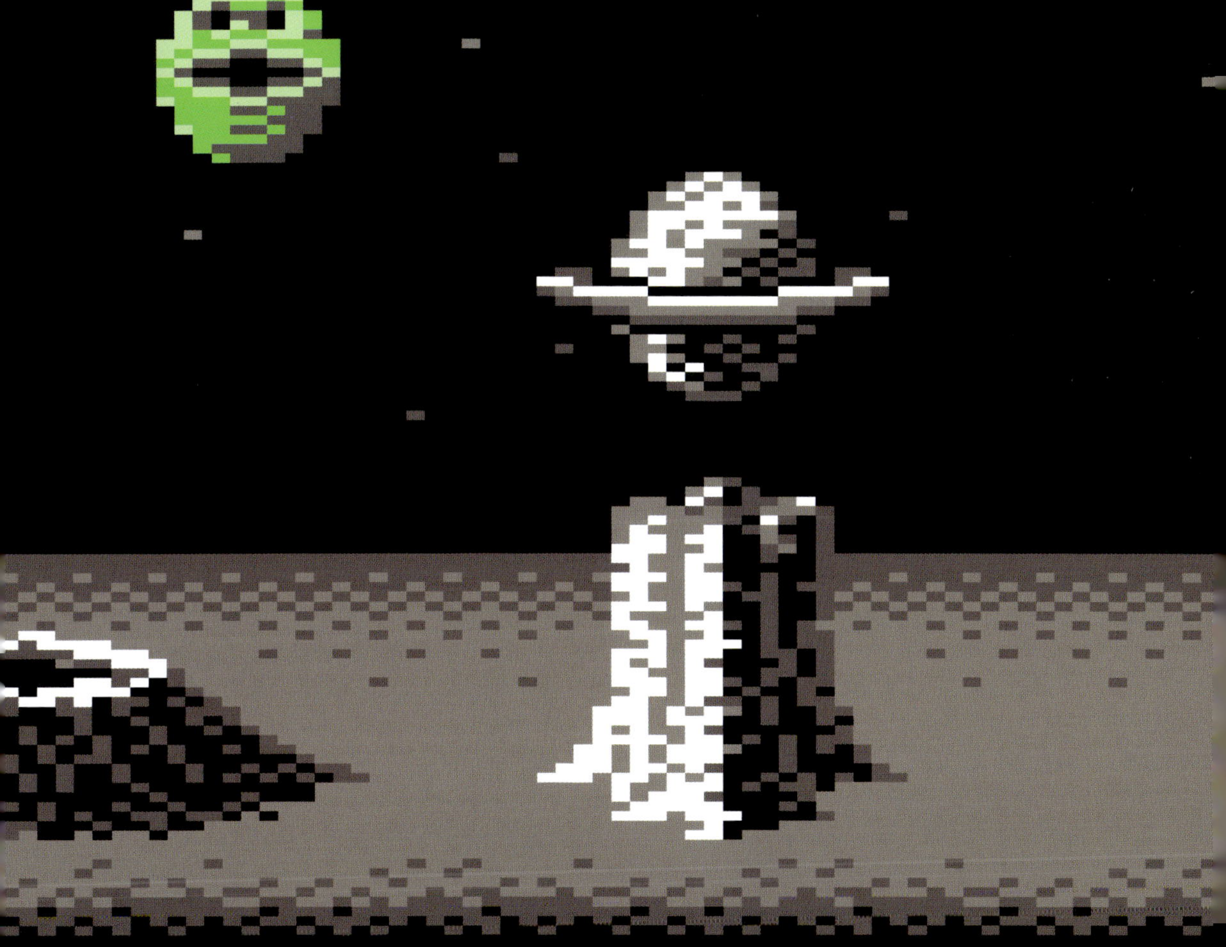

Released
1987

Genre
Puzzle adventure

Developer
Major Developments

Publisher
Incentive Software

Driller

"*Driller*, for Incentive Software, was another big turning point for me. They wanted something long and epic, not short and repetitive. Concept-wise, it was the perfect game for me. It was exactly the sort of thing I had been waiting to get my teeth into musically. It took four weeks to complete, including an almost two-week pause in the middle when the Great Storm of 1987 struck the UK, leaving us without electricity or heating for about ten or eleven days. I can remember walking down our road one dark evening, wondering if I would ever get to use the C64 again, and suddenly noticing all the neighbours' lights were finally on again. I went straight in, fired up the assembler and carried on composing."

Matt Gray, musician

"As a haunting theme with echoes of *Halloween* and *Phantom of the Opera* infiltrates your ears, the sheer vastness of the task ahead is matched with the blackness of the sky, punctuated by some really good-looking solid graphics. It's a pity they move so slowly, although that's something emulation has 'fixed' since. *Driller* was the first use of the *Freescape* engine, and future games would improve on the bar set by this release."

Mat Allen, guest reviewer

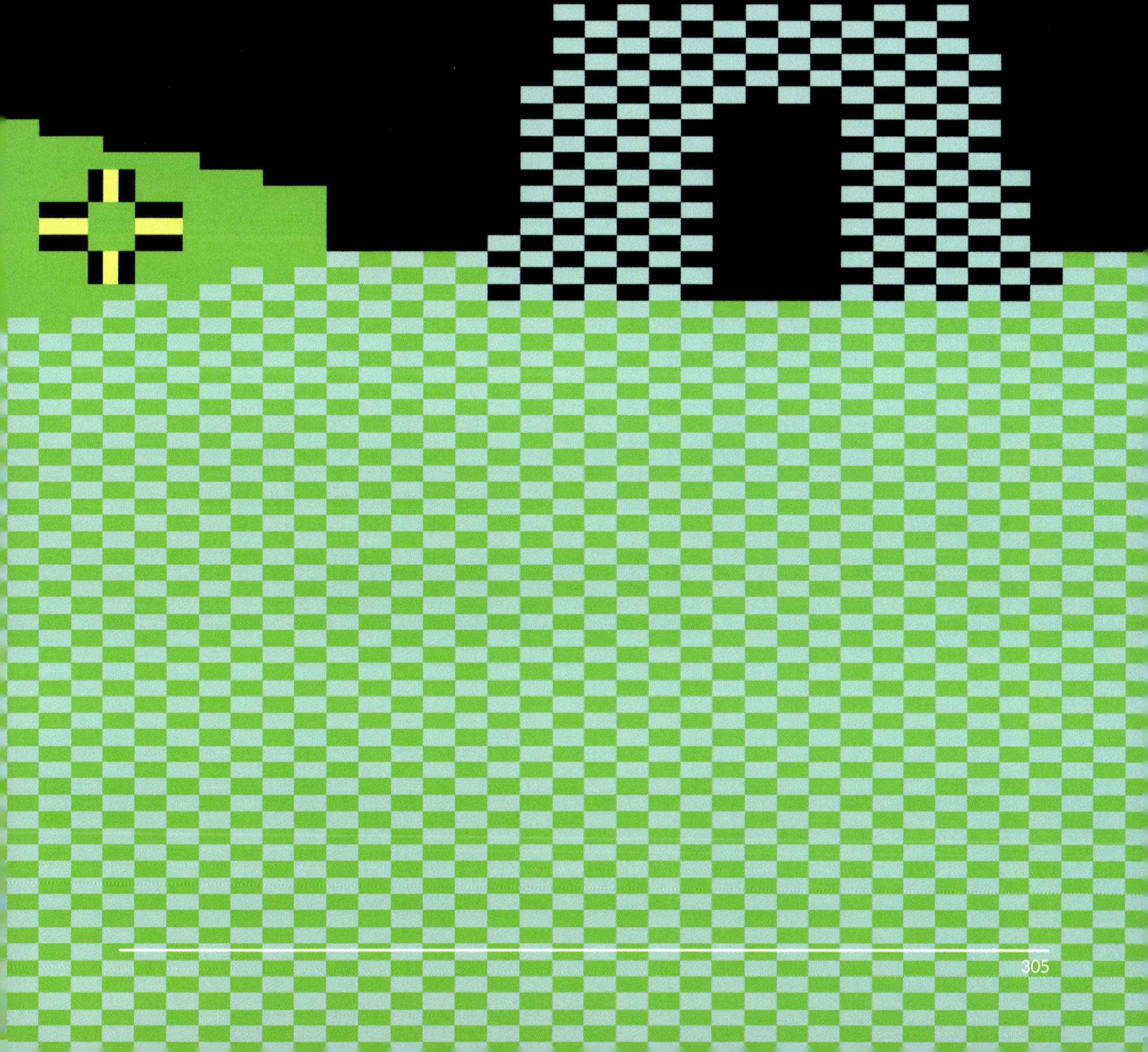

Barbarian: The Ultimate Warrior

I was given pretty much a blank canvas to do whatever I wanted after the success of the *Cauldron* games. I went to the guys with my checklist for the game that I would want to play: huge characters, brutal, over-the-top violence, laugh-out-loud moments, and cool sword fighting moves that were properly researched and animated. That's exactly how it turned out – we nailed it."

Steve Brown, designer

For me, one of the things that made *Barbarian* so special was the team – Steve Brown, Stan Schembri, Andy Fitter, Chris Stangroom, Richard Leinfellner, Sean Griffiths, Richard Joseph, and Dan Malone. We were much more than workmates; we were close friends. We literally worked and socialised together non-stop. I really feel that came through in the game."

Gary Carr, graphic artist

Released
1987

Genre
Fighting

Developer and Publisher
Palace Software

Grand Prix Simulator

"A dynamic loading screen, harking back to the early '80s and the Ferrari and McLaren clashes in F1. Based on the box art, the game was a *Supersprint*-style one with what looked like small coloured shoe boxes for cars, as I recall. The loading screens were intended to sell the budget games."

Steven Day, graphic artist

Released *1987* / **Genre** *Sports* / **Developer and Publisher** *Codemasters*

ATV Simulator

"Probably my favourite of the Codemasters screens I did. I also converted the background graphics for the game, as I recall, as a rush job with both being completed inside two days when another artist failed to deliver on time. As a general guide, most of my loading screens were completed in the eight-to-ten-hour mark in order to make them commercially viable."

Steven Day, graphic artist

Released *1987* / **Genre** *Sports* / **Developer** *Digital Persuasion* / **Publisher** *Codemasters*

Released *1988* / **Genre** *Sports* / **Developer and Publisher** *Codemasters*

Professional BMX Simulator

"This was one of a pair of screens done for the flagship game of a slightly more expensive range of Codemasters releases. When doing this screen, I used a few elements from Jim Wilson's original *BMX Simulator* loading screen in order to preserve brand continuity. My original screen read 'Super BMX Simulator', which was changed in-house to 'Professional' later (badly)."

Steven Day, graphic artist

Released *1988* / **Genre** *Sports* / **Developer** *Arcana Software Design* / **Publisher** *Codemasters*

Professional Snooker Simulator

"Generally, loading screens were based upon the cassette inlay artwork, but an exception, in this case, was *Pro Snooker*. It was my very first commissioned loading screen and was requested to be original artwork as the cassette inlay was not popular at Codemasters. The player, as I recall, was an '80s snooker player named Doug Mountjoy."

Steven Day, graphic artist

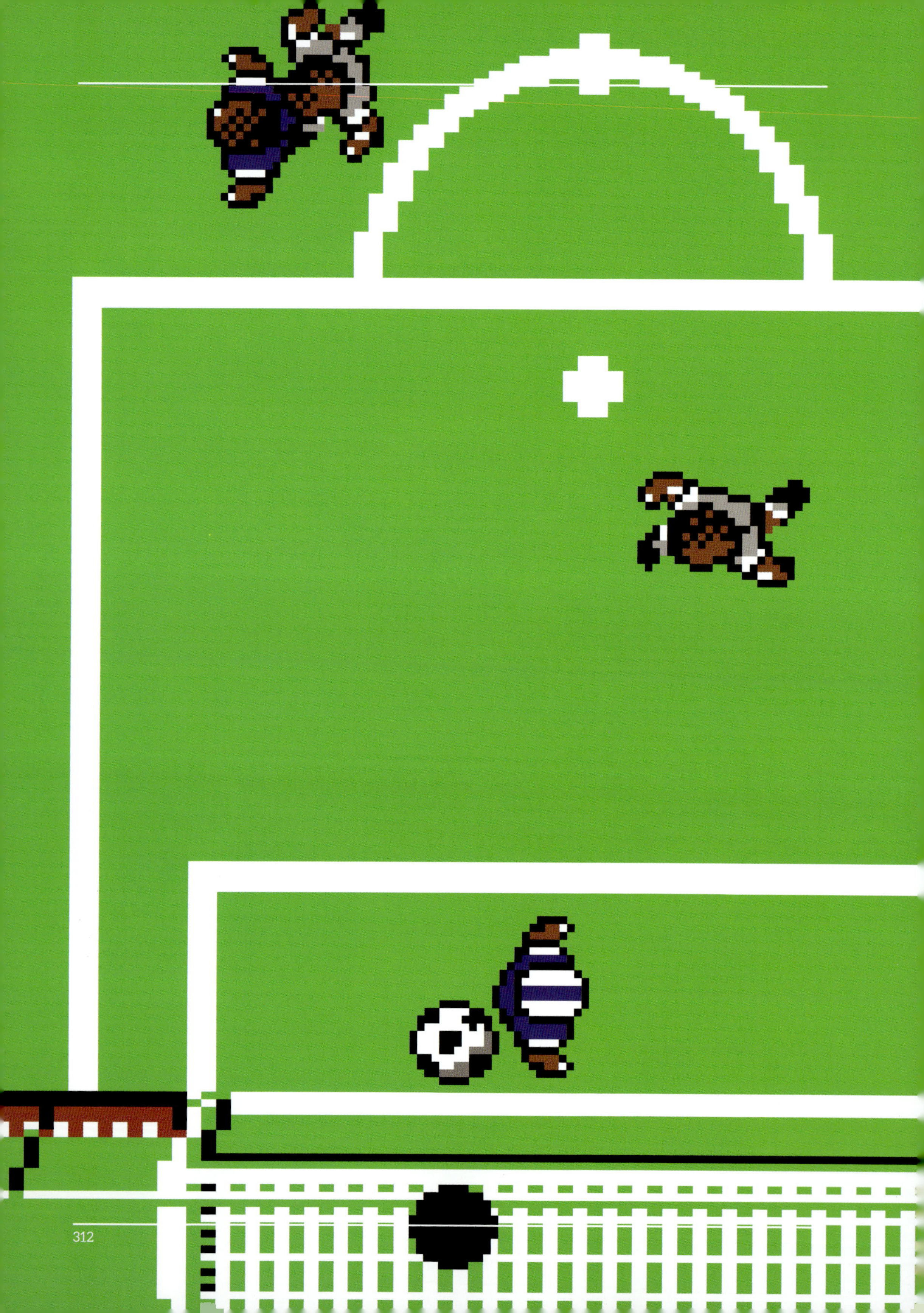

MicroProse Soccer

"In 1988, we made a C64 football game heavily inspired by the two-player trackball arcade machine *Tehkan World Cup*. We wanted to call the game *Sensible Soccer*, but our publishers MicroProse wanted to call it *MicroProse Soccer*. The company offered us a big advance, and we agreed to change the name. On its release, *MicroProse Soccer* was hailed by *C&VG* as the best sports game on any format ever. Its genre-defining features for the time included banana shots, rain, rewinding action replays, and overlaid player sprites with a sharp outline defined around the players in their team colours."

Jon Hare, co-designer and graphic artist

Released
1988

Genre
Sports

Developer
Sensible Software

Publisher
MicroProse Software

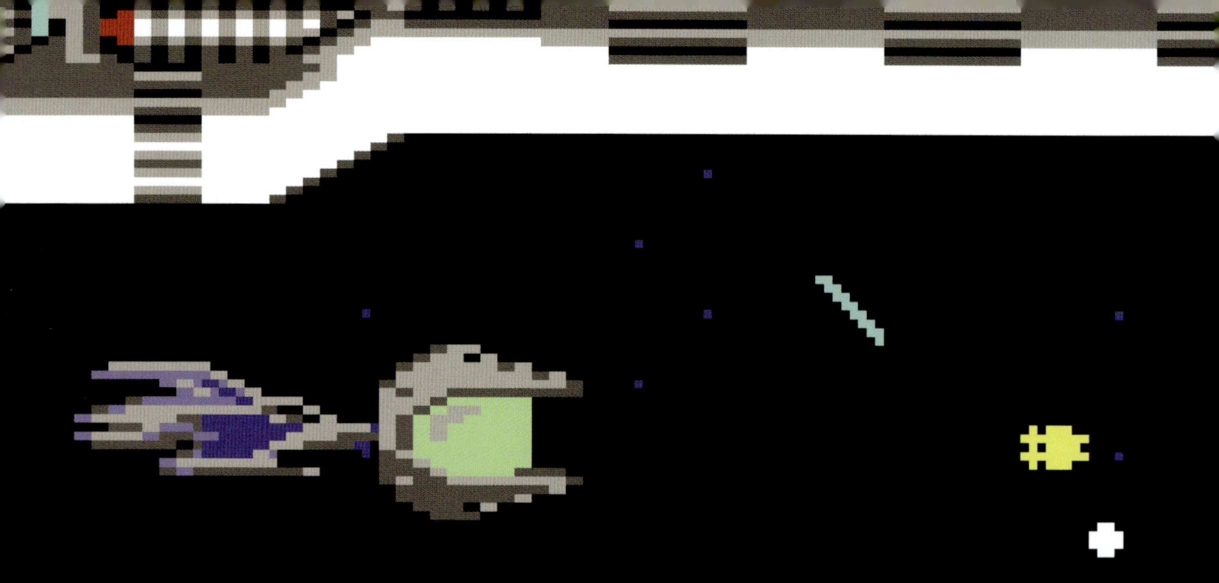

Denaris

"Manfred Trenz wrote an amazing sprite multiplexer, and we both created the graphics for the then-named *Katakis*. When released, Activision thought that it was too similar to *R-Type*, and, with the threat of legal action, it was pulled from the shelves. After some negotiations with Activision, *Katakis* was rebranded and released globally as *Denaris* – with only the name change and a few graphical tweaks, such as backgrounds and enemy sprites. The only condition from Activision was that we had to deliver the C64 and Amiga *R-Type* conversions in just six weeks!"

Andreas Escher, graphic artist

Released
1988

Genre
Scrolling shooter

Developer and publisher
Rainbow Arts

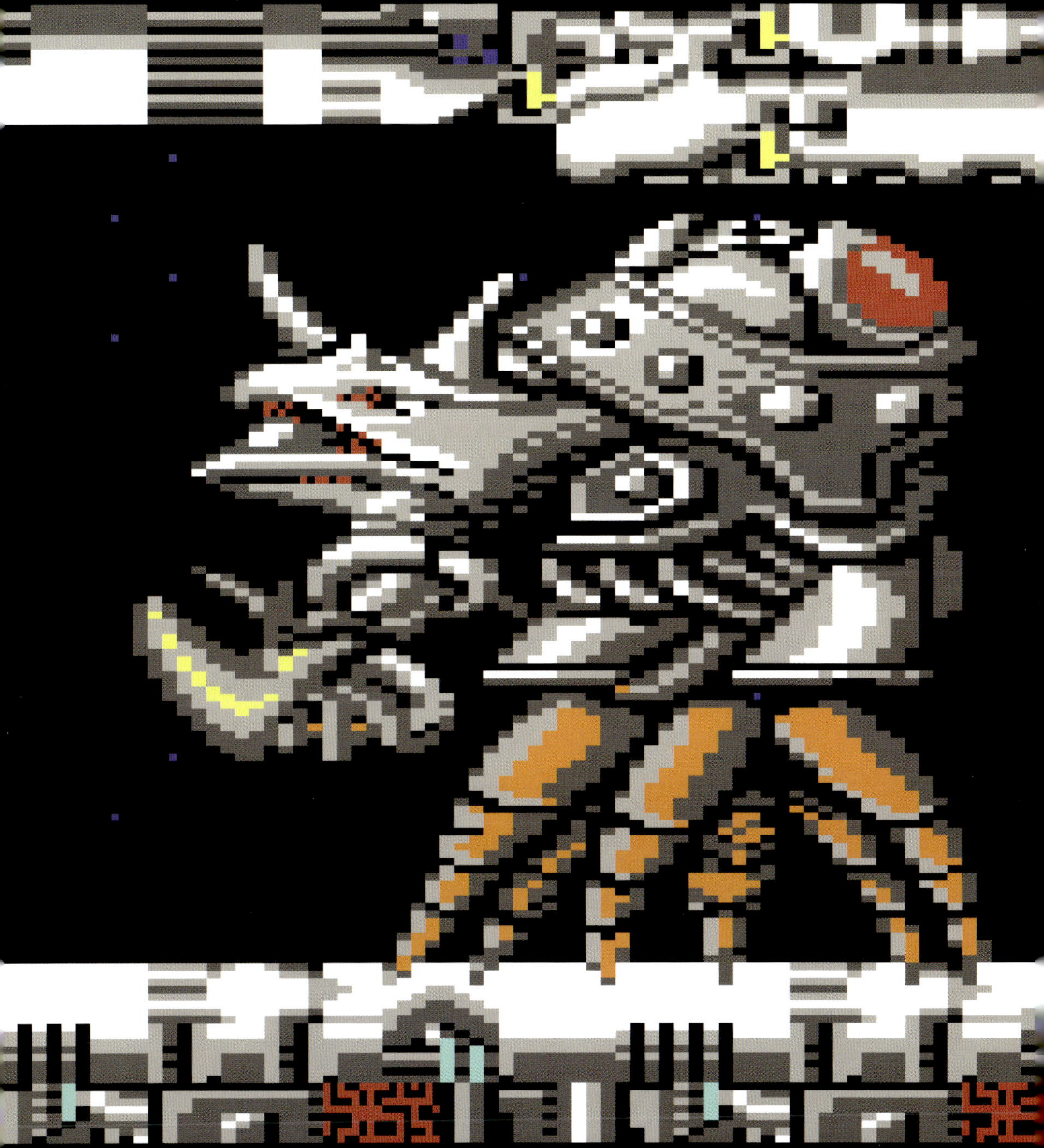

Released
1988

Genre
Action

Developer
Novotrade

Publisher
Epyx

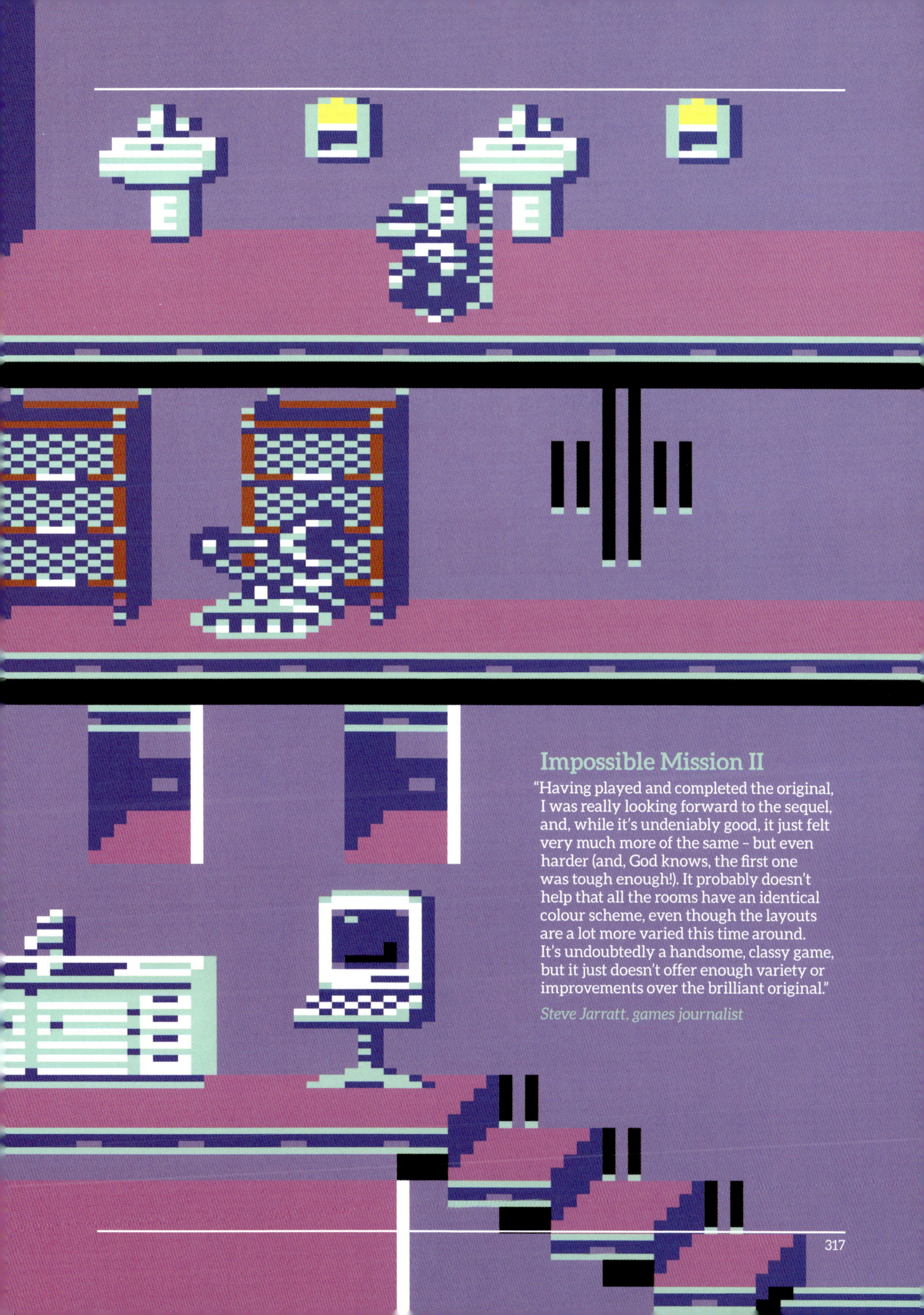

Impossible Mission II

"Having played and completed the original, I was really looking forward to the sequel, and, while it's undeniably good, it just felt very much more of the same – but even harder (and, God knows, the first one was tough enough!). It probably doesn't help that all the rooms have an identical colour scheme, even though the layouts are a lot more varied this time around. It's undoubtedly a handsome, classy game, but it just doesn't offer enough variety or improvements over the brilliant original."

Steve Jarratt, games journalist

Released
1988

Genre
Adventure

Developer
Beam Software

Publisher
Firebird

Samurai Warrior: The Battles of Usagi Yojimbo

"Based on Stan Sakai's *Usagi Yojimbo* comic book series, *Samurai Warrior*'s understated grace and beauty belied the game's outwardly cute appearance. Guiding a katana-wielding lagomorph through 17th century feudal Japan, players would need to strictly adhere to the Bushidō code of moral principles to raise their karma by means of honour, respect and kindness; otherwise, forcing the noble Miyamoto Usagi to fall to his knees and perform seppuku. Technically accomplished, beautifully presented and remarkably faithful to the comic book, Samurai Warrior is an overlooked classic."

Andy Roberts, games journalist

"The adventures of Miyamoto Usagi come to life in what is truly one of the Commodore 64's greatest games. This blend of faithful graphical representation, fitting score and authentic settings make *Samurai Warrior* a timeless classic, and, with its groundbreaking design, it remains one of the greatest comic book adaptations into video games ever made, even to this day. Stan Sakai's *Usagi Yojimbo* itself remains alive and well, being the longest current running independent comic book of all time. Well done, honoured rōnin!"

Audun Sorlie, guest reviewer

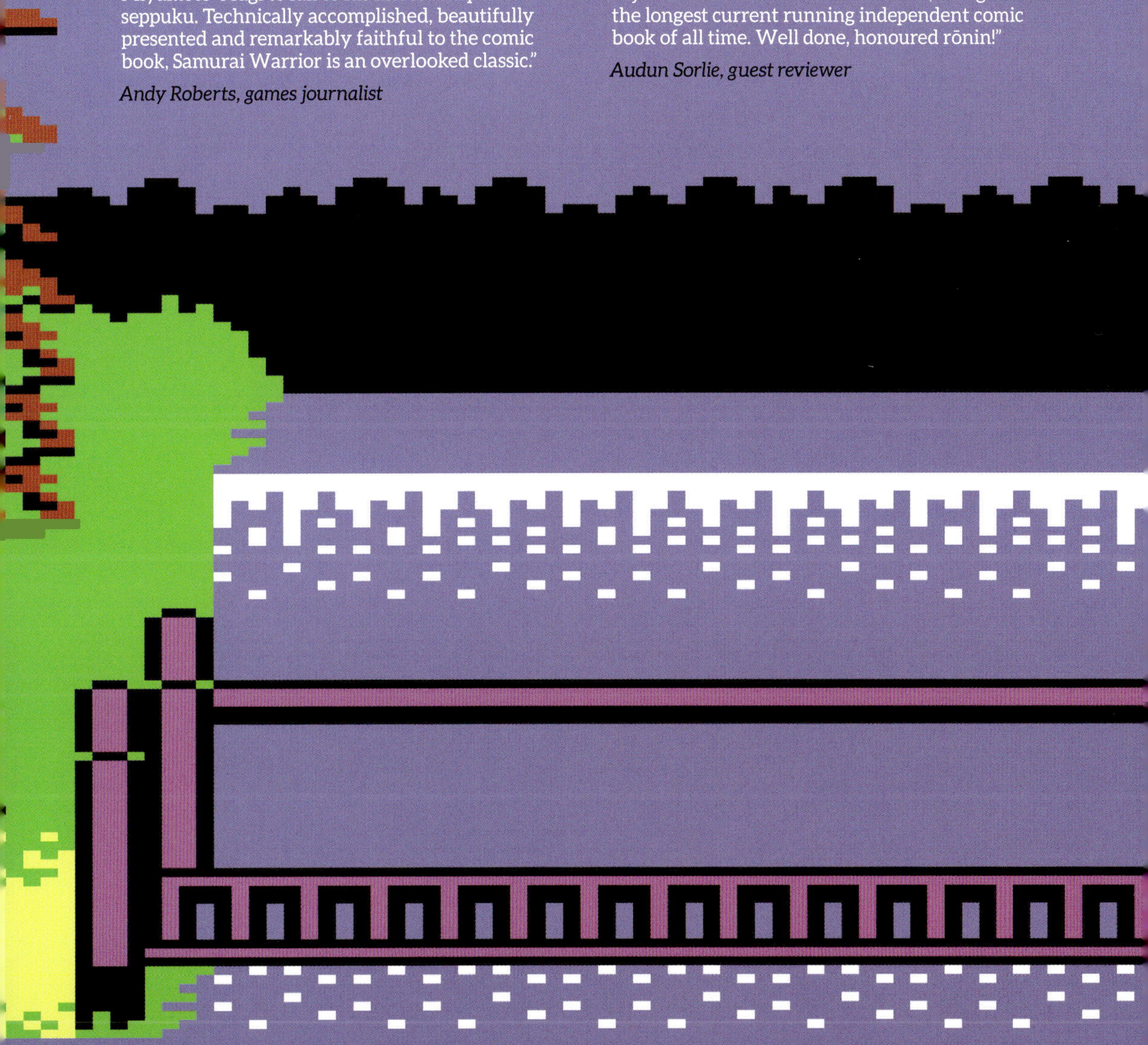

Neuromancer

"From a people perspective, *Neuromancer* was probably one of the more unusual projects that I've been involved with. The project was brought to me from my friendship with the '60s icon Timothy Leary. I was introduced to Tim through EA, and we became friends due to his heavy interest in software. Then, some years later, he came to me with a plastic surgeon's wife and two cabana boys from the Beverly Hills Hotel who had an option for *Neuromancer*. I wasn't familiar with the material, but I was immediately intrigued when I read it – and from Tim's pure excitement. It was surreal when I was having my design meetings with Timothy Leary, William Gibson and Devo."

Brian Fargo, producer

Released
1988

Genre
Adventure

Developer
Interplay Productions

Publisher
Electronic Arts

Salamander

Salamander was the first full game I completed. Three more experienced programmers refused the contract, saying it was too complicated for the C64, but I simply didn't know any better. For research, I was given £20 n ten-pence pieces and told there was a *Salamander* machine in the cafe opposite Kings Cross Station. I spent the lot and wrote reams of notes, getting funny looks from the owners and patrons alike. I then spent a happy but tiring week with pen, paper and a C64 reference manual, optimising around 40 lines of assembler code to be fast enough to draw all those sprites."

Pete Baron, programmer

Released
1988

Genre
Scrolling shooter

Developer and Publisher
Imagine

Originally by
Konami

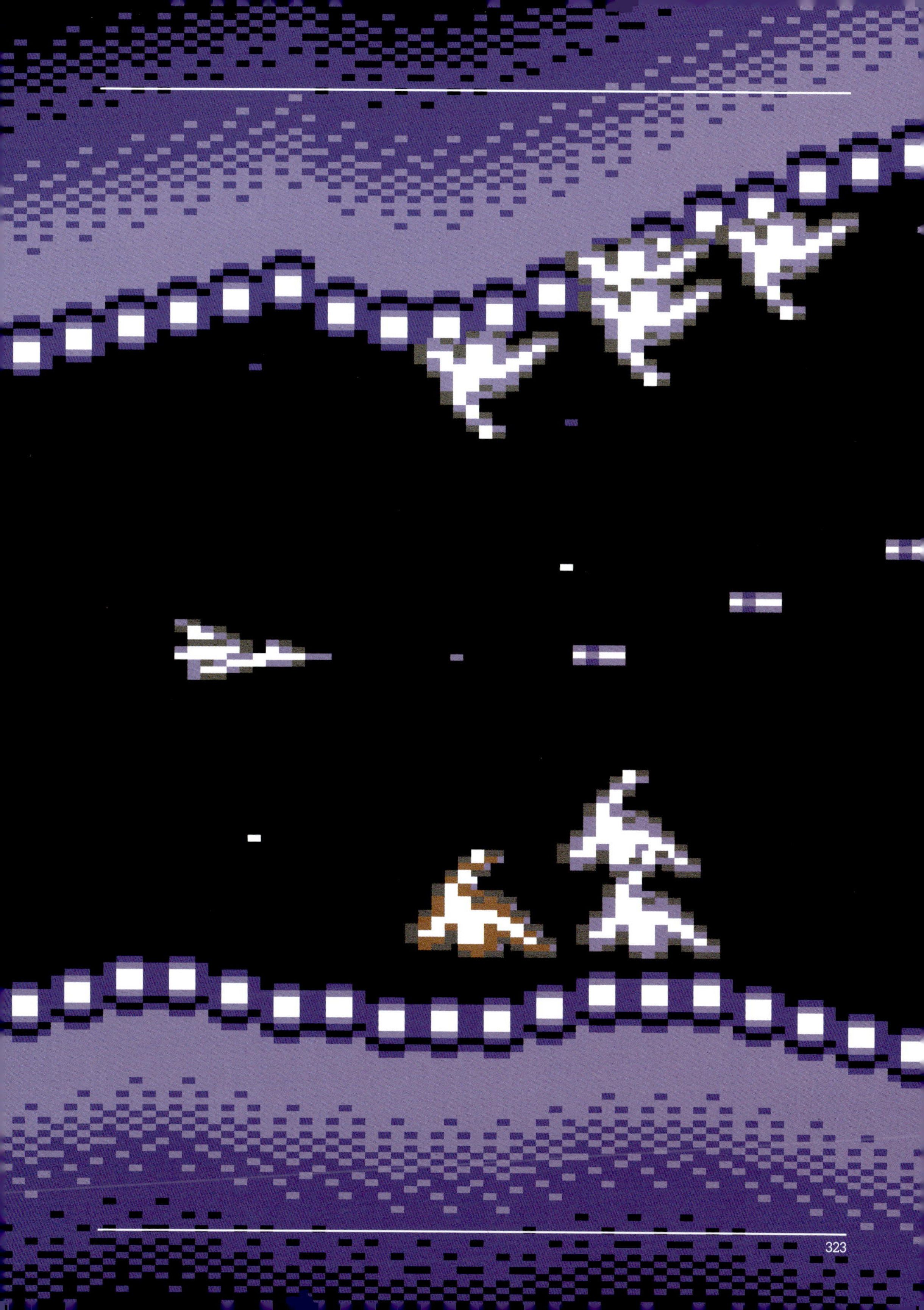

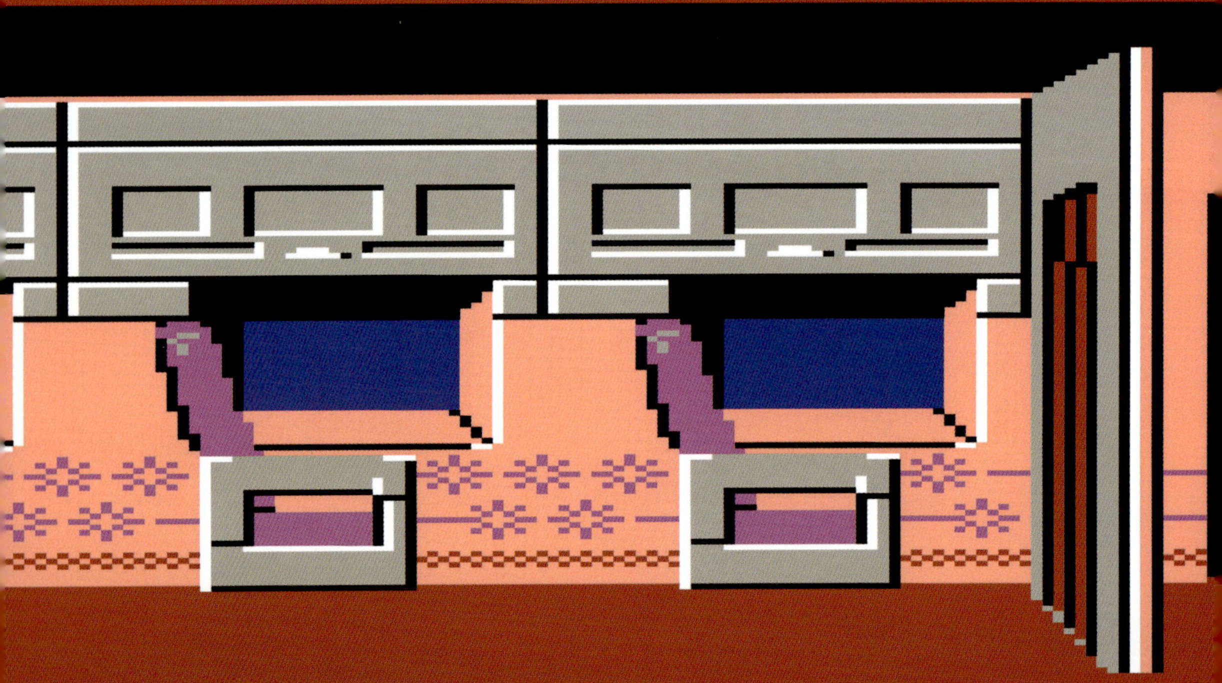

Zak McKracken and the Alien Mindbenders

"A fish in a bowl, a loaf of bread, and a Groucho Marx disguise. Just a few of the items you'll need during this highly enjoyable successor to *Maniac Mansion*, where your task is to prevent aliens taking over the Earth using a 60Hz hum. It retained all the same visual and aesthetic charm and lumped on a substantial dash of wit, sarcasm and subtle humour for good measure. Don't forget the airport codes..."

Mat Allen, guest reviewer

Released
1988

Genre
Point-and-click adventure

Developer and Publisher
Lucasfilm Games

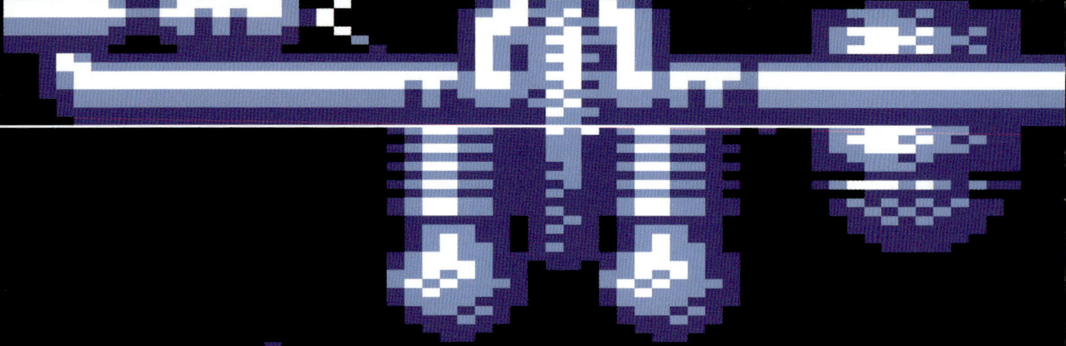

Armalyte

This was our debut game, and we wanted to make an impression. As a piece of 'art', *Armalyte* was far more than a bunch of coloured pixels positioned next to each other; it's meant to be seen in motion! As such, the art of this game was a team effort; the brilliant work by the coders, Dan and John, gave me the tools and the canvas I needed to work with to do my part, and all three of us are still proud of what we created."

Robin Levy, co-designer and graphic artist

Released
1988

Genre
Scrolling shooter

Developer
Cyberdyne Systems

Publisher
Thalamus

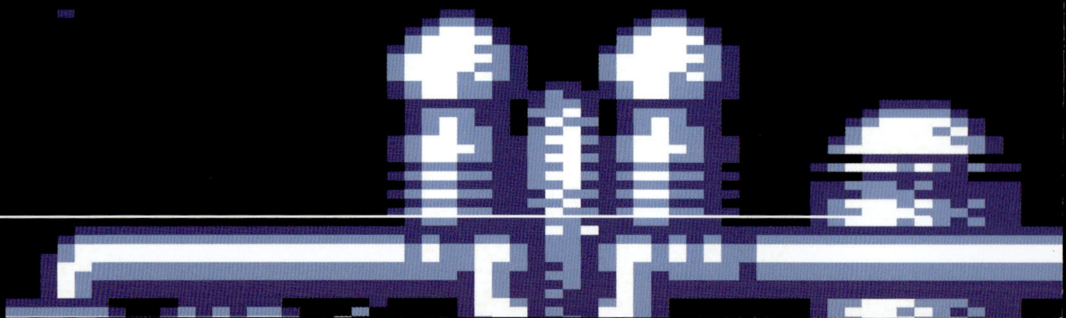

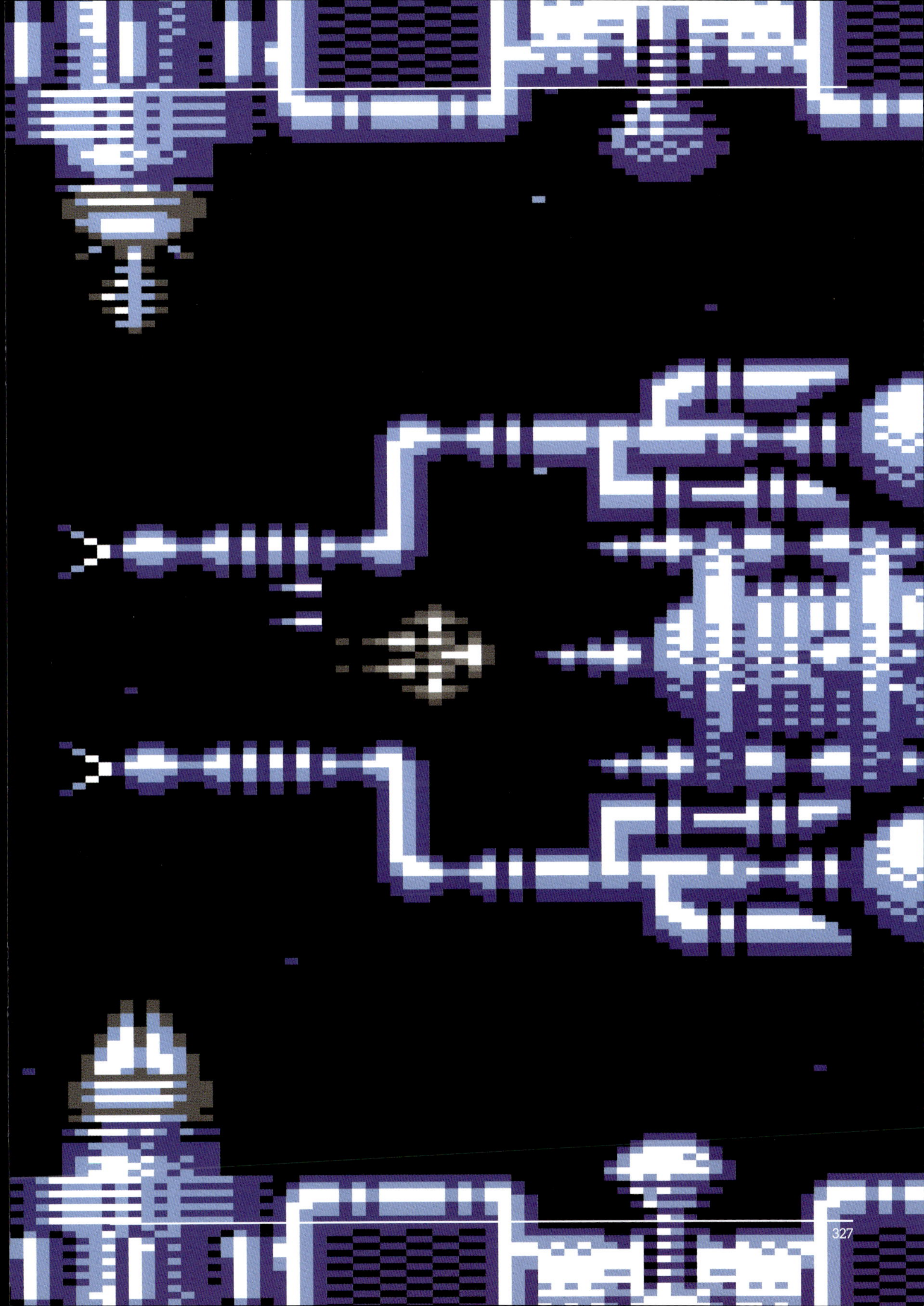

Released
1988

Genre
Action adventure

Developer and Publisher
System 3

Last Ninja 2

"*Last Ninja 2* built on the template we created for the original. The *Integrator* tool allowed me to overlay and assemble chunks of multicoloured art that I made using a mouse. The isometric 1:2 angle was unusual and challenging to animate. We didn't multiplex the sprites, so the ninja and his opponents shared the same torso and legs, with another sprite for the weapon and a 1-sprite colour overlay for the face, hands and enemy outfits. A shadow was also added to the characters in this sequel."

Hugh Riley, graphic artist

"In 1988, I created the *Last Ninja 2* soundtrack for System 3. I started with the Central Park tracks, which was important in order to stamp some sort of 'sound' on the game. It basically took from mid-January until early April to finish. It's about as big a project as you would want to undertake, but everything just seemed to work without any real hitches. I was given a fairly free hand to produce what I thought would be most suitable, and, luckily, every time I took in new tracks for each level, I got the thumbs up. It was a great time for me personally, to suddenly be working full time on C64 music. I was almost 18, but I had no real worries in the world beyond whether I could afford to buy a better car."

Matt Gray, musician

Cybernoid

Cybernoid was Raffaele Cecco's second title for us, and it was technically superb with lots of effects being thrown around on the screen. As a result, many people credited the game for helping to extend the life of the 8-bit machines with 16-bit looming on the horizon. We always believed in promoting the creators of our games, and *Cybernoid* certainly cemented Raffaele as something of a star."

Andrew Hewson, founder of Hewson Consultants

The loading screen was based on the box artwork. I found it easier to turn the box upside down and draw the ship that way, then rotate it to the right orientation! The logo and planet were drawn separately, and the ship composited on top using a nifty feature of the KoalaPainter Touch Tablet."

Stephen Robertson, graphic artist

Released *1988* / **Genre** *Shoot 'em up* / **Developer** *Raffaele Cecco* / **Publisher** *Hewson Consultants*

> **"I really enjoyed working on the C64. The graphics were usually a bit chunky, but what you lost in definition, you made up for in wonderful colour."**
>
> *Karen Davies, graphic artist*

Operation Wolf

"I was extremely pleased with this conversion. The screen itself was required to scroll horizontally left and right for about three quarters of its width, the right-hand part being devoted to ammo icons, etc., and could not scroll. Those that are familiar with the C64 scrolling capabilities will know that this could not be done in a conventional way. Either all of the screen scrolls or none of it does. I remember getting asked for years afterwards how it was done. Actually, the whole screen did scroll, but the character maps making up the 'stationary' part were manipulated in the opposite direction in sync to give the impression of a static screen for that part. The vertically multiplexed 'energy' indicator sprite hid the join. I think the graphic artists did a great job on that game, too."

Colin Porch, programmer

Released
1988

Genre
Shoot 'em up

Developer and Publisher
Ocean

Originally by
Taito

Hawkeye

Hawkeye was strongly influenced by arcade game *Rygar* (which Mario could finish in the arcades with just one guilder!). We did something which had never been done before: a multilayer parallax scroller which was held to be impossible until then on the C64. The music is by the then-unknown 14-year-old Jeroen Tel, who we introduced to the industry. It took nearly two years to build, but it was all worth it in the end as it won a gold medal award in *Zzap!64*."

Jacco Van 't Riet, graphic artist

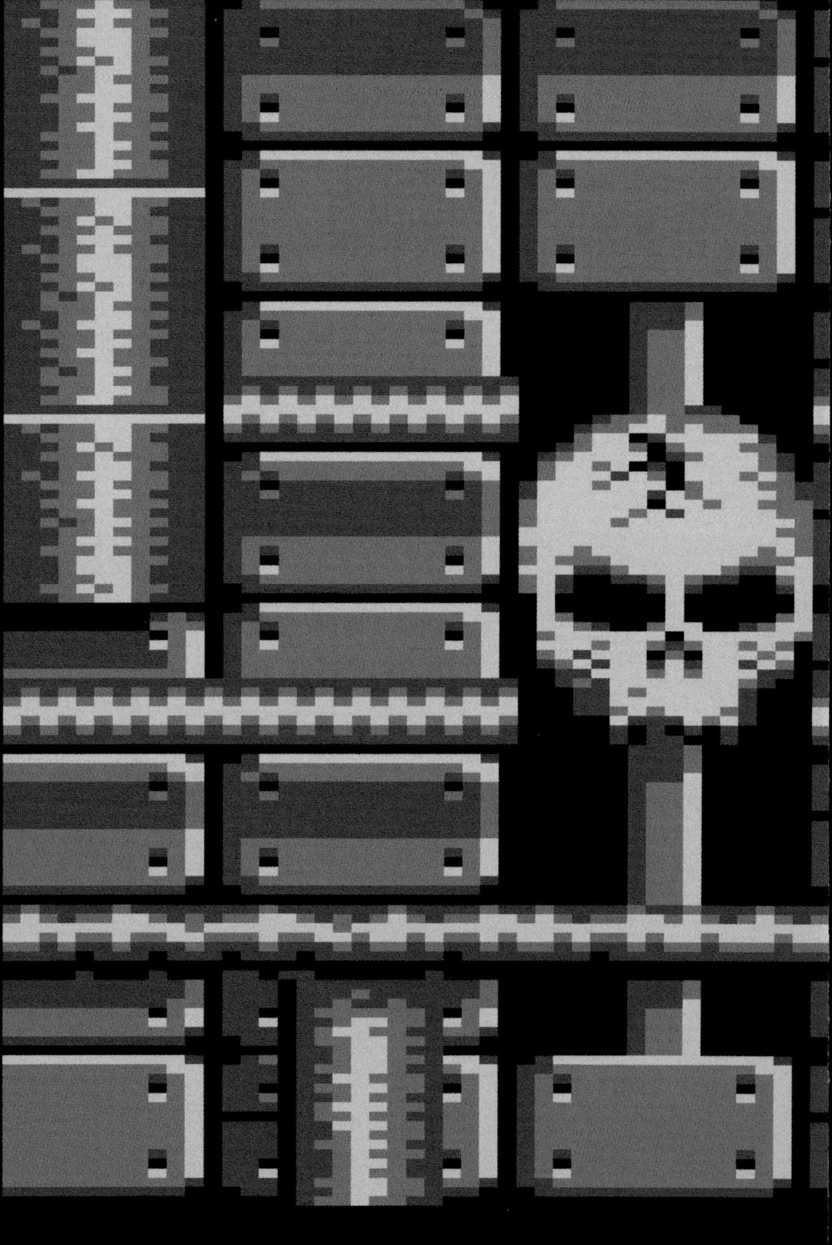

Released
1988

Genre
Run and gun

Developer
Boys Without Brains

Publisher
Thalamus

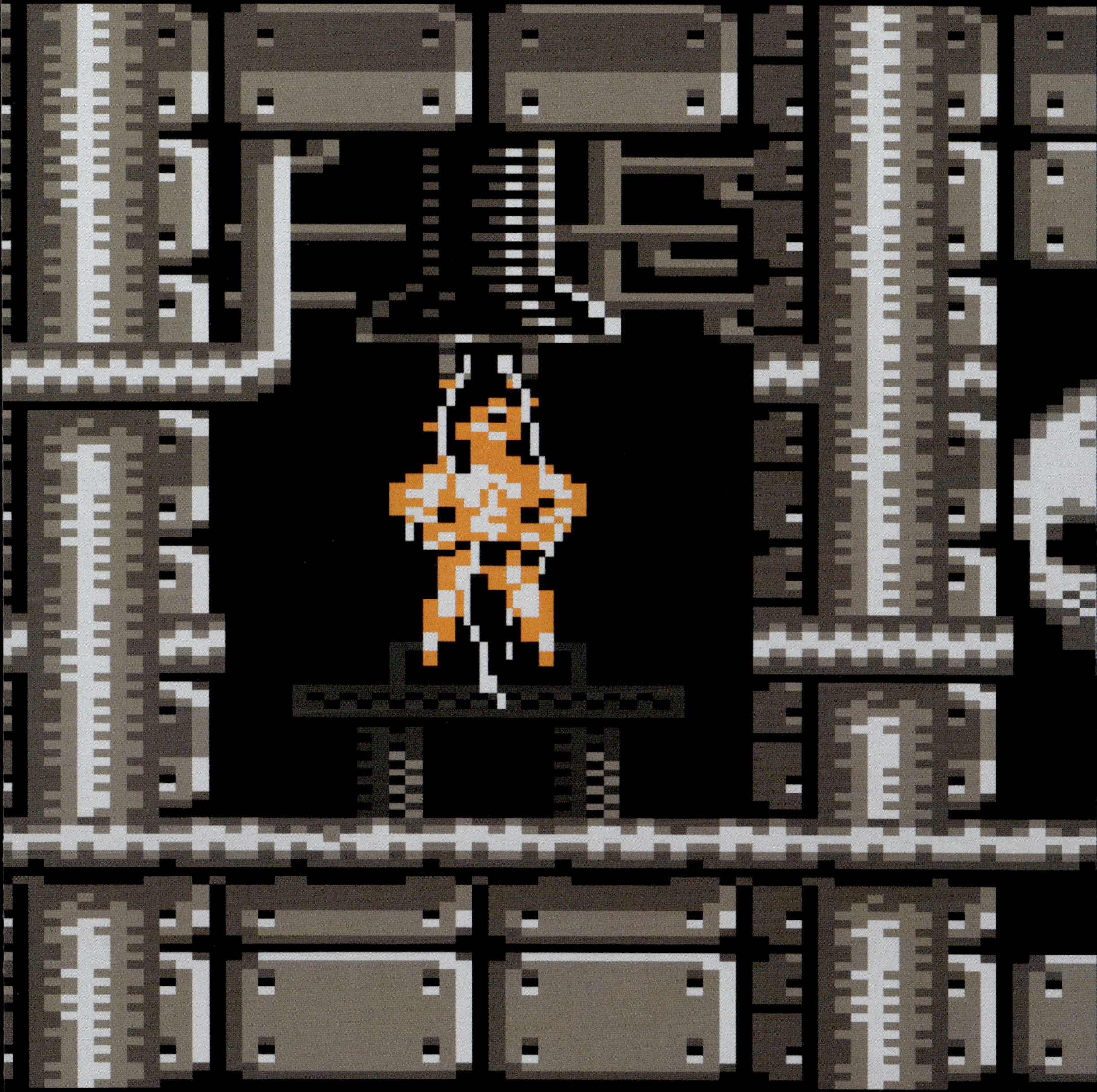

WEC Le Mans

Released
1988

Genre
Racing

Developer and Publisher
Imagine

Artwork
Oliver Frey

Katakis

Released
1988

Genre
Scrolling shooter

Developer
Manfred Trenz

Publisher
Rainbow Arts

Artwork
Oliver Frey

Batman The Movie

Ocean's interpretation of Tim Burton's much-hyped 1989 *Batman* movie sees you thrust into the role of the caped crusader as he attempts to bring down a Joker hell-bent on turning Gotham's inhabitants into grinning corpses with his 'Smylex' cosmetics. Like previous Ocean titles, each of the game's five levels has a different style of play based on specific sequences from the movie, from the platforming action of the Axis Chemical Works and Gotham City Cathedral to the side-scrolling dash through the streets of Gotham City in the Batmobile and Batwing levels. The end result is an authentic and accomplished movie tie-in that is both considerably greater than the sum of its parts and tremendous fun to boot.

"In 1989, you couldn't miss the *Batman* phenomenon. The hype was incredible. Around the film, came Ocean's adaptation which, despite being multi-load, was an enjoyable romp through Gotham City. A nice soundtrack to accompany good graphics and simple but addictive gameplay, it was assured success and is still playable today."

Robin Hogg, games journalist

Released
1989

Genre
Action

Developer and Publisher
Ocean

MYTH: History in the Making

"This was one of my favourite games that I helped create and make. It was based on a paper design that System 3 approached Peter Baron and myself to do. Pete and I had a very improvisational chemistry together. Between his code and design and my art and design, we produced some memorable moments of visual imagery and gameplay that I am still proud of."

Bob Stevenson, co-designer and graphic artist

Released
1989

Genre
Action

Developer and Publisher
System 3

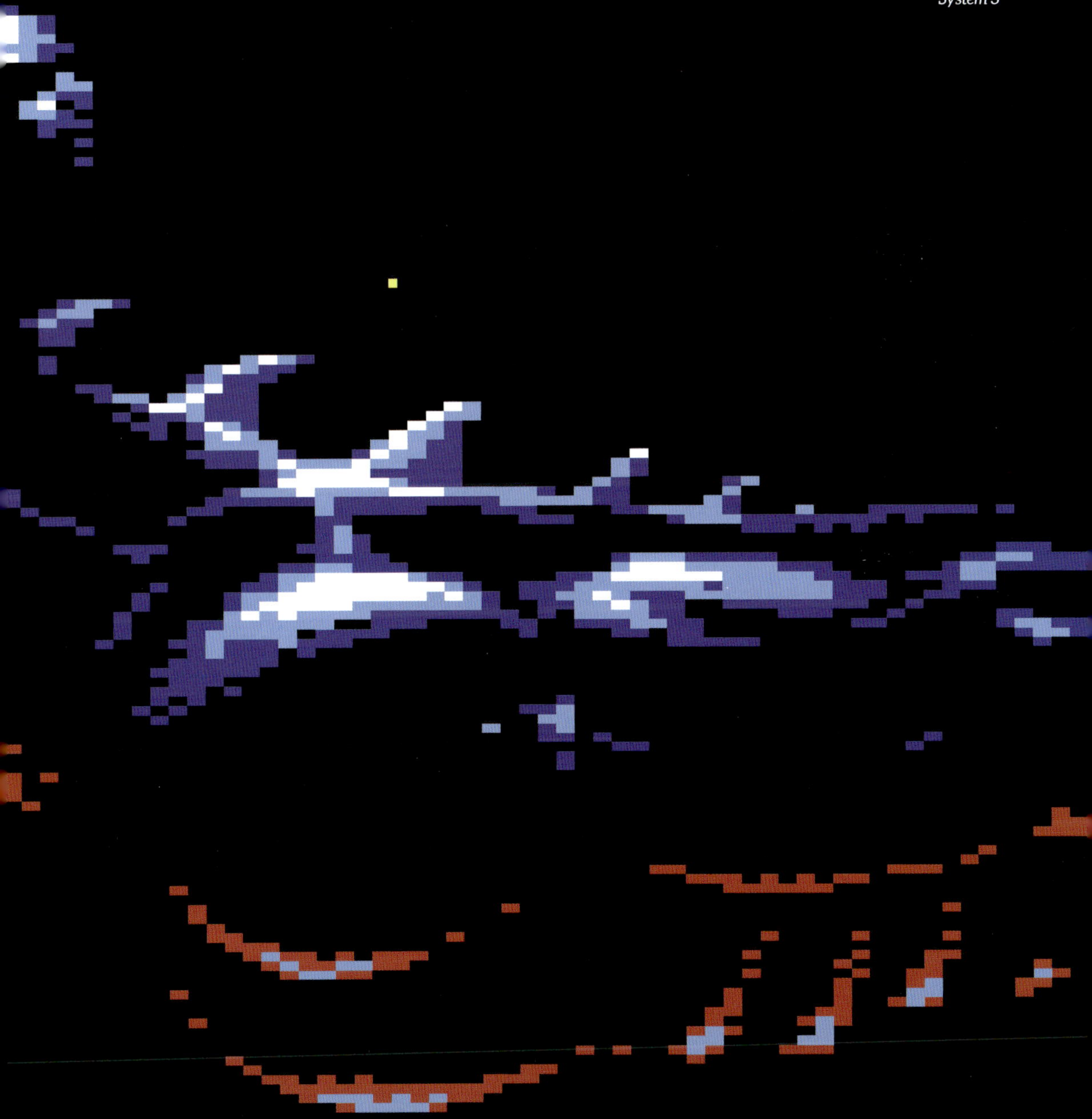

Released
1989

Genre
Racing

Developer
Probe Software

Publisher
U.S. Gold

Originally by
SEGA

Turbo Outrun

"Programmer Mark Kelly came up with this great way of displaying the track using a fantastic sprite multiplexer, but, when the player's car crashed, we had to switch off all the enemy cars to enable the crash animation to play. It was a real hack, but nobody seemed to notice! During final testing, we discovered it was possible to play the entire game in 'low' gear, making it super easy to beat. We had no time to retune the entire game, so, instead, we made the timer count down slightly quicker when in 'low' gear! It fixed the problem and, again, nobody noticed!"

Stephen Crow, graphic artist

"Fergus McGovern said to us, 'I got you guys a new project. Just one thing: they need it for Christmas!' – it was the last week of July! Two days later, the coin-op arrived in the offices, and so began a non-stop push to get the game done. 14 weeks later, we were done and heading up to U.S. Gold to get the game ready for duplication. We arrived on Monday evening and worked right through until Saturday with barely any sleep, locked away to make sure we got it done. Meanwhile, the rest of the world was watching the Berlin Wall fall!"

Mark W. J. Kelly, programmer

Ghouls 'n Ghosts

"This was my final C64 game, and, obviously, it was always going to be difficult converting a cutting-edge arcade game to the 8-bit breadbox. Fortunately, I'd worked on games requiring full-colour scrolling and baddies composed of many sprites rather than just one, which helped no end. U.S. Gold supplied an arcade board, which we played until we knew it forwards and backwards – this allowed Andy Threlfall to create fantastically accurate map layouts. The music is nothing short of amazing; Tim Follin's atmospheric masterpiece gets better and better as you play through the game."

Stephen Ruddy, programmer

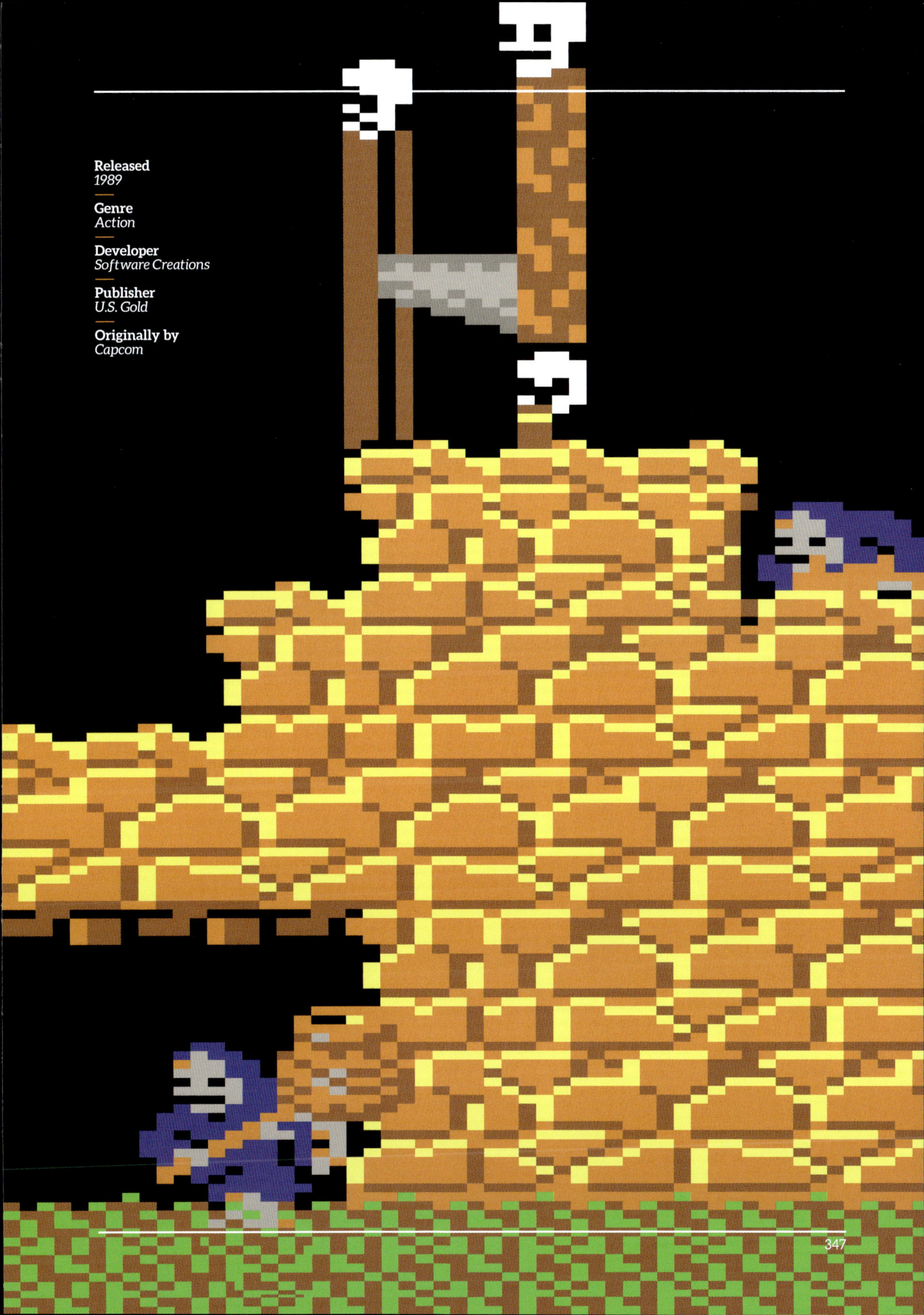

Released
1989

Genre
Action

Developer
Software Creations

Publisher
U.S. Gold

Originally by
Capcom

Graftgold

Graftgold was an independent UK games developer founded in 1983 by Steve Turner. After recruiting Andrew Braybrook, Graftgold would remain a two-man operation for several years before taking on other developers including John Cumming, Dominic Robinson, Gary J. Foreman and Jason Page. The majority of the company was later sold to Perfect Entertainment, and Graftgold eventually closed its doors for good in 1998.

Steve Turner started out as a business programmer with an interest in home computers and a passion for arcade games. Disillusioned with his career path, he established ST Software and began coding a Spectrum game in his spare time. Selling the game to Hewson gave Turner the means to quit his day job and make games full-time; Andrew Braybrook was hired, and Graftgold was born.

Despite the company's modest beginnings in Turner's dining room, Graftgold's output on the C64 between 1984 and 1990 was unprecedented, resulting in an impressive legacy of original games and arcade conversions. Indeed, Graftgold's peerless classics such as *Paradroid*, *Uridium*, *Alleykat* and *Morpheus* would propel programmer Andrew Braybrook to near-legendary status.

Graftgold's first C64 offering was *Lunattack*, a conversion of Steve Turner's 1984 Spectrum game *3D Lunattack*. A tactical shoot 'em up set on the surface of the moon, the game was an intriguing blend of strategy and violence that took weeks to master. "Only the most dogged hover pilot will be likely to better the resident high score," said *Your Commodore*, highlighting the game's steep difficulty curve. *Lunattack*'s excellent presentation and attention to detail were a taste of things to come.

Lunattack was then quickly followed by *Gribbly's Day Out*, an impossibly cute action-platformer set on the planet Blabgor. Packed with incredible detail – from Gribbly's facial expressions and evolving enemies to the innovative black and white mode – Gribbly's quest to rescue the hapless Gribblets quickly put Graftgold on the map. *Zzap!64* gave the game a 'Sizzler', calling it "one of the most original, cute and playable games to hit the 64," while *Your Commodore* simply dubbed it "a first-rate game".

> *"Andrew Braybrook was hired, and Graftgold was born."*

Paradroid / *1985*

Alleykat / *1986*

Completed in just three months, few could have predicted that Graftgold's next release, the strategic top-down shoot 'em up *Paradroid*, would become one of the C64's most pivotal games. Loosely based on Braybrook's mainframe game *Assassin*, *Paradroid*'s mix of stealth and strategy, immaculate presentation and meticulous attention to detail significantly raised the bar for C64 gaming. *Your Computer* gave the game 5/5, calling it "highly addictive," while *Zzap!64* awarded the game 97%, branding *Paradroid* "THE classic shoot 'em up" and earning Graftgold a much-deserved Gold Medal'.

Graftgold's next title was the slick, adrenaline-pumping shoot em up *Uridium*, which arrived in the spring of '86. Driven by Braybrook's desire to create a game with the smoothest scrolling possible, *Uridium* took inspiration from arcade blasters like *Starforce* and *Zaxxon*, resulting in a blisteringly fast and frenetic space battle across 15 bas-relief dreadnoughts. 'You won't drop your joystick for days," said *C&VG*, awarding *Uridium* 10/10, while *Zzap!64* gave the game a 'Sizzler', calling it "immaculate in both its execution and conception".

"Graftgold's output on the C64 between 1984 and 1990 was unprecedented."

Keen to push the boundaries, Graftgold's next C64 outing was *Alleykat*, a futuristic racing game inspired by Activision's *Pastfinder*. However, *Alleykat*'s innovative season structure and absorbing blend of gameplay styles confounded expectations, resulting in a unique user experience but a mixed reception from reviewers. Narrowly missing out on a 'Sizzler', *Zzap!64* urged readers to "try before you buy." Conversely, *C&VG* thought it "a cracking game," while *Your Computer* gave *AlleyKat* 5/5, calling it "another great game from Andrew Braybrook".

1986 concluded with the timely Christmas release of Hewson's *Uridium* and *Paradroid* double pack. The compilation featured *Uridium+*, boasting all new ships and some rather special C128-only enhancements, and the '*Competition Edition*' of *Paradroid*, which benefitted from a hefty 50% increase in speed. Awarding it 9/10, *Your Commodore* praised *Uridium+*'s "superb new ships" and thought *Paradroid* "even more enjoyable [than the original]."

1987 saw the release of *Ranarama*, a charming *Gauntlet*-inspired arcade adventure converted from the Spectrum by Graftgold newcomer Gary J. Foreman. Casting players in the role of Mervyn the frog, the aim was to explore the dungeon and wipe out the invading horde of evil Warlocks using all manner of glyphs and spells. Despite similarities to both *Gauntlet* and *Paradroid*, the reviews were unanimously positive. "A hit that shouldn't be missed," said *C&VG*, while *Zzap!64* thought it "beautifully designed, rewarding and incredibly playable".

Despite being finished towards the end of 1987, it was several months before Morpheus hit the streets due to a protracted legal dispute between Hewson and Telecomsoft. A complete departure from Braybrook's previous titles, *Morpheus* was a deep and complex strategy game wrapped around a deceptively simple premise. Highly polished and packed with subtleties, the reviews were naturally effusive. "*Morpheus* reeks of quality and professionalism," said *Commodore User*, awarding the game a coveted 'CU Superstar', while *Zzap!64* called *Morpheus* "one of the most finely constructed games ever written for the 64".

Ivan 'Ironman' Stewart's Super Off Road / *1990*

Rainbow Islands / *1990*

Hot on *Morpheus*'s heels came *Magnetron*, a strategic flick-screen shoot 'em up converted from the ZX Spectrum. A subtle blend of *Paradroid* and *Spindizzy*, the game cast the player in the role of KLF-2, a droid on a mission to save planet Earth from its imminent doom. Despite the game's slick presentation, *Magnetron*'s similarities to *Paradroid* left many reviewers with a sense of déjà vu. "If you want a *Paradroid* game, you might as well buy the real thing," said *Zzap!64*, whereas *ACE* magazine was gushing with praise, calling *Magnetron* a "terrific droid 'em up".

In contrast to the complexity of *Morpheus*, the space strategy game *Intensity* – and Braybrook's C64 full-price swansong – made its understated debut towards the end of 1988. Set on board a deep-space mining station, *Intensity* was deceptively simple but, like many Braybrook games, far greater than the sum of its parts. Expectations were high, and reviews were mixed. "Some neat touches but the gameplay is dull," said *C&VG*, while *ACE* thought it was "highly competent but uninspiring". Conversely, *Commodore User* called *Intensity* "a big and complex game that's well worth the time and effort", with *Zzap!64* adding, "[it's] an excellent game."

1988 concluded with *Soldier of Fortune*, a charming and engaging arcade adventure created by Graftgold newcomer John Cummings. With a tip of the hat to *Ghosts 'n Goblins* and *Black Tiger*, *Soldier of Fortune* immersed players in an epic quest to find the legendary Zodiac power source and banish evil from the land.

"Not Graftgold's best ever game, but excellent nonetheless," said *Commodore User*, while *ACE* magazine simply called it "addictive stuff".

Braybrook's formidable success on the C64 culminated with the budget releases of *Gribbly's Special Day Out* and *Heavy Metal Paradroid* on Hewson's Rack-It label. Sporting various nip-tucks including tweaked controls and enhanced graphics, *Zzap!64* thought Gribbly had "lost none of its charm since its release in mid-1985." Similarly, *Heavy Metal Paradroid* built on the highly successful *Competition Edition*, adding all-new *Morpheus*-inspired graphics. "Definitely a winner!" said *Commodore User*, while *Zzap!64* once again awarded the game 97% and a Silver Medal, calling *Heavy Metal Paradroid* "a game no 64 owner should be without".

Graftgold's next game for Rack-It was *Orion*, an unrelenting platform shoot 'em up in the *Hawkeye* mould. Despite *Orion*'s budget price tag, the simplistic run-and-gun gameplay – a stark contrast to the immense depth of previous Graftgold titles – garnered mixed reviews. "Orion will probably sell just because of the Graftgold name," said *Zzap!64*, while *Commodore User* thought it "more than enough to keep you occupied for your dosh".

Orion was closely followed by *Head the Ball*, a charmingly twee arcade platformer-cum-shoot 'em up which appeared on Hewson's 4th Dimension compilation (and, poignantly, the last Graftgold game that Hewson released).

> *"Ask any C64 owner for their Top 10 games list, and, chances are, there'd be a Graftgold title in the mix."*

Despite rubbing shoulders with more accomplished titles by Apex Computer Productions and Sensible Software, *Head the Ball* thankfully managed to hold its own. "Head turns out to be surprisingly addictive," said *Zzap!64*, calling it "a wolf in sheep's clothing".

Following the sale of Telecomsoft, Graftgold's next title *Bushido* made its debut on the MicroProse label. A complex and absorbing arcade-style RPG set in feudal Japan, *Bushido* boasted a wealth of characters, countless items and incredible depth of gameplay, not to mention a fast and detailed world to explore. *Your Commodore* said, "it goes for the throat in a big way," while *ACE* called *Bushido* "very fast and very playable".

Delayed due to a legal tussle between Taito and MicroProse, Graftgold's stunning conversion of *Rainbow Islands* – by Gary Foreman – was finally released in the spring of 1990. Authentic to the coin-op in almost every regard, this second sickeningly sweet adventure of Bub and Bob was nothing short of coding wizardry. *Your Commodore* gave *Rainbow Islands* 97%, calling it "dangerously addictive," while *Zzap!64* thought it "a remarkably accurate conversion in both look and feel".

Graftgold's final C64 release was *Ivan 'Ironman' Stewart's Super Off Road*, a track-based dirt racer converted from the highly successful coin-op. Another flawless conversion, the C64 incarnation of *Super Off Road* remained incredibly faithful to the original, right down to the simultaneous three-player action. *C&VG* awarded the game a 'C+VG Hit!', calling it "one of the best C64 games we've seen in a very long time," while *Zzap!64* thought Graftgold had worked wonders, branding *Super Off Road* "instantly addictive".

After leaving the 8-bit machines behind, Graftgold continued to work on numerous successful games and conversions for the Amiga, Atari ST and PC, as well as consoles including the SNES, Mega Drive, PC Engine and PlayStation. However, rising development costs coupled with multiple publisher buyouts and industry instability led to Graftgold's eventual sale to Perfect Entertainment in 1998.

Ask any C64 owner for their Top 10 games list, and, chances are, there'll be a Graftgold title in the mix. Strikingly original, technically adept, packed with depth and highly polished, anticipating the arrival of a new Graftgold game was like waiting for Christmas, each one a labour of love crafted by some of the most astute and talented developers the C64 has ever seen.

Gribbly's Day Out / *1985*

Released
1989

Genre
Shoot 'em up

Developer
Special FX

Publisher
Ocean

Originally by
TAD Corporation

Cabal

"Boy, did I love making this game. The C64 version was created by just two of us, myself and coder Robbie Tinman. As the only artist, I did everything: characters, animation, environments, objects, effects, menus, and also the title screen. I used a drawing package called *KoalaPainter*, which came with the KoalaPad, a type of basic graphics tablet. Robbie wrote some code and, with a switch and a soldering iron, created a mouse that worked with *KoalaPainter*, which, at the time, was a godsend. It was also the first time I had used an overlay sprite with an expanded underlay sprite."

Ivan Davies, graphic artist

Shinobi

"I was very excited to get a chance to work with Simon Pick, who'd just done a cracking conversion of *Nemesis* on the C64. He had proved that it was possible to successfully emulate a cool arcade machine on the C64, so we applied the same tricks to *Shinobi*. It did help quite a lot having the actual arcade machine next to my desk. I think we managed to get pretty much most of the content in there, including the giant helicopter boss, which we did by making the helicopter a scrolling background and building the foreground with static sprites."

Ned Langman, graphic artist

Released
1989

Genre
Action

Developer and publisher
Virgin Games

Originally by
SEGA

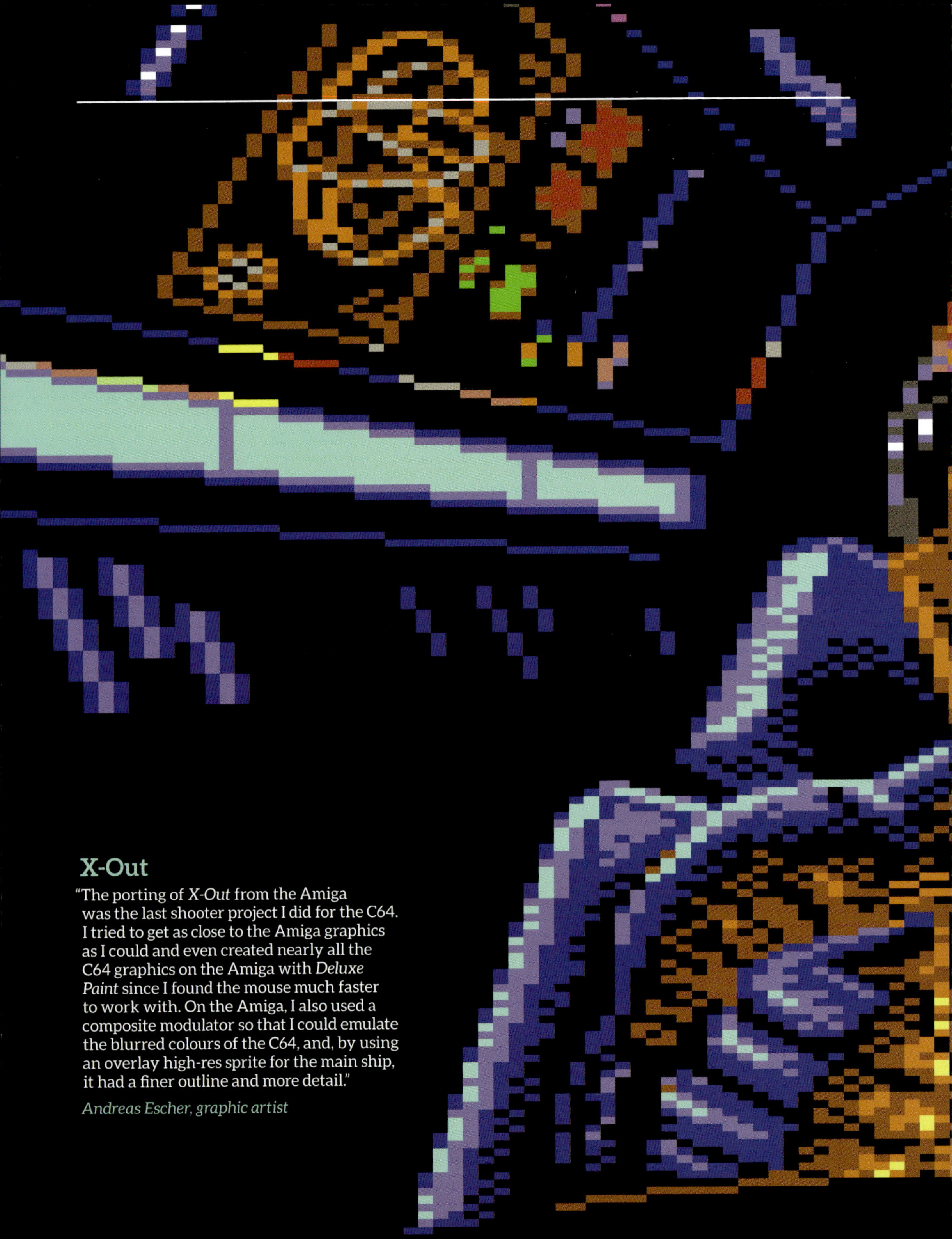

X-Out

"The porting of *X-Out* from the Amiga was the last shooter project I did for the C64. I tried to get as close to the Amiga graphics as I could and even created nearly all the C64 graphics on the Amiga with *Deluxe Paint* since I found the mouse much faster to work with. On the Amiga, I also used a composite modulator so that I could emulate the blurred colours of the C64, and, by using an overlay high-res sprite for the main ship, it had a finer outline and more detail."

Andreas Escher, graphic artist

Released
1989

Genre
Scrolling shooter

Developer and publisher
Rainbow Arts

Released
1989

Genre
Shoot 'em up

Developers
Apex Computer Productions and Transmission Software

Publisher
Thalamus

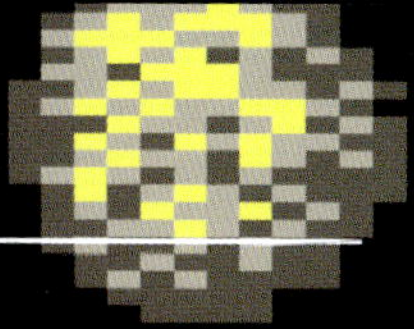

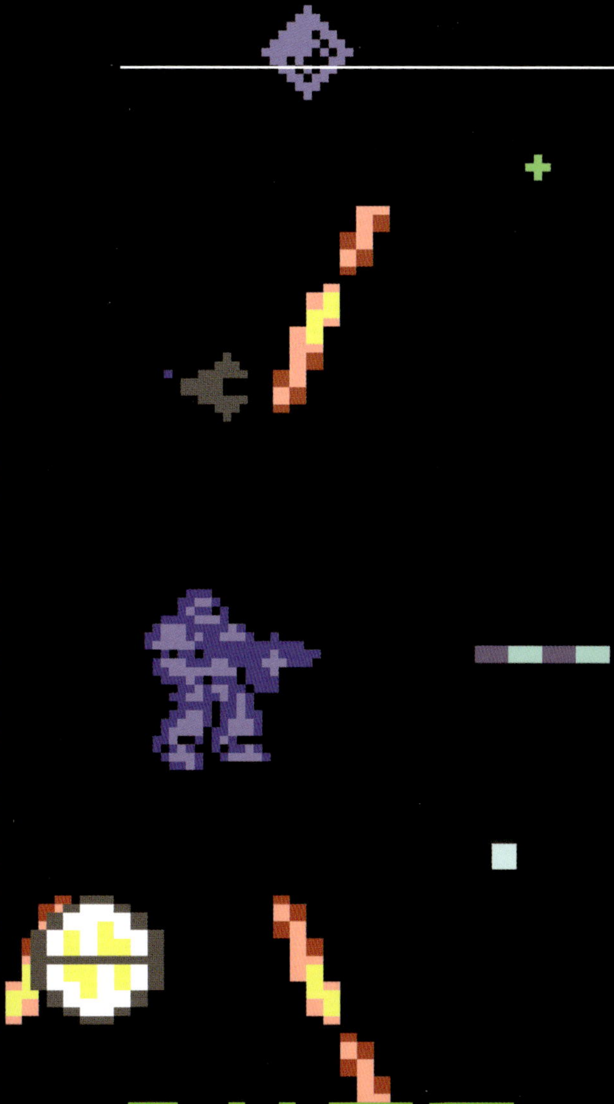

Retrograde

"Heavily influenced by the arcade titles *Hyper Dyne Side Arms* and *Forgotten Worlds*, as well as characters and environments from realms created by Games Workshop, Steve and I teamed up with our closest friend, Robin Ellis, to create a shoot 'em up on a grand scale. Although preceded by *Cyberdyne Warrior* (released on compilation through Hewson), this was our first major game. We all felt proud of the final product, particularly the unique weapons system, and equally proud of securing a publishing deal with Thalamus."

John Rowlands, designer and programmer

"Initially this horizontally scrolling blaster has you collecting credits, upgrading your primary weapons, blasting aliens and punching down robots with your powerfist, while looking for an access key to what lies beneath the planet's surface. Once you've found a way in, more blasting awaits, but now the gameplay switches to a vertical scrolling platformer. Two of these levels see the first planet destroyed, and a huge *R-Type*-style boss tries to stop your escape. This game has everything from outstanding music and well-drawn sprites to a much deeper level of gameplay than your usual 2D blaster. Well ahead of its time."

Andy Hayes, guest reviewer

Released *1989* / **Genre** *Scrolling shooter* / **Developer and publisher** *System 3*

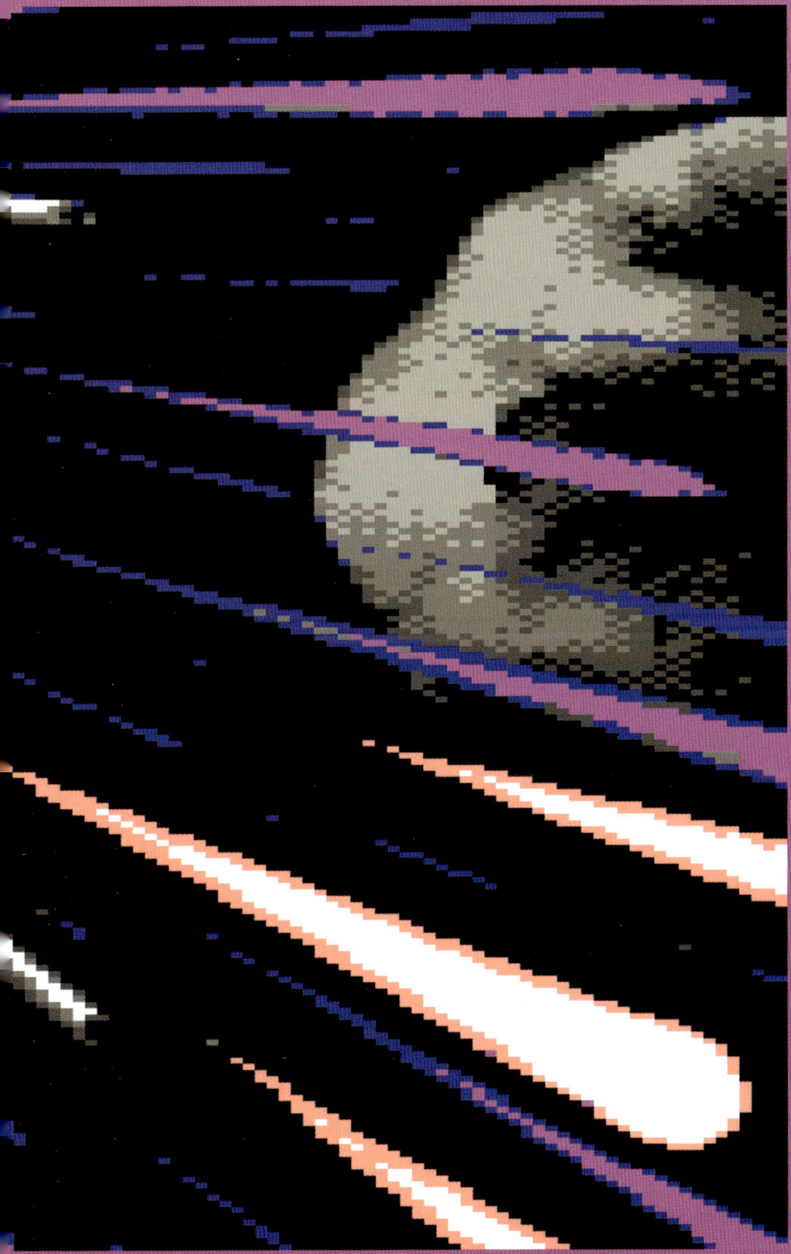

Dominator

"I was a big fan of side-scrolling shoot 'em ups, such as *Armalyte*, *Delta*, *IO* and that crazy version of *Salamander* that Bob (Stevenson) worked on. I finally got my chance to work on a shoot 'em up title at System 3 when they put me on *Dominator*. Hugh Riley had started work on it before he left to form Vivid Image, and I was brought in to create the sprite animations and loading screen. I didn't believe at the time that my style would mesh with Hugh's, but I think, in the end, it turned out quite well."

Paul Docherty, graphic artist

"When I was developing music, I had a little Casio MT-45 keyboard (the ones with all the pre-set rhythms on) which I used to work out chords and melodies with very basic sounds. I had a desk in my room that had the C64 and a portable TV on it, so I was totally isolated in my room and undisturbed. By the time I did *Dominator* for System 3, a dance-track influence was increasingly creeping into my music. This game was developed at System 3's then-new location in London. Paul Docherty was working there by then, along with Stan Schembri, who is sadly no longer with us. Stan was a real character, quick-witted and always good for a laugh. I didn't get to know everyone there very well, though, because I was still happy to work remotely from home."

Matt Gray, musician

An interview with **Robin Levy**

***A founding member of renowned C64 developer Cyberdyne Systems, Robin Levy's jaw-dropping sprites, backgrounds and level design for Thalamus's seminal title* Armalyte *quickly earned him a place among the Commodore 64's most accomplished pixel artists. After jumping ship to System 3, his impressive legacy continued on titles such as* Last Ninja 3, Turbo Charge *and the ill-fated* Deadlock.**

How did you first get interested in computers?

Video games fascinated me from the first time I saw and heard a *Space Invaders* or *Asteroids* cabinet, and, although I wasn't tall enough to get a good look at the screen, I still admired the cabinet art and was entranced by the sound effects.

It wasn't until I was old enough to get a paper round that my parents agreed to get a VIC-20 on hire purchase and let me reimburse the payments. I had a year of seeing the VIC-20 being supplanted by the C64, but, thankfully, I got a C64 the following year, just a few months before the debut issue of *Zzap!64*.

How did your career in the games industry get started?

It started in a local shop called Computerwear that was run by a very long-suffering gentleman who didn't complain too much that all the local games geeks hung around. It was there I met the other members of Cyberdyne, Dan Philips and John Kemp, as well as Rob Stevens (who went on to code *Barbarian II* for Palace). My personal breakthrough was getting *Vidcom64*, an awesomely cheap art package. I blew Dan and John away when I showed them my serpent picture (seen on the flipside of the *Hunter's Moon* disk), which was based on the *Salamander* arcade cabinet art. As I was getting to grips with C64 art, Dan and John got an optimised full-screen scroller working, and we started thinking about possibly making games.

Rob Stevens utterly floored us with his sprite multiplexor and graciously showed Dan how it worked; Dan made his own version, and we put together a demo featuring 32 sprites bouncing over a full-screen scrolling background. We showed our demo to Steve Jarratt and Julian Rignall at the Newsfield stand at a computer show, and they enthusiastically put us in touch with Paul Cooper of Thalamus.

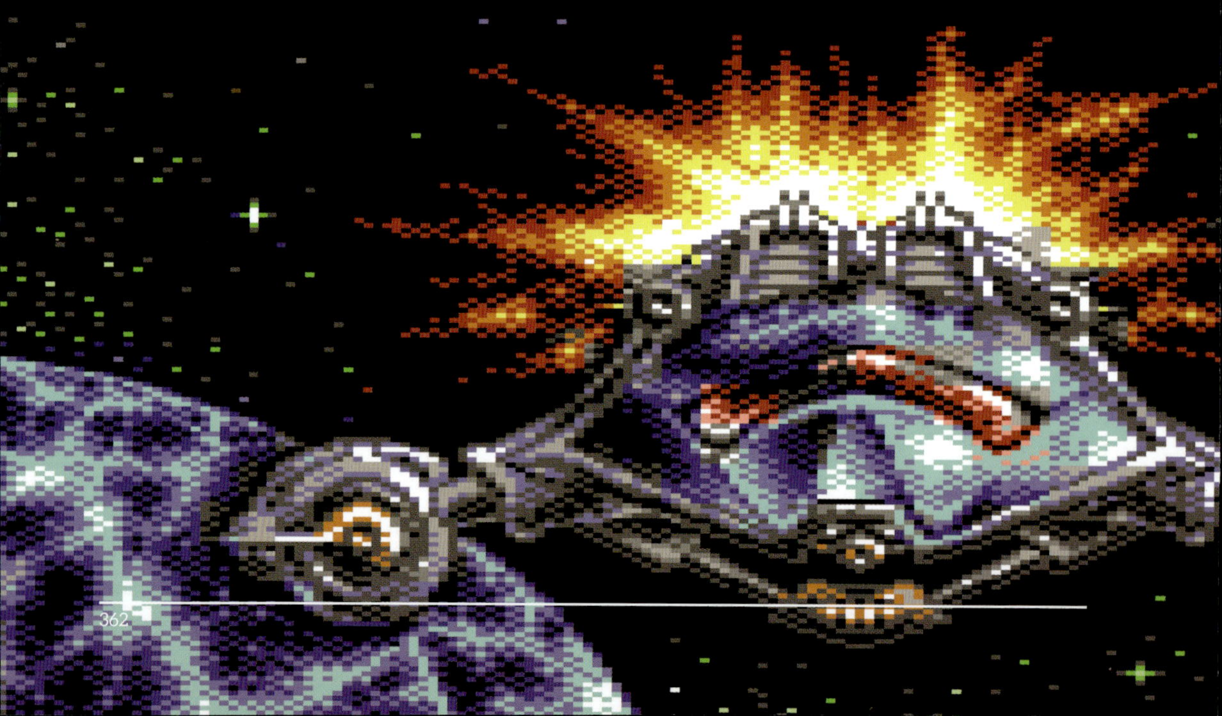

What was your first C64 project?
The first C64 game I contributed to was *Hunter's Moon*, for which I produced the loading screen and end sequence graphics.

What did a typical day in front of the computer look like for you?
Our typical working day would start mid-afternoon and carry on till daybreak the next day (or the day after that – working 24 or 36 hours straight was a common occurrence in the early days). After moving to System 3, we started working more sociable hours, although I would still occasionally pull an all-nighter, something I've only stopped doing in recent years.

You worked on several games with Martin Walker; what was the experience like?
Paul Cooper visited us and brought Martin to brief me on the *Hunter's Moon* loading screen, sound us out as a team, and discuss helping master the game (we had a custom-written fast tape loader). A month or so later, we spent four days at the duplicators creating the end sequence and mastering the game; this was the longest period I have ever stayed awake (88 hours!).

Frankly, we loved Martin. He was hugely encouraging and did a fabulous job of the *Armalyte* sounds and provided a solid piece of original theme music. Personally, he was a great mentor and introduced me to lots of music and art, as well as giving lots of creative insights. Unfortunately for Martin, I think the relationship was very one-sided as he had deep reserves of polite patience, whereas I had a poor grasp of personal boundaries and used to call him far too much!

Which programs did you use to create your C64 art?
I primarily used *Vidcom64* for bitmaps and *Steve Beats's Sprite Editor*, a fantastic program that allowed you to make sequenced animations as well as Boolean commands to combine sprites quickly and easily.

Did you use any custom tools that weren't available commercially?
I always tended to use custom editors for sequencing gameplay and creating maps. For *Armalyte*, I used a custom combination character editor, block maker and map creator for game maps and level data.

For *Last Ninja 3*, I used John Twiddy's '*Integrator*' program, which was also used by Hugh Riley and Dokk for the first two Last Ninja games and *Vendetta*. Even my copy of *Vidcom64* was modified by John Kemp to ease wear and tear on the keyboard!

What were the best and worst aspects of creating art for the C64?
The C64's drawbacks were also paradoxically its strengths and vice versa. As such, it served as a fantastic introduction to creating graphics. Everything was a trade-off with C64 art and design; the unholy trinity of memory, speed and quality had to be constantly balanced. By far the worst thing about the C64 was the change in the default colour palette during its lifetime; this realisation came late in my C64 career and made me want to move on to a new machine as soon as I could. Thanks, Commodore!

What was your process? Did you plan on paper, or jump straight in onto the computer?
I always planned my work beforehand to some degree; when embarking on a piece of C64 art you were going to be spending hours making a bitmap or committing system resources to in-game graphics, so planning was vital. Naturally, there were some situations where you could just jump in and create/edit on the fly, but, generally, if you did this from the get-go, you'd regret it further down the line.

> *"Dan Malone's* Sacred Armour of Antiriad *showed me just what an amazing artist could do with the C64."*

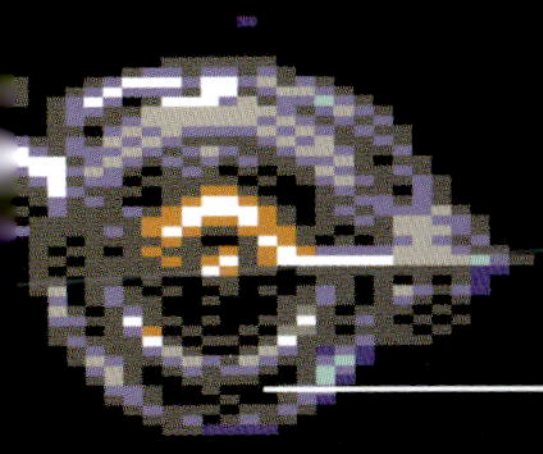

Armalyte / *1988*

How did your process change throughout your career?
It changed quite a lot although, if anything, I sketch stuff on paper even more than I did back in the '80s. Some things can be done on the fly; however, you instinctively know from experience how you want them to look before work commences.

What was the development time for a typical game?
Armalyte took us seven months from signing to finish, despite John Harries signing a contract to finish the game in a month before leaving Cyberdyne Systems to work as a project manager for Thalamus. *Deadlock* was a disaster as we didn't set ourselves any deadlines and development just went around in circles (this taught us to dispassionately evaluate what we were doing at regular intervals).

Did you receive much artistic direction, or would you say you had complete freedom?
Aside from basing some of my loading images on box art, I think the only formal art direction I ever got on the C64 was from Mark Cale's brother [Adrian] who asked me to do something like Duran Duran's *Wild Boys* video for the *Ninja 3* intro.

When creating C64 art, which aspect did you most enjoy?
Designing and testing the levels and environments.

Did you have much input in terms of game design?
I personally enjoy game design first and art second, and I have acted as both principle designer and artist on many games. *Armalyte*'s core systems weren't my design, but the levels that used them were, so, once I started using them, I would suggest refinements. Overall, it was a collaborative process, and having a clear and shared vision was vital.

Did you pay much attention to the various magazine reviews?
It depended on the project. If you were an art monkey you tended not to care as it was just a job; I felt this way about *Turbo Charge*, as I had virtually no input into the actual game. On *Armalyte*, where we worked for less money to do something we believed in, the reception from the press and end users was of vital importance.

If you had the chance to revisit any of your games, what would you change?
On the C64, there are only two games I would like to revisit: I have already done a fair bit of work on an *Armalyte* sequel but *Deadlock* would need rebuilding from the ground up.

Was there anyone in the industry whose work was inspirational to you?
Dan Malone's *Sacred Armour of Antiriad* showed me just what an amazing artist could do with the C64 and still have a game that works. Artists like Bob Stevenson, Hugh Riley, STE'86, and SIT were also a huge inspiration (Bob, in particular, was both a skilled artist and self-publicist that I could have learned a lot from had I had a more open mind). I also adored Dokk's work, which was superb technically but also had a unique energy and soul.

I was also inspired by coders that made the C64 look great; Andrew Braybrook, Jeff Minter and Tony Crowther were all very, very good graphic designers, and I sought to emulate them just as much as the dedicated artists.

What games impressed you, or had an influence on your work?
Palace, Thalamus, Graftgold, Sensible Software, Odin, Ultimate, Epyx, early EA and Llamasoft all produced games that impressed me. From a design point of view, I always end up drawing on my experiences of *Boulder Dash* and *Impossible Mission*, the first games I truly loved. Games like *Scarabaeus* and *Dropzone* I also adored visually.

Citadel / *1989*

Last Ninja Remix / *1990*

Outside of games, what were your biggest artistic influences?
I adored comics as a storytelling medium and still regularly buy *2000 AD* to this day. I had a fondness for '70s sci-fi artwork, and I have huge respect for good sci-fi concept design. One thing that has become glaringly apparent since the arrival of the Internet is the sheer wealth of talent that is out there, so, nowadays, I tend to look for stuff that has a unique feel to it.

Of all the games you've worked on, which are you most proud of and why?
By far the game I'm proudest of is *Spacelings* on iOS, which I designed, created all the art for and produced the music and sound. This had a definite 8-bit design sensibility in the same vein as *Boulder Dash*. Oh yeah, *Armalyte* too.

Were there any C64 games you worked on which sadly never saw the light of day?
Apart from *Deadlock*, not many. We were working on a *Sinistar*-esque game called *Scimitar*; created by John Kemp (the guy who wrote all of our editors), it featured a hi-res overlay ship with 'scimitar wings' moving across an amazing omnidirectional starfield. It's a shame we didn't concentrate on this instead of *Deadlock*.

What was your final C64 game? What made you decide to leave the machine behind?
My final game was *Turbo Charge*. I personally didn't like the game but really enjoyed drawing all the screens (I apologise for the distasteful end sequence!). By this point, I was getting much faster and more confident, but the colour difference between new and old C64s sucked out my enthusiasm. Oh, how I was glad to move on to the Amiga – if I ever had to draw another C64 chunk-o-vision sprite, I might have gone quite mad.

Was there a C64 game you would have loved to have created the graphics for?
Not really, although, in the early days, I would often use hacking cartridges to put my own sprites into published games to test my abilities.

Looking back, what was your favourite C64 game?
I played a lot of different C64 games for enjoyment, depending on my mood. I even had a hacked version of *IK+* that John Kemp made for me that stopped the game ending when you win; I always disliked the fact that *IK+* played so well but would end before it started getting fun.

"Braybrook, Minter and Crowther were all very, very good graphic designers, and I sought to emulate them just as much as the dedicated artists."

Do you have any standout memories from the C64 era?
Playing the first version of the first level of *Armalyte* for the first time, which landed us our first contract (produced when I was drunk for the first time – a lot of firsts there!). I also recall John Kemp calling me a bastard with a massive smirk on his face after watching me test the first draft of level five!

Why do you think the C64 is remembered so fondly?
Colourful graphics, awesome sound and some great games!

Do you still own a C64?
No, unfortunately, my last C64 died many, many years ago.

What are you up to these days?
Struggling freelance designer, artist, and musician looking for that dream job while working on my own art and music in the meantime.

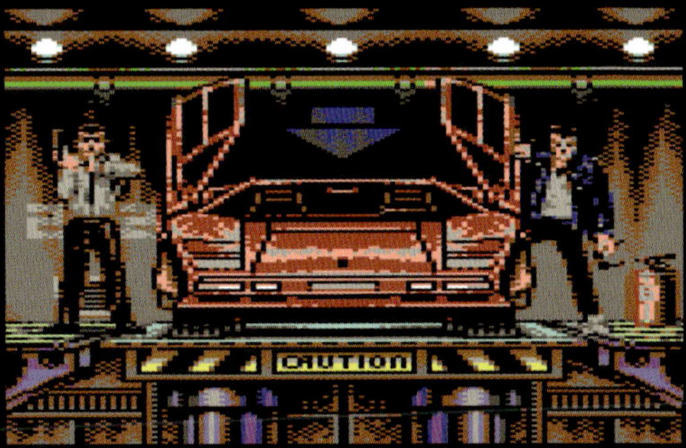

Turbo Charge / *1991*

Last Ninja 3 / *1991*

Dragon Wars

Released
1989

Genre
RPG

Developer
Interplay Productions

Publisher
Electronic Arts

The unofficial fourth game in the Bard's Tale series, *Dragon Wars* manages to shake up a tired genre with innovations such as branching paths, optional side-quests, and multiple solutions to any given predicament. After reaching the lost utopia of Dilmun, your party is accused of practising outlawed magic and imprisoned in the city of Purgatory. Here you learn of a much bigger plot to conquer the world, and thus you and your crew must escape the town and ultimately take down this unspeakable evil. Exceptionally well-crafted and presented, with a myriad of neat touches and infinite replay value, it's undoubtedly one of the best RPGs around.

"*Dragon Wars* was our attempt at merging the lessons learned from *Wasteland* and *Bard's Tale* together in an RPG. We took the party-based gameplay of *Bard's Tale* and brought in the non-linear elements that we liked so much. I think, in the very first area, there were more than four ways to get out of the prison, and people didn't realise it until after they compared notes with other players. It was also quite special that I got to work with one of my favourite artists of all time: Boris Vallejo."

Brian Fargo, co-designer

Released
1989

Genre
Racing

Developer
Magnetic Fields

Publisher
Gremlin Graphics

Super Scramble Simulator

"Many of the ideas I had for *Kikstart II* weren't right for it. At a time when you could only dream of 3D, I was impressed with the SEGA arcade game *Super Locomotive*, spending long Saturday afternoons playing it. It featured a unique dual perspective, with side and top views that were negotiated in synchrony. I combined this concept with *Kikstart*, adding the big graphics of an arcade game but wanting the feel of a simulator. It was innovative and visually impressive but lacked the fun and competition aspects of *Kikstart*. I never made that mistake again."

Andrew Morris, co-designer and graphic artist

Stunt Car Racer

Geoff Crammond's C64 swansong places you in the driving seat of a turbocharged V8 stunt car as you attempt to crush the opposition and earn your place at the top of the first division. The game boasts eight challenging tracks, each one loaded with all manner of undulating bumps, banked corners, ramps, and jumps. Thankfully, your car is equipped with long-travel suspension which allows you to land safely after catching some air, albeit with a few cracks in the chassis. Not only is the game enormous fun, it's also nail-bitingly tense; there's an incredible feeling of helplessness as your car flies through the air, and the elevated tracks add a dash of anxiety to every manoeuvre.

"While Geoff Crammond went on to focus on realistic F1 games, nothing can beat the offbeat appeal of *Stunt Car Racer*. The insane tracks, with all of their loops and jumps, provide an exhilarating rollercoaster ride. While a tad jerky, it's still an amazing technical achievement and so addictive too. The number of times I must have wrecked my car, but I kept coming back for more."

Phil King, games journalist

Released
1989

Genre
Racing

Developer
Geoff Crammond

Publisher
MicroStyle

Citadel

"Many shoot 'em up games pit you against a relentless and totally predictable onslaught of foes. *Citadel* was my stab for the 'thinking' player who occasionally wanted to stop and consider what to do next, by making all traps, weapons and gate switches triggered by proximity. By creating futuristic cities on twin levels linked by lift shafts, each choice of move and direction on their tiled floors determined what happened next, thus combining the strategy of a board game with elements of an adventure game, plus plenty of blasting action along the way."

Martin Walker, designer, musician and programmer

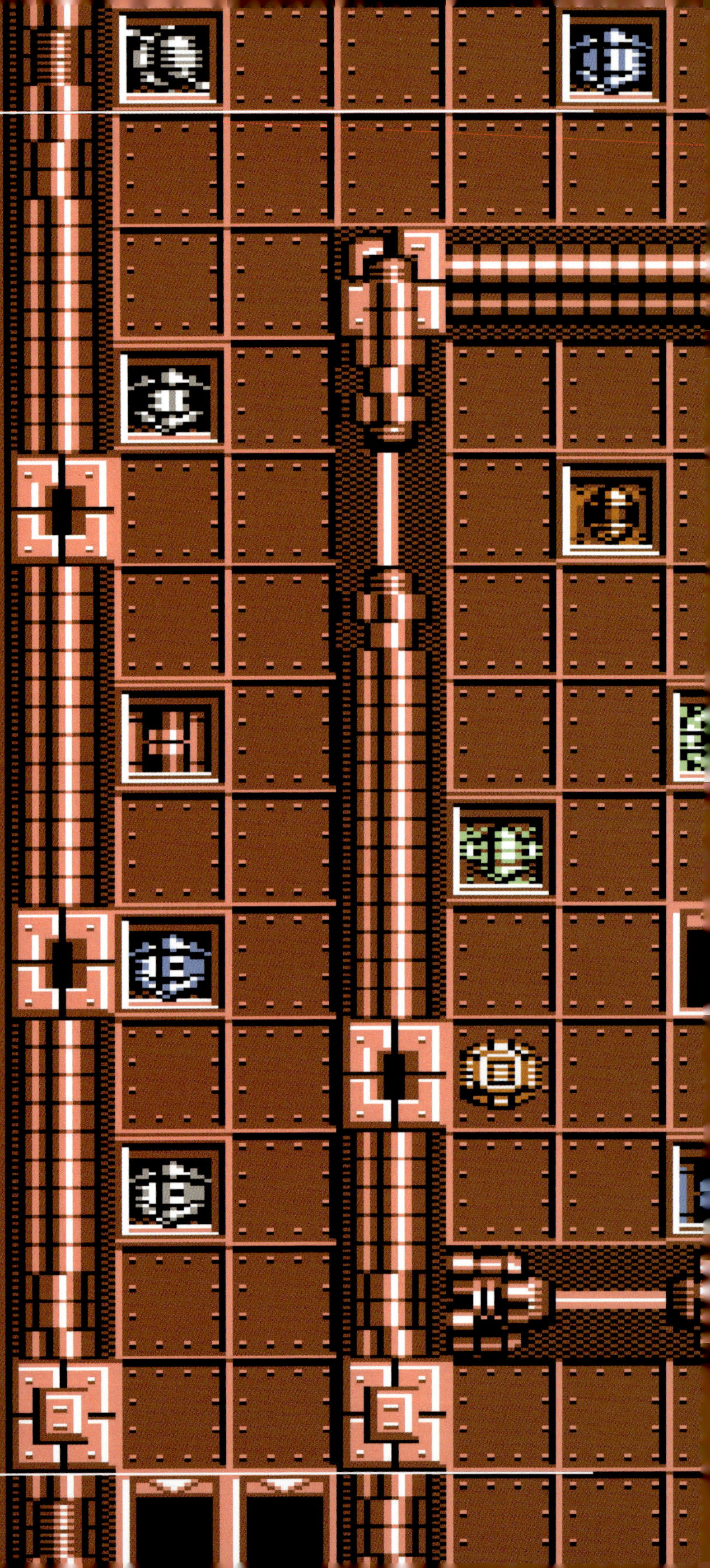

Released
1989

Genre
Puzzle shooter

Developer
Martin Walker

Publisher
Electric Dreams

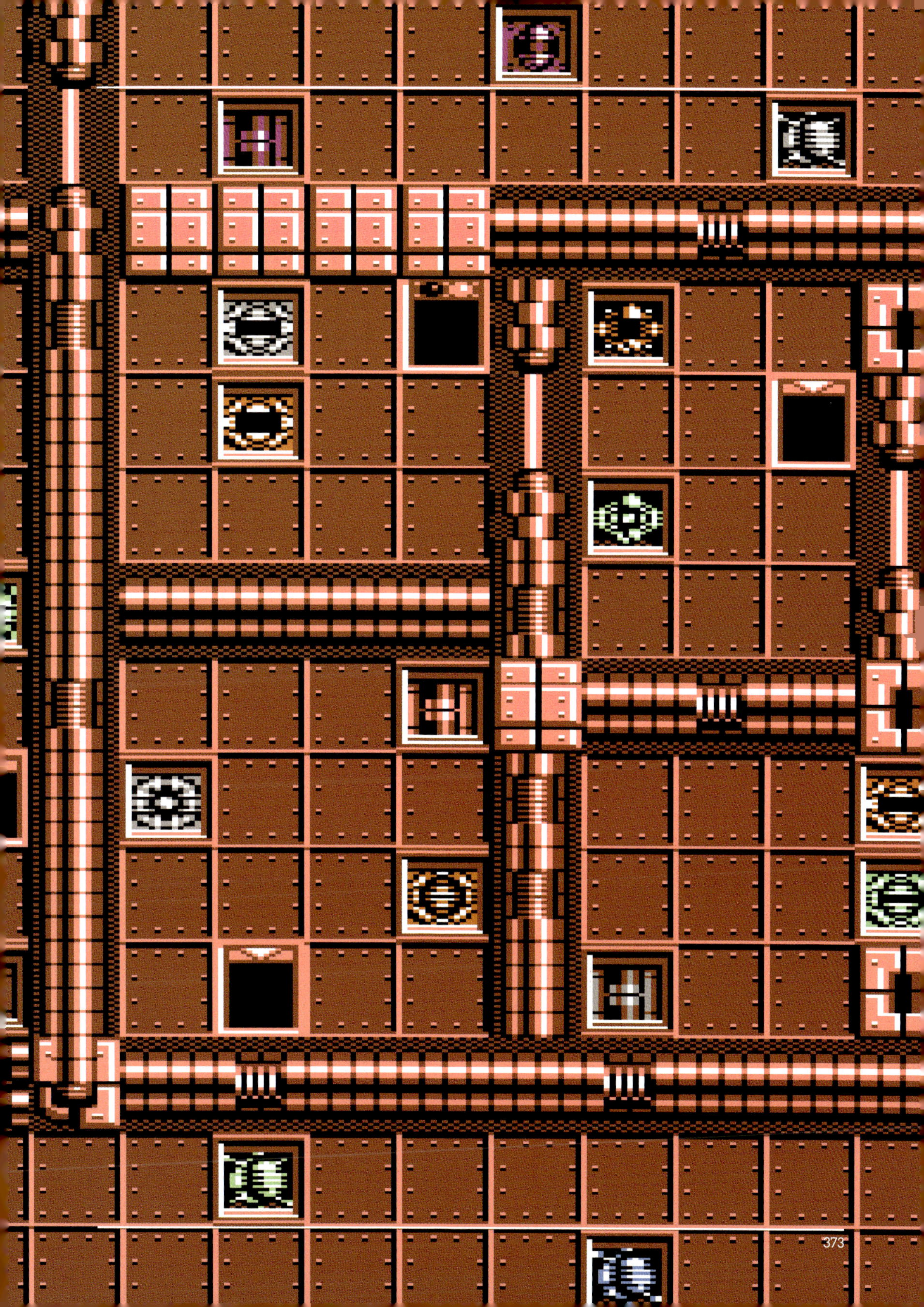

Space Rogue

There's no doubt that Origin knows its stuff when it comes to RPGs, and *Space Rogue*'s blend of 2D sci-fi RPG and 3D space flight simulation propels the genre to another level entirely. After your ship is wiped out during a recon mission, you find yourself alone in deep space, contemplating your next move. From here, you have complete freedom to explore the various star systems, visiting planets, bases, and space stations and undertaking missions to earn valuable resources. While *Elite* is often regarded as the definitive space trading game, *Space Rogue*'s sophistication and depth undoubtedly make it a worthy contender for the crown.

"It took until 1989 for a worthy successor to *Elite* to emerge, and *Space Rogue* did just that, taking the strong storyline of an Origin adventure and putting it into the limitless possibilities of space, adding gripping combat to boot. A well-deserved Gold Medal in *Zzap!64*, *Space Rogue* remains an underappreciated classic."

Robin Hogg, games journalist

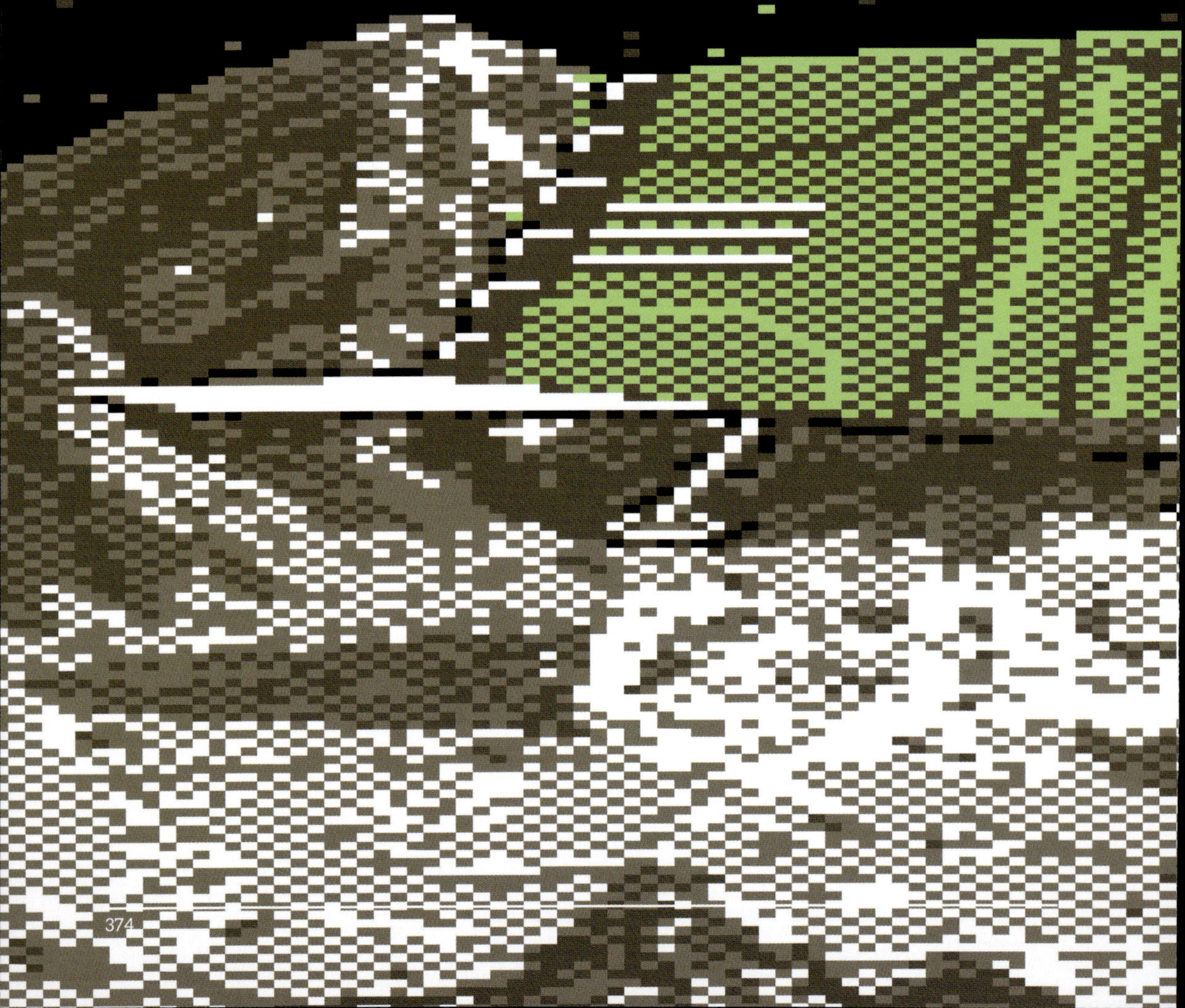

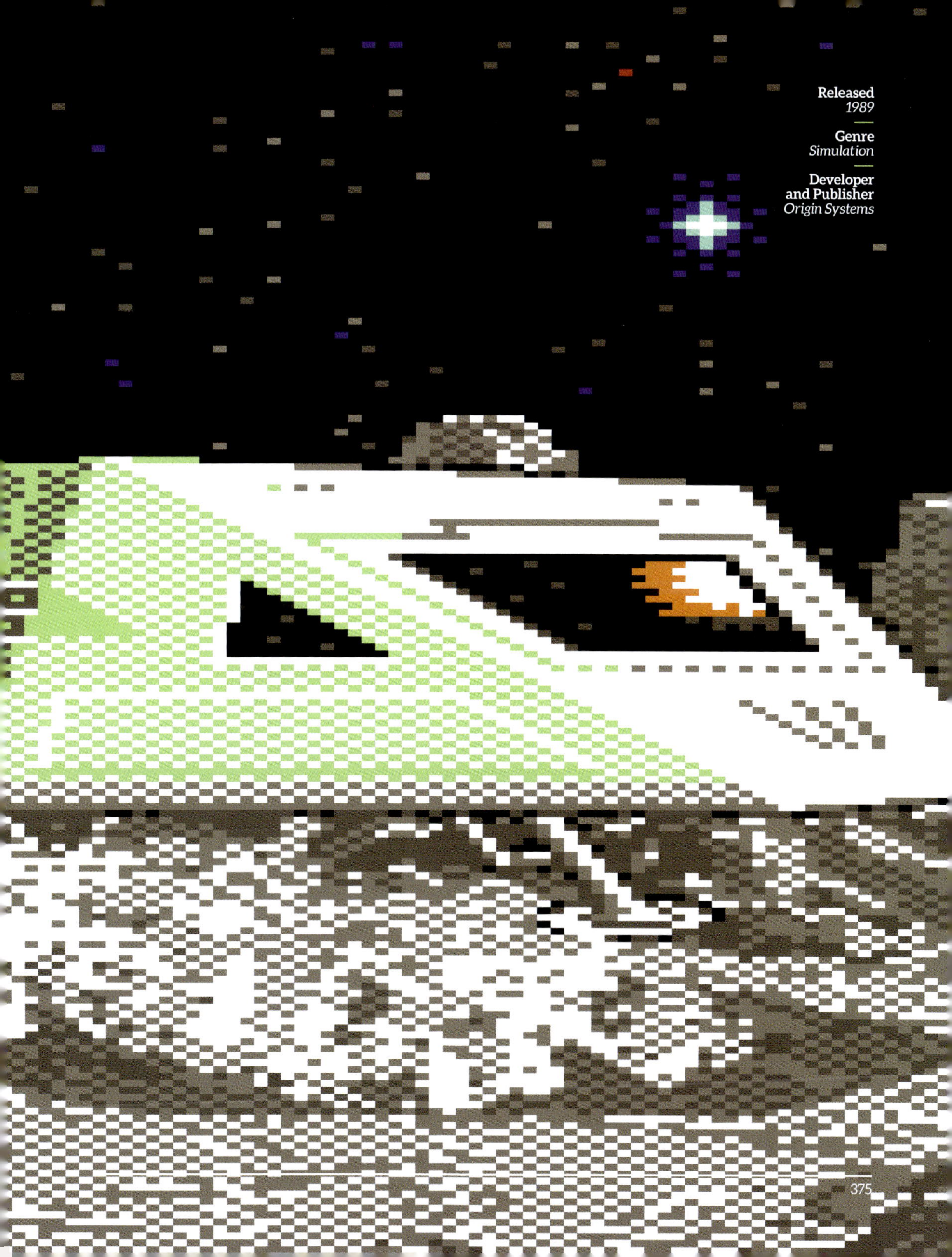

Released
1989

Genre
Simulation

Developer and Publisher
Origin Systems

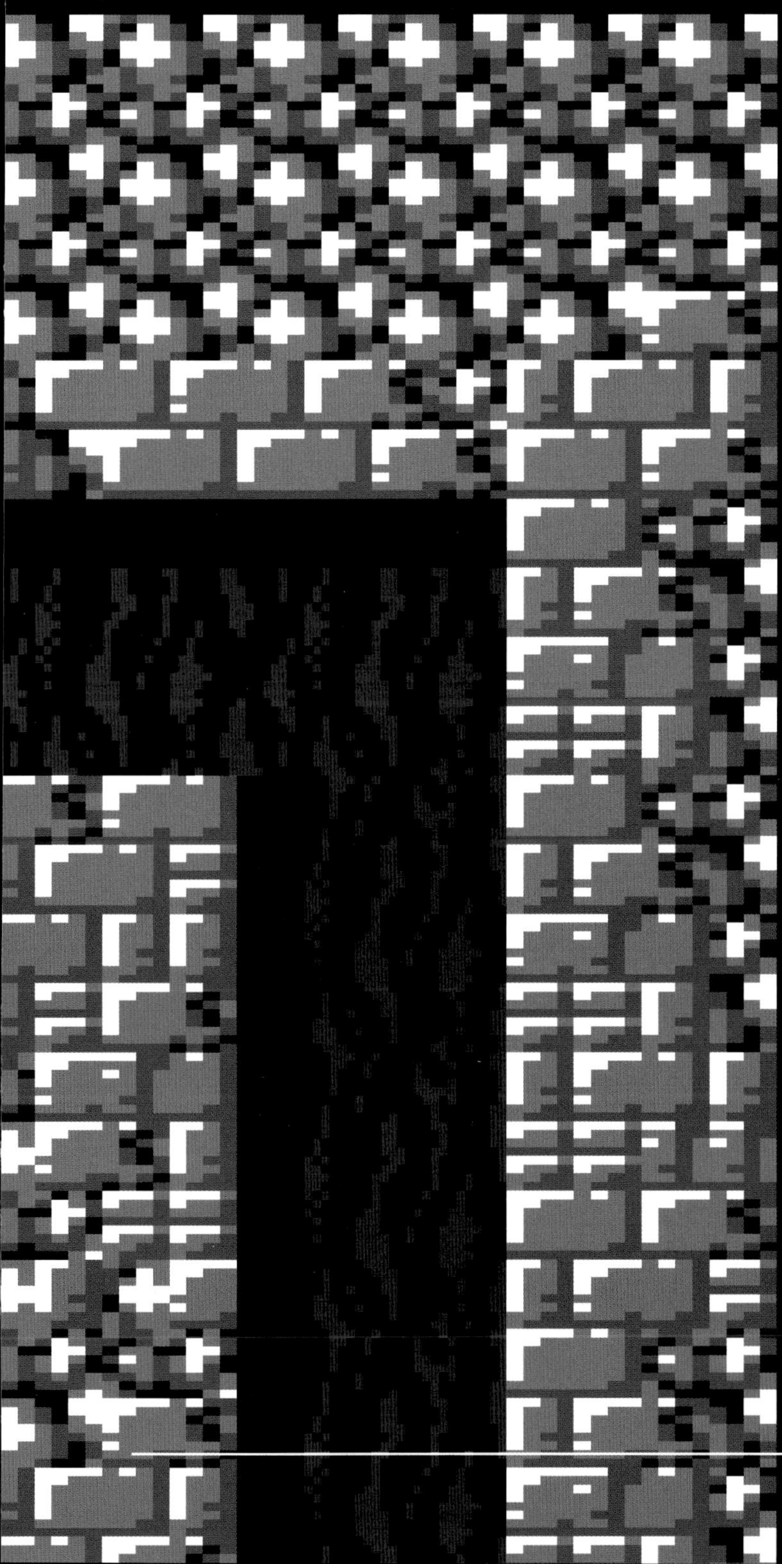

Rick Dangerous

A love letter to *Raiders of the Lost Ark*, *Rick Dangerous* is an action platformer in which our fedora-festooned hero must travel to various locations around the globe in search of adventure. Gameplay involves traversing multiple trap-laden screens spread across four vertically scrolling levels, but, fortunately, Rick has an arsenal of tricks up his sleeve: enemies can be dispatched with the revolver (or pointy stick), while the dynamite is handy for removing obstacles which block the way. Throw in a wacky plot and some entertaining cartoon interludes, and you have the perfect recipe for one of the most maddeningly addictive games on the C64.

"The C64's 24x21 pixel hardware sprites had the biggest impact on the design of *Rick Dangerous* across all formats. To build the game for five different systems in under four months, Terry Lloyd and I realised that the most efficient way to go was to draw everything so it would work on the C64. Although inspired by the art of Guillermo Mordillo, the squashed look of Rick and his enemies owes much to the VIC-II chip's limitations more than anything else."

Simon Phipps, co-designer and graphic artist

Released
1989

Genre
Action

Developer
Core Design

Publisher
Firebird

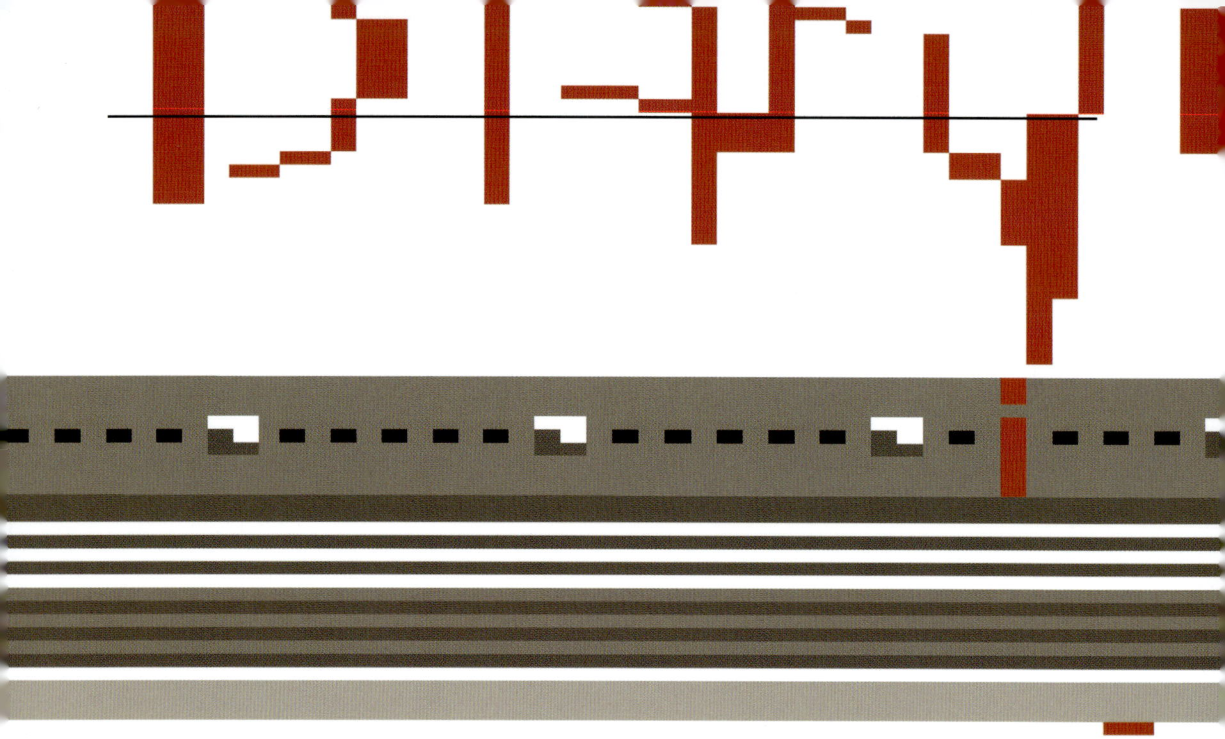

Project Firestart

"Survival horror – the early years. *Project Firestart* is a great homage to films like *Alien* and made a real mark (albeit not commercially) with an engaging plot, disturbing cutscenes and fearful atmosphere. Along with multiple endings, you've got the recipe for a great next-gen game right there."

Robin Hogg, games journalist

Released
1989

Genre
Action adventure

Developer
Dynamix

Publisher
Electronic Arts

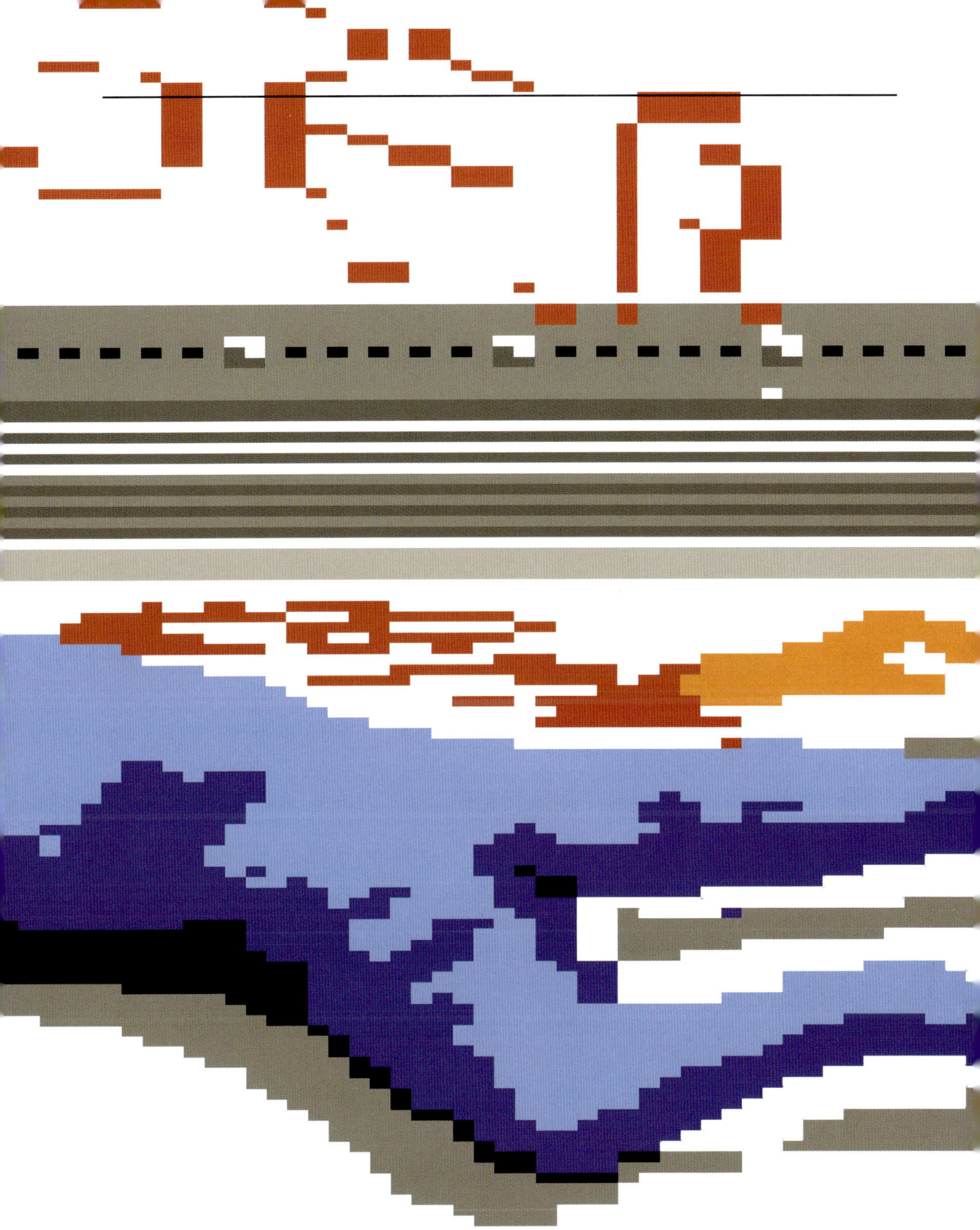

Released *1989* / **Genre** *Action* / **Developer and Publisher** *Ocean*

RoboCop

"I remember going to a computer show at Earls Court armed with a newly created *RoboCop* bitmap. By unbelievable chance, Ocean was looking for an artist for its new *RoboCop* game. Gary Bracey saw my image, and I got the job on the spot! At literally the last minute, I had to add some blurb about the video release and, until a few months ago, I had never noticed the typo. Oh dear!"

Stephen Ian Thomson, grahic artist

Released *1989* / **Genre** *Action* / **Developer and Publisher** *Ocean*

The Untouchables

"I had to make a lot of likeness tweaks to actors due to copyright issues. I believe this was the reason Bob Wakelin was commissioned to paint an alternative cover for the game. This was never used, but it looked so cool, I had to use it as the title page! Due to the resolution issue on the C64, I did a small section from the centre."

Stephen Ian Thomson, grahic artist

Released *1990* / Genre *Action* / Developer and Publisher *Ocean*

Navy SEALs

"For the title screen, I really wanted to do a sort of graphic novel which essentially would be a flipbook of screens. I don't think this had been done before. With the game being on a cartridge, we were able to fit a lot more on – unfortunately, time was against us, and I was unable to do this. We settled on the logo for the title screen. It came out OK, but I hate the lack of anti-aliasing!"

Stephen Ian Thomson, grahic artist

Released *1990* / Genre *Shoot 'em up* / Developer and Publisher *Ocean*

Operation Thunderbolt

"This was a 'get it done now' project. I think we had about six weeks start to end to complete the whole thing. I don't think they even wanted a loading screen, but I ended up doing one in my own time while the game was being tested. Paul Hughes slipped it in at the last minute. I think I copied this from a movie poster. Can you guess which one?!"

Stephen Ian Thomson, grahic artist

Turrican

In this vast action-packed run and gun set across thirteen sprawling levels, our hero must hunt down Morgul, an unspeakable three-headed beast responsible for all of humanity's fears and nightmares. Like any self-respecting shoot 'em up, there's plenty of fodder to annihilate along the way, huge end-of-level bosses to tackle, and a multitude of ways to upgrade your firepower. You can also transform into a *Metroid*-style gyroscope, which allows you to roll through the level relatively unhindered. The brainchild of Manfred Trenz, *Turrican* is an absolute tour de force, both in terms of scope and sheer technical mastery, and one of the greatest C64 games of all time.

"I have a vivid memory of first seeing *Turrican* in the *Zzap!64* office. We were all blown away by it, particularly the graphical variety of the vast labyrinthine levels and some awesome bosses. This is matched by the amazing arsenal of the hero, including the trademark rotating power beam and innovative gyroscope. The gameplay is superbly designed and well balanced."

Phil King, games journalist

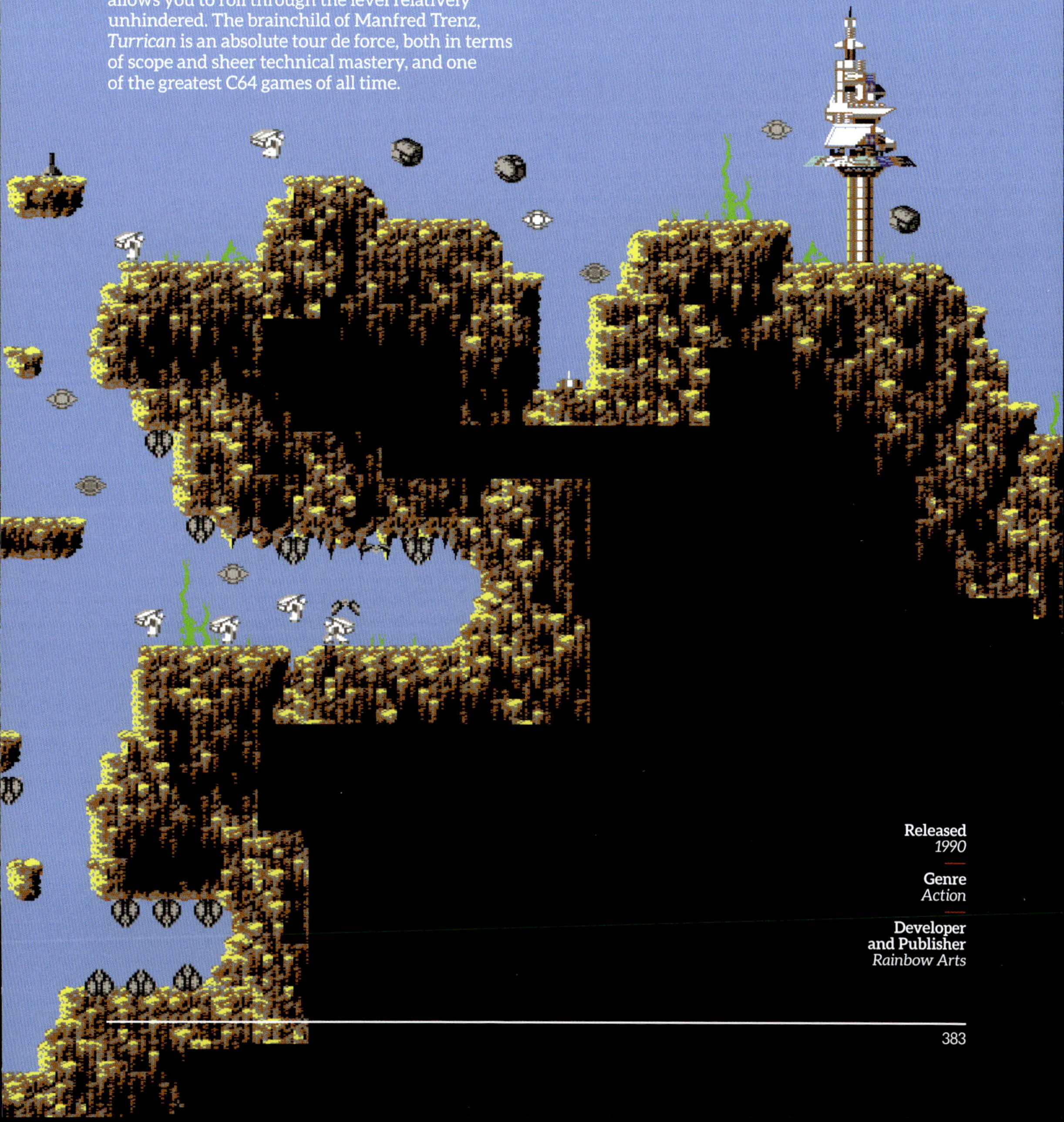

Released
1990

Genre
Action

Developer and Publisher
Rainbow Arts

PLAY

PLAY

Vendetta

A stunning intro sequence sets the scene for System 3's sprawling flick-screen action adventure, in which the hero must race against the clock to rescue his kidnapped relatives from the clutches of an evil terrorist organisation. While comparisons with *The Last Ninja* are inevitable, *Vendetta* is a very different beast, with suitably macho sprites, a plethora of firearms, combat moves and melee weapons, and a strong emphasis on gathering clues and evidence vital to the success of the mission. Add in some turbocharged racing sections between levels, and you'd almost swear you were playing a movie tie-in based on some obscure '80s action movie.

Released
1990

Genre
Action adventure

Developer and Publisher
System 3

"In 1989, I did *Vendetta* for System 3. The first track I did for this was a cover of *Infected* by The The. Paul Docherty introduced me to it as a reference, but I took it a little too literally. I had to make a lot of use of the filters on this game, to keep the mood. This was actually my last game for System 3, sometime around March 1989. I think the Maniacs of Noise had rolled into town by then!"

Matt Gray, musician

Released
1990

Genre
Adventure

Developer
The Oliver Twins

Publisher
Codemasters

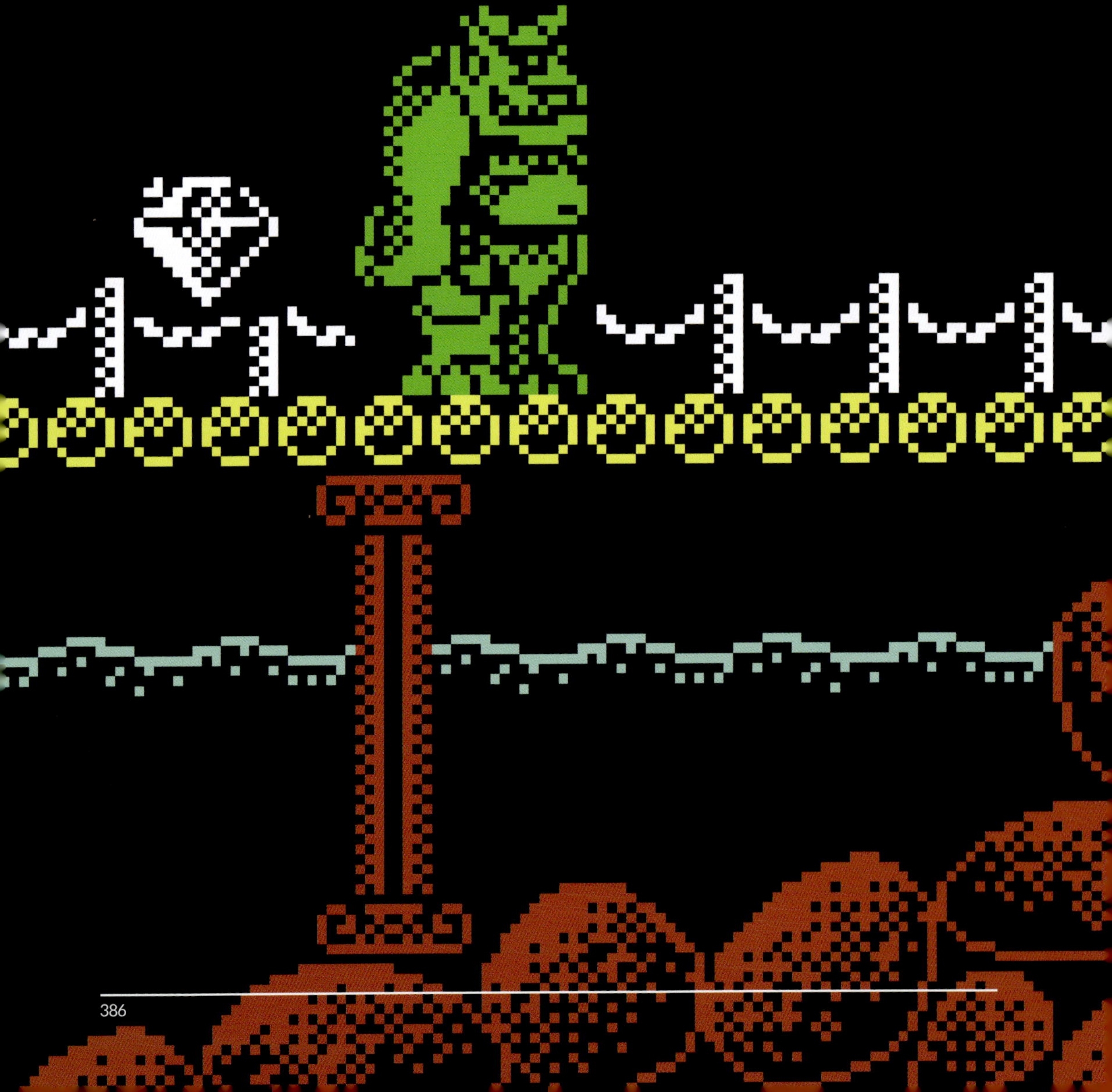

Magicland Dizzy

"In this fifth game of the incredibly popular Dizzy series, The Evil Wizard Zaks has cast spells on six members of the Yolkfolk, transporting them to Magicland, and Dizzy must set about rescuing them. Dylan is transfigured into a thorny bush, Denzil is frozen in ice, Dozy is put into an enchanted and perhaps everlasting sleep, Dora is turned into a frog, Daisy is enlarged and imprisoned inside Zaks's oubliette, and Grand-Dizzy is trapped inside a magic mirror. Developed originally on the Spectrum and Amstrad by Big Red Software, the C64 version was expertly converted by Ian Grey, who was responsible for all the C64 Dizzy games."

Philip Oliver, co-designer

Rainbow Islands

"It was as colourful and cute as anything from Nintendo and superbly judged in its trickiness. The premise was simply to reach for the sky by conjuring rainbows that could briefly support your weight, and trap or kill bugs, or grab things… just like, y'know, real rainbows do. Ocean's conversion of Taito's arcade original was one of its finest moments. *Rainbow Islands* is still playable and still addictive. Just one warning: its rendition of the saccharine *Somewhere over the Rainbow* is both a programming achievement and a crime against the SID 6581 at the same time."

Sean Masterson, games journalist

Released
1990

Genre
Arcade

Developer
Graftgold

Publisher
Ocean

Originally by
Taito

Midnight Resistance

"Made by Special FX in Liverpool in 1990, this was my favourite C64 game of all time. It was a side-scrolling, two-player, co-op arcade conversion, although we were restricted to a single player on the C64. This was another two-man development, working alongside Robbie Tinman. For this one, I actually stopped saving my artwork to audio cassettes and upgraded to a 5.25-inch floppy disk drive. The game included several different locations, so there was more variety in the graphics I was producing, and what other game has a huge floating head spitting out small brains as the end boss?"

Ivan Davies, graphic artist

Released 1990 / **Genre** Run and gun / **Developer** Special FX / **Publisher** Ocean / **Originally by** Data East

"It's the opening bars of music on level one: the way they come crashing in the second you hit the fire button and begin your rampage; it jolts you into action. You twist your joystick as wave after wave of enemies run at you, armed and full of intent. You find a shop and stock up on flame-throwers or grenades and set out again, helicopters swooping above and tanks patrolling the ground. I once saw the same game running on a friend's Amstrad. It was neutered; virtually monochrome and mute. *Midnight Resistance* did what I thought was impossible: it made me love the Commodore 64 even more."

Neil Grayson, guest reviewer

Murder!

Released
Unreleased

Genre
Adventure

Developer
Kingsley Harrison

Publisher
U.S. Gold

Artwork
Oliver Frey

Ferrari Formula One

Released
1990

Genre
Racing

Developer
Rick Koenig

Publisher
Electronic Arts

Artwork
Oliver Frey

Fantasy World Dizzy

"Development started on 1st September, 1989, and was completed by the end of the month. *Fantasy World Dizzy* was considered the Oliver Twins' best Dizzy game ever. It was a fun period of our lives ... amazingly productive. We'd got loads of money from previous games royalties; we'd bought a house, turned one of the rooms into an office and had no distractions. We'd mastered all the technology and were able to create games very fast and in very high quality. The gamers loved them, and we were pretty assured that each would go on to sell hundreds of thousands of copies and become bestsellers."

Philip Oliver, co-designer

Released
1990

Genre
Adventure

Developer
The Oliver Twins

Publisher
Codemasters

Hammerfist

"I originally created this on the Atari ST and reproduced it by hand on the C64. I was an admirer of the Vivid Image team, and Hugh Riley, in particular, was a graphics hero of mine, so it felt like an honour. The game was gritty and complex, but the central idea of swapping characters during play was absolutely at the heart of the game, and what I wanted to convey in the title screen."

Paul Docherty, graphic artist

"This was the first game we made as Vivid Image. The core idea was to ease the pain of dying and then restarting as, when your health was low, you could switch to the alternate character while the other recharged. The tough male and the athletic female had different but complementary skills that needed to be used strategically throughout."

Hugh Riley, graphic artist

Released
1990

Genre
Action

Developer
Vivid Image

Publisher
Activision

Creatures

"Conceived while we were doing the dishes, *Creatures* marked a departure from our previous shoot 'em up games and set the tone for the remaining C64 titles that we would create. We worked tirelessly on this title, working 18-hour days for the last six weeks of production and going without any sleep over the final five days! We have fond memories of the Thalamus stand at one of the computer shows being literally ripped apart by fans clamouring for the promotional fluffy fuzzy bugs."

John Rowlands, co-designer and programmer

Released
1990

Genre
Puzzle platformer

Developer
Apex Computer Productions

Publisher
Thalamus

"Compunet really thrived on user content and interactions, so there was this incredible competition to upload better and better content."

Stephen Robertson, graphic artist

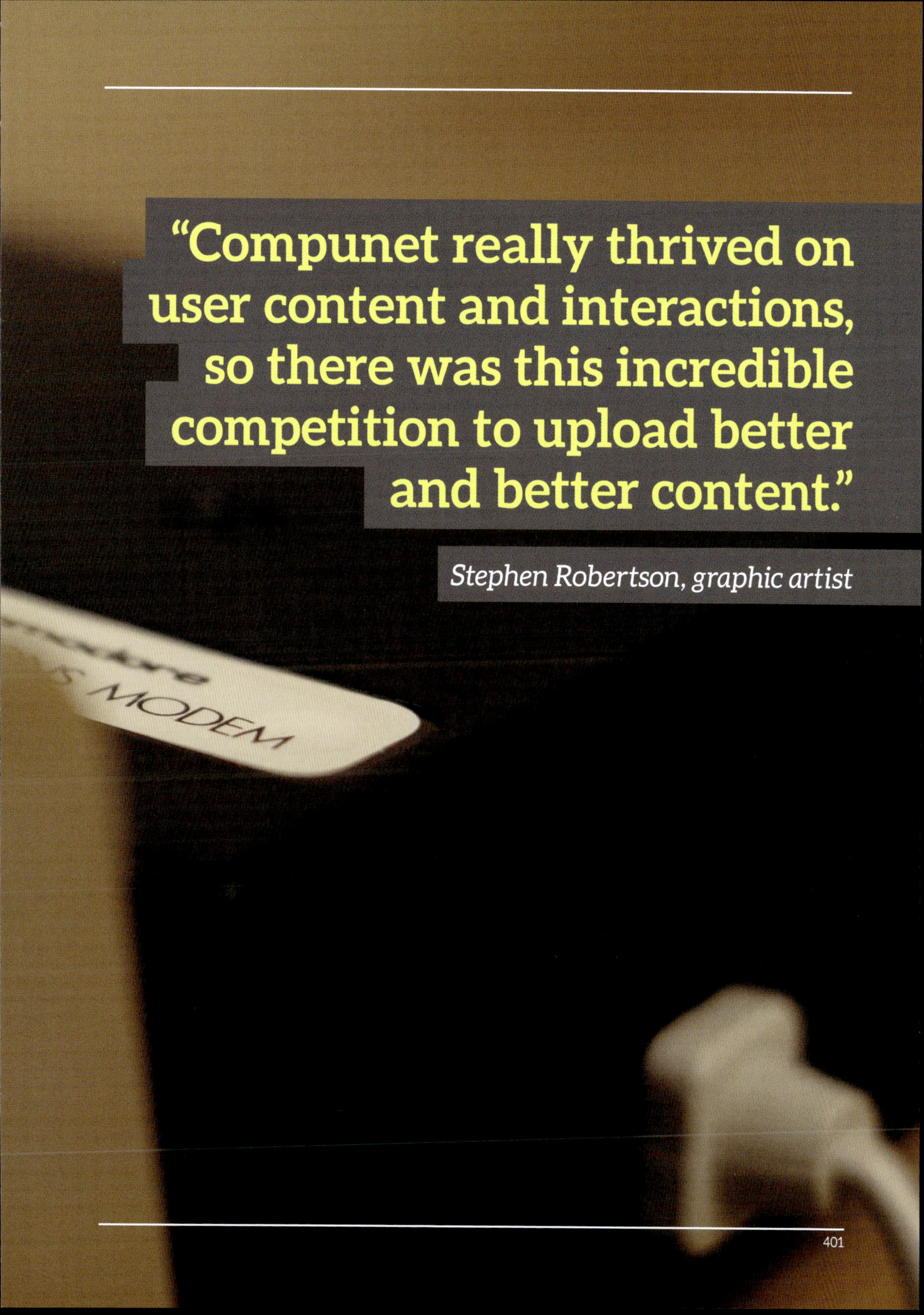

The demo scene

The C64 demo scene was born from the controversial cracking scene of the early '80s. Thanks to the likes of Compunet, the demo scene became a hotbed of creativity, and, over time, C64 demos evolved from simple, single-screen intros to spectacular showcases of artistry and technical prowess. Indeed, many of the scene's best-loved programmers, artists and musicians would go on to enjoy successful careers in games development.

Think Twice IV / *The Judges / 1987*

Digital Acid! / *Ash & Dave / 1987*

My first experience of the demo scene (aside from watching them) was The Party 3. I had a blast, and it was like nothing I had seen before. I ended up in third place with a picture I had originally pixelled for a *64'er* magazine graphics competition, and I met so many legendary people there for the first time. I remember barbecuing inside the hall at various events, countless chats I had with scene legends, and reading Finnish poems from a book to drunk Finns without speaking a single word of the language. Crazy days!"

Daniel Kottmair (DeeKay)

"The party lines were a good way to trade information, rag on people or just talk nonsense. I was chatting with some guys from the UK, and one of them turned out to be Jade from Dominators, and we got onto the subject of working on a game called *Shatterlands* together. We actually used the party line to transfer data: I called from Australia to the USA, Jade called from the UK to the USA, we connected our C64 modems and transferred the C64 programs. For the time, it was kind of special and very unusual – and it worked!"

David Simmons (Jazzcat)

"Joining Fairlight back in 1988 was like being signed by Barcelona FC!"

"I remember my first meeting with Jacco Van 't Riet (Jaws) at a C64 show in London '86 when Carl 'Claka' Clarke came up to me in a rush at the bar and asked, 'Have you pissed off any Europeans lately? Because there's an enormous Viking looking for you downstairs!'. It turned out Jacco had been wanting to meet me after seeing the *Karate Kid* artwork. After this meeting, I was frequently called (usually) on a Sunday night by Jacco and several of the other Boys Without Brains members on hijacked conference call phone lines for a group chat."

Steven Day (Ste'86)

Aliens / *Scoop* / *1986*

"Joining Fairlight back in 1988 was like being signed by Barcelona FC! My early experiences were coming from the UK sceners who were doing some cool stuff. Stoat & Tim, Ian & Mic, and Tony 'Ratt' Crowther all spring to mind – amazing craftsmanship. I actually owe a lot to the demo scene and the activities back then as it has hugely influenced the successful career that I have built today. All in all, it boils down to what I still have with me – loads of experiences, skills learned and friends gained. What an amazing thing to be a part of."

Pontus Berg (Bacchus)

"My interest in demos started when Ben Daglish and I teamed up to form 'We Music' (an acronym for WE Make Use of Sound In Computers). We created a disk featuring multiple music tracks that we could use to advertise our skills at creating music, so the demos were originally for financial gain, but, sometimes, the demos were experiments to try out techniques we could use in games. When we discovered demos could be uploaded to Compunet, I found myself uploading demos we created in our spare time."

Antony Crowther (Ratt)

"My first real exposure to the demo scene was around 1985-86, even though I'd owned a C64 since the end of 1982. A friend of mine dropped off a few floppies containing these things called 'demos', and one of the very first ones I saw was the *Smalltown Boy* music demo by The Mighty Bogg. Wow, this was fantastic! Another disk had *Thrust Concert* by Stoat & Tim. I was blown away after seeing it and knew I had to get into this 'scene' somehow. The best route at that time in the UK was Compunet."

Mike Berry (Kernal)

com

"My highlight of being part of the scene? I guess it had to be Compunet, one of the first iterations of the World Wide Web, but my interest tailed off after I got a huge phone bill! When I was no longer using Compunet, the distribution channel was gone, and so the demos made it into my games instead. I did a book demo in Challenge of the Gobots, and the demo in *Trap* of course. *Kettle* had a Windows-type front-end and I liked to put 'Test Card' demos in my games too (I think there was one in *William Wobbler*)."

Antony Crowther (Ratt)

"My first experiences of the demo scene were when the first of the Compunet demos began to appear at my local computer club. Up to that point, I had seen many small animations and 'cracked by' messages done in different ways, but these were the first standalone pieces done for no other reason than to showcase talent. I particularly remember the early Bob Stevenson art like *Hendrix* and *Rambo*. All this was a few months before I began doing C64 art in January '86 and several months before our first foray onto Compunet."

Steven Day (Ste'86)

"I like to think that the folk writing demos to upload onto places like Compunet were pioneers of sorts. Of course, our work simply cannot compete technically with some of the amazing stuff being produced today, but I remember that period of time with great affection and consider it the 'golden years', not only of the demo scene but of the C64 in general. My favourite ever Compunet-era demo was '*Circlesque*' by Stoat & Tim."

Mike Berry (Kernal)

unet

GOLD

"At the time, and especially in the UK and Ireland, one of the best ways to share demos (and just about anything else Commodore 64 related) was Compunet. It was extremely popular in the early days and was a wonderful place to share Commodore 64 music, demos and information, and socialise with like-minded folk. I absolutely loved it – easily the best years of my C64 life! Sadly, due to alleged mismanagement resulting in huge debts, it closed down in 1993. By then, many of the great coders had moved on to commercial games production or just lost interest."

Mike Berry (Kernal)

"I used the demo scene as a springboard to joining the games industry as, in the UK, it was a well-trodden path into paid employment. Compunet basically brought together the entire UK scene and gave us a mini Internet about ten years before the real thing. Along with the Compunet activity came all the other things such as the computer shows where I'd meet the other guys in the scene (usually at the bar or around the *Zzap!64* or Compunet stands), and a huge personal highlight for me was my art appearing in *Zzap!64*."

Steven Day (Ste'86)

"Looking back, it's actually amazing how ahead of its time Compunet was. You had email, real-time chat rooms, news, the ability to upload content, such as graphics, demos, and so on for other people to download and the ability to charge for it too. Paid downloadable content on the C64 in 1986 – amazing! I wrote an app for Compunet that made it really easy to make cool ASCII art and sold it for a few quid. I think I made about three thousand pounds!"

Doug Hare (MACH81)

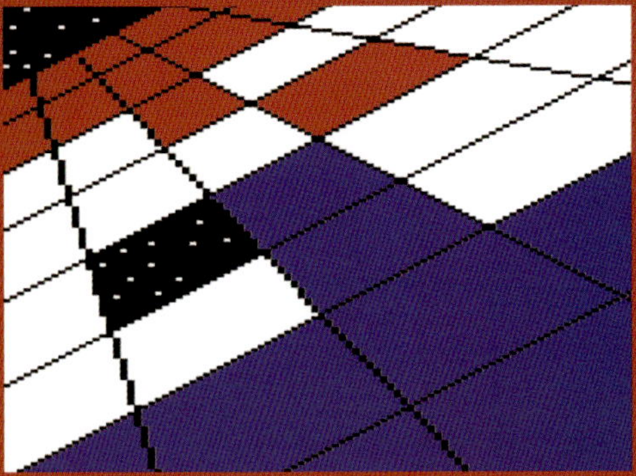

The Final Edge / *1001 Crew / 1986*

That's the Way It Is / *Scoop / 1988*

Vision / *Mist 2 / 1990*

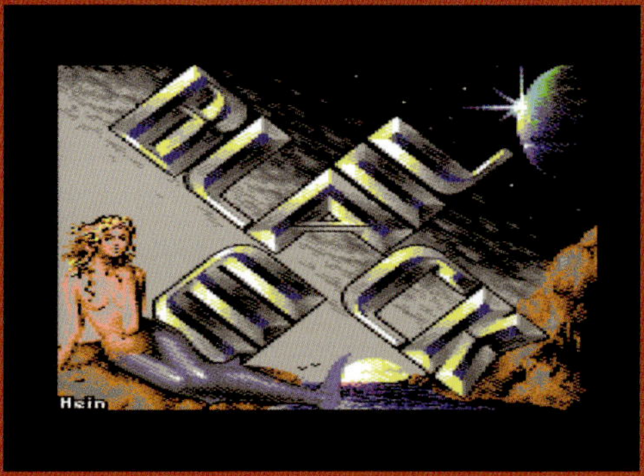

Dutch Breeze / *Black Mail / 1991*

"For some years, I was actively swapping with over 200 people. It was crazy: cheating stamps, wrapping packs, cataloguing and requesting wares, watching your collection grow; it was like the C64 scene version of a pen pal. I remember some days that I would come home and have dozens of packages waiting for me. Being a swapper was considered lowly by the elite, but, without swappers, the scene would have been very different. In fact, many of the scene wares you can download from the net today came from the diskettes of a swapper."

David Simmons (Jazzcat)

"Seeing *Zzap!64* starting to cover Compunet encouraged me to up my game as a demo coder. I remember shortly after I'd done the *VSP&IK+* demo, I went for an interview at a local software house. They introduced me to their in-house C64 coder, who decided to show off his skills to me. We gathered around his computer, and he started displaying his latest code, which was basically one of my demos with the picture and scroll text changed. I then opened my disk box with all the Meanteam demos and handed it to him. Realisation and apologies followed!"

Pete Dabbs (JCB/Meanteam)

"Being a swapper was considered lowly by the elite, but, without swappers, the scene would have been very different."

Access Denied / *Reflex / 1994*

Mathematica / *Reflex / 1995*

Deus Ex Machina / *Crest & Oxyron / 2000*

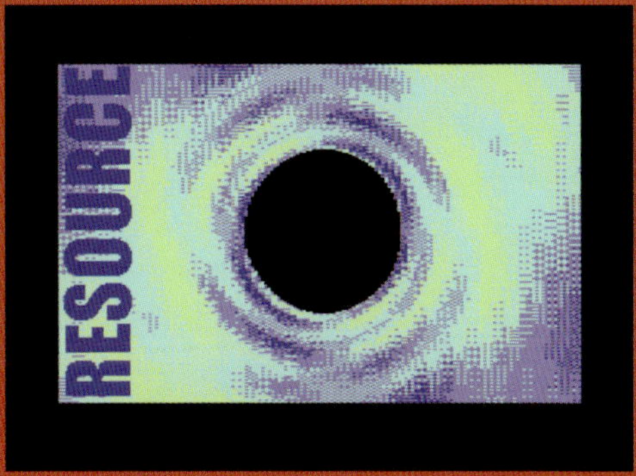

Soiled Legacy / *Resource /2001*

Edge of Disgrace / *Booze Design / 2008*

Coma Light 13 / *Oxyron* / *2012*

"*Trap* would have to be my favourite demo – it's the demo that everyone seems to mention. It used the existing music from the game, but had a few extra kilobytes for the font and graphics. The game was completed before the demo was started, so the game wasn't compromised – the challenge was to actually fit a demo into such a small space. In the game's box, there were two tapes, one with an audio recording of the *Trap* music. We used three synchronised C64s to produce it, resulting in a nine-voice version of the music."

Antony Crowther (Ratt)

"I was a coder and a swapper but overall an organiser. It was a sort of social network that we created before the ones we all know nowadays. Being part of the demo scene was crazy as we gave so much importance to things that most of the world didn't care about. Our micro-universe was so damn important for us, and we were (and still are) addicted to our daily dose of 8-bit pleasure! Italy has always had some very good talented sceners but were mainly code rippers – nothing special compared to the European and world scene where all the cool stuff was coming from."

Enrico Sturaro (E$G)

"One of the craziest pixel art projects I've worked on is probably the lady in the water at the start of the *Deus Ex Machina* demo. I remember, when creating that, Crossbow and I were working on it over the Christmas holidays, and he was away from university so didn't have any access to email. He had no dial-up at home, so I was having to fax the sprite data to him – crazy! An outstanding moment was the demo coming in first place at Mekka & Symposium 2000. It took two years to create, and I'm still immensely proud of it."

Daniel Kottmair (DeeKay)

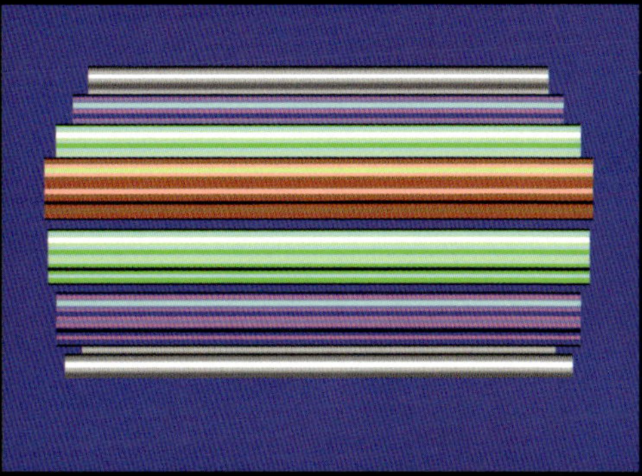

Desert Dream / *Chorus & Resource / 2007*

Wonderland XII / *Censor Design / 2013*

Uncensored / *Booze Design / 2014*

GoatLight / *Fairlight / 2015*

I'm not sure I could pick just one demo as my favourite. As a group, we specialised in music ripping and being the first to get the best game music into a demo and onto Compunet. If I had to go with just one, it would be *VSP&IK+*. It was the first demo of its kind and was the first routine to use a hardware bug to scroll a really large bitmap screen using very little CPU. This trick was later famously used in the game *Mayhem in Monsterland* seven years later. Another highlight was getting to know a great bunch of guys, some of who are still great friends today."

Pete Dabbs (JCB/Meanteam)

"I was never on Compunet personally, but I regularly received demos from people that were (usually simple one-file productions or 'rips' which stole the latest music and graphics from commercial games). I remember getting stuff from traders who had the privilege of being on Compunet and managed to connect to the group consisting of Jeff Minter, Rob Hubbard and various members of the demo scene such as Bob Stevenson and Dokk."

David Simmons (Jazzcat)

> *"We gave so much importance to things that most of the world didn't care about."*

The Sarge

Part of the demo scene for almost 30 years, Swedish-born Joachim Ljunggren, a.k.a. 'The Sarge', is one of the C64's most prolific pixel artists. A former member of infamous groups such as Fairlight and Triad, he created graphics for in excess of 80 demos, as well as numerous commercial games such as No Mercy *and the critically acclaimed* Rubicon.

Ha Ha / *Triad* / *1987*

I started doing graphics on my first computer (Texas TI-99/4A), it was very limited in what it could do, and there was no way to save anything to tape. There were no programs for painting on it, so, when I got my first Commodore 64, I dived in straight with KoalaPainter and started creating pixel art using my Tac-2 joystick. I've always been interested in technological breakthroughs, and I was fast to jump onto the C64 when it appeared – it felt so advanced."

My first swapping friend and I started a group called Mutants 2001, and we released a couple of simple demos that got some attention in the scene. Soon I jumped over to a demo group called Front where I stayed for a short while until Ixion called and asked me to become a member of Triad. I still remember the phone call and how shocked I was that one of my heroes in the scene called me. I stayed in Triad a couple of years and then became a member of Fairlight."

"Even though I never went to any copy parties or met a lot of sceners, it was the community spirit that made the demo scene feel so special. There were many phone calls, lots of talking and meeting new friends going on. The feeling of contributing to the scene with graphics, and getting them out there for people to see and to comment on, was great and a huge buzz. Getting that occasional feedback on your work was the big driving force for me."

"At Triad, we received many letters over the years, but I remember one funny letter I got from a fan who was complimenting us for having created a hit song that was huge on TV and radio here in Sweden at the time called *Tänd ett ljus* (Light a Candle). He really liked it and was wondering who I was in the group as he didn't recognise my name. But, of course, it wasn't us; it was by a pop group also called Triad!"

"Back then, we hardly had any software or hardware to work with – it was very basic. All the recent technical discoveries, such as the graphic modes and opening up the borders, were just not possible (or at least we didn't think they were). So when I look from a graphical point of view at some of the amazing new demos that get released today, I find it really hard to compare them as we couldn't do those things back when we started out."

"A lot of older guys and girls that started our careers on the C64 like to keep an eye on, or even do something new on, the computer that gave us so many good memories. I know when I start up my C64 and look at all the old demos and graphics, I'm right back there in my dorm with all those feelings and memories. Apart from the Amiga, it's the only computer with a real soul. There hasn't been a computer since that was as unique as the C64."

> *"The feeling of contributing to the scene with graphics, and getting them out there for people to see and to comment on, was great and a huge buzz."*

Esfpetanof / *Triad / 1987*

Robocop Demo / *Fairlight / 1988*

Rutig banan / *Fairlight / 1989*

The Sarge #1 / *Fairlight / 1991*

Golden Axe

"We didn't have access to the coin-op, just a big box of circuit boards, connectors, joysticks, buttons and instructions in Japanese! Once assembled, we set about taking pictures of every frame of graphics in the game. I believe we shot over 20 rolls of film! To get the characters big on the C64 screen, I did a little hardware trick called sprite multiplexing, where I would re-use the same sprite on the screen after the upper portion had finished drawing. Overall, it was a fun game to work on and was quite a challenge, but it won us our second 'Gold Medal' from *Zzap!64*."

Mark W. J. Kelly, programmer

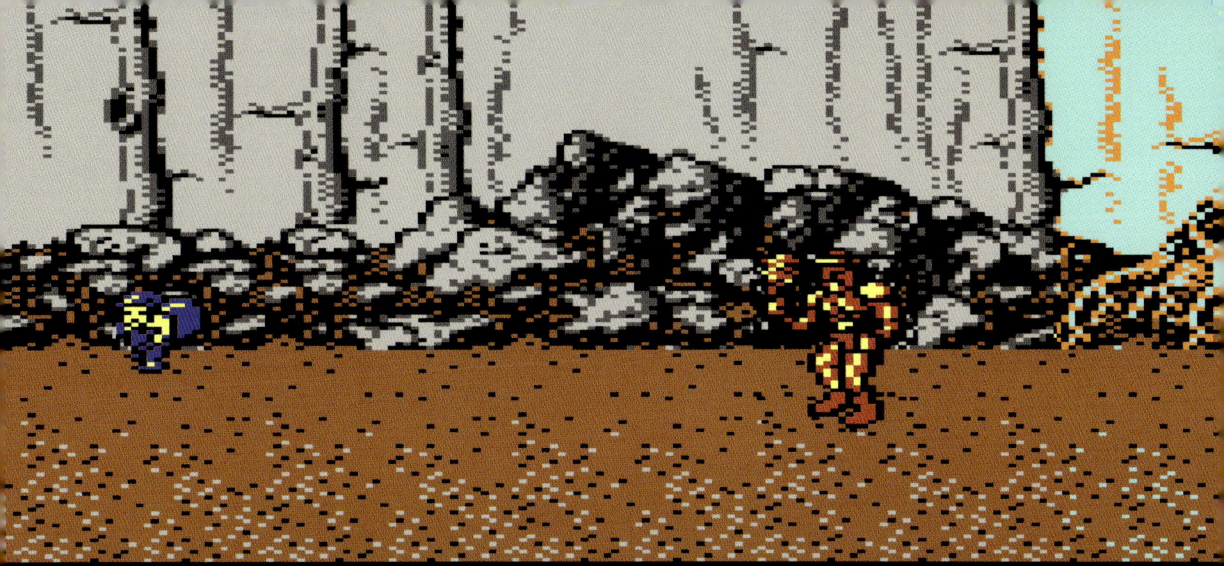

Released
1990

Genre
Scrolling beat 'em up

Developer
Probe Software

Publisher
Virgin

Originally by
SEGA

Flimbo's Quest

"The Amiga had just come onto the market, and we were unsure which machine to initially program *Flimbo's Quest* on. We had such a good development system on the C64, so we chose that. During development, we had a bit of a crisis as Mario moved to Germany, and I started to work for a design agency. In the end, Laurens did a terrific job in programming *Flimbo's Quest*, and it became a sort of cult game that was successful on both the C64 and Amiga."

Jacco Van 't Riet, graphic artist

Released
1990

Genre
Platformer

Developer and Publisher
System 3

Chase HQ II

Released
1990

Genre
Racing

Developer
Probe Software

Publisher
Ocean

Originally by
Taito

Artwork
Oliver Frey

Turrican II

Released
1991

Genre
Platformer

Developer and Publisher
Rainbow Arts

Artwork
Oliver Frey

The Ocean Loader

From the distinctive opening bars of Martin Galway's legendary loading music to the majestic sweeping reveal of the loading screen, Ocean turned the tedium of cassette loading into an experience. Aided by musicians Peter Clarke, Jonathan Dunn and a slew of talented artists, Paul Hughes's 'Freeload' system would go on to push the boundaries of Ocean's loading sequences even further.

"I always loved the loading screens on the ZX Spectrum – they always nicely set up the anticipation for what was to come. A good loading screen always set high expectations for the player. The Commodore 64, alas, had to switch the screen off during its heinously slow loading routines.

After creating Freeload (what is now affectionately known as 'The Ocean Loader'), the first thing I did was to ensure I didn't need to turn the screen off. Once I had the screen on with reliable fast loading, it would be churlish not to have a lovely multicolour loading screen to give the Spectrum a run for its money!

Ocean had some incredible in-house artists, many of which made jaw-dropping loading screens for the C64. With such stunning imagery in hand, complemented by the musical delights of Messrs Galway, Clarke, Dunn and Cannon, the now infamous Ocean loading sequence was born: smooth-scrolling credits messages, SID soundtracks blasting away in the background, and 32,000 lovingly crafted pixels displayed during the four-minute turboload sequence.

Freeload was designed to do much more while the loading was going on, and so, when Steve Wahid did a little sprite animation sequence of twinkling stars designed to pulse over the *Rastan* logo on Martin MacDonald's bitmap, I thought it would be neat to have it run over the loading screen during the sequence.

Like Richard Aplin of Interceptor Micros fame, I had a bunch of 'Load-a-Games' written that you could play while the main games were loading. Unfortunately, as Ocean always officially licensed its titles, it wasn't considered appropriate or indeed ethical to have a *Space Invaders* or *Breakout* clone playing during the load sequence.

Tape loaders were always a game of cat and mouse with the hackers; I'd leave little messages buried in the different layers of protection to tease them and then be in awe of their ingenuity as I typed in their infinite lives pokes from *Zzap!64* to see how they had gotten around the protection. The next release would seal up that exploit, and so the cycle continued!"

Paul Hughes, game designer and programmer

> *"Tape loaders were always a game of cat and mouse with the hackers; I'd leave little messages buried in the different layers of protection to tease them."*

Total Recall / *1991*

Released
1991

Genre
RPG

Developer and publisher
Strategic Simulations Inc.

Death Knights of Krynn

"The gold box series of *AD&D* titles were some of the most recognisable games on the C64, partly due to the packaging, and partly due to their quality. *Death Knights* was the culmination of several attempts to tweak the formula, a winding tale of intrigue, dragons and redemption set within the realm of Krynn. With a substantial main storyline and plenty of side-quests to undertake, this game had legs ... and arms ... and most other bones, given that skeletons were a frequent enemy! The only pity is that SSI never completed any RPG series on the C64."

Mat Allen, guest reviewer

Released
1991

Genre
Sports

Developer and publisher
Image Works

Originally by
The Bitmap Brothers

Speedball 2: Brutal Deluxe

"This conversion from the hugely popular Amiga game was a great surprise to many C64 owners back in 1991, as was the fact that it was so well done despite the obvious limitations of the nine-year-old machine. Although the game lost the digitised speech and metallic graphics of the Amiga version (replaced with a primarily purple colour scheme), it lost none of the addictive playability of the original. Taking your ten-man 'Brutal Deluxe' team through the 14-week league option was a marathon exercise in strategy, frantic gameplay and massive amounts of extreme physical violence. Brilliant!"

Tim Nicholls, guest reviewer

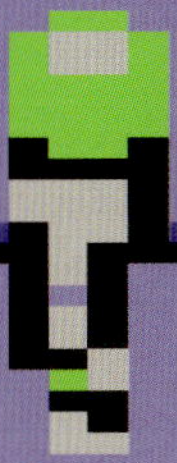

Released
1991

Genre
Platformer

Developer
The Sales Curve

Publisher
Storm

Originally by
Jaleco

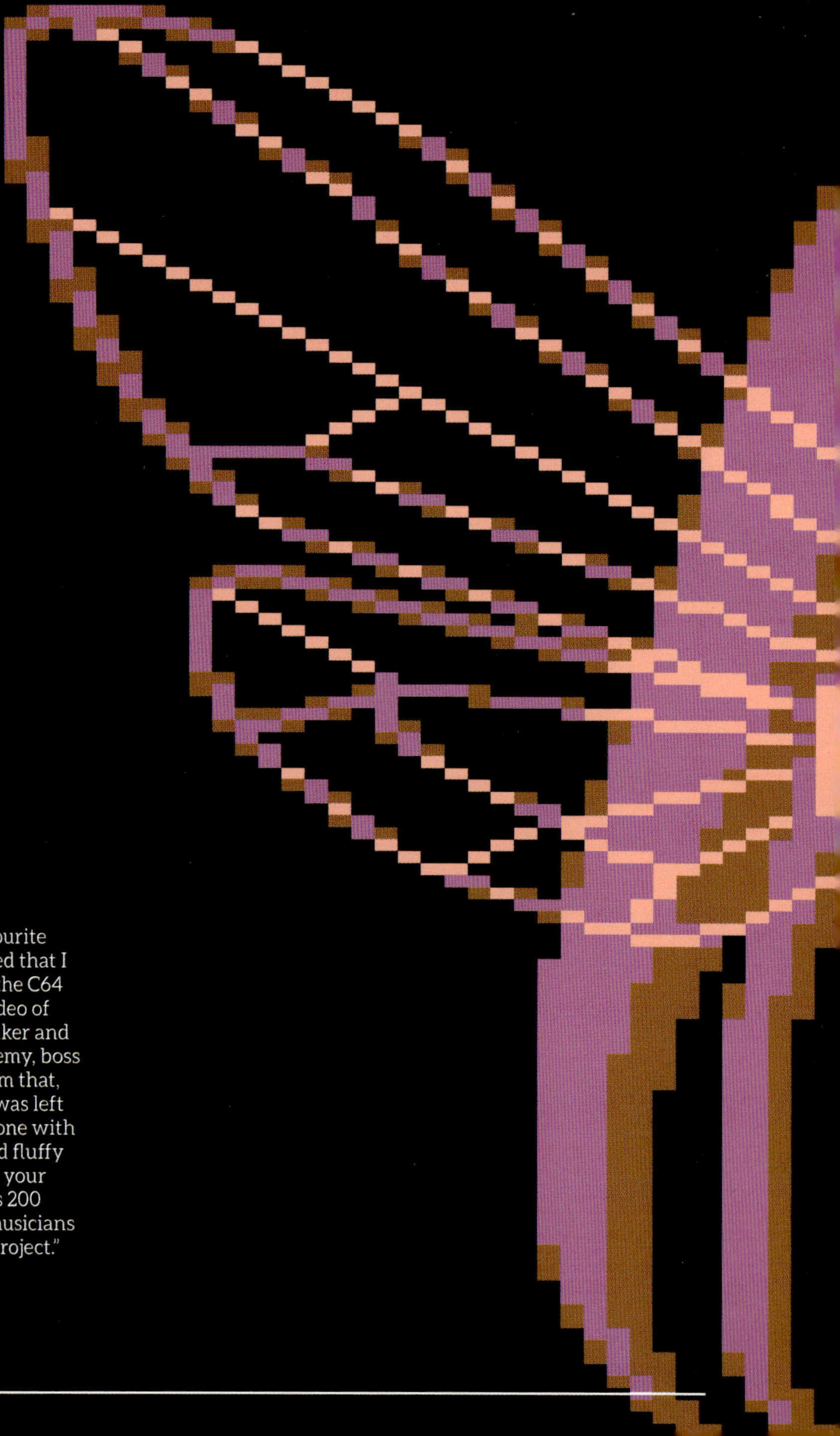

Rodland

"*Rodland* is in my top three favourite projects I've ever done. I insisted that I got to write it because I loved the C64 so much. Armed with just a video of the arcade original, Rob Whitaker and I discussed how the player, enemy, boss art, etc. would work. Aside from that, I left him alone to draw, and I was left alone to code. But being left alone with nothing but fairies, flowers and fluffy bunnies does strange things to your brain. The high-score table has 200 random names of actors and musicians that kept me sane during the project."

Steve Snake, programmer

Released
1991

Genre
Platformer

Developers
CTA Developments and 221b Software Developments

Publisher
Titus Software

The Blues Brothers

"In the early '90s, C64 owners were duty-bound to laugh at anybody with a console. Secretly, though, we all wanted to play something a bit like *Mario*, and *The Blues Brothers* was probably as close as we got. Instead of coins, there are rotating records; instead of shells, your weapons of choice were crates. But, most impressive of all was its size, and, with a thumping, bass-heavy soundtrack and tons of variety, it proved that a machine knocking on for its tenth birthday could still cut it."

Neil Grayson, guest reviewer

An interview with **Gary Winnick**

Gary Winnick was the first artist to join George Lucas's fledgling development company Lucasfilm Games, and cut his teeth on classic C64 titles such as **Labyrinth, Rescue on Fractalus!, Koronis Rift** ***and*** **The Eidolon.** ***After partnering with Ron Gilbert, the duo would go on to pioneer an entire genre with the groundbreaking point-and-click adventure*** **Maniac Mansion.**

Do you remember how you first got interested in art and design?
As far back as I can remember, I was enamoured with comic book art and animated cartoons, so I started creating and drawing my own characters before I was in my teens.

Did you take any formal art training or education?
I majored in both Art and Business at Monterey Peninsula College. I was considering going on to art school but ended up getting a job in the computer industry before making that leap.

How did you first get interested in computers?
The art store I was working at started selling Atari computers, so I bought an Atari 800 with the idea of learning how to program, and that eventually led to a job creating game graphics at Atari.

How did your career in the games industry get started?
I believe I answered a couple of job ads in the newspaper. Both Atari and Imagic were companies close to my home and were looking for artists; I interviewed with them and was offered jobs by both within the same week. I decided on Atari, partly because I owned an Atari home computer at the time.

How did you end up working for Lucasfilm Games?
A good friend introduced me to some folks from Apple, one of them being Charlie Kellner, who went on to become one of the first members of the Lucasfilm Games division. At that time the group was pretty small and only about six months old when they realised they needed a full-time art resource. Charlie recommended that I talk to the group, as I had experience creating graphics on the Atari 800 (which was their initial target machine). They gave me a test to create the animated 'Jaggi' alien for *Rescue on Fractalus!* and I guess they liked what I did since they offered me a job soon after. I ultimately ended up as the first artist that Lucasfilm Games hired.

You worked on several hit games with Ron Gilbert; what was the experience like?
Ron was hired to do the C64 conversion of *Koronis Rift*, and, at that time, the group was still pretty small, and we all worked together on the same floor. We all hung out with each other and got to know each other pretty well. Ron and I, in particular, shared a similar (sick) sense of humour and enjoyed the same TV shows, movies, and so on. We always worked well together, particularly when designing stories and characters. On top of that, I couldn't program, and Ron couldn't draw, so we had clear roles when working together.

> *“I really looked to Ron to understand the capabilities of the C64 and how we could enhance the experience.”*

What was the first original C64 title you worked on?
Ron had been hired to port games to the C64, so when we decided we'd design and pitch an original title at Lucasfilm, it was logical for us to begin on the C64. That idea ultimately became *Maniac Mansion*.

What did a typical day in front of the computer look like?
On *Maniac Mansion*, Ron and I would typically meet in the morning and go over what we wanted to focus on for the day. This usually involved some sketching on paper.

All of the rooms had to be created within the confines of the Commodore's character set, so I'd use the 'Skedit' character set editor that Ron wrote. First, we'd define the room layout, screen size, objects and paths through the room, then, using my sketch and Ron's notes, I'd block in the basic shapes with flat blocks of colour. Then I'd proceed to add some more detail, working from the walls forwards, adding in the objects, rudimentary light sources, and final touches. Once I had a reasonable-looking image, I'd run that through the *Skedit* character crunching feature, which would take the image and crunch it down to the necessary 256 characters by comparing and replacing similar characters. I would then touch up the image and re-run the crunch feature successively until I ultimately got a version we were happy with.

Which programs did you use to create your C64 art?
At the time we started on the C64, I don't recall anything commercially available that was close to what we wanted, and since we'd already developed our own art tools for conversions (as well as creating *Labyrinth: The Computer Game*), we just continued to refine those.

Did you ever use any custom tools that weren't available commercially?
While working on *Maniac Mansion*, we developed our own proprietary in-house tools (Ron wrote and refined these over the course of the project). There were two main art tools: '*Skedit*', which was for background art and served as the character set editor and '*Byle*', which was the sprite animation editor.

Looking back, what were the best and worst aspects of creating art for the C64?
At that time, getting to work on the C64 felt like a step up from our prior constraints, and, certainly, I remember feeling like the scrolling backgrounds were unique and state-of-the-art when we were creating them. I don't consider anything to be particularly bad about developing graphics for the C64. Rather, it was just a challenge to get the graphics looking as good as possible given the obvious constraints of pixel resolution, colour, frame rate etc.

What was your process? Did you plan on paper, or jump straight in onto the computer?
On *Maniac Mansion*, I'd just sketch out everything on paper first, including character designs, environments, storyboards, and so on. For some items, I'd also lay

out versions on grid paper (based on the process I'd learned creating graphics for the Atari). Another thing I'd do (as we didn't have scanners at the time) was take a clear piece of acetate and trace an image using a black Sharpie marker. I'd then tape the acetate to the front of my monitor and trace a rough version of it onto the screen. Once I had a reasonable representation on the screen I'd refine from there.

Did your process change throughout your career?
Over my time at Lucasfilm, which was close to a decade, the process, technology and number of people involved changed dramatically: commercial tools such as *DPaint* become more available, better and more cost-effective, and the advent of consumer-oriented scanner technology was also a turning point. Another important development was being allowed to bring in other art resources as the business grew, first as independent contractors, then as in-house resources.

What was the development time for a typical game?
Probably anywhere from one to two years, depending on the overall complexity. As far as deadlines went, before the advent of online sales, it was critical to get your games into the retail outlets in enough time prior to the Christmas shopping season. Schedules were important but weren't insane – common sense did tend to prevail (at least that's how I remember it!).

Did you receive much artistic direction, or would you say you had complete freedom?
Within each development team, there was a Project Leader, who usually conceived the project and held the creative vision for it. Project Leaders were pretty much the final authority for the game's content and were intimately involved working on the project. In the case of *Maniac Mansion*, Ron and I were the co-designers/project leaders, and I think we got along pretty well (a major reason we reunited to work on *Thimbleweed Park*).

When creating C64 art, which aspect did you most enjoy?
Probably my favourite part about making games back then – and still to this day – was developing and creating new characters (including their personalities and backstory) then designing and animating them.

Did you have much input in terms of game design?
Yes, very much so. Given the company culture, which was established early on, we were a fairly small tight-knit group, and it remained pretty much that way until the time I left. As such, the process tended to be pretty organic and collaborative.

Did you pay much attention to the various magazine reviews?
In those pre-Internet days, it took a while to see an actual printed review (usually months after we shipped something) so we were usually on to the next project before we saw anything. I remember generally getting positive reviews, which was certainly nice and helped reaffirm the effort and attention to detail we had tried to incorporate.

If you had the chance to revisit any of your games, what would you change?
Ron and I have always talked about potentially eliminating the unintentional dead ends in *Maniac Mansion*...

> *“Ron and I put a lot of ourselves into both the humour and look of the game.”*

Was there anyone in the industry whose work was inspirational to you?
A lot of the artists I was fortunate enough to work with at Lucas, including Ken Macklin, Steve Purcell, Mark Ferrari, and Iain McCaig.

What C64 games at the time impressed you, or had an influence on your work?
The first people in the group who really had their finger on the pulse of the C64 were Ron Gilbert and Aric Wilmunder who came in to do those early conversions from the Atari. I really looked to Ron to understand the capabilities of the C64 and how we could enhance the experience.

Outside of games, what were your biggest artistic influences?
I started out as a comic book guy (mainly Marvel) in the '60s and '70s, so definitely the comic art of that era. Many of the comic book, fantasy and animation artists of those times were also influential, including Jack Kirby, Neal Adams, Jim Steranko, Frank Frazetta and Eyvind Earle, to name but a few.

If you had to pick just one game to include in your portfolio, which would it be?
It would have to be *Maniac Mansion* because it was fairly revolutionary at the time (multiple playable characters, multiple endings, the introduction of cutscenes, etc.). Also, Ron and I put a lot of ourselves into both the humour and look of the game.

Were there any C64 games you worked on which sadly never saw the light of day?
I think the closest may have been the legendary *Habitat* (the complete version as Chip Morningstar and Randy Farmer envisioned it), which was only run as a limited test version. At the time, it ended up taking too much bandwidth, so a dramatically scaled-down version called *Club Caribe* is what ultimately ended up being released.

What made you decide to leave the machine behind?
I think the proliferation of the IBM PC at the time caused most of the industry to focus their development onto that platform.

Did you have a favourite Commodore 64 game?
I think I got a bit addicted to some of the arcade conversions on the C64, and *Qix* was one of those I remember in particular. Honestly, I just liked the abstract/2D simplicity of it.

The Eidolon / *1985*

Maniac Mansion / *1987*

Was there a C64 game you would have loved to have created the graphics for?
I might have liked to have fleshed out some of the C64 graphic adventures we created in more detail. Overall, I've always enjoyed character-and story-driven games and feel I've had an opportunity to participate in that renaissance, both on the C64 and other platforms.

Any standout memories?
I remember *Maniac Mansion* as one of the few times in my life when I received unconditional creative support. Ron and I were free to try almost any idea and approach we could imagine, and we were supported in our vision by both the other members of our group and our boss Steve Arnold. And of course, working at Skywalker Ranch was pretty amazing.

Why do you think the C64 is remembered so fondly?
A lot of innovative programs and games were first developed on the C64; it was a very good and reasonably priced platform for the time and, as such, there's a good-sized base of dedicated users from that period that have a great nostalgia for the hardware and software that was in their homes while growing up.

Do you still own a C64?
No, I pretty much gave up my older hardware a couple of moves back. I really wasn't using it for anything, so I gave everything to a good home.

What are you up to these days?
At the end of 2014, I ran a successful Kickstarter with my good friend and Lucas alumni Ron Gilbert for *Thimbleweed Park*, a brand-new adventure game in the style of *Maniac Mansion*. That project went well and can be seen in all its glory at thimbleweedpark.com.

Total Recall

"*Total Recall* was another 'get it done' project! I had already made a lot of screens for the game, some of which I had to draw from memory. Almost at the very end of the project, we got some production stills from the movie, one of which was the eye bulge scene. I had seen the movie by this point and had to include the Cohaagen death scene. It's one of the funniest things I've ever seen and still makes me laugh to this day."

Stephen Ian Thomson, graphic artist

Released
1991

Genre
Action

Developer and Publisher
Ocean

Supremacy

"*Supremacy* (*Overlord* in the US) was an 8-bit conversion of a 16-bit game with masses of data to display in text and icons. There was no animation, so it was an interesting break for me. The tricky part was getting the look and feel of the original while losing none of the functionality. It was very satisfying to get the layout to maximum efficiency and squeeze it all into the C64."

Hugh Riley, graphic artist

Released
1991

Genre
Strategy

Developer
Probe Software

Publisher
Melbourne House

“We helped with the initial bunch of games that were put on the C64GS. It was a great idea, but, unfortunately, Commodore couldn’t quite pull it off.”

Mevlut Dinc, Vivid Image

Exile

"This was the last loading screen I created for the C64. I was a huge fan of Jeremy Smith's *Thrust*, so there was no chance I was going to turn the opportunity down! For the astronaut, I wanted to evoke a shiny helmeted face, and the brown blobs on the helmet are supposed to be reflections of approaching aliens. It was tough to return to the C64's limitations after working for a year on the 16-bit platforms."

Paul Docherty, graphic artist

Released
1991

Genre
Action adventure

Developer and Publisher
Audiogenic

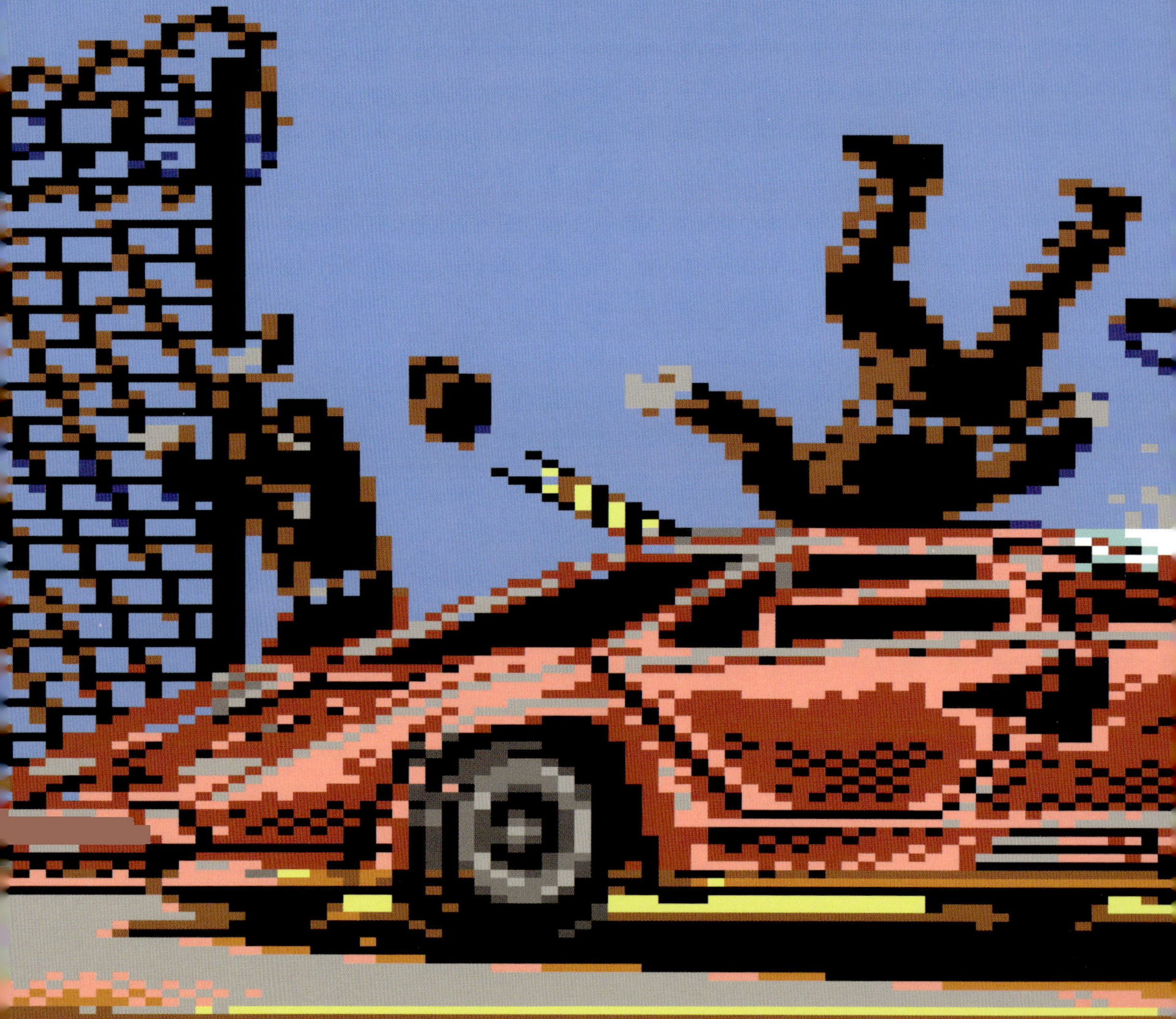

Turbo Charge

"While I'm not a huge fan of the game, I hugely enjoyed producing all of the artwork. It was probably the closest I got to comic work at the time as I had the freedom to create imagery that illustrated one small aspect of a bigger story. In this image, we show the player smashing through a border. Not so sure about the depiction of the car, but I really like what I did with the three cops, especially the poor fellow rolling over the bonnet!"

Robin Levy, graphic artist

Released
1991

Genre
Racing

Developer and Publisher
System 3

Last Ninja 3

"*Last Ninja 3* was an event for me when it finally came out and was available in stores. The controls and gameplay were quirky, but the series and games as a whole are the absolute example of artistic achievement from the C64. There was not a part of these games that wasn't the best the medium could offer – the art, the music, even down to the covers of the games themselves. A design triumph that stands tall amongst games of today and likely forever."

Marc Bell, guest reviewer

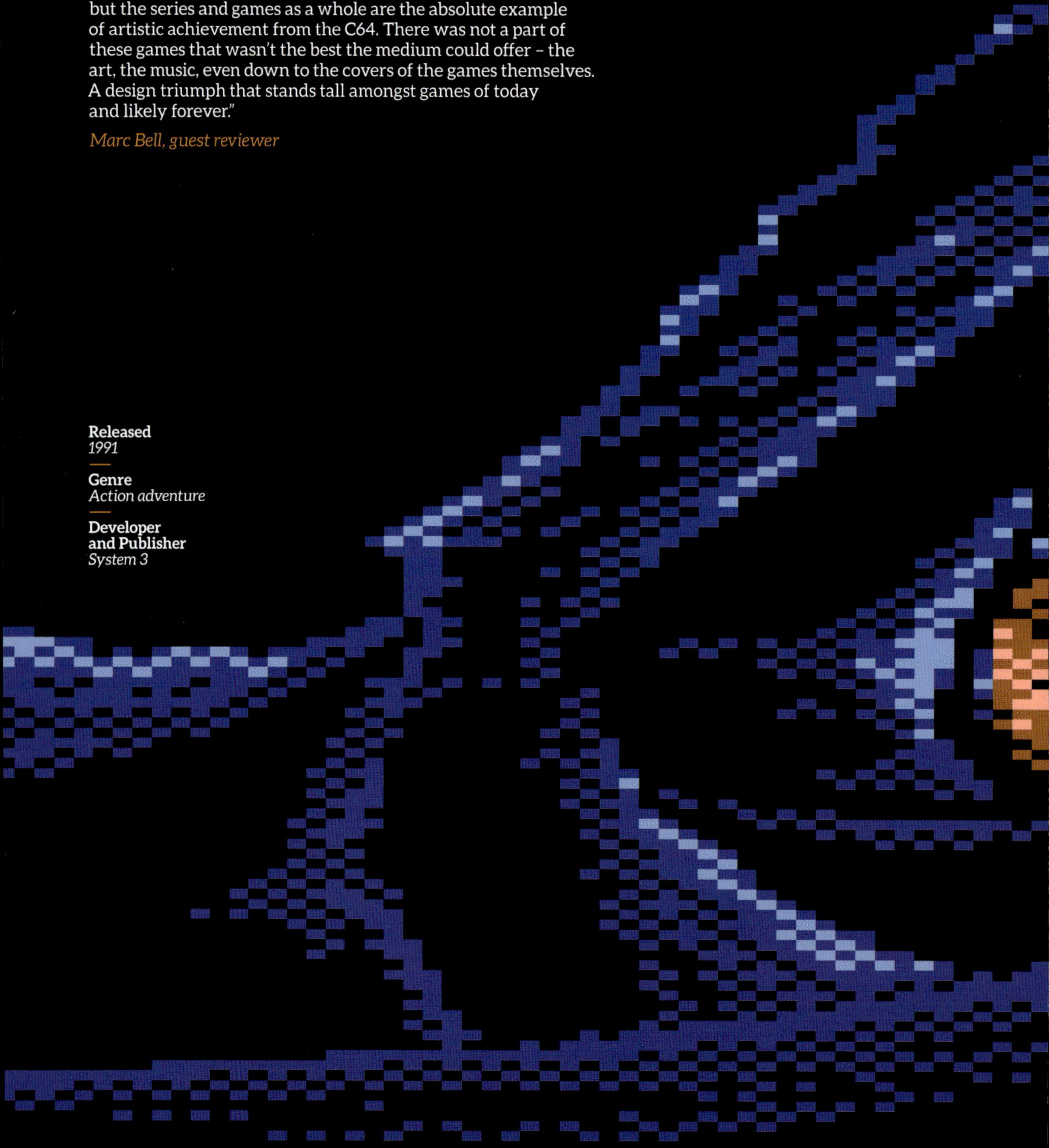

Released
1991

Genre
Action adventure

Developer and Publisher
System 3

CJ's Elephant Antics

"I was asked to think of a cute character, so I came up with an elephant with big floppy ears, and, just to throw the cuteness upside down, we had him chuck bombs and spit out peanuts. As for the maps and enemies, well, I always wanted to draw the Eiffel Tower, the Pyramids and a snowy level with a cute snow monster! The intro was a nod to my all-time favourite Indiana Jones film where CJ bursts out of a plane flying through the air."

Jonathan Smyth Temples,
co-designer and graphic artist

Released
1991

Genre
Platformer

Developer
Genesis Software

Publisher
Codemasters

SMASH
TV

Smash TV

"The original *Smash TV* arcade machine (made in 1990 by veteran game designer Eugene Jarvis at Williams) tried to predict what TV would be like far off in the future of 1999. It had a fun game design mechanic which (amusingly) became the core DNA of many reality TV shows today. (You'd work as a team in multiplayer mode, but, when the prizes show up, it's an absolute grab-fest!) Watch out for Mutoid man!"

Dave Perry, programmer

Released
1991

Genre
Run and gun

Developer
Probe Software

Publisher
Ocean

Originally by
Williams

North & South

Released
1991

Genre
Strategy

Developer
Probe Software

Publisher
Infogrames

Artwork
Oliver Frey

Space Gun

Released
1992

Genre
Shoot 'em up

Developer and publisher
Ocean

Artwork
Oliver Frey

Slicks

"In 1992, Codemasters published a great top-down F1 racing game for the C64. *Slicks* features six tracks, multiplayer, six unique F1 cars, smooth scrolling, ruthless AI and a Career mode which persisted with your team for the next season. Just like real F1, you have to try to get a ride in your opponents' superior F1 teams like Brabham and McLaren. It's easy to see why Codemasters are still creating amazing racing games today."

Andy Hayes, guest reviewer

Released
1992

Genre
Racing

Developer
Digital Design

Publisher
Codemasters

Nobby the Aardvark

"*Nobby* was our pièce de résistance. It had multicoloured, full-scrolling backgrounds with huge enemy sprites and a great soundtrack for each level. My only regret is the space station level, which was originally a castle garden, but Thalamus changed it at the last minute. I wasn't going to get paid for the change so didn't put much effort into it. This has come to haunt me in later life as it's an almost perfect game bar that level. All our own games received rave reviews, but *Nobby* was the highest with a 'Gold Medal' award from *Zzap!64*."

Jonathan Smyth Temples, co-designer and graphic artist

Released
1992

Genre
Platformer

Developers
Genesis Software

Publisher
Thalamus

Creatures II

"With the critical and financial success of *Creatures*, a sequel was inevitable. It was easy to recognise that the most innovative elements of the original title were the torture screens, so these would naturally form the backbone of the sequel's design. A departure from side-scrolling levels allowed us to add several different types of sub-game, resulting in yet another massive multi-load product and another 'Gold Medal' from *Zzap!64*."

John Rowlands, co-designer and programmer

Released
1992

Genre
Puzzle platformer

Developer
Apex Computer Productions

Publisher
Thalamus

"I came to the C64 in 1992 and was immediately sold on *Creatures 2* while reading *Commodore Format*'s developer diary. I'd played Nintendo and SEGA, but the Rowlands' original and hugely varied gameplay was a revelation. I'd also never experienced such truly atmospheric and downright funny presentation before, which only added to an already perfect game. I could spend just as long listening to the catchy 'Get Ready!' music as playing amongst all the cute and fluffy gore. To me it's the C64's mascot title and remains my favourite videogame on any system to this day."

Philip Boyce, guest reviewer

Released
1992

Genre
Action

Developer
Vivid Image

Publisher
Image Works

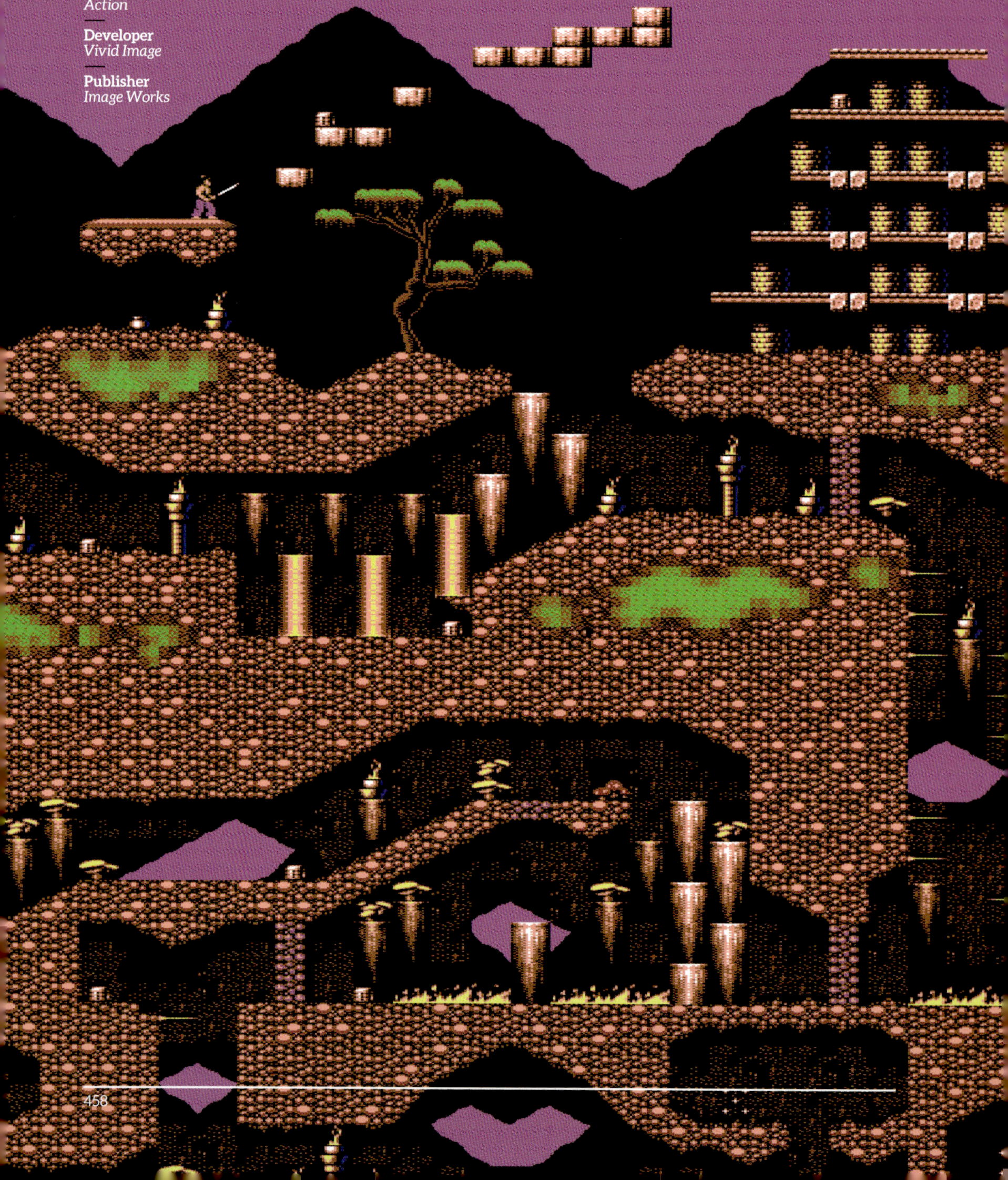

First Samurai

"*First Samurai* is one of the most remembered and respected games ever and was voted the Game of the Year in 1991. It involved so many great programmers and graphic artists. The Amiga was the lead version, and we did a great job of fully capturing the game on the C64. We were very lucky to have Jon Williams to code and Mat Sneap to do the graphics for the C64 version."

Mevlut Dinc, designer

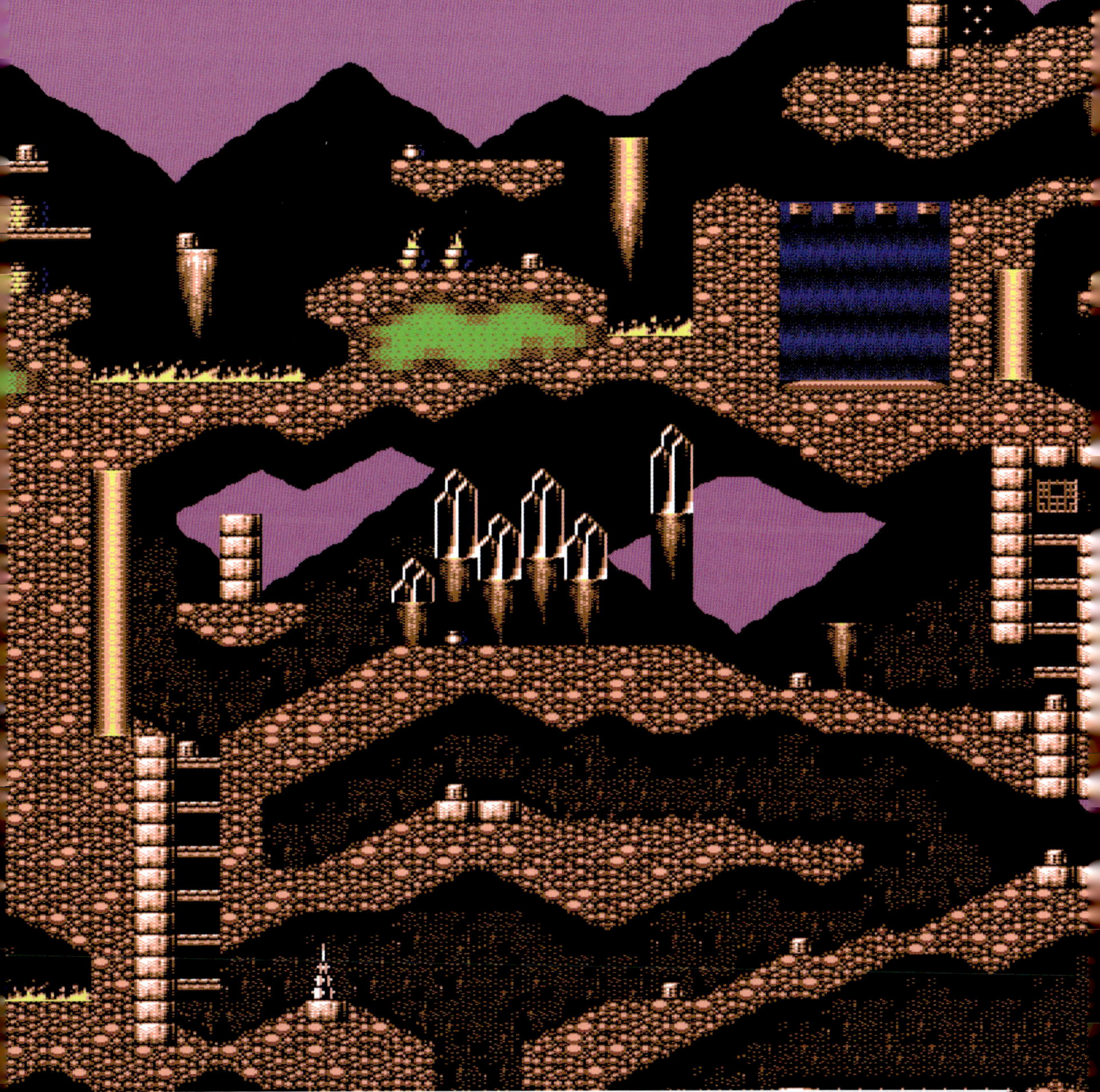

Released
1992

Genre
Platformer

Developer
Data Designs

Publisher
Millenium

James Pond 2: RoboCod

"The guys who programmed 16-bit *RoboCod* told the C64 crew that the platformer couldn't be done on an 8-bit micro. But Data Designs thumbed their noses and achieved something incredible: C64 *RoboCod* is the whole thing. There are ten massive, multi-scrolling levels with the backgrounds ported directly from the Amiga. They're laden with thousands of collectables and secret rooms, often accessed by extending the Cod's body many screens high to reach a ledge. Add in the real-world inertia, cute animation and dozens of enemies, and the only thing you're left raging at are the truly dreadful puns."

Neil Grayson, guest reviewer

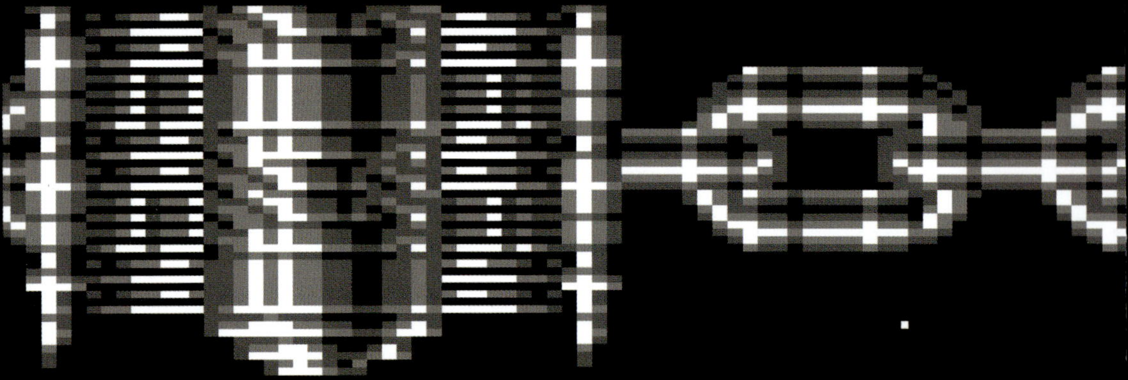

Lions of the Universe

This is one of the best-remembered games developed by members of the former demo group Cosmos Designs who were well-known sceners in the early '90s. *Lions of the Universe* is an *Armalyte*-inspired, technically perfect horizontally scrolling shooter boasting a simultaneous two-player mode, weapon upgrades and huge end-of-level bosses. Large numbers of enemy sprites on-screen in varied formations were possible using the complex 'sprite multiplexing' coding technique. With this game, the boys from Austria delivered something that many fans count among their top-ten scrolling shooters – especially those gamers after a serious challenge!"

Arnold Blueml, guest reviewer

Released
1993

Genre
Scrolling shooter

Developer
Cosmos Designs

Publisher
CP Verlag

Mayhem in Monsterland

"We poured so much love and attention into every aspect of its design that this is the game we're most proud of. We pushed the VIC chip to its limit with the user interface, gameplay and graphics. And, although awarded 100% by *Commodore Format*, which caused many to discuss whether any game could indeed be perfect, it was the perfect swansong for us."

John Rowlands, co-designer and programmer

Released
1993

Genre
Platformer

Developer and Publisher
Apex Computer Productions

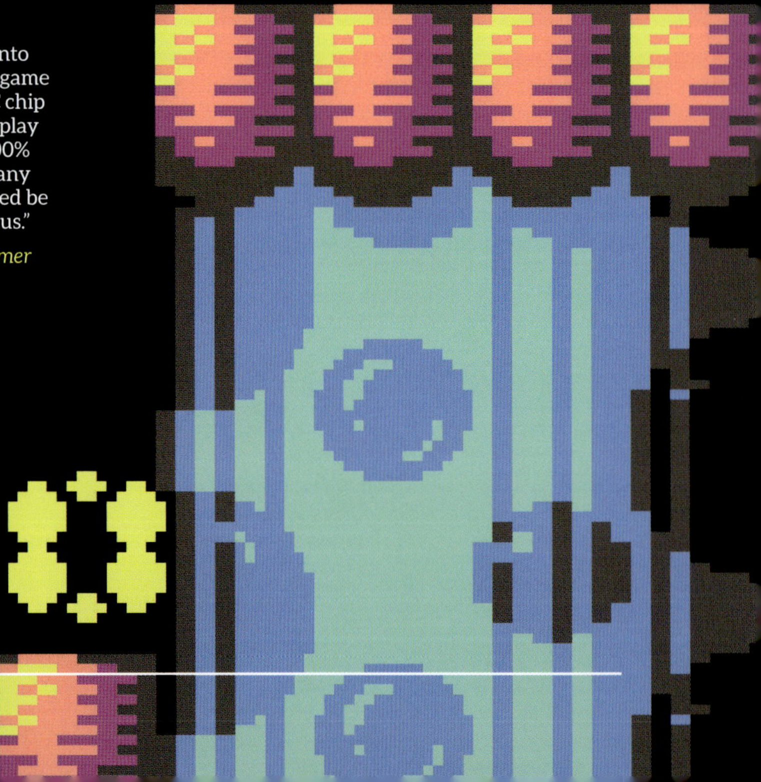

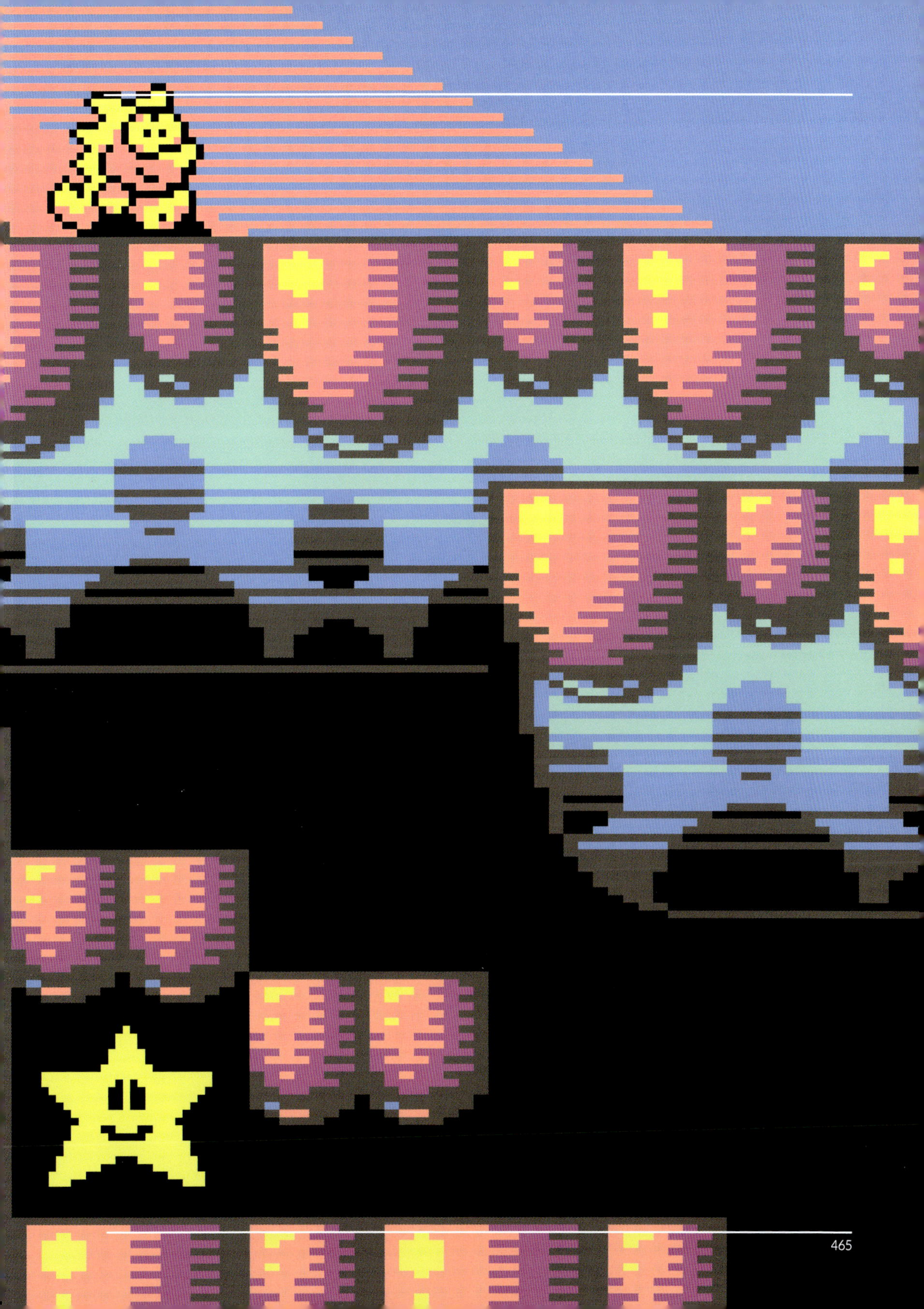

Released
1994

Genre
Puzzle

Developer
E & E Software

Publisher
Psygnosis

Originally by
DMA Design

Lemmings

"The trapdoor opens and here they come! Argh! Gotta be fast! There's loads of them. Yes, *Lemmings* is a race against the clock. How do they pack such jaunty personality into a handful of pixels? It's a work of genius… no! I need a blocker! They're heading towards the lava! It's hard to write a review whilst trying to save them all. And, believe me, I do want to save them all – *Lemmings* does that to you."

James Leach, games journalist

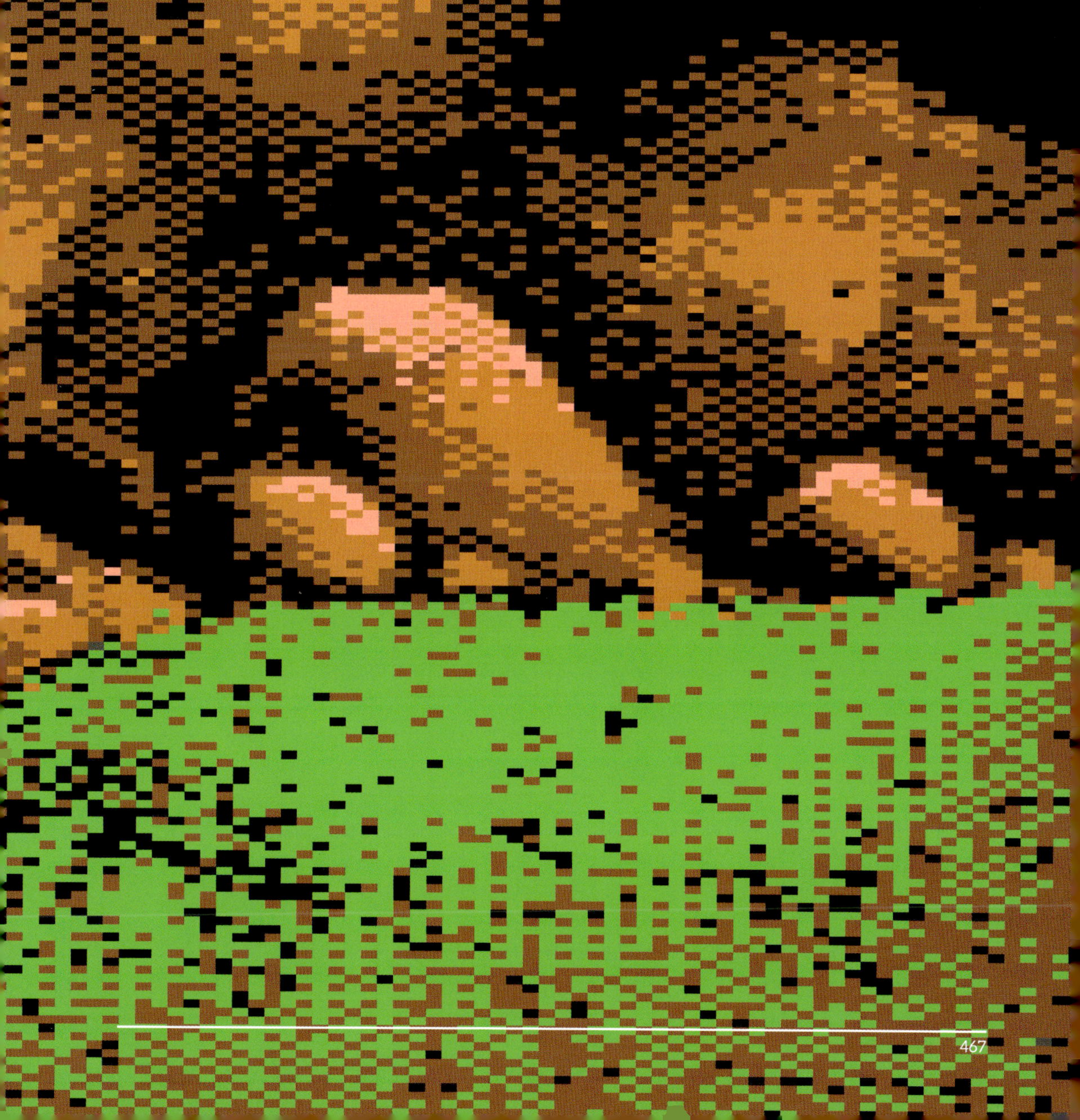

Prince of Persia

"Several people were talking about the viability of a C64 version at the time, and my intention was to create some game assets for possible public domain use. Coincidently, a programmer named Andreas Varga had also been creating *Prince* for the C64 on a cartridge, but he lacked finished graphics. By that happy coincidence, the C64 finally got *Prince of Persia*, albeit 20 years late! I was very happy with the 'Sizzler' rating in *Retro Gamer* magazine and original creator Jordan Mechner praising it on the development blog."

Steven Day, graphic artist

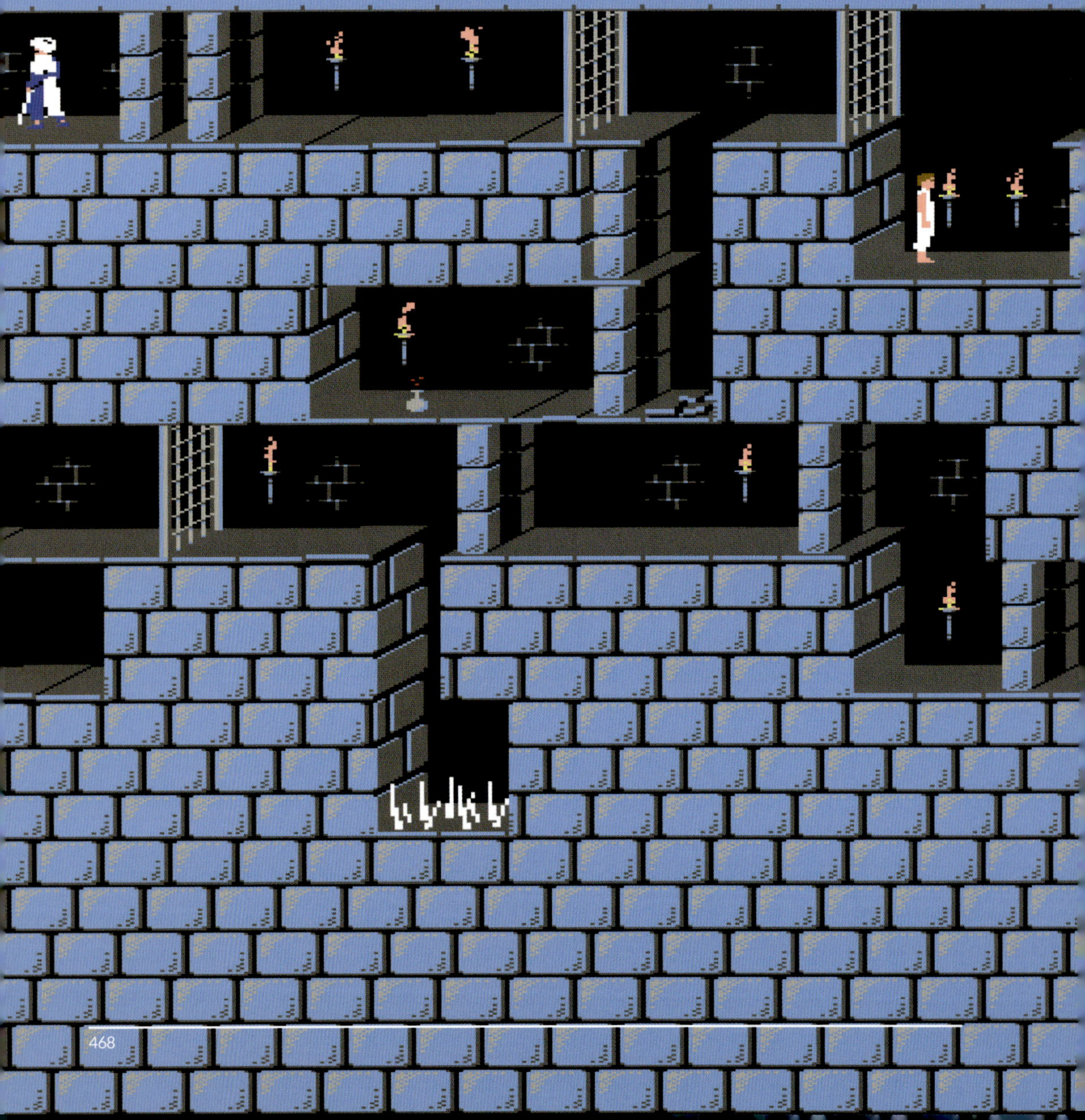

Released
2011

Genre
Platformer

Developer
Andreas Varga

Publisher
Public Domain

Originally by
Brøderbund

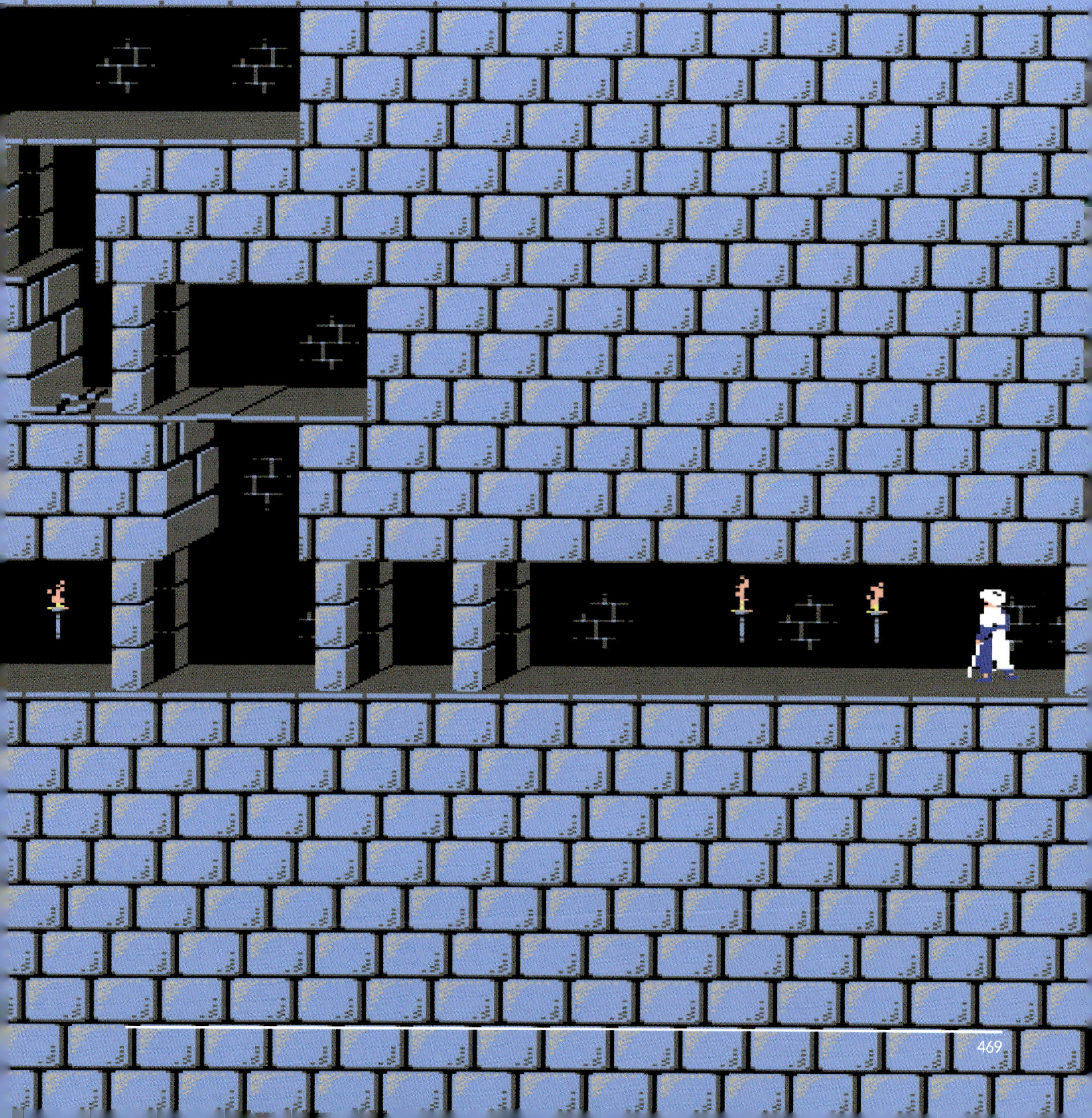

C64anabalt

"After playing the Flash version of *Canabalt* in 2009, I knew it would be fun to try to convert it to the C64. The gameplay, as well as the grey colour scheme, was something that would work well on the breadbox. Most importantly, the scale of the game was small enough for me not to lose motivation halfway through. Unfortunately, some things from the original that I wanted to include did not make it to the final game due to memory limitations."

Paul Koller, programmer and graphic artist

Released
2011

Genre
Endless runner

Developer
Paul Koller

Publisher
RGCD

Originally by
Kittehface Software

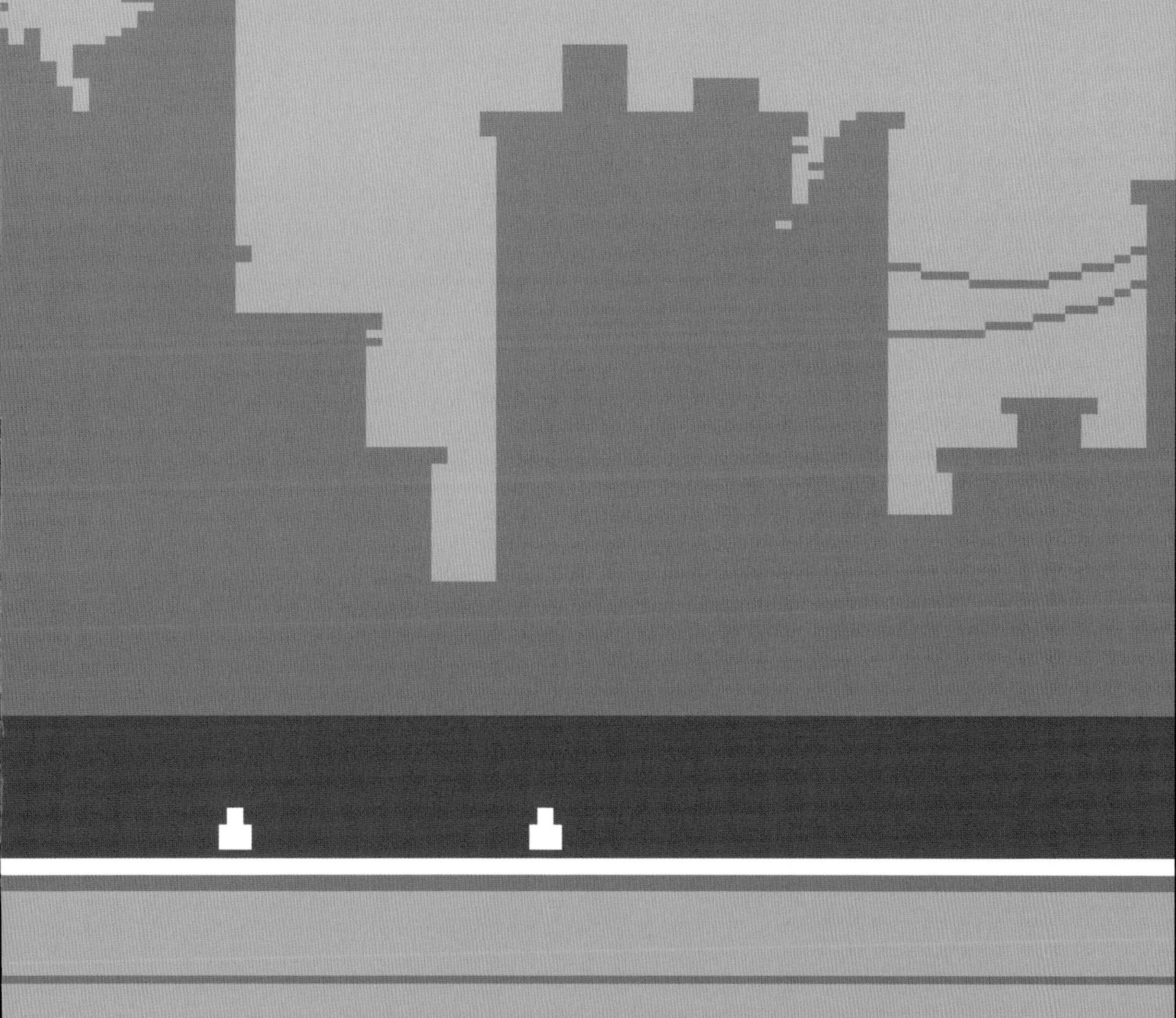

Super Bread Box

"The 2010 game *Super Crate Box* is often described by Vlambeer themselves as a game that could have existed in the '80s. Well, I proved to them that, indeed, their concept is very well possible on an 8-bit machine. Besides the obvious multiplexor and weapon effects, the playable characters were also a challenge to implement. It was not easy to convert the characters to only six double-sized pixels across, but, in the end, I think I succeeded nicely!"

Paul Koller, programmer and graphic artist

Released
2013

Genre
Action

Developer
Paul Koller

Publisher
RGCD

Originally by
Vlambeer

Bomberland

"This game was quite a considerable part of my life. The time between the first line of code typed and the last was longer than the entire official life of the Commodore 64! It was worth it, though, and the library of games on the C64 has been enriched with a fully fledged entry of the Bomberman series."

Michal Okowicki, programmer and graphic artist

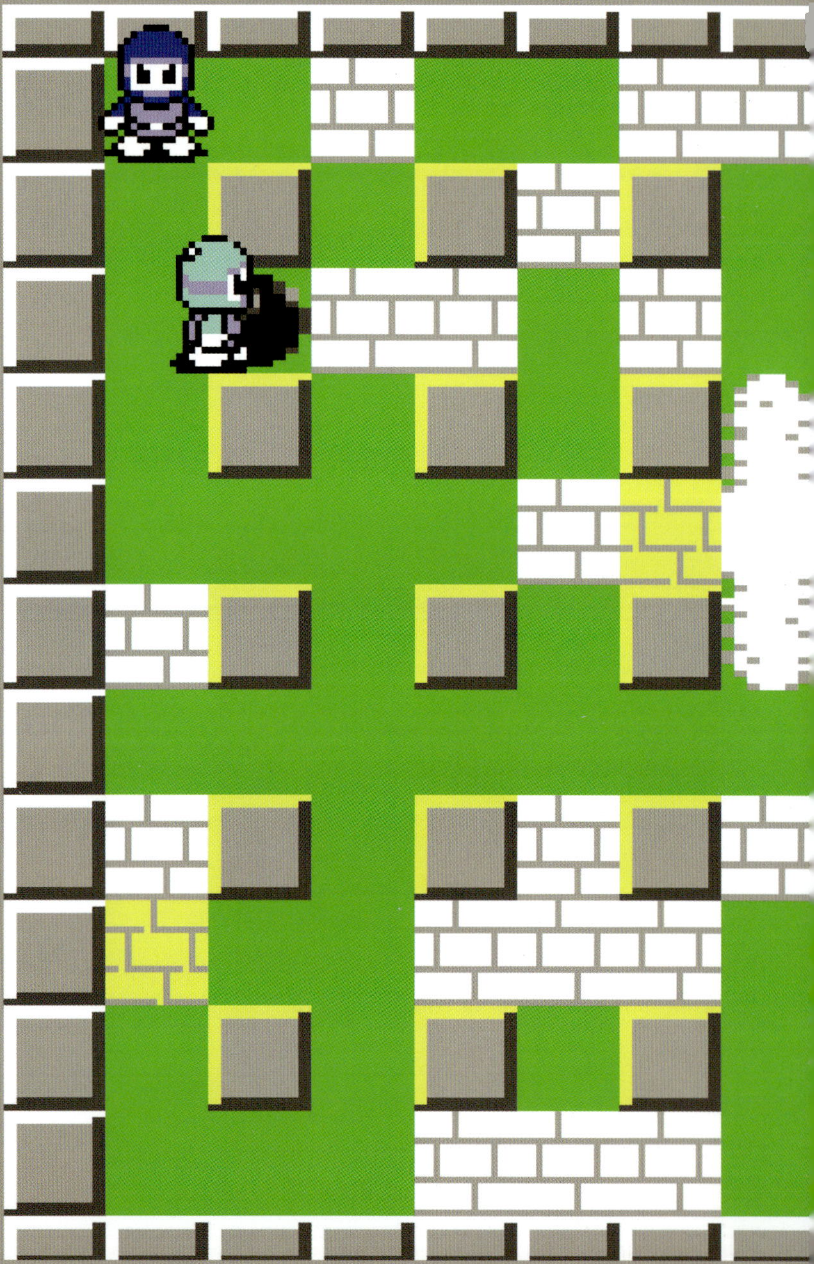

Released
2013

Genre
Action

Developer
Michal Okowicki

Publisher
RGCD

Micro Hexagon

"I always wanted to try my hand at a vector-type game but without the slow movement usually associated with such games on the C64. *Super Hexagon* is a fantastic twitch-style arcade game that intrigued me to see whether I could pull something off like this. After releasing the game in December 2013, I was overwhelmed by the attention this port received!"

Paul Koller, programmer and graphic artist

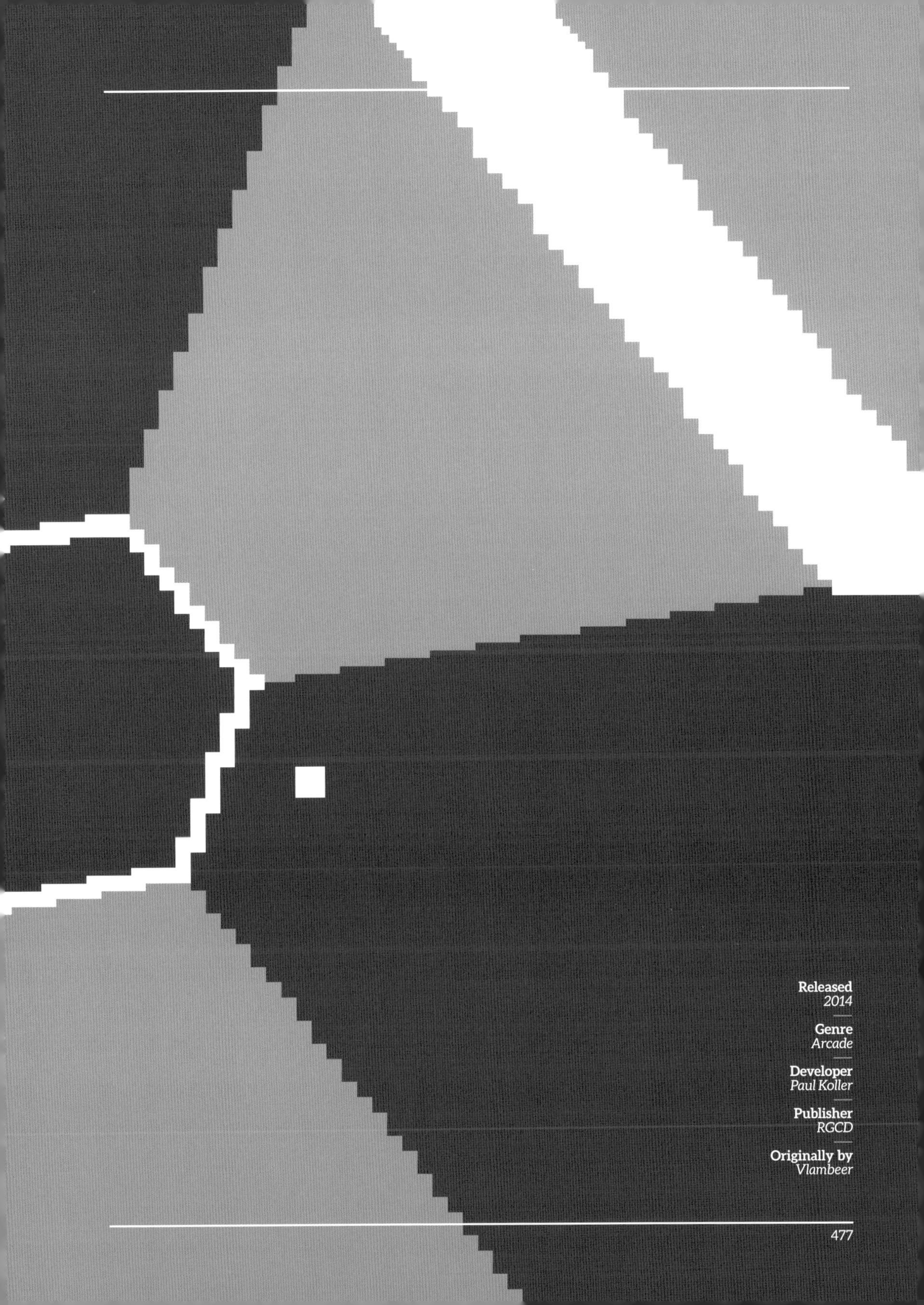

Released
2014

Genre
Arcade

Developer
Paul Koller

Publisher
RGCD

Originally by
Vlambeer

COMMA

Commando

"I endeavoured to produce a screen with the feel of a much-expanded version. The main image had exactly what I needed: a '*Band of Brothers*' worn-looking soldier with a netted helmet and festooned with grenades and ammo clips (just like the game). Around him, I added as many of the familiar game elements as I could, with special attention to the palm trees and the newly added helicopter, which are what most people remember from the arcade game."

Steven Day, graphic artist

Released
2014

Genre
Run and gun

Developer
Nostalgia

Publisher
Public Domain

Originally by
Capcom

Knight 'n' Grail

Knight 'n' Grail started as a single screen mockup posted to a big pixel art site in 2008. During my ten-month parental leave, I wanted a small project to work on, so I took that mockup and made something out of it. Later into the project, Håkon Repstad (Archmage) made a whole level full of enemies and also drew the ending sequences as well as the cover art. Hans Axelsson, a co-worker of mine at the time and an old C64 scener, made the lovely music. And, as can be clearly seen, the game was heavily inspired by the Castlevania series."

Mikael Tillander, designer, programmer and graphic artist

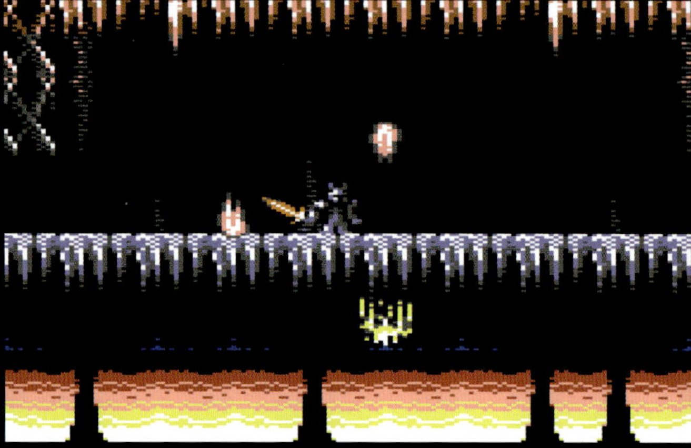

Released *2009* / **Genre** *Action adventure*
Developer *Mikael Tillander*
Publisher *Psytronik Software*

Soulless

I've always had a love for Commodore 64 platform games, so, when I approached Georg (Rottensteiner) with the idea for *Soulless*, I got stuck right in as soon as he said yes! Graphically, the game is heavily influenced by *Draconus*, with the search gameplay mechanic taken from *Impossible Mission*. I started by creating the game map in *Photoshop* until Georg supplied me with a lovely map editor, and, once the map was in, the rest of the game came together really quickly. Georg spent the last few months cramming all the new art I kept on chucking at him into memory; then, once it fitted, I would throw even more at him!"

Trevor Storey, co-designer and graphic artist

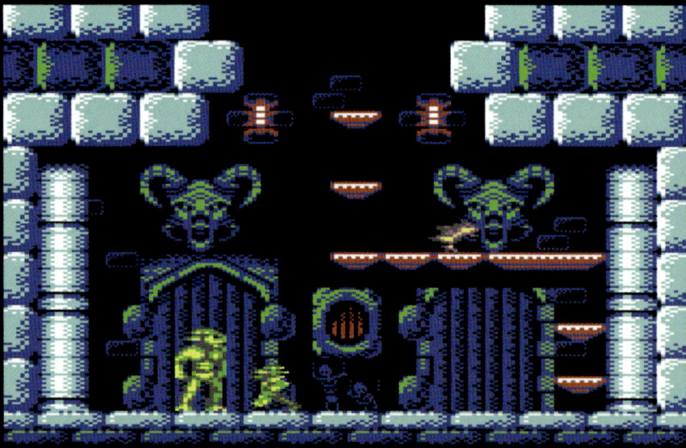

Released *2012* / **Genre** *Action adventure*
Developers *Georg Rottensteiner and Trevor Storey*
Publisher *Psytronik Software*

Released *2014* / Genre *Arcade*
Developer *Nostolgia*
Publisher *Public Domain* / Originally by *Nintendo*

Donkey Kong Jr.

"The initial graphics began life in 2012, but it wasn't until 2014 that coder Andreas Varga picked up the gauntlet. When Andreas began coding, he decided to use bitmap mode, and the opportunity was taken to reimagine the game with background visuals more suited to the C64. The cartoon look was inspired by *Congo Bongo*, with a dash of Core Design (*Rick Dangerous*, *Chuck Rock*) thrown in. Consequently, the game isn't an arcade-perfect port but more of a late-life C64 reboot. It plays exactly like the Atari 7800 version, which is considered one of the best home versions but, in my (biased) opinion, looks prettier!"

Steven Day, graphic artist

Released *2015* / Genre *Point-and-click adventure*
Developer *Prior Art*
Publisher *Public Domain*

Caren and the Tangled Tentacles

"This point-and-click adventure features the main character Caren, a female lab assistant who is out to solve a gruesome murder. The small development team of Martin Wendt, Kamil Wolnikowski and myself meant that we had enormous flexibility and creative freedom, and the positive feedback during development was overwhelming. As well as winning a couple of competitions, it recently won first place at the Meteoriks (like a demo scene Oscar). It was amazing seeing people playing and enjoying *Caren* at the recent Gamescom expo in Cologne, and chatting to Ron Gilbert about it was a personal highlight."

Oliver Lindau, co-designer and graphic artist

The Bear Essentials

"*The Bear Essentials* was developed in around two years after digging my C64 out from the loft and getting enthusiastic about coding on old computers again. It took me a while to relearn machine language and find the right tools and approach, but the struggle was completely worth it. I wanted to make a platform game and eventually settled on a collect 'em up, like *Manic Miner*/*Jet Set Willy*, but using the C64's graphics to make it look like something along the lines of *Creatures*. In fact, I started with the Clyde sprite from *Creatures* and drew a bear over the top; then I figured he would probably want to collect apples, and then came the idea of stockpiling enough apples for his family to last the winter. It took a lot of effort to get the game up to the standard I was looking for. Lots of polishing, testing, redrawing graphics, rewriting routines. Working with Pond to prepare the physical copies of the game was just a really brilliant experience. They would update me every day on all the different countries the game had shipped to, and I really treasure those memories of my game venturing out into the wild!"

Graham Axten, designer, programmer and graphic artist

Released
2016

Genre
Platformer

Developer
Graham Axten

Publisher
Pond Software

Planet Golf

"I was playing with the idea of implementing faithful physics on the C64 with no specific game in mind. I just wanted to create a credible ballistic engine, and a ball bouncing on an irregular surface was meant to be a proof of concept for that experiment. When I finally saw that ball moving on the screen, I thought I'd build a game on top of that, and golf was the obvious choice. It came from my love for the history of space exploration. The game is a homage to astronaut Alan Shepard who actually played golf on the Moon in 1971! The ballistics was definitely the most difficult part. It was quite easy to implement it in the first place, but, once I started building a game around that engine, adding other moving objects and the whole game logic to the mix, I immediately hit the C64's limitations. From there, it was a long and delicate process of optimisation before I had everything run the way I wanted to."

Antonio Savona, designer, programmer and graphic artist

Released
2017

Genre
Sports

Developer
Antonio Savona

Publishers
Psytronik Software and RGCD

Sam's Journey

"Being big fans of side-scrolling platform games, we realised that most great titles of that genre had been released on video game consoles, like Nintendo's NES and SEGA's Master System, but rarely on home computers. Being big fans of the Commodore 64, we decided to take the challenge of creating a console-style platform game for that very computer.

"Sam finds himself on an unexpected journey in a strange world. He has a lot of basic moves in stock, such as running, jumping, climbing, swimming, and carrying items. But, if Sam collects a special costume, he changes his appearance completely and even gains additional skills! While the fast free-directional scrolling, the huge levels, the many enemy creatures or Sam's transformation from a ninja to a pirate were quite tricky to implement, the hardest part was actually to fit all those game mechanics and features into the limited memory of the C64."

Chester Kollschen, designer and programmer

Released
2017

Genre
Platformer

Developer
Knights of Bytes

Publisher
Protovision

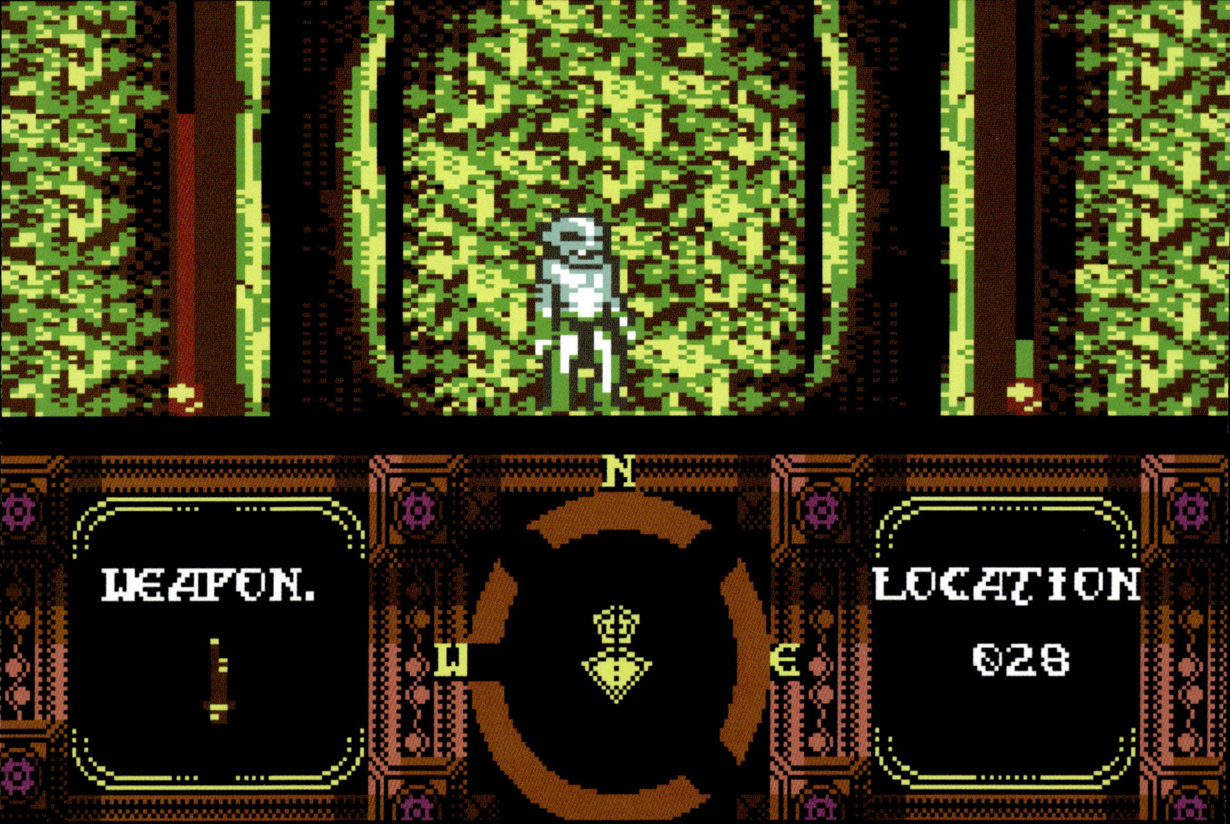

Argus

"The initial idea was to create a *Dungeon Master*-style game with large mazes to negotiate and creatures to battle. Like *Dungeon Master* and *Eye of the Beholder*, it started out as you'd 'jump' to locations when exploring, but we wanted to animate the corridors. It took a lot of fiddling to get it looking right, but I was really pleased with how it turned out once we got there. Creating the map with all the links took a lot of time and head-scratching. Poor Achim (Volkers) had to get it all into the code, so I think I got off lightly! The hardest part was testing; checking every location's links took so much time as there were 1,500 to go through. Again, Saul Cross came up with a really nice soundtrack – I asked for a *Master of Magic*-style, and that's what he delivered. It's amazing how quickly we got this one done; I'm really proud of that."

Trevor Storey, co-designer and graphic artist

Released
2017

Genre
RPG

Developer
Icon64

Publisher
Psytronik Software

Rocky Memphis - The Legend Of Atlantis

"I wanted to create a platformer with a character that could run, attack, climb over edges, jump and climb ladders. I've always been a huge fan of archaeology and the *Tales of Atlantis* and wanted to do a game with that idea. In creating the temple, I really wanted it to be high-res, so I set the background colour to dark brown so I could use more colours on the detail – it worked really well. One highlight was how we could get the character animation looking relatively smooth, considering there were four sprites per frame. Additionally, coming up with and then cramming all the puzzles in took some doing, but, with some tweaking here and there, myself and Stu (Collier) managed to do it. Saul Cross yet again came up with a really nice soundtrack to the game. In the end, it all came together great and won three Game of the Year awards."

Trevor Storey, co-designer and graphic artist

Released
2018

Genre
Adventure

Developer
Icon64

Publisher
Psytronik Software

Hunter's Moon

Hunter's Moon Remastered

"*Hunter's Moon Remastered* was undoubtedly a labour of love; I'm incredibly proud that we managed to tick off all the additions on our wishlist, and working with Martin Walker was a definite career highlight. The incredible intro sequence was very much a team effort, with Robin Levy handling the animations, Ste Day and myself designing the logos, Matt Gray providing the music, and Martin Piper's incredible animation technology holding the whole thing together. However, even running from cartridge the animation system needed a little time to initiate, so we threw in the Cyberload message to hide the nine-second delay!"

Andy Roberts, producer

Released
2018

Genre
Shoot 'em up

Developer and Publisher
Thalamus Digital

Keystone Kapers

"This conversion is my letter of love to the pioneering Activision coders of the early '80s and to the incredible pieces of entertainment they managed to create with such a limited set of resources. It was Steven Day's idea. He showed me some preliminary graphics he had done for a potential conversion of some Activision games, *Keystone Kapers* being one of them, told me that Saul Cross would also be on board for music and sound, and asked me if I fancied joining the team. I jumped at the chance of doing something with them because they are legends in the industry, and I'd code anything they wanted me to. The improvements are in the graphics and in the sound, and they reflect the superior hardware capabilities of the Commodore 64. The gameplay, instead, remained identical to the original, because that is just perfect the way it is. I'm really proud of the messages we received from Garry and Dan Kitchen, praising our work."

Antonio Savona, programmer

Released
2019

Genre
Arcade

Developers
Saul Cross, Steven Day and Antonio Savona

Originally by
Activision

Unreleased games

Despite playing host to thousands of games throughout its mighty reign, the C64 also had its fair share of titles that would unfortunately never see the light of day. Whether too technically ambitious or simply dropped for financial reasons, these games would ultimately be confined to the scrapheap of history, destined never to see a commercial release.

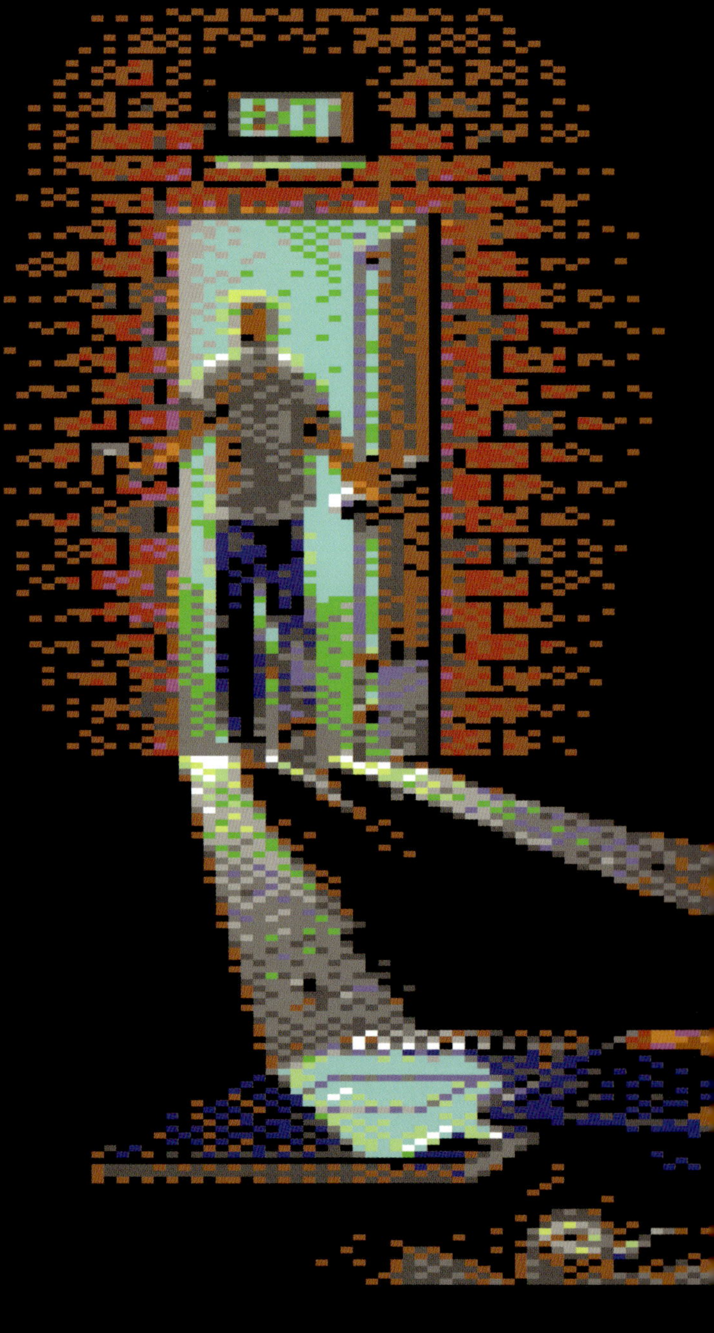

Games That Weren't by Robin Levy / 2016

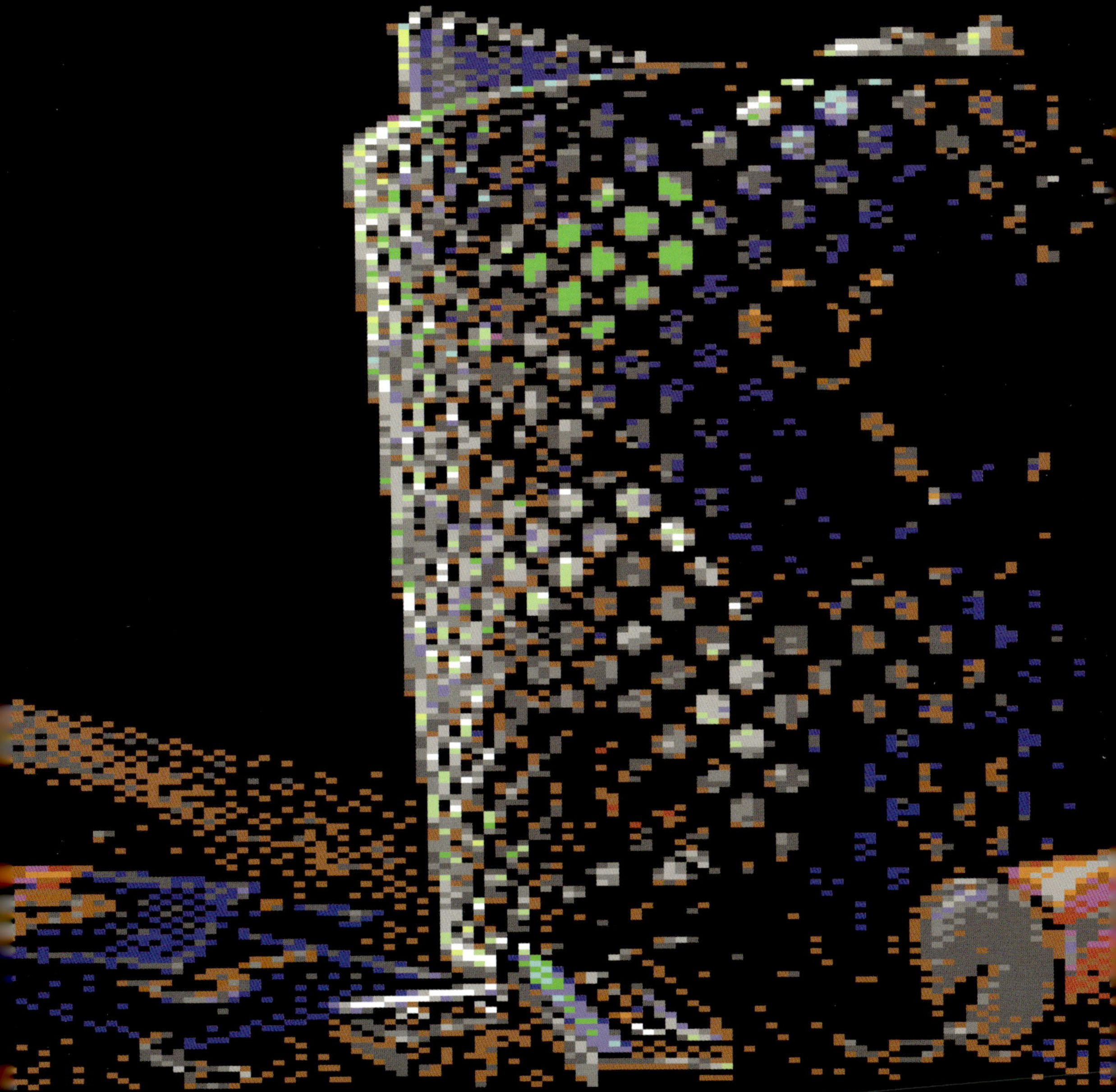

Deadlock

Robin Levy dazzled us with this graphical masterpiece, presented in *Zzap!64* as an exciting indication of what was next from *Armalyte*'s creators. Inspiration was drawn from titles such as *Impossible Mission*, *Obliterator* and *Baal* – but improving on them with depth and stunning visuals to set it apart from other games at the time. However, a gluttonous character sprite count and over-focus on its look resulted in limited agility, too few enemies to destroy and a distinct lack of fun, which ultimately killed the game. Had *Metroid* been a key inspiration, the outcome could well have been very different indeed.

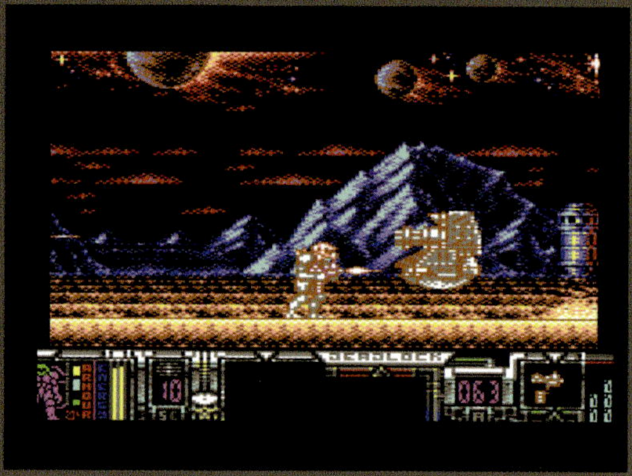

Daffy Duck and the Great Paint Caper

We know just how Elmer Fudd felt, trying to catch that darn duck and always falling short! *Zzap!*'s Sizzler review and Hi-Tec's subsequent demise transformed *Daffy Duck* into arguably the most sought-after of unreleased C64 titles ever. A laborious 18-year search succeeded where Elmer failed, finally delivering the game to an excited community. It's a vibrant kids' platformer, with puzzle-solving elements across seven varied and graphically rich worlds, including City, Desert, Forest and Mars scenarios. It wasn't quite the stellar game we all expected, but it was still fun and exciting to play nonetheless.

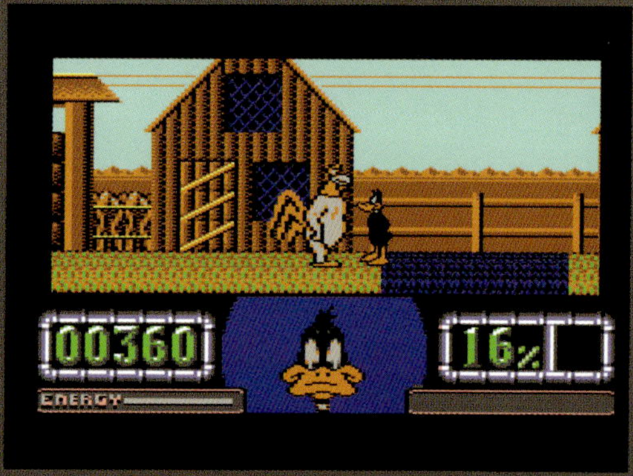

Fuzzball

This game's young wizard surely failed his chemistry exams! After turning yourself into a Fuzzball and accidentally filling a castle full of the furry creatures, you must work through 50 devious levels and destroy all the Fuzzballs so you can return to your human form. *Commodore Format*'s preview looked and played every bit as good as the released Amiga version – with many anticipating the final release. However, a legal dispute with another publisher meant the developer had to suddenly stop working on the game. After a delay, artist Jed Adams attempted to finish proceedings, but by now the market had deteriorated and System 3 decided to quietly retire the game.

Solar Jetman:

Hunt for the Golden Warpship

When searching for unreleased games, remember to check behind your radiator. Haydn Dalton did and helped recover a complete C64 version of *Solar Jetman*. Due for release across several platforms by Software Creations, this is a brilliant conversion of one of the best NES games of all time. Sure, it's missing the cutscenes and features slightly shrunken levels – but it otherwise faithfully retains the look and soul of the original. Tragically, Sales Curve decided that the game wouldn't sell well and decided not to release any of its conversions – a decision that doesn't make sense to this day.

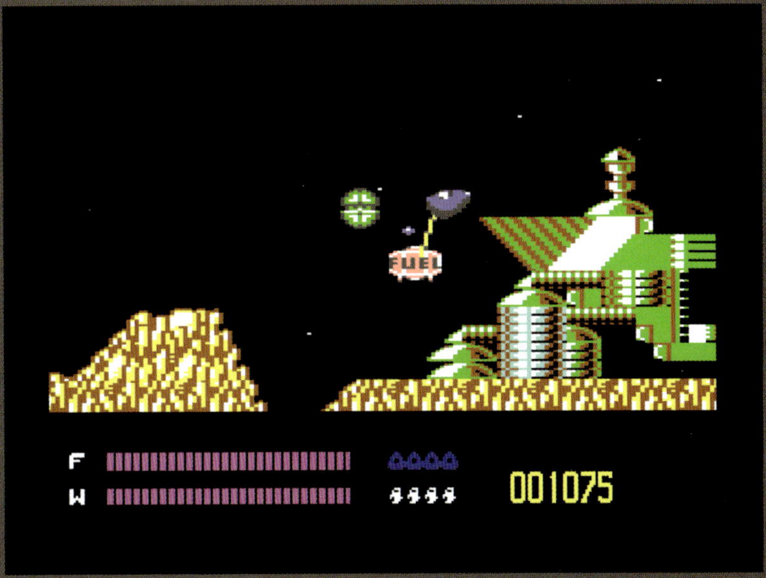

“When searching for unreleased games, remember to check behind your radiator. Haydn Dalton did and helped recover a complete C64 version of Solar Jetman.*”*

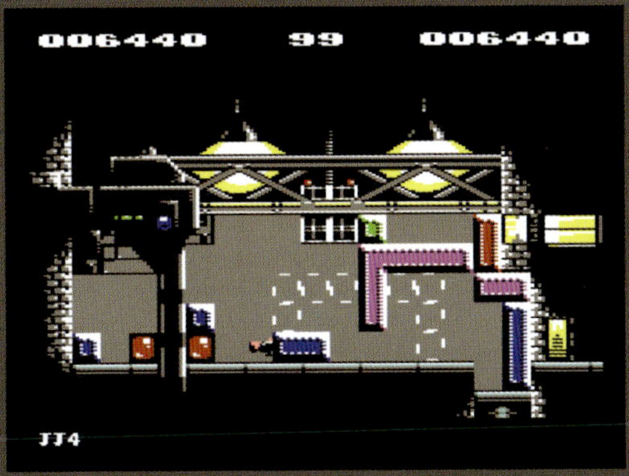

Devious Designs

From the developers of *Myth*, came this intriguing puzzler featuring J.J. Maverick, who must defeat Dr. Devious and his plan to transform the Earth into a cube. Each level has you reconstructing world-famous structures from cubic deformation against a time limit and while avoiding enemies. The game was canned quite late in development due to Imageworks' feeling that the C64 market had disappeared. Recovered a while back, there are several levels to enjoy, featuring impressive artwork by Bob Stevenson. The controls were deemed far too complex and were heavily toned down for the 16-bit version that eventually surfaced.

Spellcast

The developers of *CJ's Elephant Antics* demonstrated their skills with this impressive NES-like *Castlevania/Ghosts 'n Goblins* hybrid. A polished single level was shown to publishers, but amazingly never got signed up – resulting in an eventual release on *Zzap!64*'s covermount tape. Featuring a large map, various weapons, flying dragons, bees, snakes, floating logs and treacherous jumps, there was plenty of fun to be had. The title screen (with reference to the *Ghosts 'n Goblin*'s map) is an indication of a game that could have been very special.

Time Crystal

The visuals are startling when you consider the early development date – but unsurprising considering the involvement of Amiga legend, Jim Sachs. Following his impressive-looking *Saucer Attack*, this was planned as a full-blown cinematic experience. After a scintillating introduction, you are transported to a world where dinosaurs roam – though with not much to do apart from land your craft. Jim became disillusioned with piracy and was then entranced by the Amiga, resulting in *Time Crystal*'s early cancellation. It later resurfaced on the NES (with Power Glove compatibility), but that also never quite made it.

"The visuals are startling when you consider the early development date – but unsurprising considering the involvement of Amiga legend, Jim Sachs."

Troddlers

When a conversion of this *Lemmings*-inspired puzzler was announced in 1993, fans were sceptical that it would be anything more than vapourware. In fact, there were two teams competing for a contract, and this was the chosen effort. When compared with its 16-bit counterparts, the conversion looks very impressive indeed, with many *Troddlers* on screen and no major slowness. Realising it was late in the C64's life, the game was cancelled not long into development. Intriguingly, a new preview from the original developers was released not long ago, suggesting that it could still be finished one day.

Escape from Colditz

Based on the popular 1973 board game, this isometric 3D title has you guiding four prisoners to freedom. Things didn't start well, with early developer switches causing initial delays, with the next developer also struggling to finish. The Amiga edition snuck out just before Digital Magic's demise, but development delays resulted in C64 owners ultimately missing out. Remains of the game were leaked, and, evidently, there is a solid conversion taking shape. However, you'll periodically get stuck in the background, and there is a distinct lack of interaction at this stage, meaning (ironically) escape is pretty much impossible.

Tyger Tyger

Gary Liddon's *Black Tiger* clone, coupled with Paul Docherty's wonderful pixelling, looked exciting at the time. Press hype suggested that Firebird had another classic on its hands, but then it just completely disappeared. There are suggestions that it was cancelled due to copyright infringement fears, but it was more likely due to very slow progress, with MicroProse probably retiring it following its takeover of TelecomSoft. Rebuilt from recovered source code, the game is currently around 60% complete but is more a graphical demo than a game. With four levels, limited enemies, platform jumping and swimming, it's a teasing glimpse of a once promising title.

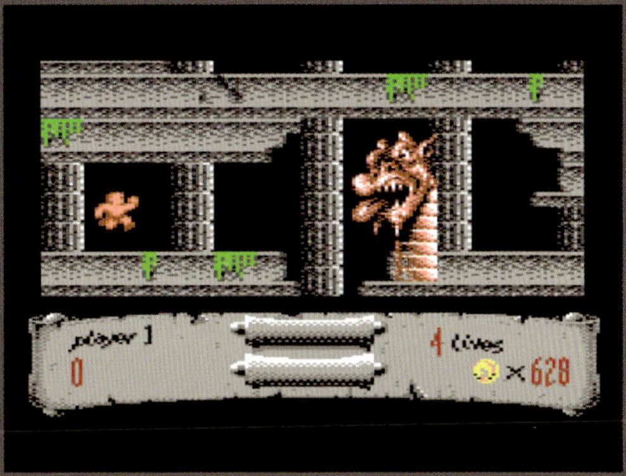

Thanks to everyone who made this book happen.

To purchase your copy and more titles visit www.bitmapbooks.com

Thanks to Steve Jarratt for the writing, editing, reviews and advice. Andy Roberts for the writing, reviews, artist interviews, company profiles, encouragement and contacts. Al Busby for the *Commodore Format* magazines. Frank Gasking for the Unreleased Games section. Benjamin Wimmer for permission to print his game maps. Amanda Purdom for the proofreading. Roger Kean and Bob Wakelin for the high-resolution artwork. C64.com for the interview permissions. Matt Wilsher and Chris Daw for the awesome photography and finally to Sally, Izzy and Tommy for their patience while this project was put together.

First published in 2014 by Bitmap Books Ltd
Extended Edition published in 2016 by Bitmap Books Ltd
Second Edition published in 2020 by Bitmap Books Ltd

A CIP catalogue record for this book is available from the British Library.

To get in touch, please email us at hello@bitmapbooks.com

Accept no imitations ... we are the world's no. 1!